S0-BWT-477

THE INTERNATIONAL ENCYCLOPEDIA OF CATS

Edited by G. N. Henderson and D. J. Coffey
Consultant Leslie S. Smith

Photographs by Anne Cumbers
Drawings by Annabel Milne

THE INTERNATIONAL ENCYCLOPEDIA OF **CATS**

McGRAW-HILL
BOOK COMPANY

New York St. Louis
San Francisco
Mexico Panama
Toronto

First published 1973
Reprinted 1974

This book was designed and produced by
Rainbird Reference Books Limited
Marble Arch House, 44 Edgware Road, London W2
for McGraw-Hill Book Company
1221 Avenue of the Americas, New York, N.Y. 10020

Designer: Margaret Thomas

Library of Congress Cataloging in Publication Data
Henderson, G. N.
The international encyclopedia of cats.

1. Cats–Dictionaries. I. Coffey, D. J., joint author. II. Title.
SF442.2.H46 636.8′003 72–10958
ISBN 0–07–028163–7

Printed in Japan

CONTRIBUTORS

Muriel Calder, M.R.C.V.S.,
Veterinary surgeon, judge and long-hair breeder, U.K.;

Lorna Connor,
Hon. Secretary and a founder of the Northern Ireland Cat Club;

Eldon V. Davies, Ph.D.,
Research Scientist, television broadcaster and contributor to scientific journals, U.S.A.;

Elizabeth Dobbs,
Secretary Governing Council of the Cat Fancy of Ireland, Siamese Cat breeder;

Caroline Franklin,
Lecturer in Animal Nursing, writer, U.K.;

Joan O. Joshua, F.R.C.V.S.,
Veterinary surgeon, University teacher, broadcaster and author, U.K.;

Joan Judd,
Founder of the Feline Advisory Bureau and Central Fund for Feline Research, Vice-President of the Havana Cat Club, writer, U.K.;

Camilla McColm,
Show Manager, editor, Siamese Cat breeder, U.K.;

Grace Pond, F.Z.S.,
International judge, breeder, author of many books, show organiser, broadcaster, U.K.;

Dr Ivor Raleigh,
Chairman Governing Council of the Cat Fancy, International judge, author, U.K.;

Dr Patricia Scott,
University Reader in Physiology, author, U.K.;

M. A. Simpson,
Secretary and Show Manager, All Breeds judge, South Africa;

R. C. Smith,
U.S.A.;

G. T. Wilkinson, M.V.Sc., B.V.Sc., M.R.C.V.S.,
Veterinary surgeon, broadcaster, author, U.K.;

H. D. Williamson, D.V.R.,
Author, radiographer, U.K.;

L. S. Winstock, M.A., Dip.Ed.,
Author, U.K.

ACKNOWLEDGMENTS

The photographer and producers wish to thank the many owners who so kindly provided facilities and allowed their cats to be photographed. Colour plates: Mrs Amphlett, 31, 33; Mrs Ashford, 23; Mrs Aslin, 2, 44, 46; Mrs Britton, 17; Mrs Butcher, 36, 62; Mrs Buttery, 42; Mr Chapman, 50, 52; Mrs Cunis, 32; Mrs Dell, 14, 16; Mrs Ellis, 18; Mrs Ford, 11; Mrs Gamble, 39; Mrs Goodwin, 20; Mrs Gowdy, 19; Mrs Greenwood, 55; Mrs Harding, 29, 30, 35; Mrs Hillam, 12; Mrs Howes, 61; Mrs Hyde, 26; Mrs Johnson, 7, 10, 57; Mrs Kite, 45; Mrs LeRoy-Lewis, 38; Mrs Menezes, 49; Miss Munford, 34; Mrs Nicolas, 28; Mrs Philpot, 40, 41; Mrs Pocock, 15; Mrs J. Richards, 13; Mrs R. Richards, 5; Mrs Roden, 48; Mrs Sayer, 24, 25, 27, 53; Mrs Shepard, 6, 37, 56; Mrs Tidmarsh, 60; Miss Tosswill, 51; Mrs Wade, 9, 22; Mrs Weaver, 21; Mrs White, 43, 47; Miss Wiseman, 1; Miss Woodifield, 3, 4, 58, 59.

Black and white photographs: Mrs Absalom, Brown Spotted and Brown Tabby Long-hair; Mrs Ashford, Rex kittens; Mrs Aslin, Siamese Tabby Point; Mrs Beever, British Blue; Miss Brown, Himalayan Blue Point; Mrs Chapman, Silver Tabby Long-hairs; Mrs Fisher, Birman and Devon Rex kittens; Mrs Greenwood, Silver Tabby Short-hair; Mrs Howes, Cream Long-hair; Mrs Johnson, British Blue Cream; Mrs LeRoy-Lewis, Russian Blue; Mrs Menezes, Abyssinian kittens and Silver Spotted; Mrs Pears, Siamese kittens; Mrs Roden, Chinchilla; Mrs Sayer, Egyptian Maus, Foreign Lilacs and Havanas; Mrs Shepard, Red Self kittens; Miss Stock, Blue Burmese and Cornish Rex Brown; Mrs Thompson, Blue Long-hair and Cream Long-hair; Miss Woodifield, Bi-colour Long-hair; Miss Woodthorpe, Tortoiseshell Long-hair.

Uropets Ltd, London, generously provided a selection of dishes, collars and other accessories for the black and white plates.

COLOR PLATES

Numbers in **bold** refer to plate numbers, and *italics* to page numbers

1 Abyssinian *17*
2 Abyssinian, Red *18*
3 Bi-coloured Long-hair *35*
4 Bi-coloured Short-hair *35*
5 Birman and kitten *36*
6 Black Long-hair *45*
7 Black Short-hair *45*
8 Blue Chinchilla *46*
9 Blue Cream Long-hair *47*
10 Blue Cream Short-hair *47*
11 Blue Long-hair *47*
12 British Blue *47*
13 British Cream *48*
14 Burmese Blue *48*
15 Burmese Brown *48*
16 Burmese Cream *48*
17 Cameo, Shaded *73*
18 Cameo kittens, Shaded, Red and Shell *73*
19 Chinchilla *73*
20 Cornish Rex *73*
21 Cream Long-hair *74*
22 Cream Long-hair kitten *74*
23 Devon Rex *91*
24 Egyptian Mau *92*
25 Foreign Lilac *117*
26 Foreign White *118*
27 Havana Foreign *118*
28 Himalayan (Colourpoint) Chocolate Point *118*
29 Himalayan (Colourpoint) Blue Point *118*
30 Himalayan (Colourpoint) Lilac Point *119*
31 Himalayan (Colourpoint) Red Point kittens *120*
32 Himalayan (Colourpoint) Seal Point *120*
33 Himalayan (Colourpoint) Tortie Point *120*
34 Korat *120*
35 Lilac Self *129*
36 Manx *130*
37 Red Self, Premier and female Champion *147*
38 Russian Blue *148*
39 Scottish Fold, father and daughter *173*
40 Siamese Blue Point *174*
41 Siamese Chocolate Point *175*
42 Siamese Lilac Point *175*
43 Siamese Red Point *176*
44 Siamese Seal Point *201*
45 Siamese Seal Point kitten *201*
46 Siamese Tortie Point *201*
47 Siamese Tabby Point *201*
48 Smoke Long-hair *202*
49 Spotted, Silver kitten *219*
50 Tabby Long-hair Brown *220*
51 Tabby Long-hair Red and kittens *220*
52 Tabby Long-hair Silver *245*
53 Tabby Short-hair Brown *245*
54 Tabby Short-hair Red *245*
55 Tabby Short-hair Silver *245*
56 Tortoiseshell Long-hair *246*
57 Tortoiseshell Short-hair *246*
58 Tortoiseshell and White Short-hair *246*
59 Tortoiseshell and White Long-hair *246*
60 Turkish *247*
61 White Long-hair, Orange-eyed *248*
62 White Short-hair, Odd-eyed *248*

Abscess An abscess forms when foreign substances, including germs, gain entry to the body. Large numbers of white blood cells migrate to the infected area around which a wall of tissue forms, preventing the spread of the germs. A high proportion of the white blood cells die after engulfing the germs, and the resulting liquid is known as pus. If the abscess is deep-seated a narrow tract, known as a fistula, may form connecting the abscess to the surface or to one of the body cavities. This allows the discharge of pus. If the abscess is near the surface, it becomes increasingly tense and more painful until it 'points'. Finally it bursts, discharging its contents to the exterior. In slow forming abscesses fluid may be withdrawn from the abscess contents, resulting in almost solid pus. This is known as inspissation. Abscesses are commonly the result of puncture wounds inflicted by cats' teeth during fights. Other causes include thorns, needles, glass and wood splinters and other infected foreign objects. Some infectious diseases are characterized by abscess formation. The best treatment for abscesses is to encourage pointing by frequent bathing with warm salt water. This should be as hot as the patient will tolerate. When they eventually burst, the contents should be gently wiped or flushed out, and bathing should be continued for four or five days. Veterinary attention should be sought when an abscess is suspected since serious complications can occur. The formation of abscesses is a normal body reaction to defend the body.

Abnormal Behaviour see BEHAVIOUR

Abnormalities see BREEDING ABNORMALITIES

Abortion Abortion is the premature expulsion from the womb of the unborn kittens. Apart from infective disease, little is known concerning the cause of abortion. The whole process of pregnancy from conception to birth is under extremely delicate hormonal control and any upset in this balance may lead to abortion. The so-called 'hormone of pregnancy', progesterone, is known to be important for the maintenance of pregnancy. Damage or inflammatory changes in the placenta may cause death of the foetus due to interference with the passage of oxygen from the maternal blood to the foetus. There is evidence that a genetic factor may be involved in some cases of abortion.

In human medicine there is an increasing tendency to abortion with advancing maternal age. This probably applies equally in the cat. The chances of abortion rise with the number of previous pregnancies. Inadequate nutrition may be a factor of abortion. Severe injury to the mother may precipitate abortion, but normal activities, such as tree climbing do not increase the chances of abortion.

The treatment of abortion depends upon an accurate diagnosis of the cause. Affected queens and their aborted kittens should be subjected to a careful examination to determine the presence of possible infection. Postmortem examination of aborted kittens may be useful.

Abyssinian

Abyssinian Said to resemble closely both in outline and appearance the cats so beloved by the Ancient Egyptians, the Abyssinians differ from the other Short-hairs with their distinctive ticked fur. At various times they have been known as 'Ticked', 'Bunny', or 'Rabbit' cats, because of their fur colouring.

There are two recognized varieties, the one referred to as Normal, having ruddy brown fur, with each hair having two or three bands of black or dark brown colouring, while the other, the Red, has similar tickings, but the fur is a rich copper red, doubly or trebly ticked with darker colouring. It is also possible to have Abyssinians with coats of bluish-grey, the fur being banded with darker colouring. Cream Abyssinians are also being bred but have not yet been granted recognition. They have been seen in the U.S.A. and on the Continent, but are not recognized as yet.

The type is Foreign, but the outline is not so long and svelte as that of the Siamese, or the head so long and pointed. The body should be slender and the tail longish and tapering. The large expressive eyes may be green, yellow or hazel and the sharp ears comparatively large. The coat texture should be fine and close.

Bars and markings are considered bad faults, but a dark line along the spine is permitted. Any white

Abyssinian kittens

marks are frowned on, and white chins are considered undesirable, but do tend to keep appearing.

Still comparatively rare, as they are not prolific breeders, the Abyssinians make delightful pets, proving most affectionate, loving attention, and disliking close confinement.

See colour plate 1, *page 17 and* 2 *page 18.*

Accidents Without doubt the commonest accident to befall the cat is the road accident. The severity varies from mild abrasions to extensive physical damage. All accidents however apparently slight should be examined as soon as possible by a veterinary surgeon. Internal haemorrhage or hidden bleeding can occur. Undiagnosed it can cause death up to 24 hours after the accident.

Cats which have suffered a severe road accident should be handled with care. Place one hand flat under the shoulders and the other similarly under the pelvis. The cat should be then lifted, altering its position as little as possible, in case broken bones pierce a vital organ. It should be placed on a soft bed and covered with a warm blanket to combat shock. Severe arterial bleeding should be arrested before removal to the veterinary surgeon. Time should not however be wasted cleaning minor skin wounds, since more serious conditions may require immediate veterinary attention. In general the splinting of fractured legs should not be undertaken by amateurs but left until professional help is obtained in the surgery. Speed in obtaining veterinary help is the essence of successful accident treatment.

Burns and Scalds Occasionally cats are burnt with hot water. The damage in these cases is not always apparent, as it is in the human, since the fur obscures the skin. Treatment depends on the severity but includes antibiotics to prevent infection, antihistamines and in some cases skin grafts. The area of skin burnt may well die and slough off, leaving a large raw area which requires careful and hygienic nursing. Modern drugs have considerably improved the chance of recovery following severe burning.

Dangerous liquids on skin Cats not infrequently become covered in oil, tar, creosote or kerosene/paraffin. Some of these substances are absorbed through the skin and are highly poisonous. The cat will almost certainly attempt to remove them by licking causing further extensive damage to its alimentary canal. Benzene substitute will remove creosote and paraffin readily. If unavailable mild soap solution, olive oil or liquid paraffin will cleanse the fur of creosote. Paraffin will also be removed by mild detergent such as washing up liquid, being careful to rinse carefully. Veterinary advice should always be sought before or after first aid treatment. See also ARTERIAL BLEEDING and NEEDLES.

Accommodation Pet cats usually have access to the house, where they rapidly adapt to family life. They vary their sleeping-places, choosing perhaps a sunny windowsill in daytime and a warm spot near lagged pipes at night. It is important, however, to provide your cat with its own bed, where it can feel secure. This should be in a dry, draughtproof place where it will not be disturbed.

Baskets and Beds Wicker baskets are still popular as beds for cats. Although reasonably suitable for pet cats, they are hard to disinfect. Nor do they exclude draughts so well as wood, cardboard or PVC beds.

Probably the best bed is made of PVC, and is round in shape, with vertical sides about eight inches

ACCOMMODATION, BASKETS
A deep, partially roofed basket ideal for litters

ACCOMMODATION, BASKETS
left A sleeping basket with raised base to avoid draughts

high. It can be collapsed for storage, and is easily washed and disinfected.

A wooden box-bed on legs may be made to suit your specifications by a handyman. If disinfection of this is necessary, it should be effected by thorough scrubbing with a solution of bleach.

Cardboard grocery boxes also make very adequate beds for cats, and may be burned when they become soiled.

Newspaper and old towels or small woollen or nylon blankets make ideal bedding materials. Imitation fur fabric is now available by the yard from department stores, is easily washable and very cosy.

Cattery A cattery is any establishment devoted to the housing of cats. Catteries are designed according to one or two basic plans:

1. *Indoor Cattery* This comprises rooms containing hutches, pens or cages for the cats. An ultraviolet, bacteriocidal lamp is used in some catteries, to help reduce airborne infection. The cages are often fitted to permanent shelving. The advantages of this type of cattery are that it is comfortable to work in. It is easy to clean and heat and relatively cheap to establish. The disadvantage of indoor catteries is that it enhances the spread of cat flu from one infected animal to the other occupants. Provision should be made for exercising the cats, and tree trunks are useful for this purpose. Cats kept indoors will not suffer from boredom if they have plenty of toys and companionship.

2. *Outdoor Cattery* The outdoor cattery consists of individual houses, preferably each with its own attached exercise yard surrounded by wire mesh. Although expensive to establish and labour intensive, it has the great advantage that airborne infection is reduced.

Artificial heat is usually necessary in catteries during the winter months in order to maintain the ambient or environmental temperature in the optimum range of between 55°–75°F. If possible, the artificial heat should be supplied by water-filled radiators connected to a central boiler, but electric storage heaters, oil-filled electric radiators and tubular electric heaters are equally acceptable. Oil heaters should not be used as the fumes may predispose the cats to respiratory infections. They also present a fire hazard as do electric and gas fires. If additional heat is required for a litter or a sick cat,

ACCOMMODATION, CATTERY
right A well constructed stud-house

ACCOMMODATION, CATTERY
top left A boarding cattery,
bottom left a nursery pen,
right accommodation for a
breeding colony

dull-emitter infra-red lamps suspended about four feet above the bed are effective. Local heat may also be supplied in the form of electric heating pads for the beds, but care must be taken to ensure that these are covered with a waterproof, impervious material. A maximum and minimum thermometer should always be used to indicate the daily fluctuations in temperature and a room thermostat provides an economic means of maintaining a stable ambient temperature.

Accommodation of Pupils The term accommodation applied to the eyes strictly means changes in the lens which occur to enable cats to view near or far objects. It is also used in connection with the pupil of the eye when it refers to the constriction or dilatation of the pupil in varying conditions of light. When light falls upon the retina at the back of the eye, the pupil constricts to a vertical slit in the cat. In dark surroundings the pupils dilate. The green eyes seen when cats are caught in car headlights at night is due to reflected light from the retina. These are purely reflex actions and are not under voluntary controls by the cat. This reflex is used by the veterinary surgeon in some examinations of the cat. See also EYE ANATOMY.

Acetylsalicylic acid see ASPIRIN

Achondroplasia Achondroplasia is a defective formation of the cartilage of the long bones before birth. These bones do not increase in length as the body grows and the affected kitten is a dwarf. The condition is thought to be genetic in origin. It is very uncommon in the cat and affected kittens are usually put down at birth.

Acid Milk This condition is said to occur when the kittens are between four and eight weeks old. The kittens either suddenly refuse to suckle altogether or vomit after suckling. They may show ulceration of the tongue. The milk gives an acid reaction to litmus. The administration of milk of magnesia to the queen apparently corrects the condition and restores the milk's normal reaction. Some veterinary surgeons doubt the existence of this condition.

Acinonyx jubatus see CHEETAH

Acne, Feline see SUB-MENTAL ORGAN INFECTION

Adoption see FOSTER MOTHER

Aelurostrongylus abstrusus see Lungworms under WORMS

Affixes and Prefixes An affix is a distinguishing cattery name used after the name of a cat, such as 'Bill of the Den', 'Bill' being the cat's name and 'of the Den' the affix. New affixes are not now approved in Britain although they were once in common usage, and breeders who registered them many years ago are still permitted to use them. They are still permitted on the Continent.

A prefix is used before the name of the cat, such as 'Bluestar Timothy', with 'Bluestar' being the prefix and 'Timothy' the cat's individual name.

Any prefix chosen is subject to the approval of the Governing Council of the Cat Fancy in Britain and once it has been approved and the necessary fee paid, it may only be used by the breeder registering it and only for kittens bred by him. Care is taken that there is no duplication of prefixes, and to prevent confusion that they are not too close to any existing ones. Affixes are allowed in the U.S.A. but both affixes and prefixes are usually referred to as 'cattery names'. These have to be registered with the appropriate governing body, being subject to much the same conditions as in Britain.

For anyone intending to go in for breeding and exhibiting seriously, a prefix is an essential. It will be used on the pedigrees of any kittens sold and should stock bearing the prefix win constantly at the shows, they will soon be in demand. A prefix, therefore, is another form of advertising.

African Lion see LION

African Wild Cat *Felis libyca* is reported to be slightly larger than the domestic cat, although differences of opinion exist and records are somewhat sketchy. Some authorities refer to it as a sub-species of the European Wild Cat, *F. silvestris libyca.*

Coat pattern resembles the tabby (mackerel tabby) although it is slightly lighter in colouring, the female being lighter as a rule than the male. The tail is ringed, but not so distinctively as the European Wild Cat and the tip is not nearly so thick or blunt. The underparts are yellowish and backs of ears are reddish. It has a wide range in Africa, being found in most areas except the great deserts and equatorial forests, but is also found in Arabia – which forms part of the Ethiopian Region – and its range extends to Syria and thence eastwards to India. Geographical races of the same species may be found in Crete, Sardinia, Corsica and Majorca. Thus, with such a wide distribution diversity in descriptions must be expected. It also breeds freely with domestic cats within this range.

While generally accepted to be nocturnal, cool cloudy days entice it out to hunt birds and small mammals. It is also known as the Bush Cat.

Afterbirth The afterbirth is the mass, composed of the placenta and the associated foetal membranes, which is expelled from the uterus following the birth of the kitten. Afterbirths may be expelled individually after each kitten is born, or two or three kittens may be delivered followed by a mass consisting of their afterbirths. In the cat the placenta is of the zonary type and develops in a belt around the middle

colour 1 Abyssinian

2

colour 2 Abyssinian, Red

right Afterbirth and kitten

of the chorionic sac. The edges of this belt are stained brown due to the presence of accumulations of a blood pigment. See BEHAVIOUR and BIRTH.

Ageing In the cat old age or senescence can be said to commence at 9 years of age. One investigator found the cat to be the longest-lived of the small domestic animals, living in exceptional cases for 25–30 years.

As the cat approaches old age care should be taken to ensure its comfort. Warm dry comfortable beds, good quality nourishing food and grooming enhance the longevity of any animal, and are especially enjoyed by the cat. Old animals tend to take less exercise while continuing to enjoy overeating. Obesity is as dangerous for old cats as for man, and should be controlled by diet.

Like most animals older cats tend to suffer from a number of diseases and disorders particularly kidney disease, neoplasia and arthritis. Unusual behaviour or symptoms like increased thirst, loss of appetite, constipation, diarrhoea, diminished sense of taste or smell, stiffness when moving, sudden loss of lifelong house training should be viewed with concern and veterinary advice sought immediately.

Regular yearly veterinary examinations of old cats will help to identify disease in its early stages when treatment is likely to prove more successful.

Ailurophobia The cat is probably capable of inspiring a greater degree of loathing than any other animal and when this sentiment becomes acute – often resulting in sweating, paleness, nausea, hysteria, and even fainting – it is called ailurophobia.

Julius Caesar was among the great men who abhorred cats. Two French kings, Henri II and Charles IX, swooned if a cat came too close. One issue of Addison's *Spectator* contains a lengthy discussion on unfavourable reactions to the cat. Napoleon sweated profusely in the presence of cats, and Field-Marshal Lord Roberts, the hero of Afghanistan and the South African War, could not breathe properly in their company.

Ronsard, the gentle and civilized poet, said of himself that 'there does not live a man in the world who so greatly detests cats'.

Albinos Albinism occurs occasionally in cats. Albinos are characterized by their white hair, absence of skin pigment, and pink eyes. Deafness is rather more common in albino animals than in others, and is thought to be a linked factor. It is usual for breeders to cull stock showing a tendency to produce albino offspring. See SIAMESE.

Allergy Allergy is the term used to describe a variety of inflammatory reactions that occur in the animal as a result of its exposure to foreign proteins and other agents known as allergens. A severe allergic reaction may be fatal, a mild one may only show as slight reddening of the skin or rash formation. Examples of allergies affecting the cat are penicillin-allergy; flea allergy; food allergy.

Treatments include antihistamines, anti-inflammatory and sympathominetic drugs.

Although very time-consuming, in cases of persistent allergy, identification of, and isolation from, the cause is rewarding.

Aloofness A trait often criticized by doglovers, who think that cats should be indiscriminately friendly, like dogs. In fact, the initial aloofness of a strange cat is a manifestation of his reserved nature. It is especially gratifying for his human friends when he abandons his aloofness and shows affection towards them. Aloofness may often be expressed by meticulous washing procedures, or by sitting with the back turned to the 'audience'. Aloofness is also often displayed towards other species, particularly dogs and horses, and usually when the cat is in a safe position, up a tree or on a windowsill. Cats frequently tend to be aloof (sulk) after they have been annoyed by humans behaving in an inconsiderate manner, but really it is a means of recovering their amour-propre.

Alopecia Alopecia is a loss of hair from the skin. In the cat the condition results commonly from hormonal imbalance. The loss of hair commences on the inside of the thighs and spreads to the back of the thighs, the perineum and to the undersurface of the abdomen. Usually there is no sign of itchiness or inflammation of the skin, which remains covered by a short, silky, down-like coat. Only a small proportion of cats are affected and treatment consists of administration of appropriate hormones.

There is also an hereditary form of hairlessness or *Alopecia congenita*. In this condition the loss of hair is usually not total, various parts of the body being nude whilst the remainder is covered by fine down. It becomes progressively worse with age, the skin becoming bare and wrinkled. See also BALDNESS and MOULT.

American Blue see RUSSIAN BLUE

American Short-hair Once looked on as household pets only, they are believed to be the descendants of the cats that accompanied the Pilgrim Fathers on their voyage to North America. Granted recognition in recent years, they are now of full pedigree and are rapidly increasing in numbers. In appearance they are very like the British Short-hairs in Britain, but the coat is not so plushy and the noses are slightly longer. Muscular cats with short thick even fur, medium to large bodies on legs of good substance, their heads are large with well developed cheeks and noses of medium length. The ears are medium in size, with rounded tips and the eyes are large and round. The colours are similar to those of the Persians. Faults are too fluffy coats, tails out of proportion in length to the body, that is too long or too short, and noses that are too snub. Points are:

30 Head
20 Type
10 Coat
10 Condition
20 Colour
10 Eye colour

The American Short-hairs should not be confused with the Exotic Short-hairs, also recognized by the Cat Fanciers' Association in the U.S.A., which has more Persian type. See EXOTIC SHORT-HAIRS.

American Society for the Prevention of Cruelty to Animals see A.S.P.C.A.

A.S.P.C.A. In 1865 animals in the United States were not protected from cruelty by law. They were regarded legally and by most people as property. As a result, they were horribly abused.

While on a world tour that year Henry Bergh, a wealthy native of New York City, came in contact with officials of the Royal S.P.C.A. in London. Bergh, who had been appalled by the animals' suffering he had witnessed in New York and elsewhere, decided to make an attempt to alleviate the situation. His efforts as an individual were futile and he realized that only an organization could obtain fruitful results. Bergh, socially powerful, enlisted the help of a number of prominent New Yorkers. The group issued a strong public statement endorsing the need for protecting animals from cruelty. More importantly, Bergh, supported by the group, obtained passage of a bill in the New York legislature making the more blatant acts of cruelty to animals illegal and subject to fine and imprisonment. It was the first such bill passed in America and gave limited police power to proposed private humane societies.

After months of planning, in April 1866, Bergh organized the American Society for the Prevention of Cruelty to Animals. He was elected president. At first, few convictions were obtained but gradually the Society made its influence felt.

The A.S.P.C.A. had problems financially for the first few years and Bergh spent much of his own money. He also raised enough donations to keep the Society. Today, the A.S.P.C.A. is a large, flourishing organization with chapters in every major city. It shelters more than a quarter of a million animals a year.

The A.S.P.C.A. investigates thousands of reported acts of cruelty and neglect annually for the purpose of enforcing humane laws and to prevent abuse to animals. It also rescues trapped or endangered animals – threatened by man or nature. Trained officers and ambulances are ready for any emergency, including stranded cats. The Society also has films, literature, lectures and demonstrations as well as its annual 'Be Kind to Animals' week to educate the public. Special consideration is given by the A.S.P.C.A. in placing thousands of cats, dogs and other animals into suitable homes every year. The Society is actively working to gain passage of better local, state and federal humane laws.

The Society, in order to place special emphasis on cats, introduced its cat safety identification tag. It was the first organization to do so. It has also developed special equipment for rescuing cats from trees. Another Society innovation was a Certificate of Examination, which allows anyone adopting one of its animals to take it to any veterinarian for a complete physical.

In placing cats and other animals, the Society emphasizes responsible ownership. Prospective owners

AMPUTATION A cat balancing well after the loss of a limb

are given medical information and an attempt is made to screen them.

Employees of the A.S.P.C.A. are selected in part on the basis of an understanding and humane attitude toward animals and an enthusiasm for the Society's work.

American Standards The American standards for pedigree cats are very similar to those of the British Cat Fancy, but are probably better in some respects in that they go into detail more fully. There are a number of registering bodies in the U.S.A., the largest being the Cat Fanciers' Association Inc. and the majority publish their own set standards, which may vary slightly from one association to another. They may not recognize all the same breeds; for example not all Associations recognize the Exotic Short-hairs.

A standard gives in full the characteristics required for what would be considered the perfect specimen of each variety, with points being allocated for each characteristic, totalling one hundred in all. It is the yardstick by which cats are judged, but it is almost impossible for a cat to be so perfect that it cannot be faulted in some way.

The Cat Fanciers' Association Inc. divides its required standards into two main sections, the Long-hairs and the Short-hairs. The former being sub-divided into the Angora, the Balinese, the Birman, Himalayan and Persian, while the Short-hairs are divided into the Abyssinian, American Short-hair, Burmese, Colorpoint Short-hair, Exotic Short-hair, Havana Brown, Korat, Manx, Rex, Russian Blue and the Siamese.

Amputation Amputation is the term applied to the surgical removal of the whole or part of a limb, or tail. The indications for amputation include gross infection, or severe damage, resulting in immobility and insensitivity of the affected part.

Amputation involves the severing of large blood vessels with the possibility of some degree of shock. Amputation is now, however, using modern surgical techniques, undertaken with the very minimum of ill-effects.

Some owners become extremely distressed at the thought of the operation and prefer to have their pets put to sleep, rather than allowing them to undergo amputation.

The ability of animals to readjust and live a normal life after amputation is however quite remarkable, especially in cats.

Anaemia Anaemia is a reduction in the normal number of the red blood cells and/or the concentration of haemoglobin in the blood. The end result is a diminution in its oxygen-carrying capacity. Anaemia is not uncommon in the cat, particularly in older animals, and usually occurs as a secondary feature of other disease conditions. The symptoms vary according to the cause and the severity of the anaemia. Generally there is pallor of the conjunctiva, gums, tongue, and the inside of the ears and the nose. There may be weakness and listlessness and in very severe cases the cat may be breathless and lie on its side panting. Dropsical swelling of the abdomen and the limbs may also occur in long standing cases.

Anaemia may develop in three main ways:

1. Loss of blood due to an accident or surgical wounds; chronic haemorrhage resulting from ulceration of the gastro-intestinal tract, from bleeding tumours, enteritis or coccidiosis; blood-sucking parasites such as hookworms, ticks, fleas or lice.

2. Increased red cell destruction (haemolytic anaemia). Destruction of red blood cells takes place constantly at a fairly fixed rate in the normal animal but accelerated haemolysis may occur due to: (a) Infection with the blood parasite *Eperythrozoon (Haemobartonella) felis,* or with certain bacteria such as staphylococci and streptococci. (b) Poisons such as phenols, snake venom, bacterial toxins, or lead.

3. Decreased blood formation. This may result from a variety of factors including organic diseases such as cancer, chronic nephritis; or infectious diseases.

Treatment depends upon the cause of the anaemia. This is often extremely difficult to establish. See also FELINE INFECTIOUS ANAEMIA.

Anaemia, Feline Infectious see FELINE INFECTIOUS ANAEMIA.

Anaesthetics The main purpose of anaesthetics is to render the patient insensitive to pain. Anaesthetics fall into two main groups, local and general.

Local anaesthetics Small areas of the body are anaesthetized by injecting a local anaesthetic around the nerve which communicates pain from the area to the brain. Modern local anaesthetics are derivatives of the original substances used, cocaine. This technique is very rarely used in veterinary surgery for cats.

General anaesthetics General anaesthetics affect the brain and cause the patient to become unconscious. This may be administered in various ways, as an injection, as a gas through a mask or in tablet form. Chloroform, one of the first substances used, has largely been superseded by more modern drugs but ether still retains a useful role.

Barbiturates have been employed in veterinary medicine for many years and have greatly improved anaesthetic facilities.

Providing the animal is healthy the risk from anaesthetic death has now been reduced to a very low level indeed. The risk however always remains. See also SEDATIVES.

Anal glands Lying either side of and slightly below the anus are two small glands, the anal glands. The secretion formed by them is passed through small tubes or ducts to the anal ring during defaecation. In the dog they are thought to have a communication function by adding a characteristic odour to the faeces, but since cats bury their faeces this is unlikely to be significant in modern domestic felines.

The glands may become impacted, to be followed in some cases by abscess formation but this is uncommon in cats.

Anatomy Anatomy is the study and science of the structure of the animal body and the relationship of its various parts to each other. The study is largely based on dissection, the name being derived from the Greek (ana + temnein – to cut). For anatomical description the body can be divided conveniently into systems either because of functional or structural relationship.

Alimentary System Mouth, pharynx, oesophagus, stomach, duodenum, jejunum, ileum, caecum, colon, rectum, anus, and the associated organs of salivary glands, liver and pancreas.

Respiratory System Nostrils, nasal passages, pharynx, larynx, trachea, bronchi, lungs and pleura.

Urinary System Kidney, ureters, bladder and urethra.

Reproductive System MALE: Scrotum, testicles, vas deferens, seminal vesicules, prostate, prepuce and penis. FEMALE: Ovaries, fallopian tubes, uterus, cervix, vagina, vulva and mammary glands.

ANATOMY The heart

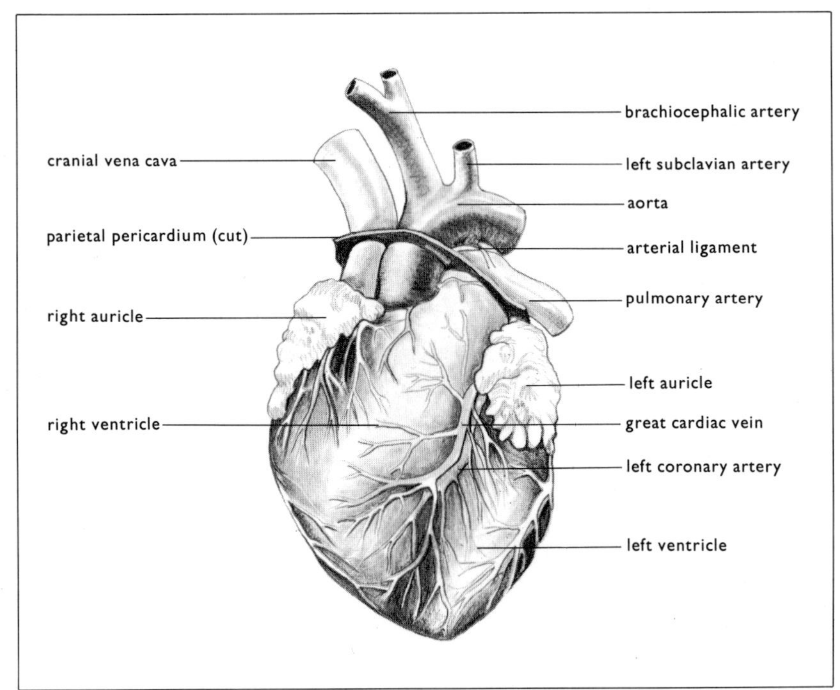

Endocrine System Pituitary gland, thyroid gland, adrenal gland, pancreas, ovaries and testicles.

Circulatory System Heart, pericardium, arteries, veins, arterioles, venules and capillaries.

Lymphatic System Thoracic duct, lymphatic duct, lymphatic vessels, lymph nodes, spleen and thymus.

Nervous System Brain, spinal cord, cranial nerves, spinal nerves, and sympathetic nervous system.

Locomotor System Bones, joints, muscles, tendons and ligaments.

Integumentary System Skin, subcutis, footpads and claws.

Haemopoietic System Bone marrow and spleen.

Sense Organs Eyes, ears, olfactory, gustatory and tactile apparatus.

Peritoneum.

It will be noted that some organs enter into more than one group. This is due to the fact that they possess more than one function, as in the pancreas with a digestive and an endocrine function.

Ancestors see DOMESTICATION

Ancylostoma tubaeforme see Hookworms under WORMS

Andean Cat see MOUNTAIN CAT

Angora The first cats with long fur seen in Europe were said to have been the Angoras, brought there by travellers from Angora, the capital of Turkey, now Ankara. Their long flowing silky coats were pure white, and their eyes were amber; blue; or one blue and one amber. It was discovered that those with blue eyes frequently suffered from deafness. Their heads were small, with upright ears and the bodies and tails long. Other cats with long coats were also introduced from Persia. These had broader heads, orange eyes, and the fur was fuller, but less silky. With the start of cat shows and the general interest in pedigree cats, the Persian type came to be preferred and cross-breeding followed, with the result that the Angoras died out. A few Angoras still existed in Turkey where they were thought much of, but where there was little interest in breeding, and so no records were kept, and they were not known elsewhere.

In the 1950's in Britain, some cats were imported from Turkey, which were known eventually as 'Turkish'. They were white with bright auburn markings on the face and tail, and it was soon realized that their type was similar to that of the early Angoras

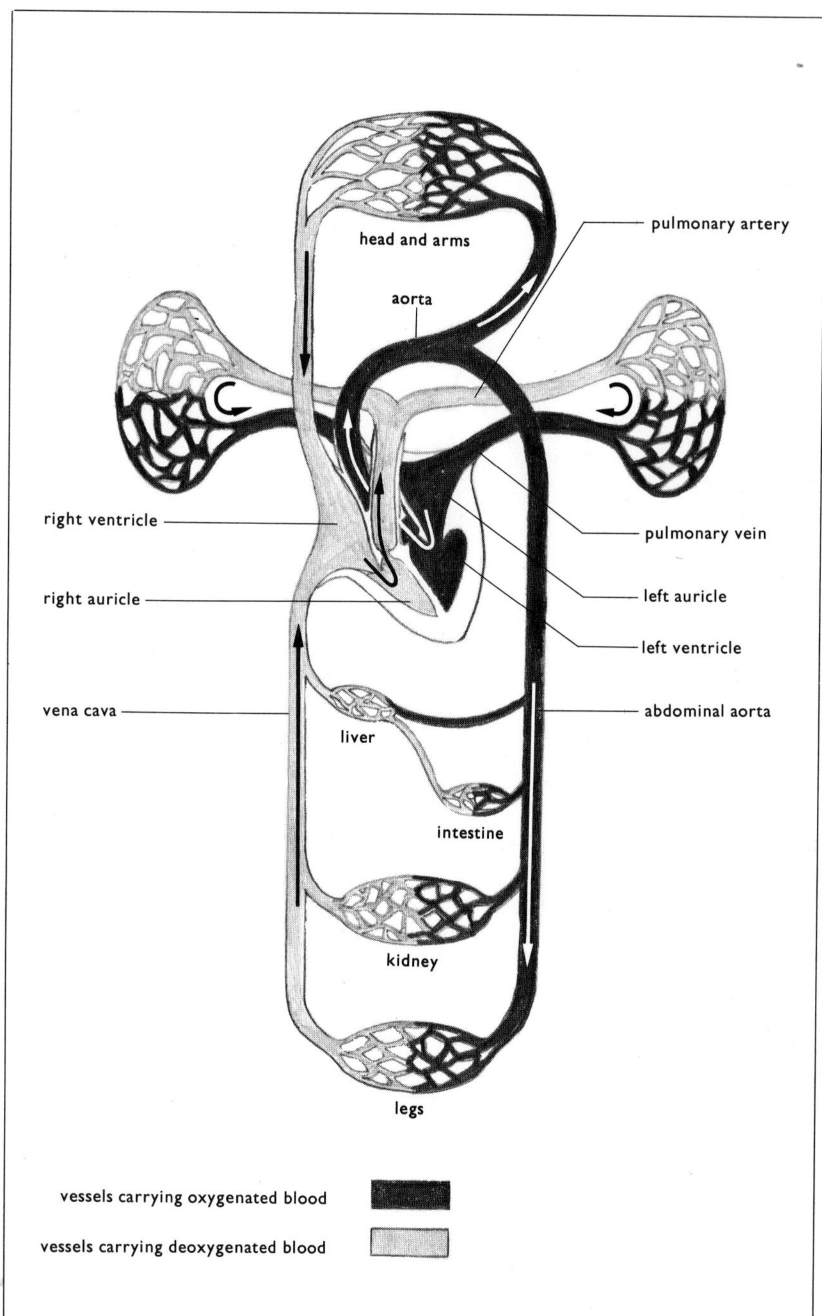

ANATOMY A diagrammatic representation of the circulatory system

although they differed in having markings. These are now being bred by a number of fanciers in Britain but there are as yet no Angoras similar to those now seen in the U.S.A. A few years ago, some Angoras were imported into the States direct from the Zoo at Ankara, where the Turkish authorities were carrying out a small breeding programme, having realized that the variety was practically extinct.

They are white, with eyes of blue, or amber, or one of each colour, and have type similar to that of the original long-hairs. Great interest has been shown in them, and as they have been breeding true and were obviously a distinct variety, they were recognised in 1970 by the Cat Fanciers' Association in the U.S.A. and now have a provisional standard.

Ankyloblepharon This word is used to describe the union of the upper and lower eyelid margins. The condition is normal in newborn kittens – which are unable to open their eyes. When the animal is 10 to 12 days old, the eyelid margins should separate, thus exposing the eyeball to light and permitting the development of normal vision. If the eyelid margins are still joined when the kitten reaches 16 days, it is necessary to seek veterinary advice. Cases of persistent ankyloblepharon can often be treated by a very quick and simple operation. Occasionally, however, surgical destruction of the adhesions between the margins of the lids only serves to reveal complicating disease conditions of the orbit. One such condition is symblepharon, adhesion of two parts of the conjunctiva. Again, surgical correction is possible, but is complex. There is some evidence that ankyloblepharon, and other eye disorders associated with it, may be a heritable condition, and thus it is unwise to continue breeding from a queen that persistently produces kittens with this disorder.

Ankylosis see ARTHRITIS

Anoestrus see OESTRUS

Anophthalmus see BREEDING ABNORMALITIES

Antibiotics Antibiotics are products of bacteria and moulds which, when brought into contact with disease producing organisms, inhibit their growth or kill them. Only small quantities of the antibiotic is required to obtain an effect. Antibiotics have been found to affect bacteria, rickettsia, viruses, fungi and flatworm groups.

Large numbers of antibiotics have been investigated, but only a small proportion are suitable for use in the human and veterinary medicine. The first antibiotic discovered was needless to say penicillin.

Commercial production of antibiotics for therapeutic use consists of growing the moulds and bacteria that produce them on or in special nutrient substances under controlled conditions. They are then removed, purified, and finally prepared for marketing. Before release from the factory, each batch of antibiotic must be checked by extensive laboratory trials.

Because of the dangers involved in the use of antibiotics they should be used only under veterinary supervision.

Antidotes Antidotes counteract poisons. They act either by combining chemically with the poison to form a non-poisonous substance, or by rendering ineffective the action of the poison.

Anus The anus is the external opening of the alimentary canal. It is formed by a muscular ring which relaxes when faeces are passed.

Few problems relate to the anus of the cat. It rarely develops irritation as a result of worms.

Any Other Colour There are many charming cats around that conform to no set standard. They may have resulted from mis-matings, cross-breeding, or from a definite breeding pattern. Ever since cat shows were started, such cats have been shown as 'Any Other Variety or Colour'. In the Long-hairs, a cat that differs from any other may be registered as 'Any Other Colour', and exhibited in the classes for this, but may not compete with the recognized varieties. Three generations of pure breeding are required before consideration can be given by the Governing Council of the Cat Fancy to the giving of a breed number and an agreed standard, and any one endeavouring to produce a new colour or pattern can exhibit such a cat under the 'Any Other Colour' heading until pure breeding can be proved and the standard recognized.

As a cat registered as 'Any Other Colour' may be of any colour or type, there can be no recognized standard, and such a cat is not eligible for a challenge certificate and therefore cannot become a champion.

Such cats are known as 'Experimental' or 'Any Other Variety' in North America, while on the Continent they would have to be shown in the class known as 'Novice' for unrecognized varieties.

Any Other Variety At the first cat shows held in Britain, there were few classifications for the cats, the majority being shown under the general heading of 'Any Other Colour' for the Long-hairs and 'Any Other Variety' for the Short-hairs. As more and more breeds were given standards, the numbers in the 'Any Other Variety' classes grew less and less and it seemed as though such a class would be of little use eventually. It has been allowed to remain, however, as it has been found most useful for cats with short fur that do not conform to any recognized standard, and whose characteristics differ in some way from the varieties already known.

As 'Any Other Variety' is not a specific breed, there can be no set characteristics given as to the body structure, build, type or colouring. However, such a breed number is useful, in that it enables any short-coated cat that is different to be registered and exhibited in the special classes at the show for this breed number. In this way, breeders endeavouring to produce a new variety may show the results of such selective or experimental breeding, and new cross-breeds or cats of unusual colouring can be exhibited. Prizes are given for the 'Any Other Variety' classes, but no challenge certificates are awarded, so there can be no champions. Many of the popular breeds today, such as the Rex, made their debut before the public in this way. Once a standard and a breed number has been given, of course, such cats may be entered in their own classes and even become champions.

In the U.S.A. such cats are known as 'Experimental' or 'Any Other Variety' and may appear at the shows in such classes. They are, of course, not given championship status.

Aortic thrombosis see HEART DISEASE

Aphrodisiacs Aphrodisiacs are drugs which increase sexual appetite and libido. They are rarely necessary in veterinary work, since animals kept in a healthy environment should have an adequate natural desire to reproduce their kind. Furthermore, genetically and physically sound animals that refuse to mate for psychological reasons may pass on this behaviour to their progeny. They are therefore better not bred.

Hormone preparations have been used particularly in senile males.

Non-hormone aphrodisiacs that have been employed in the past include strychnine, yohimbine and cantharides.

Appetite A cat's appetite is extremely capricious, and may easily be lost altogether during illness or emotional upset.

Cats will not eat if they cannot smell the food. Highly scented foods like herrings, kippers and sardines may be offered to cat 'flu patients.

The B vitamins are important in the maintenance of appetite. Meat flavoured yeast products may be added to the food, or smeared on the cat's nose so forcing him to lick it off. Liver is also a rich source of B vitamins.

Cats are fastidious eaters, and will refuse food if it is stale or on dirty dishes. It is better not to offer huge amounts of food, as cats prefer to eat relatively small quantities at a time.

Depraved appetite This term has been used to describe the eating by an animal of its own faeces. The condition is fortunately extremely rare in cats. If it is encountered, the usual policy is to feed a good balanced diet, with vitamin and mineral supplements to the animal, so as to ensure that there are no deficiencies in the food. It is also helpful to remove the cat's dirt tray immediately after use, as this will help to break the habit.

Archangel see MALTESE and RUSSIAN BLUE

Arterial Bleeding This term refers to the escape of blood through a hole or break in the continuity of an artery or arteriole, and its occurrence is a top priority first aid situation. It is most likely to be seen following a severe cut or road accident.

Arterial bleeding is characterized by being very forceful, the flood often being projected some distance from the cat, occurring in rhythmic spurts. The oxygenated blood is bright red in colour.

An attempt should be made to control the haemorrhage by application of a pressure bandage. Do not waste time trying to clean the wound, but place a pad of cotton wool, gauze, lint or a folded handkerchief on the bleeding point. Then bind this tightly into place with a bandage. If blood seeps through the dressing, it is usually better to place more binding over the top than to remove the original one and start again. Should bandaging fail, a tourniquet may be used. This may be improvised from soft string, a bandage or a length of rubber tubing. A loop is placed around the leg or tail on the side of the wound nearest the heart, and the rest of the material twisted until haemorrhage ceases. A pencil or stick may be used to facilitate the twisting action. The tourniquet is then tied in position, but it should be released gently after fifteen minutes, and re-applied five minutes after that if necessary. Avoid covering up a tourniquet with a bandage, as this may lead to its being overlooked. A tourniquet left in position for too long causes severe tissue damage. Once the haemorrhage is under control, veterinary treatment should be sought. If arterial haemorrhage of the internal type occurs – the patient usually goes into a state of shock, the membranes of the lips, gums and eyes appear very pale. Such cases should also be rushed to the veterinary surgeon immediately.

Arthritis Arthritis means inflammation of the joint. Severity can vary from very mild transient attacks to a very persistent painful condition. Fortunately this condition, so common in ageing man and dog, is rarely a problem in cats. It is however a common sequel to cat bites which have penetrated the joint, causing often severe suppurative infection. Occasionally such extensive changes occur in the structure of the tissue that normal function is lost resulting in ankylosis – a stiff unusable joint.

Artificial Insemination Artificial insemination denotes the deposition of the semen of the male into the vagina of the female by artificial means. This technique is widely used in cattle as the semen obtained in a single ejaculation from a valuable bull, suitably diluted, may be used to inseminate several cows thus increasing the propagation of the bull's desirable traits. The procedure has limited use in the dog mainly for inseminating a bitch widely separated by distance from the desired stud dog, but has not been used to any extent in the cat.

Artificial Respiration This is a first aid measure to be applied when a cat is unable to breathe. Breathing is normally controlled by an almost foolproof nervous mechanism, so that it only ceases when there is severe damage to the lungs or thorax, blockage of the windpipe, or loss of consciousness. Loss of consciousness could result from any of the following: poisoning by fumes and gas, poisoning by a substance the cat has eaten; severe electric shock; concussion; stroke (brain haemorrhage); fits; severe shock, as after a road accident; drowning.

The first aider should follow this procedure:

First, make sure air can enter the lungs, removing any fluids or objects that have entered the mouth. If you suspect there is mucus or fluid which you cannot reach with your fingers or a piece of cotton wool, do not be afraid to hold the unconscious cat up by the hindlegs and swing it gently between your legs to make the fluid fall out.

Lay the cat on its side on a flat surface. Pull the head so the neck is stretched out straight, and pull out the tongue so it does not fall back and block the airway. Place one hand flat on the ribs and press down briskly towards the table. Do not apply so much pressure that you break the ribs, but push firmly so that you hear the air coming out of the cat. Then take your hand off the cat and let the chest expand. Carry out 25–30 artificial respirations per minute. Keep going until the cat moves its tongue and start breathing of its own accord, or until help arrives. Do not give brandy or any other substance by mouth, as this could choke the patient.

Ascarids see Roundworms under WORMS

Ascites Ascites is the abnormal accumulation of fluid in the abdominal cavity known as dropsy. In the cat this occurs as a result of congestive heart failure, cirrhosis of the liver, or feline infectious peritonitis. In the first two conditions, the fluid is forced out of the abdominal veins because of interference with the return of blood to the liver. In the case of feline infectious peritonitis, the fluid represents an outpouring of serum from the blood vessels of the abdomen as a result of the action of the infecting virus.

Whatever the cause of the condition, the clinical signs are similar and consist of a gradual distension of the abdomen with an associated loss of flesh over the loins and the fore and hindquarters. If one hand is placed against the abdomen and the other side gently tapped, a fluid trill can be appreciated passing through the ascitic fluid.

Treatment is usually unrewarding. The fluid can be removed by puncture of the abdomen (paracentesis) but unless the cause is removed it will soon re-accumulate. Drugs to remove the fluid in the urine (diuretics) may be prescribed and the blood circulation improved.

Chylous ascites is the accumulation of a milky fluid in the abdominal cavity due to rupture or leakage from the lymph vessels. These vessels carry the fat-containing lymph from the intestine via the thoracic duct to the great veins in the chest. There is no practicable treatment for this condition. See also POT BELLY.

Aspirin Aspirin is a proprietary name for the drug, Acetylsalicylic acid. This drug is very poisonous to cats and it has been found that when cats were given the usual recommended dose of 5 grains daily, the majority died within an average period of 12 days. When given half this dosage, the animals lost their appetites, became depressed and vomited. Post-mortem examination revealed damage to the liver and the bone marrow. In view of these findings, Aspirin should never be given to cats.

Asthma Although there are not a great many reports of this condition occurring in the cat, observations by those who have studied it indicate that it may be more common than records suggest. The bronchi and the bronchioles – the fine tubular branches of the lung – contract, reducing their internal diameter and restricting airflow. Simultaneously, large quantities of mucus collect in the air passages effectively reducing the space still further. Therefore, air stagnates in the lungs instead of being breathed out, and the small air sacs, the alveoli, eventually become distended and may be permanently damaged. Causes of asthma include allergy, sinusitis and bronchitis. Treatment consists of administering substances which relax the bronchi and vapours to reduce the mucus. Oxygen is given by mask in severe attacks. One of the biggest problems for the veterinarian treating asthmatic patients is the prevention of the permanent lung damage that can result from repeated attacks. Sometimes it is advisable to send the cat away to an environment free from the agent responsible for the allergic response.

Atavism The recurrence of hereditary characteristics which have skipped one or more generations. These characteristics may be physical, such as coat-colour, coat length, shape of head, or deformities such as umbilical hernia. The genetic mechanisms whereby various characteristics are transmitted from one generation to another are extremely complex, and not yet fully understood. It is, however, always a good plan to look at the parents and, if possible, the grandparents of any cat which you intend to buy for breeding, or at least to find out all you can about its forebears. If you are attempting to establish a breeding strain, breed for five or six generations in order to discover any undesirable atavistic traits.

Ataxia This term describes the inco-ordination of movement which often accompanies weakness or nervous disorders. It may result from severe debilitating illness or nervous disorders. Ataxia is only a symptom and the diagnosis of the underlying condition can be difficult. Veterinary advice should be sought when the symptom occurs. See also Cerebellar Hypoplasia under PANLEUCOPAENIA.

Atony see BLADDER DISORDERS

Atrophy Tissues or organs which are unused are commonly seen to become reduced in size. This is atrophy. Perhaps the commonest cause of atrophy results from muscle disuse following fractured legs. Here the muscles waste away. On removal of a plaster the leg will appear much thinner than its normal fellow. The situation will rectify as the leg again comes into normal use.

Less commonly damage to nerves supplying muscles will cause muscles to atrophy. The cause is the same. Since the muscles have no nerve supply they cannot function normally.

Aujeszky's Disease see PSEUDORABIES

Australian There are no cats indigenous to Australia, and the so-called Australian cats exhibited in America at the end of the last and the beginning of this century were said to have resulted from a mutation from a Siamese introduced into Australia from Britain; the offspring being re-imported to that country and sent from there to the U.S.A.

Describing them, one writer said 'they were funny little beasts, sitting up like squirrels, and with much the same shape of head . . . (they) do not seem to live long.' Another wrote that 'they were delicate as kittens, the mother rarely having more than one at a time . . . they are very partial to heat, but cannot stand cold weather.' They were said to be very sleek coated, with small pointed heads, long noses and big ears. The colours were various. An old photograph shows a cat with most definite striping.

They were exhibited at a number of shows in the U.S.A. in the late 1890's winning many prizes, one cat being valued as high as $600. They appeared to die out quite suddenly, probably because of the low birth rate and extreme delicacy, and so vanished from the cat scene.

Autumn Litters Litters born in the autumn are the result of queens coming 'on call' towards the end of the breeding season in the summer. Such litters have the disadvantage that the kittens will be reared during the winter months when inclement weather is likely to curtail their outdoors activities and render house-training more difficult.

B

Bad Temper If a cat is bad tempered or irritable, it usually has a good reason. It may have earache, or have had its tail shut in a door, or had a dead rat confiscated. However, some strains of long-haired cat are notoriously bad-tempered, and this may be the reason for some owners not being persuaded to groom their cats. On the whole, though, cats are no worse tempered than any other species, including humans. When upset, they are more likely to nurse their injured pride than fly into a rage.

Bad temper is most commonly shown when they are unjustifiably attacked by another cat, or a dog or other animal; when prevented from going outdoors or eating a favourite item of food; when confined to a box and transported by road or rail; when taken to the vet and forcibly restrained for some reason, such as the taking of temperature, or when badly hurt.

Baldness Baldness is a condition in the rex breeds of cat in which there is a tendency to lose the fur, sometimes temporarily in the form of a premature moult but occasionally more permanently in elderly animals. The condition is part of the rex coat characteristics. In these breeds the guard hairs of the coat are abortive and the undercoat, or down hairs, are sparse. In some cats this coat anomaly is intensified so as to produce a deficiency of the down hairs. The constant grooming activities of the cat may also produce baldness by pulling the down hairs from the defective hair follicles. In some cases the baldness may be due to breaking off of the down hairs. Cats of the Devon rex breed are more frequently affected than the Cornish rex, possibly because of the greater fragility of their down hair fibres. See also ALOPECIA and MOULT.

Bali Tiger see TIGER

Balinese Popular in North America, but unknown in Britain or the Continent, this variety is said to have arisen in the first place through a mutation, with a kitten with a longer coat than usual being born in a litter of Siamese. Similar kittens appeared in other litters and these mated to one another bred true. The Balinese has definite Siamese type and colouring but the soft silky fur is two inches or more in length. They should not be confused with the Himalayans or Colourpoints, which also have the Siamese coat pattern but are of Persian type with very long coats.

Long graceful cats with well defined points colouring of Seal. Chocolate, Blue or Lilac, with pale body colouring in keeping, as given in the Siamese standards, any similarity to a Persian is considered a bad fault. The heads are modified wedge-shaped, with large ears, wide at the base, and the almond shaped eyes should be deep vivid blue.

Their characters are very similar to those of the Siamese and their voices sound very much the same. Less demanding, highly intelligent and certainly most affectionate, their great asset is that while being very decorative, their coats require comparatively little attention.

Bandaging Bandaging of a cat may be required for various reasons to protect a wound; to support a fractured or dislocated bone; or to stop a cat scratching itself.

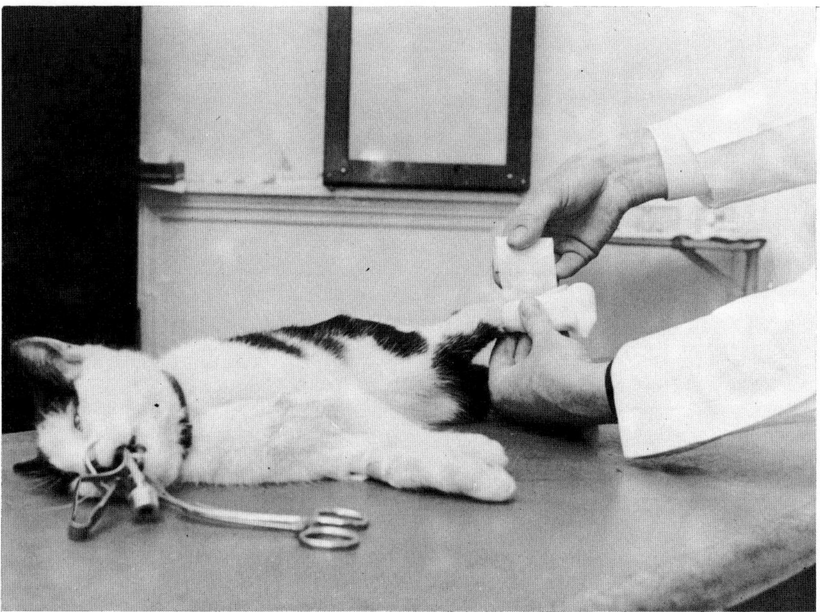

Bandaging an anaesthetized cat. The tube protruding from the cat's mouth may be used for anaesthetic gasses or oxygen

Two main types of bandage are used: crepe and white open wove cotton. In addition, a white stockinette is now available in small sizes suitable for cats' legs and tails. Bandages should always be secured with adhesive tape, not safety pins. It is best to apply the tape in such a way that the sticky surface is half on the cat's coat and half on the bandage.

Bandages should be applied firmly without interfering with the circulation.

Baskets see CARRIER BASKETS and ACCOMMODATION

Bathing Since cats in good health wash and groom themselves efficiently, bathing is only required for disease conditions, or when the coat becomes covered in a noxious substance such as tar or paraffin, which would be dangerous for him to lick off. Contrary to general belief most cats are often co-operative when bathed, provided they are firmly handled.

It is most important to have the water at a comfortable temperature. Fill the sink or tub first and test the temperature with your elbow; the water should feel lukewarm. Then, holding the cat by the scruff of the neck and supporting his hindquarters, lift him gently and submerge all but his head in the water. The shampoo or medicament should then be applied. The cat can then be held on the draining-board while the sink is refilled preparatory to the final rinse. The cat should be wrapped in a towel in order to remove excess moisture from the coat, and put in a warm place to dry.

After an insecticidal bath for the elimination of fleas or other pests, the cat is usually not rinsed out, but left to dry and then thoroughly brushed out. It is essential to prevent the cat licking his coat before the powder is removed, such as by an Elizabethan collar.

Sulphur-based compounds to cure skin conditions are normally rinsed out after application.

Fungicidal shampoos are applied in the same way as human shampoos.

If the cat has oil in its coat, a weak solution of mild detergent, such as washing-up liquid may be used. It is important to rinse this out very thoroughly.

Carbolic soap should never be used for bathing cats.

Bay Lynx see BOBCAT

Beds see ACCOMMODATION

Behaviour The ancestors of our domestic cats developed, structurally and behaviourally, in the wild to become lone, territory loving, hunters. Unlike dogs they form no family or pack system and social contact with their own kind is restricted either to that between a mother and her young or for mating.

However like all animals they are able to adapt to a variety of environments and we therefore find that cats can adjust, within limits, to life in close contact with human beings. Indeed many become so well adapted that they would be reluctant to face the harsher realities of life in the raw.

In spite of centuries of domestication the cat has escaped many of the adverse effects of selective breeding for behavioural characteristics so apparent in the dog.

The domestic cat remains in essence a lone hunter, whose territory is more important than social relationships. It is important for owners to understand cat behaviour and the tenuous relationship they enjoy with human beings.

Mothering A few days before the onset of birth a female cat seeks a secluded corner in which she apparently feels secure. She prepares the nest and awaits the birth of her young. As each kitten is born the mother frees it from the water bag, if it has not already burst, licks up the fluids, severs the umbilical cord and eats the placenta. She then licks the newborn kitten which has the effect of both cleaning it and stimulating normal breathing. Experienced mothers are usually more attentive to their young than those with a first litter.

When all the births are complete she retrieves any kittens that may have wandered away from the nest, and lying down, positions herself on her side, presenting her mammary glands to the young, and encircles them with her legs. Young kittens, as soon as they are born, instinctively move forward waving their head from side to side. This inherent ability, aided by the mothers position eventually leads them to a nipple. Having once received a reward of warm milk they quickly learn for future reference where to find this source of food and comfort and can thereafter make directly for the bar. During the first two weeks of life each kitten chooses one nipple and

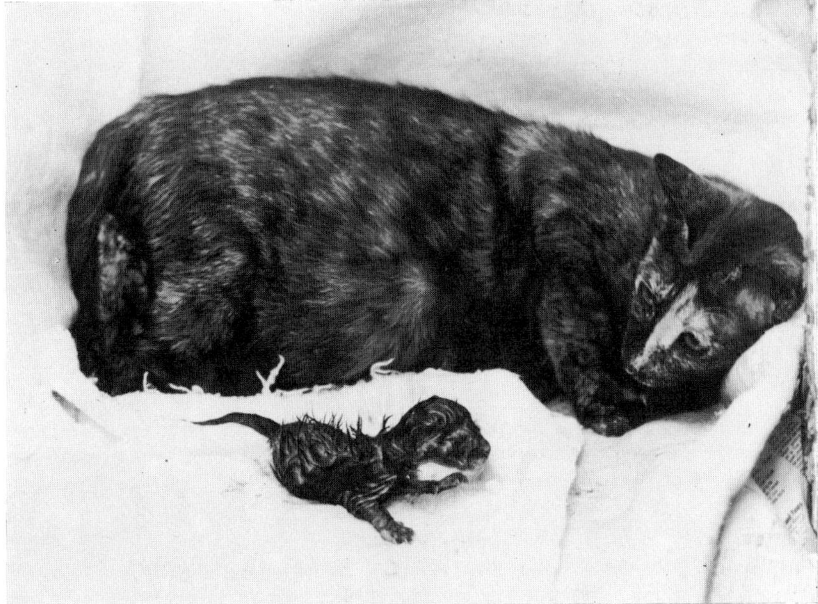

The first kitten free of its mother

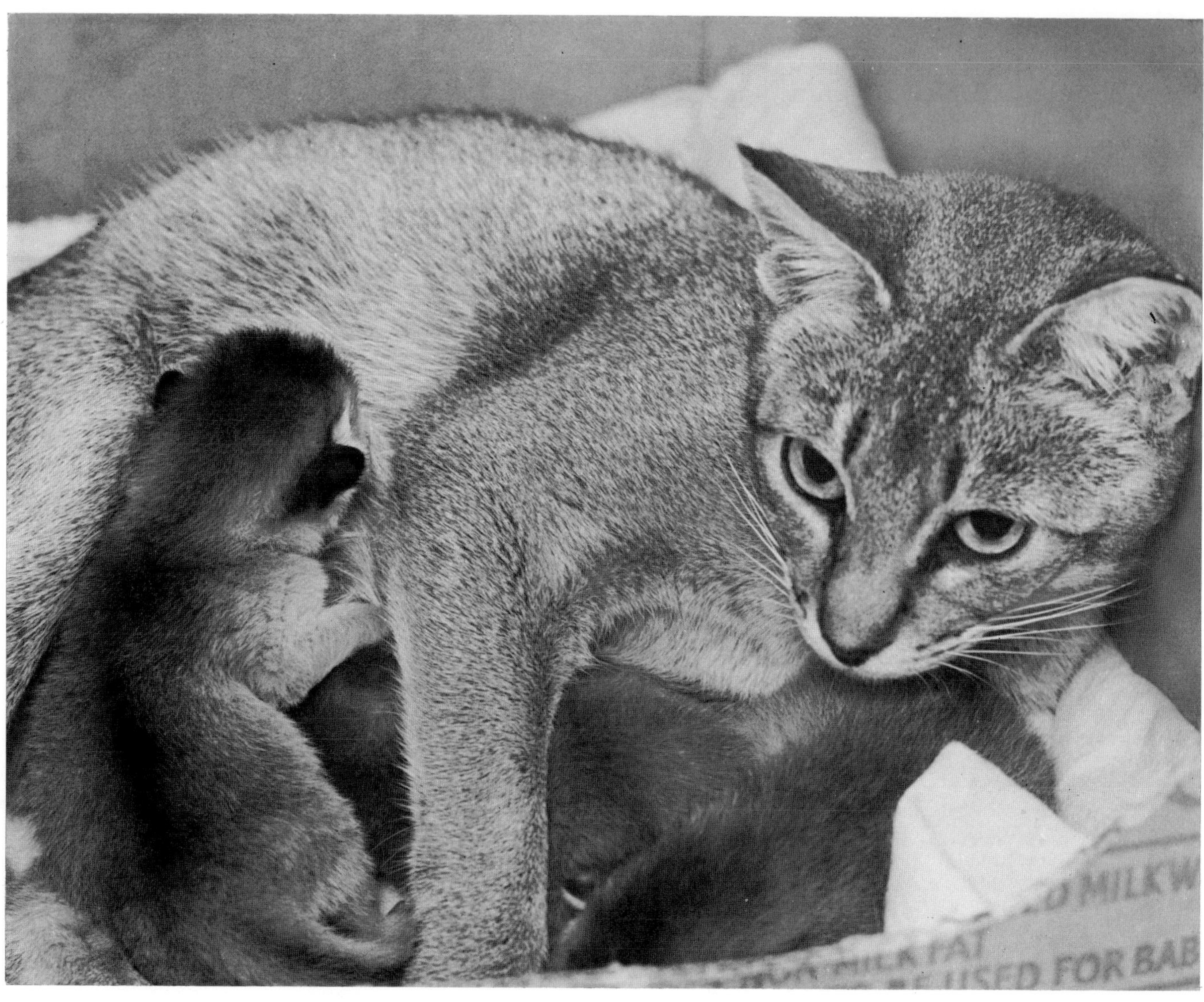

Suckling

feeds from the same one each time. Later they become less selective and freely explore the alternatives.

During the first two weeks the mother licks the anal and genital region of each kitten. This is essential to stimulate normal urination and defecation. It is very important therefore when hand rearing orphaned kittens, to remember to simulate the mothers actions by rubbing these areas gently with cotton wool.

At first during the lactation period the mother returns to the young to allow them to feed. Later when their eyes open, between 9 to 12 days, and they are able to move about the mother stands still some distance from the nest encouraging the kittens to go to her to suckle. Towards the end of lactation, as the sharp teeth get beyond a joke, the mother becomes increasingly reluctant to suckle her young and it requires persistent pursuit by the kittens.

Weaning begins towards the end of the 5th week and is usually complete by the 8th. In some domestic situations however, it is not unusual to see kittens still suckling from their mother up to a year of age. Such behaviour, seemingly offensive to some owners, causes no physical harm to either party and is apparently pleasurable to both.

Hunting behaviour After 5 weeks of age the kittens begin to follow their mother further from the nest. She brings back her kills for them to eat. About this time the kittens begin to play intensively and many of the components of hunting behaviour are observed in the games. As they grow they follow the mother on her expeditions to learn the necessary skills of hunting. Clearly contact with their mother and litter mates is essential in order to develop skill as a hunter. It could be deduced, and has been proved experimentally, that to produce good 'mousers' kittens should not be removed too early from their mother or litter mates. Interestingly, the father has no function in the rearing of kittens, this duty being entirely delegated to the mother.

From the play of infancy then the kitten learns how to hunt and kill. On sighting its prey a cat approaches with a smooth gliding movement, keeping close to the ground, making use of any available cover. Attaining a position close to the prey it hides, crouches for the attack and with a sudden rush pounces, attempting to trap the victim with its claws and bite the nape of its neck. Having made the kill it seeks a quiet place for consumption of the meal. In the well-fed domestic cat only partial sequences may be seen. The pouncing and grabbing components remain but killing is often postponed. Hunting behaviour is obviously pleasurable and rewarding to the cat, but in the wild its hunger precipitates the finality of the kill. Since the domestic cat is usually well fed the motivation to kill is less intense and the hunting is consequently prolonged. Thus we see cats 'playing' with mice and birds.

Territorial Behaviour In nature cats space themselves territorially, one cat to an area. The size of the territory depends among other things on the availability of suitable food in the area, for example the density of the rodent population. The domestic cat is however subjected to territories imposed by man. While they usually learn to adjust to this situation, the initial stages may be accompanied by fierce fighting which often produces unpleasant and debilitating abscesses.

Spraying Spraying is the term used to denote emission of jets of urine at particular objects, such as walls, curtains. It is a method of demarcating territory or to inform female cats of the presence of a male available for mating. This activity is performed by male cats, frequently but by no means always, by entire males; it is completely under voluntary control of the individual and is not related to a desire to empty a full bladder.

The act of spraying is characteristic. The tail is raised and often quivers; the cat directs its hindquarters in such a way that the backward facing penis, which may be seen protruding from the sheath, is aimed, often with a high degree of accuracy, at the object to be marked with urine; a jet of urine is emitted for a few seconds only. The posture adopted is quite different from the squatting position during normal urination.

A change in family circumstances, such as the advent of a baby or another cat, has frequently led to the development of spraying by neutered males. Siamese cats are particularly prone to this reaction. This would appear to reinforce the cats feeling of territorial security.

Because the urine of entire male cats and of those castrated after sexual maturity has a characteristic and to most people an offensive odour, the habit of spraying is unpleasant and can lead to friction in areas of dense population.

Sexual Behaviour Sexual behaviour in the female usually commences between 6 to 8 months of age. Males do not usually exhibit full mating behaviour before 10 months.

Female cats in the northern hemisphere show two main peaks of sexual activity in the year, January to March and again in May and June. During these months non-pregnant animals will come into 'heat' every 2 or 3 weeks and remain receptive or 'calling' for 4 to 10 days. While the female is calling she will roll on the floor, appear unstable on her hind legs and rub against the floor emitting a howling cry. To the uninitiated it may appear that she is in intense pain, and veterinary advice is often sought at this time. The only pain she is experiencing results from the psychological misery of sexual frustration.

Egyptian Mau kitten playing

Bi-colour Long-hair

Males range over considerable distances to contact receptive females. Before initiating copulation the male investigates the area, rubbing the scenting areas on his face, neck and tail against surrounding objects, spraying a highly scented secretion from two small anal glands, and occasionally urinating. This produces a very offensive smell, unacceptable to most human beings.

The male then examines the female, utters a specific call and finally grips the back of her neck. She may call, rub the floor, roll over and finally on being gripped by the neck assumes a crouching position. Taking a position astride the female the mating is quickly completed, accompanied by a unique cry from the female. As the male dismounts he is faced by unprovoked aggression from the discourteous female. Both then sit cleaning themselves for a time after which mating commonly recurs. Up to ten sequential matings in an hour have been observed between a pair. Males will mate with any receptive female while there is evidence that females may show discretion and demonstrate preference.

To prevent the problems associated with sexual behaviour it is common for cats to be neutered. Female cats are spayed, that is removal of the uterus and ovaries, while the testicles are extracted from the male, called castration. In the female, spaying at any age is effective but males castrated after the beginning of sexual behaviour, or puberty, show variable results from complete decline of sexual behaviour to the retention of many of its components including roaming, fighting and sterile mating. It does not, however, always remove the offensive smell of the male.

Abnormal Behaviour Abnormalities of behaviour are not infrequently presented to the veterinary surgeon for attention. Since behaviour may be the manifestation of an organic illness it is important that a full physical examination be made before purely behavioural possibilities are considered.

We have seen that the environment is very important to the cat and any change may precipitate alterations in behaviour. Thus the disappearance or death of an owner, change of house, introduction of a new baby or pet can cause a cat to stop eating, become listless and hide away, show aggression, anxiety – recognized by dilation of the pupils – or make attempts to escape. Many of these symptoms regress spontaneously after a few days but the situation can be aided by gentle handling and occasionally by medicament.

Cats born in semi-wild situations, out of contact with human beings until several weeks of age, often make timid, poorly socialized pets. Gentle handling and patience can again improve them but these animals rarely make ideal pets.

The provision of toys and moving objects has been said to eliminate the expensive attacks on nylon stockinged legs in flat-dwelling cats, thought to result from a frustrated hunting drive.

The introduction of a new cat or other pet may cause a house-trained cat to become dirty in the house. This is probably due to territory marking behaviour which usually resolves spontaneously.

Orphaned kittens with frustrated suckling needs have been known to develop a persistent habit of sucking soft furnishing.

The damage done to furniture by claws may be alleviated by the provision of a log or scratching post, although it needs to be introduced while the cat is young to be successful. The cutting of claws does not help since scratching is initiated when claws need sharpening and cutting will therefore exacerbate the condition.

The more we understand of the behaviour and 'thinking' of a cat, the more pleasure will we obtain from its presence and companionship.

Bells Small bells are attached by some owners to their cats' collars. This may be in order that the cats cannot stalk small birds and other prey in silence, or it may be to help the owners locate their recalcitrant cats when they want to bring them indoors. Since cats are so well adapted to moving about noiselessly, it seems a little unfair to saddle them with a tinkling sound from which they cannot escape. Bells are not recommended, except for use by people who cannot bear their cats to hunt birds.

An old fable tells of how a family of mice decided to hang a bell around the neck of their enemy, the cat, hence the expression, 'belling the cat'.

Bell's Palsy see FACIAL PARALYSIS

Bengal Tiger see TIGER

Bent tails see BREEDING ABNORMALITIES

Bi-coloured Cats with coats of two colours were entered in many of the early shows; the black and white being known as Magpies. In more recent times they have appeared at the shows in the Any Other Colour class (Long-hairs) and in the Any Other Variety class (Short-hairs), and as it was soon realized that they would be most useful in the breeding of Tortoiseshell and Whites and possibly other varieties, they were granted recognition, and given their own classes.

An old standard was revived requiring the markings to be similar to those of the Dutch rabbit, requiring a most distinct and concise division of the colour. This proved to be too exacting and almost impossible to reproduce, and the standard was amended to

> Any solid colour and white; the patches of colour to be clear and evenly distributed. Not more than two-thirds of the cat's coat to be coloured and not more than one half to be white.

The colours may be any solid colour and white, with the type as for the appropriate variety. The big round eyes may be deep orange or copper in colour.

left Blue and Seal Point Birman kittens

Tabby markings in the coat would be faulted, as would yellow or green eyes.

The new colour standards have been found much easier to produce and more are now appearing on the show benches. They are also known in the U.S.A. as Parti-colored.

See colour plates 3 *and* 4, *page 35.*

Bilateral luxation see BLINDNESS

Biliousness Biliousness is a popular term used to denote a condition of general malaise associated with lassitude, nausea, vomiting, especially of yellowish fluid, constipation or diarrhoea and loss of appetite. The condition, as the name implies, is usually ascribed to some disorder of the biliary secretions and gall bladder, but is more often due to a digestive upset in the cat.

See also GASTRO-ENTERITIS

Bird-chasing To humans, the most distressing aspect of bird-chasing – and mouse-, rat- and shrew-chasing likewise – is the way the cat tortures its prey, worrying, patting and even throwing it into the air for a considerable time before killing and eating it. Some people confiscate the prey from their cats, but it is probably more advisable to kill the animal and then give it back to the cat. After all, the cat is likely to be extremely mortified and puzzled at having his prey removed. Cats, furthermore, cannot be taught to refrain from bird-chasing; they can only be prevented from killing by confinement to the house. Bells may be used as a last resort, for those who find the destruction of wild birds insufferable; but it should be borne in mind that wild birds have many natural enemies, such as hawks, rats, foxes, and that one cat more or less will not have much effect on their welfare. See also BEHAVIOUR.

Birman The Birman, known also as the Sacred Cat of Burma, has no connection with the short-coated Burmese, having long fur and a Siamese coat pattern. Legend has it that they are descended from the Sacred cats that were the guardians of the temples in Burma. The standard differs from other long-haired cats, the body being long on low legs, the head wide and round with full cheeks, the eyes a bright china blue and the tail longish but bushy. The most distinctive feature, not found in any other variety, is the white paws, like gloves on all four feet; with those on the back legs coming to a point like a gauntlet. The colouring of the fur is as given for the Siamese – light coloured body with contrasting points. There are several point colourings being bred, Seal, Blue, Lilac and Chocolate.

Although the Birmans have been bred and exhibited on the Continent for more than thirty years, it is only comparatively recently that they have been introduced into Britain and into the U.S.A. but the numbers are increasing rapidly, with the kittens being much in demand.

See colour plate 5, *page 36.*

colour 3 Bi-coloured Long-hair
4 Bi-coloured Short-hair

3

4

colour 5 Birman and kitten

Birth By nature, cats prefer to give birth in an undisturbed and private environment, but it is, nevertheless, wise to observe them at intervals during the process of parturition so as to ensure nothing is amiss.

The average gestation period of the cat is usually considered to be 65 days, although a tendency to both longer and shorter gestations have been noted in some individual animals. A cat frequently shows a number of signs which will assist the owner in assessing when the kittening is likely to occur. For example, a drop in temperature of 1 or 2 degrees Fahrenheit occurs 1 or 2 days before the onset of parturition. The cat may cease feeding, seek solitude and start to make a nest for the litter. Swelling of the external genitalia, accompanied by mucus production, may be evident. The production of mammary secretion, which since it may take place several days before kittening, is an unreliable guide.

Parturition is generally considered to consist of 3 stages, the primary, secondary stage and tertiary. The primary stage is when involuntary contractions of the uterus are taking place, and this may cause the animal a little discomfort and restlessness. This stage takes anything from 2 to 24 hours. During the secondary stage, uterine contractions become much more powerful and frequent and are accompanied by voluntary straining on the part of the cat. She may pant a little or even make small grunting noises. A fluid-filled sac, known as the water bag is presented in the vulva, and usually breaks as the kitten is born.

The passage of the afterbirth (placenta) which normally follows each kitten is called the third or tertiary stage. The mother-cat knows instinctively that the membranes must be licked away from the face of each of her young offspring in order for them to breathe, and that she must bite the umbilical cord if it does not break, in order to sever the connection between the kitten and the placenta. In the rare event of the queen failing to carry out these maternal duties, the cat's owner should perform them for her. The membranes can be removed by hand or with a soft old towel; the umbilical cord is best cut about 4 inches from the kitten with clean blunt scissors, although people with sufficient experience may tear it while applying pressure with the thumb nails. Great caution must be exercised to avoid pulling on the kitten's umbilicus and causing herniation or even rupture of the abdomen. There is usually a resting period of variable length following the arrival of each kitten.

Kittens may be born head or tail first. The latter known as breech birth or a butt ended kitten is so common as to be regarded as normal by most authorities. In the event of prolonged straining occurring without a kitten being produced, or if part of a kitten is visible with little sign of the rest following, veterinary advice should be sought. The production of a greenish-black discharge without any kittens is also a sign that all is not well.

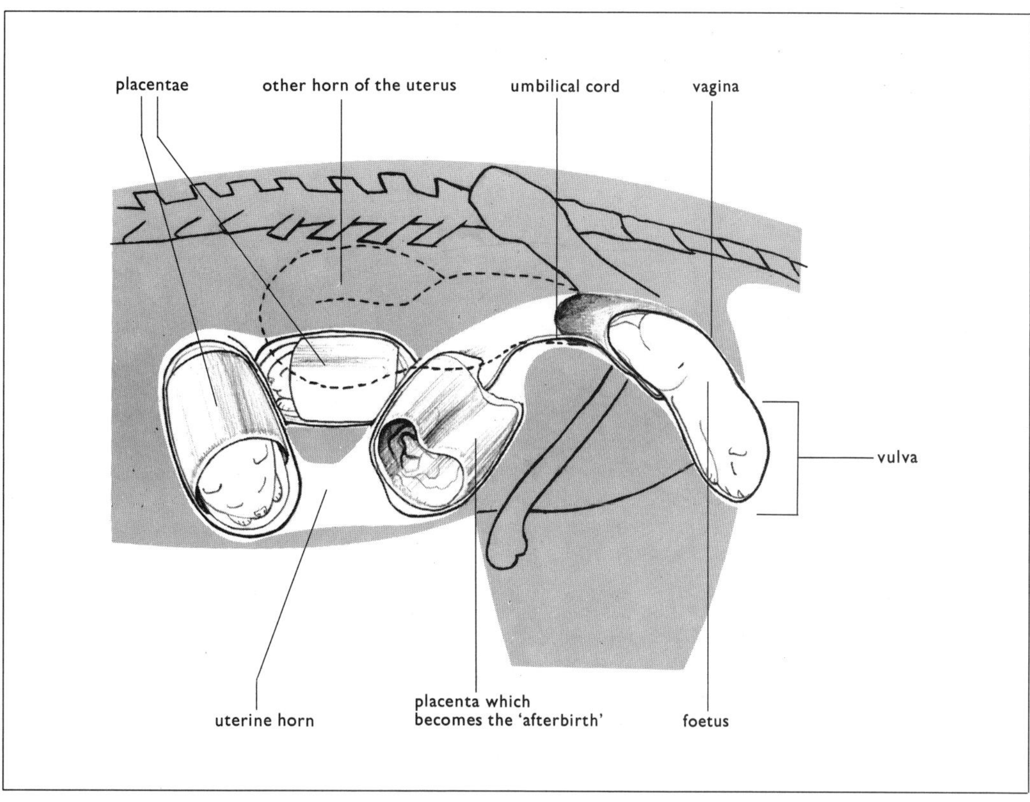

right Parturition of the first foetus and position of the remaining developed foetus

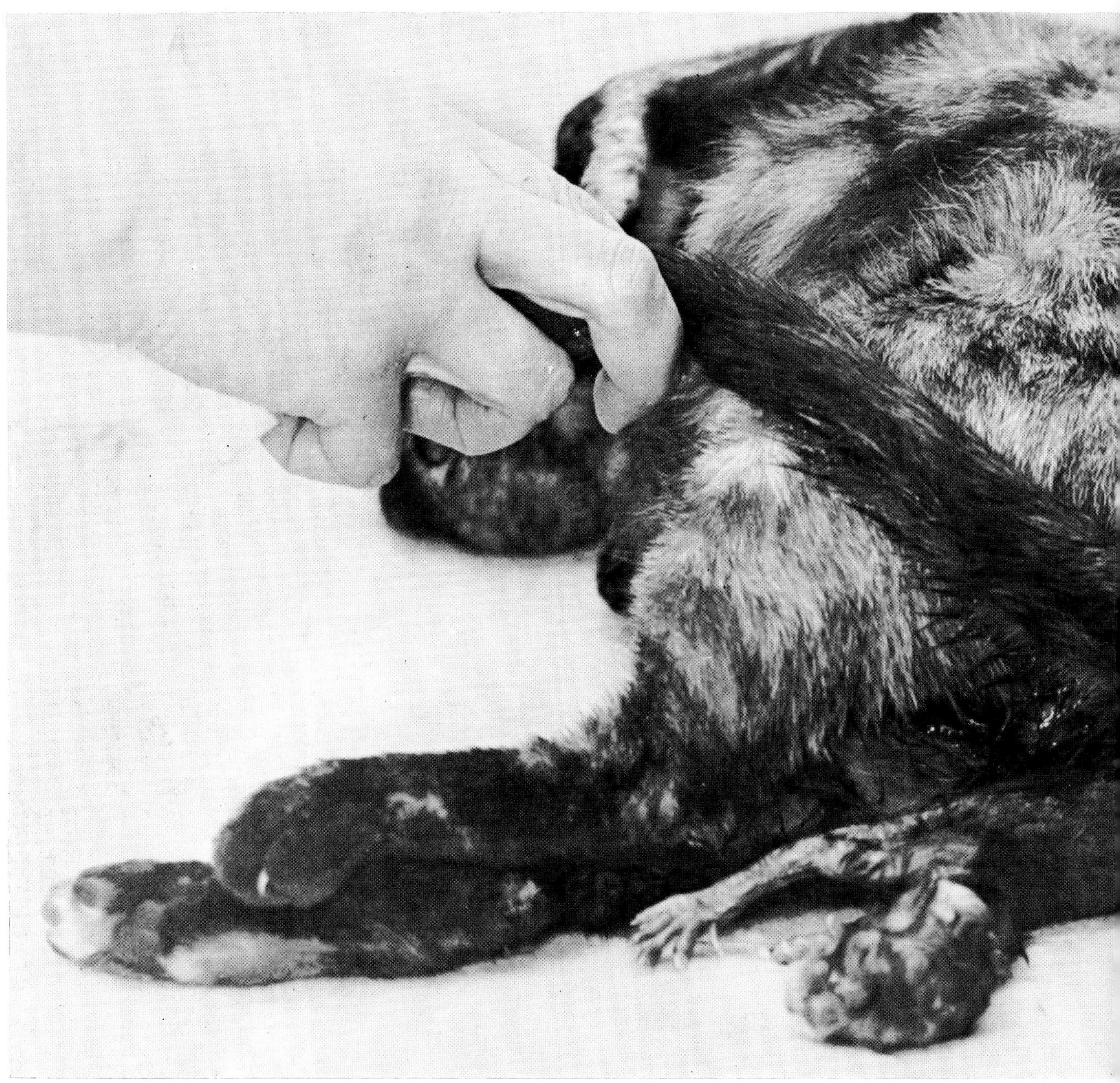

The mother eats the membranes produced during parturition. Undue disturbance of the mother should be avoided, and changing of the bedding material is inadvisable in the period immediately following kittening. It is far better to place clean bedding on top of the material that has been soiled.

Delayed Birth The term 'delayed birth' may be used to describe a long gestation period (pregnancy), or a delay in the birth of kittens once actual kittening has commenced.

A long gestation period appears to be an inherited characteristic as certain strains of cats will always carry their litters for longer than the average.

Delay in kittening may be said to occur when a kitten has not appeared after 45 minutes of purposeful straining on the part of the queen, and veterinary advice should be sought. Intervals between the birth of kittens are variable but usually comparatively short, ranging from 10 to 60 minutes. With small litters these intervals may be more prolonged. A type of interrupted labour sometimes occurs in the

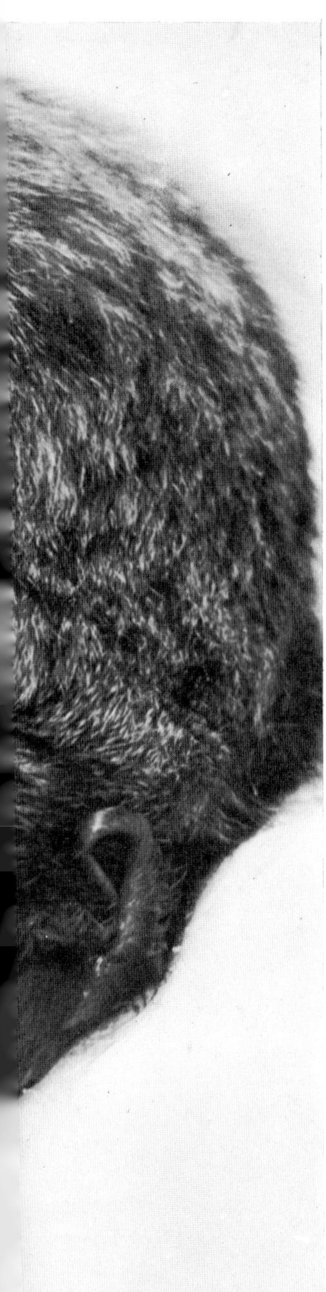

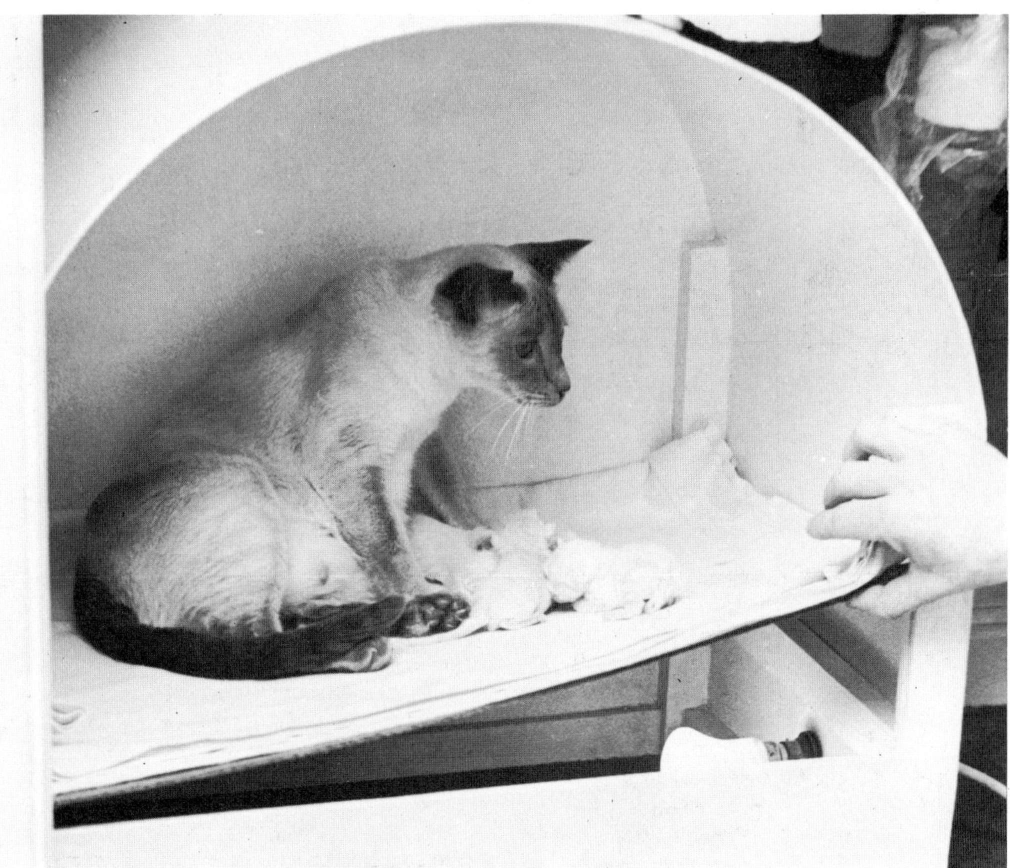

top left Some 60 per cent of kittens are born head first; *top right* a few hours old and searching for their mother's nipples; *bottom right* a whelping box with underfloor heating to prevent chills

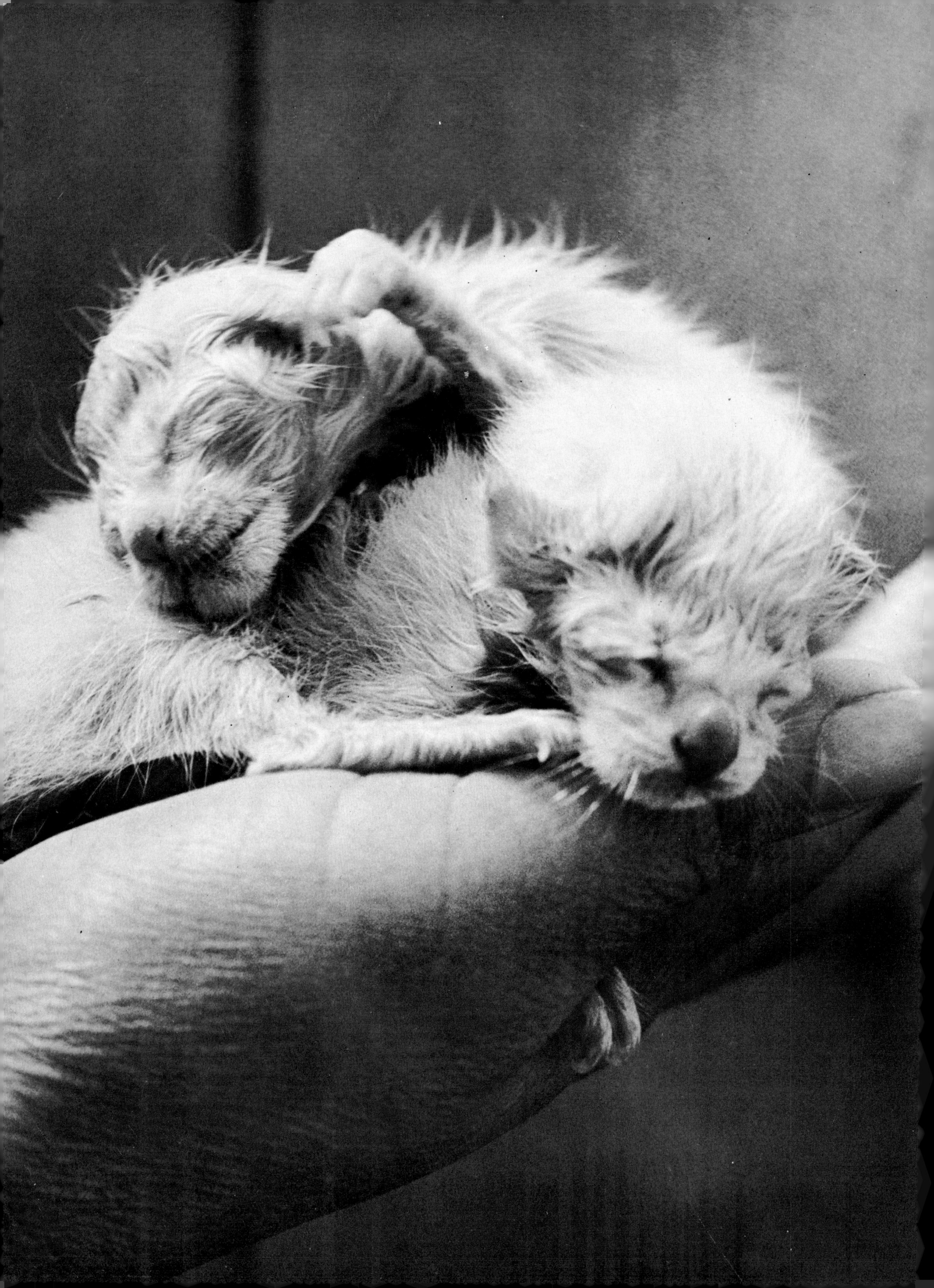

Just born Siamese

cat in which part of the litter is delivered normally, and there is then an interval of from 12 to 24 hours in which the queen apparently rests and generally behaves as though kittening is complete. At the end of this period, labour is resumed and the remainder of the litter is delivered without difficulty.

See also BEHAVIOUR, Mothering and CAESARIAN.

Birth Control The simplest method of birth control and the most commonly employed is to surgically remove the female reproductive apparatus. This is called spaying.

More recently however drugs in injectable and tablet form have become available which will prevent conception. Their use is mainly restricted to pedigree breeding females who are not required to produce young at certain times. These drugs should only be used on veterinary advice.

Biscuit Meal see COMMERCIAL CATFOODS

Bites A bite from another cat is probably the most common reason for a cat's attendance at the veterinary surgery. Since they are usually infected, bites will often cause painful abscesses on the body, commonly the head, legs and base of tail.

They usually occur during disagreements over territorial rights or breeding. See also BEHAVIOUR and ABSCESS.

Black Long-hair The Black Long-hairs are one of the oldest pedigree colours known, but there has never been a very large increase in the numbers appearing at the shows, although an outstanding Black has been Best in Show many times.

A well groomed adult cat with jet black fur and copper coloured eyes is very beautiful, but the would-be purchaser of a kitten of about ten weeks old may be put off by the rusty appearance. It is not always realized that sometimes it is not until the kitten reaches adult age that the coat becomes the dense shining black so much admired, many young kittens having brownish, greyish fur.

If a Black is to be exhibited, great care will be needed to keep the coat in show condition, as it tends to react both to strong sunshine and the damp, giving a sunburnt appearance, which would be penalized by the judge at the show.

In the past, many good Blacks have resulted from cross-breeding with blues, and an occasional outcross with this colour is still recommended to improve the type and eye colour. Blacks are useful in the breeding of Tortoiseshells, Tortoiseshell and Whites, Whites and the Bi-Colours.

The standard required is as given for the long-hairs, the faults being white hairs and rustiness of the coat.
See colour plate 6, page 45.

Black Panther see LEOPARD

Black Short-hair There are many black cats with short fur, but the majority are pets of unknown parentage. Most attractive, they may be, but there can be no comparison with a good pedigree specimen with jet black coat and typical British or American Short-hair type.

The pedigree Black should have a shining glossy coat, with no signs of white hairs. The fur should be black right down to the roots with no rusty or brown shadings, although the kittens may have a brownish tinge to their coats when young. The large round eyes should be a deep copper or orange in colour, with no trace of green. In the British standard, 25 points are allowed for the coat colour and 25 for the shape and eye colour.

By cross-mating, outstanding Blacks may be produced from the British Blues. The Black males make useful mates for the all-female Tortoiseshells and the Tortoiseshell and Whites. They have also been used to produce the old, but recently re-recognized Bi-colours, the cats with two coloured coats, once referred to as the Magpies.

There are many superstitions connected with Black cats, some people looking on them as unlucky, but others insisting they are lucky and refusing to turn one away should it come to their house.
See colour plate 7, page 45.

Black-footed Cat *Felis nigripes* is slightly smaller than the average domestic cat, and has a pale tawny-brown coat with white underparts; the body is marked with rather indistinct spots which darken towards the legs fusing together to form three rings. The head, neck and shoulders are striped. The soles of the feet are black which led to the designation of its name, but since many British tabbies possess this feature it is not outstanding. Type rather resembles the domestic cat and successful crosses have been reported.

Now very rare, its range includes the Kalahari Desert, Botswana and the western districts of the Orange Free State and parts of the Transvaal and eastern Cape.

Generally hunting at night like most wild cats, the Black-footed Cat is thought to take as its prey birds, small reptiles and the like. Zoologists are in agreement that our knowledge of this species as well as other small cats of Africa needs further study.

Bladder Disorders *Cystitis* Cystitis or inflammation of the urinary bladder is common in the cat. The cat makes frequent attempts to urinate but succeeds in passing only small amounts of urine. Outside the cat will dig a hole, strain for a while, cover up the hole and dig another one to repeat the process. The urine may be blood-stained and usually has an increased smell of ammonia. Sometimes there is a mild fever and the cat will often show signs of increased thirst. There may be stiffness of the hind-quarters and the animal may walk with a rather straddle-legged gait. The fur around the hindquarters may become soiled and stained with urine, again the ammoniacal odour being noticeable.

Treatment is by the administration of the broad-spectrum antibiotics or the urinary sulphonamides. Any obstruction to the free flow of urine should receive the most urgent attention. An increased water intake will serve to dilute the urine and the infection. It can be assured by mixing water with the cat's food, by adding salt to the diet, or by giving salt tablets.

Bladder Sand Bladder sand causes obstruction to the passage of urine through the urethra, the passage leading from the bladder to the exterior of the body. It occurs quite frequently in both entire and neutered male cats. The obstruction is caused by the accumulation in the bladder of struvite (magnesium ammonium phosphate hexahydrate) in the form of sand-like crystals or sabulous plugs. This material precipitates out of the urine, then passes down the urethra where it becomes impacted at the narrowest part causing a progressive obstruction back to the bladder. The actual cause of the condition remains unknown. There is some suggestion that a virus may be concerned in the causation of the condition.

Symptoms are that the cat makes frequent attemps to pass urine, sitting on its sanitary tray or over holes in the garden for several minutes at a time without success. There is usually obvious straining and sometimes this is accompanied by a low moan of apparent pain. Often the penis is extruded from its sheath and the cat will frequently lick the tip of the organ sometimes resulting in quite severe damage to the delicate skin. The owner often wrongly supposes that the cat is constipated and will administer aperients, with the result that valuable time is lost before the cat is presented for treatment. If the obstruction is not relieved, the animal loses its appetite and becomes apathetic and listless. With the build up of waste products in the blood stream there is vomiting, dehydration, coma and death. Inflammatory changes occur in the lining of the bladder due to secondary bacterial infection of the retained contents and there may be considerable haemorrhage into the urine.

Treatment is surgical and comprises the removal of the obstruction. When the obstruction cannot be relieved it may be treated by by-passing the penile part of the urethra by connecting the bladder directly to the exterior of the body.

Prevention of recurrence of obstruction is of prime importance and can be achieved by lowering the specific gravity of the urine by increasing the water intake, and by adjusting the diet to exclude foods rich in magnesium. The water intake of the cat can be increased by mashing one-third of a teacupful of water to each meal. Most meats and fish have a high magnesium content, whereas a low magnesium level is found in milk, eggs, tripe, tinned luncheon meat, beef dripping and carrots. Some foods which are high in magnesium are also high in calcium which means that a lower urinary magnesium level is produced. Some proprietary tinned cat foods fall into this category. These dietary restrictions should, of course, only be applied to known 'stone formers', 'non-stone formers' should have as varied a diet as possible.

Cystic Calculi Cystic (Vesical) calculi, or stones in the bladder, are not very common in the cat and when they do occur are usually seen in the female rather than the male. The stones may be single or multiple. The symptoms are very similar to those seen in cystitis and are, in fact, reflections of the irritation and inflammation induced in the bladder lining by the presence of the stone(s). There is generally more straining when the cat urinates and the urine is more often blood-stained. Treatment is essentially surgical and consists of the removal of the stones from the bladder via an abdominal incision. Prevention of recurrence depends upon control of urinary tract infection, dilution of the urine by increased water intake, acidification of the urine by means of drugs, and feeding the cat a low-ash diet.

Atony of the Bladder Atony or loss of tone of the muscular wall of the bladder may occur following upon urethral obstruction, particularly where the obstruction has been partial and the gradual onset has led to prolonged overdistention of the organ with consequent overstretching and fatigue of the muscle fibres. It may also occur where there has been damage to the nervous control of the bladder, usually a consequence of a road accident and sometimes accompanied by paralysis of the tail or even of the whole of the hindquarters. The symptoms are that the cat's abdomen becomes distended as the bladder fills up and this is followed by the dribbling of small quantities of urine from the overfull organ. The fur of the hindquarters becomes soiled with urine and the constant wetting may lead to chapping of the skin of the area. There is a noticeable smell of ammonia due to bacterial decomposition of the urine retained in the fur. If the abdomen is gently pressed urine will escape fairly freely. Treatment is difficult, especially where the nervous control is involved, and consists mainly of the frequent manual emptying of the bladder combined with the administration of antibiotics to avert a retention cystitis supervening.

The cat should be kept as clean and as comfortable as possible until normal bladder function is regained.

See also HAEMATURIA.

Bladder Sand see BLADDER DISORDERS

Bleeding see ARTERIAL BLEEDING and HAEMORRHAGE

Blind Teats see TEATS

Blindness This condition is fortunately not commonly reported in the cat but may be due to a number of causes:

1. Microphthalmia when the eyeball components are reduced in size and some may be absent. In very severe cases, vision is impossible.
2. Bilateral luxation of the eyeball is very unusual, as it is almost always one eyeball that is displaced. In the event of its occurring, however, total blindness would ensue unless very prompt skilled treatment was available to replace both eyeballs in their sockets before irreversible damage had taken place.
3. Malignant neoplasms (cancers) that invade the eye tissue.
4. Cataracts if allowed to progress, will frequently cause total loss of vision. Cataracts are caused by a number of factors, including microphthalmia, inflammatory or degenerative diseases of the eye, or diabetes mellitus.
5. Severe infection of the eye usually acquired at the time of a cat fight.

Although normal cats have great acuity of vision, both in daylight and in the dark, blindness or partial blindness is not so great a disability as to necessitate humane destruction in all cases. Sympathetic and imaginative management of a cat whose vision has been impaired will often enable it to continue a contented existence. For example, the owner should take care always to keep the cat's bed or basket in exactly the same place, should avoid changing the layout of furniture in the house too frequently, and protect the cat from possible dangers that he cannot perceive by means of vibrations, smell or sound. See also EYES AND EYELID DISORDERS.

Blow-fly Strike see MYIASIS

Blue Burmese see BURMESE

Blue Chinchilla As yet an unrecognized variety in Britain, Blue Chinchillas are produced by mating a Chinchilla with a Blue Long-hair. The type is as for other long-hairs, the coat long and silky, with blue replacing the white of the Chinchillas, but with typical tickings on the head, flanks, back and tail. The Chinchilla has sea-green eyes and the Blues deep orange and copper, but the former colouring is lost, with those of the Blue Chinchilla normally being orange or amber. They may also be produced from matings with Blacks and Smokes. There should be no tabby markings.

The Blue Chinchillas seen in Britain should not be confused with the Shaded Silvers recognized in North America and other parts of the world. These are a pure bred form a darker Chinchillas, but it will take some time to reproduce the Blue Chinchillas with the required number of generations of pure breeding. Once this is done, application will probably be made to the Governing Council of the Cat Fancy for recognition and a breed number. At the moment, they may only be shown in the Any Other Colour classes. Although known in the U.S.A. and on the Continent, there are, as yet, no recognized standards.
See colour plate 8, page 46.

Blue Cream Burmese see BURMESE, NEW COLOURS

Blue Cream Long-hair Produced from Blue and Cream matings, ideally this most attractive variety should have a coat with blue and cream softly intermingled, giving a shot-silk effect. It is difficult to produce such a coat to perfection, and frequently there may be patches of colours, which is liked in North America, but is a fault in Britain and on the Continent.

The Blue Cream males are a rarity and invariably sterile. Although Blue Creams may appear in litters from Tortoiseshells, they are usually produced by cross-breeding the Blue Long-hairs with the Creams. A Blue Cream mated to a Cream male may produce Blue Cream females, Blue males, Cream males and Cream females. Mated to a Blue, she could have Blue Cream females, Blue males and females and Cream males.

As the two colours used in the production of this variety are known for their good type, the best Blue Creams are outstanding in this respect, having good broad heads, neat ears and big round eyes of deep orange or copper.

A cream blaze, a mark running down from the forehead, is liked by breeders and certainly adds to the attractiveness of the face. Faults are any red colouring in the coat, solid paws (of one colour rather than intermingled) and definite patches of blue or cream. In the U.S.A. definite patches of blue and cream are called for in the standard. The shot-silk effect is considered a fault.
See colour plate 9, page 47.

Blue Cream Point see SIAMESE, ANY OTHER COLOUR

Blue Cream Short-hair An all-female variety, any males born invariably proving to be sterile, the Blue Creams are produced in the first place from Blue and Cream matings (see CREAM SHORT-HAIRS). They appear also occasionally from Tortoiseshell breeding.

The British and Continental standards require the pastel shades of the fur to be of blue and cream softly intermingled, with no patching. This is exceedingly difficult to produce and most specimens seen at the British shows have some form of patching. The American and Canadian standards call for the coat to be blue with patches of solid cream, the patching to be well defined. Any sign of tabby markings is regarded as a serious fault by any standard.

In the British standard 40 points are given for type alone, which is usually very good; 35 points are given for the colour; 20 for the eyes, which may be copper, orange or yellow, never green. The coat texture is important. It must be short and fine, never coarse or harsh to the touch. For American standard see AMERICAN SHORT-HAIR.

Breeders like the Blue Creams not only for their equable temperament, but also for the charming variety of kittens it is possible for them to produce, according to the stud used.
See colour plate 10, *page 47.*

Blue Cross The Blue Cross, which incorporates Our Dumb Friends League, is an animal welfare organization in the U.K. It provides facilities for the treatment of animals by qualified veterinarians and assists in collection and disposal of stray animals. Several well-equipped modern hospital complexes have been built by this organization.

Blue Long-hair The most popular of the Long-haired varieties, and also for a very long time, the variety considered to be nearest to the set standard, but now possibly the Whites and the Creams are also coming very close. The Blues have been used in the past to improve nearly all the self-coloured Long-hairs and have also been used in planned breeding for the production of new varieties, such as the Colourpoints. They are also known as Blue Persians.

left Blue Long-hair kitten

The characteristics required are as given for all Long-hairs, and the champions seen at the shows with their broad heads, well-placed small ears, round copper coloured eyes, firm chins with enormous ruffs forming halos around the head are certainly very near perfection. Any shade of blue is permissible, as long as it is even all over, but many prefer the paler shades. White hairs in the coats are faults, as are green rims to the eyes, and kinks in the tails. Over-typing, that is extra short noses, should be avoided, as it may cause weepy eyes.

The kittens are usually born with tabby markings, which disappear as the fur grows, and in a very short while they become most attractive and very photogenic, their pictures frequently appearing on chocolate boxes.
See colour plate 11, *page 47.*

Blue Persian see BLUE LONG-HAIR

Blue Point see HIMALAYAN and SIAMESE

Blue Russian see MALTESE and RUSSIAN BLUE

Blue Smoke see SMOKE LONG-HAIR

Blue Tabby see TABBY LONG-HAIR and TABBY SHORT-HAIR

Blue Tortie Point see SIAMESE, ANY OTHER COLOUR

Blue Tortoiseshell and White see TORTOISE-SHELL AND WHITE LONG-HAIR.

Boarding Since cats relate to territories rather than people it is kinder to leave them in their own surroundings providing adequate supervision is available from a friend or neighbour.

When this is impossible it becomes necessary to board in a cattery. Great care should be exercised when selecting a cattery since they are very variable in quality. Examine the establishment before booking and make sure it is clean, efficiently run and that it is under some form of veterinary supervision. The best boarding establishments insist on adequate vaccination certificates. It is essential therefore to consult your veterinary surgeon to ensure your compliance.

Acquaint the cattery owner with particular food preferences of your cat and if possible leave an address where you can be contacted.

Bobcat *Felis rufa,* referred to also as the Bay Lynx on account of the colour, is closely related to the Northern Lynx, and the head and facial markings are almost identical. The short 'bobtail', responsible for its name, is only about 5–7 in. long and is dark on the upper part with white underneath; this is unlike the Lynx whose tail tip is entirely black which assists greatly in identification.

colour 6 Black Long-hair
7 Black Short-hair

overleaf 8 Blue Chinchilla
9 Blue Cream Long-hair
10 Blue Cream Short-hair
11 Blue Long-hair
12 British Blue

6

7

◁ 8

10

12

colour 13 British Cream
14 Burmese Blue
15 Burmese Brown
16 Burmese Cream

below right The Bobcat, *Felis rufa*

The Bobcats' colouring is reddish-brown on the back which gradually shades to creamy white on the underparts, but lighter specimens occur which are pale brown and the density and distribution of spotting is variable. This no doubt occurs on account of its distribution which covers the U.S.A. well into Canada and most of Mexico, and the wide difference in climatic conditions of which it has a great tolerance, but genetic study would be of interest. The fur is of little commercial value as it is considered much too brittle.

Comparing the size to that of the Northern Lynx, again great variation is noted but the Bobcat is usually the smaller of the two and unlike the Northern Lynx, has small paws. Some sizes quoted for males give a length of 32–50 in. and for females 28–48 in. In some instances 48 in. are quoted for the Northern Lynx but the latter is somewhat higher to the shoulder. It is only to be expected that with man's devastation to the wildcats environment great deviation in sizes and mode of life will be found from now on.

The Bobcat prefers more open country to the lynx, but may sometimes be found in dense forest. Prey usually consists of small mammals and birds although occasionally bigger prey such as White-tailed deer, sheep or calves are taken and, like many other cats, raids on domestic poultry yards are not
14 unknown. An excellent climber, it may be dis-
16 covered resting on the limbs of a tree during the day.

Bobtail see JAPANESE BOBTAIL.

Bombay In the U.S.A., there is a new variety known as the Bombay, bred originally from cross-matings between the Burmese and the American Short-hair.

The Bombay is a short-coated black cat, with the fur having almost a patent leather sheen. The head should be round, the ears medium in size with slightly rounded tips, and the wide-apart eyes may be yellow to copper in colour. The muscular body should be medium in size, with the males being slightly larger than the females. The tail too should be of medium length, without kink.

Bone Disorders *Broken* Causes of breakage (fracture) of bones of cats fall into two broad categories; mechanical causes, which include direct impact, and spontaneous or pathological causes, which renders the bone extremely fragile, so that it breaks on a normally harmless impact. This last cause is very rare in the cat.

Fractures vary enormously in their complexity, from single fissure and greenstick type, to those involving damage to nerves, blood vessels and possibly even organs such as the bladder or lungs. Sometimes a single bone is crushed into a large number of fragments, and pieces of bone may pierce the skin. There is then a grave danger of infection of the bone occurring. Modern surgical techniques, now mean that it

is practical to attempt treatment of the majority of broken bones.

Antibiotics are often employed to reduce the risk of infection which retards healing.

Neoplasia The commonest neoplasia of cat bone is the osteosarcoma, a malignant growth which often becomes large enough to affect normal function and to exert pressure on surrounding soft tissues. It may occur in any bone of the body. Secondary tumours – known as metastases – are often associated with osteosarcomas. They may occur in the lungs, with fatal consequences. Osteosarcoma is an extremely malignant tumour, and surgical treatment is extremely difficult and unlikely to effect any long-lasting relief.

Chondrosarcomas, malignant tumours of the cartilage found at the ends of bones, are sometimes seen in joints such as the hock and shoulder. Again, metastases are common.

Another type of tumour affecting the skeleton is known as periosteal fibrosarcoma. This is a tumour involving the fibrous tissue of the periosteum – a strong membrane surrounding the bone, and responsible for its nourishment. These neoplasms are frequently extremely large, but fortunately rarely form metastases.

Osteomyelitis Osteomyelitis is infection of the bone. It is a serious condition which usually requires extensive surgical treatment and may result in amputation where this is possible. Antibiotics have greatly improved the chance of successful treatment but it remains a difficult and dangerous condition.

See also DISLOCATIONS.

Bonemeal Bonemeal, which is produced by the grinding to flour of sterilized animal bones, is a valuable source of calcium and phosphorus in the diet of growing, pregnant and lactating cats.

Since, however, there is a danger of feeding too much calcium and phosphorus it is wise to consult a veterinarian before adding bonemeal to your cat's diet.

Boots Boots or overshoes are a necessary item of equipment wherever a number of cats are maintained and a high standard of cleanliness has to be observed as they control the spread of infection. They are invaluable to breeding, boarding and quarantine establishments.

There are several types of footwear to suit individual requirements which range from disposable overboots to full length rubber thigh boots with cleated soles, three-quarter length thigh boots or half wellingtons. The latter range stand up well to hard wear and to walking through disinfectant trays at cattery entrances.

Disposable type shoes should always be available for the use of Public Health Inspectors, Veterinary

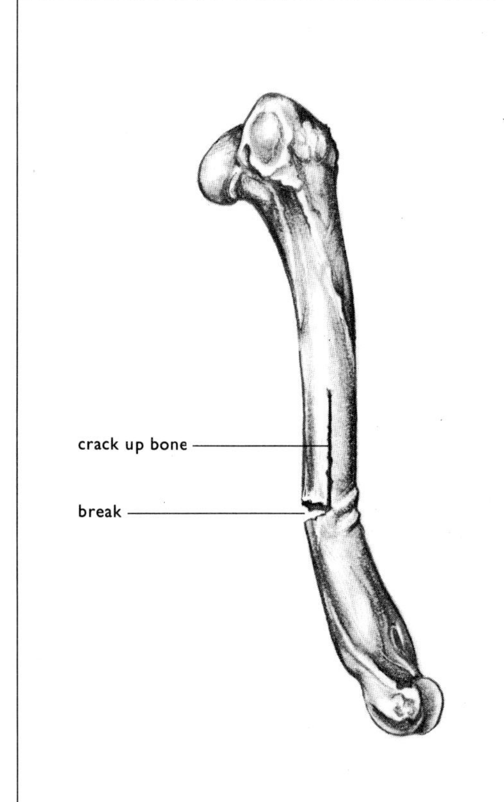

BONES, BROKEN *right* A greenstick fracture; *below left* a transverse fracture; *below right* a comminuted fracture

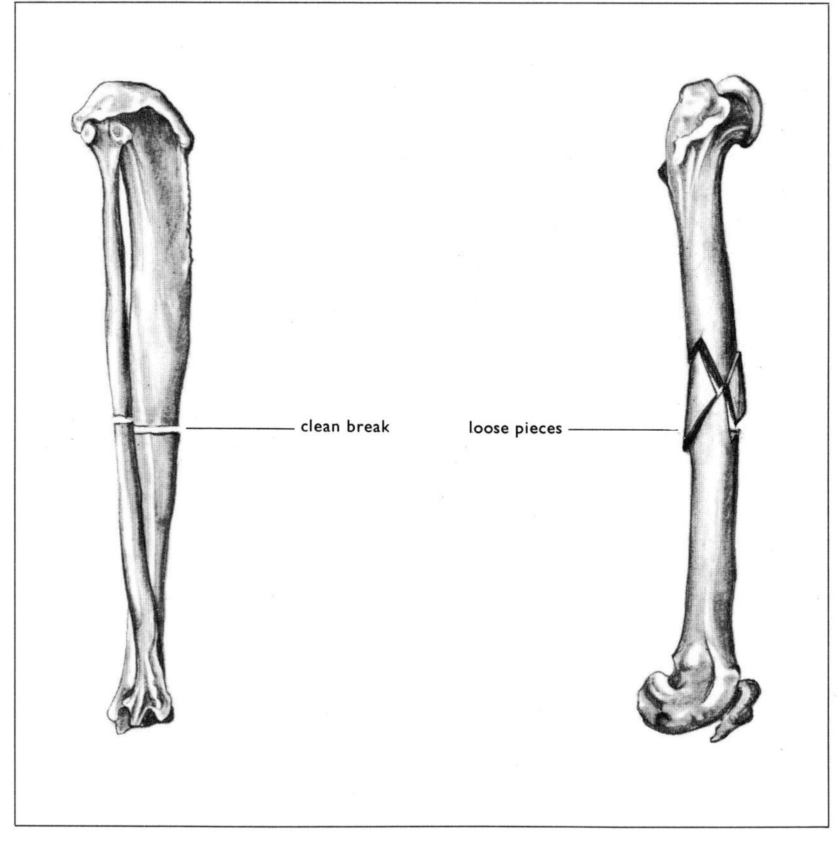

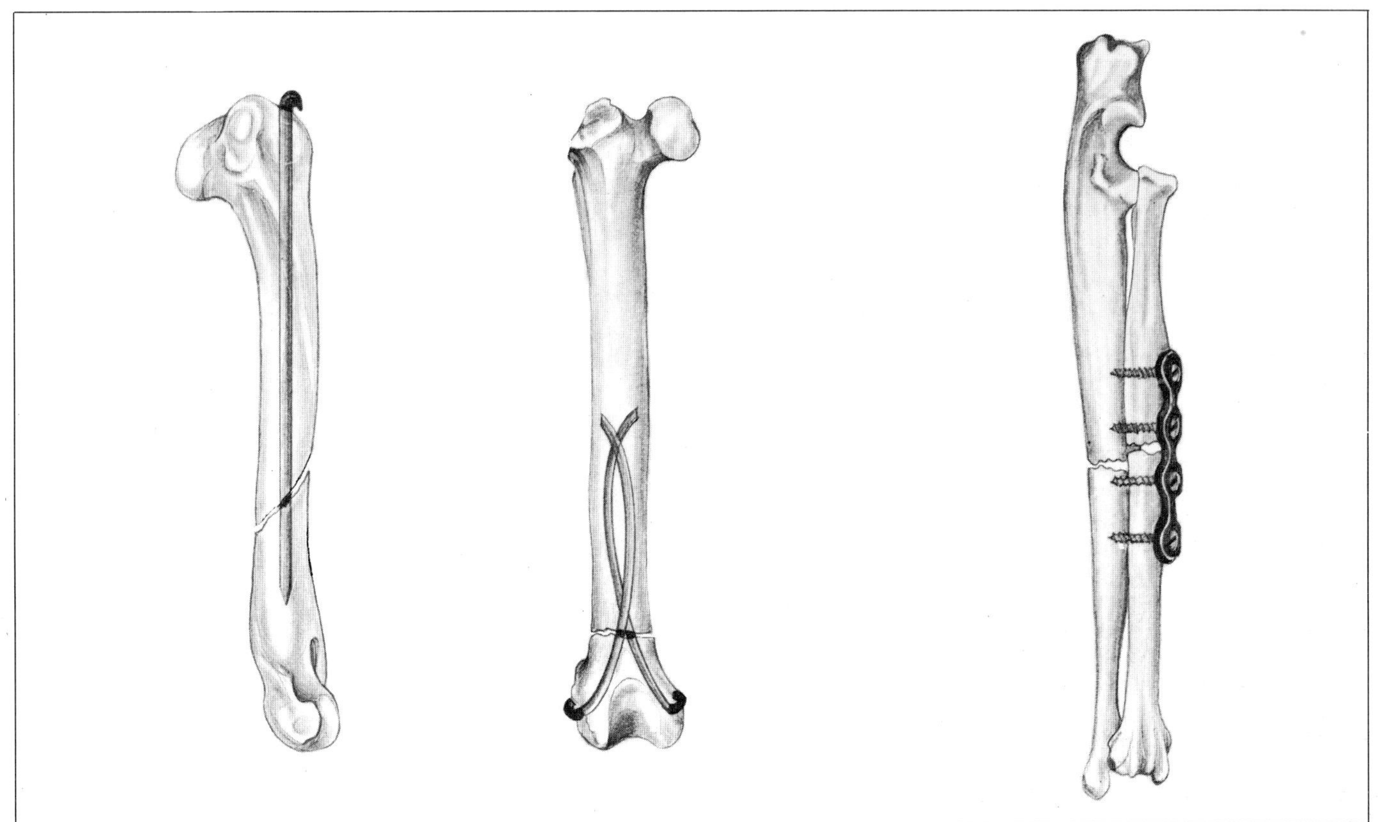

Surgeons, Clients, or where an outbreak of infection has taken place, whether in cattery or home.

They are obtainable from suppliers of veterinary protective clothing and shops specializing in feline accessories.

BONES, BROKEN *above* Three repair methods: *left* retrograde pinning of the humerus with an intermedullary pin; *centre* two rush-type pins used to repair a supracondyloid fracture of the femur; *right* a bone plate repair of radius and ulna

Brain Disorders The brain is a very sensitive organ which is extremely susceptible to damage. Fortunately it is housed in a container of bone. Damage occurs as a result of accidents, infections or poisons and should always be treated by veterinary surgeons.

Since the brain controls all the body's functions damage to it may cause a wide variety of symptoms. The commonest include, fits, inco-ordination of movement, circling, changed behaviour and unconsciousness.

Fits A fit is a loss of consciousness accompanied by rhythmic involuntary movements on the part of the patient. Violent paddling action of the limbs, thrashing of the tail, twitching of the facial muscles and champing of the jaws are commonly observed. Salivation, defaecation and urination may occur. Fits are the result of brain abnormalities which may be temporary or permanent in nature. Although fits are extremely distressing for the owner, the fact that loss of consciousness is involved means that they are not so for the cat, the main risk to the patient is choking, or injury by colliding with surrounding objects. It is best thus to remove the animal to a dark quiet room in which there is little furniture. Veterinary advice should be sought in all cases of fits.

Concussion Concussion is caused by the transmission of the impact of a blow on the skull to the brain. It involves a degree of loss of consciousness, varying from dizziness and inco-ordination to collapse and loss of reflexes. Concussion may follow compressed fracture of the skull. It may be immediate or delayed. Recovery is possible if the condition is correctly treated. Minor behavioural changes are, however, sometimes observed after recovery of consciousness, and it would appear that post-concussion amnesia cannot be ruled out. See also NYSTAGMUS.

Encephalitis This term refers to inflammation of the brain. A wide variety of behavioural changes may occur, often accompanied by general symptoms of illness. The condition usually results from infections. Treatment is difficult owing to the difficulty of getting drugs to the brain.

Epilepsy This condition is extremely rare in the cat. Epileptic fits occur often without warning. The cat is unaware of its actions during the attack and all that should be done is to prevent it from injuring itself. Following the fit it may appear somewhat dazed. Treatment is possible but depends on the severity and frequency of the attacks.

Neoplasia The effect of a growth in the brain depends entirely on the part affected and so affects the relevant part of the body.

Breaking Wind see FLATULENCE

Breast Bone see STERNUM

Breathing Breathing, or external respiration, is the name given to the alternating filling and emptying of the lungs with air. This is a continuous process in all living mammals.

Air entering through the nose passes into the naso-pharynx, the pharynx and thus into the trachea (windpipe). The trachea branches into two bronchii, which in turn split up into a lot of smaller pipes called bronchioles. These terminate in the tiny air sacs or alveoli.

The lungs have an excellent blood supply which takes oxygen from the inspired air in the air sacs, to all parts of the body where it is used to release energy.

Breathing is an involuntary action, the cat making no conscious effort to breathe. The lungs continually fill and empty.

Breathing difficulty see DYSPNOEA

Breed A breed is a variety of cat, which has characteristics distinguishing it from other members of the species and which are consistent when two members of the same breed are mated to produce a litter.

Breed Clubs and Societies Among the many cat clubs and societies in Britain, there are a number known as the specialist or breed clubs. These, such as the Siamese Cat Club, which is the largest, look after the interests of a particular variety or varieties rather than catering for all breeds.

The specialist clubs may nominate fanciers they consider would make good judges of the variety for which they cater, for approval by the Governing Council of the Cat Fancy. If it is considered necessary, a specialist club may suggest certain alterations to the standard of points, for instance the Black and White Cat Club have recently had 'an undershot jaw shall be considered a defect' added to the description of the head shapes required for the Black and the White Long-hairs.

Several of the specialist clubs run a show for cats and kittens of their variety, with the Blue Persian Society running one for Blue Long-hairs only, and several of the Siamese Clubs for Siamese only.

Breeder The term breeder is non-specific. No qualifications are required and no special knowledge needed before the title is assumed. There is therefore a wide cross-section of breeders from the well informed to the totally inept. Aspiring breeders should join one of the cat fancy clubs before embarking on breeding and should seek the advice of their veterinarian.

Breeding Breeding, since it incorporates certain restrictions of normal mating, requires knowledge and understanding of the feline reproductive procedure.

Stud Management For stud management to be described as successful or even satisfactory a high conception rate amongst visiting queens must be achieved. High conception rates can only result if the breeding cycle of the species is fully understood; this is particularly important in cats.

In the female cat ovulation (the shedding of ripe, fertilisable eggs from the ovary) is *not* spontaneous; it results from a suitable stimulus, usually the act of mating. Ovulation occurs 24–36 hours later.

Pre-mating behaviour plays a part in getting the ova (eggs) in the ovary ready for discharge. The queen herself must take an active part in the act of coitus, hence controlled matings such as are carried out with some other animals are not feasible.

It is quite obvious that pre-mating behaviour cannot be entirely simulated when dealing with pedigree stud cats.

The queen should be allowed to remain in close proximity to the chosen stud during her pro-oestrous phase with the tom being allowed access to her occasionally under supervision to test her receptivity. When she is willing to be mated it is preferable to allow the male and female to remain together so that several services daily can take place. Conception frequently does not follow a single service and may not follow two but usually results after three or more services within a 24-hour period.

Stud cats in popular demand are often not allowed to serve a queen as often as is desirable to prevent overtiring. It is far better to allow multiple matings however and get a high conception rate rather than risk many queens missing; if need be a higher stud fee should be charged.

In the breeding season tom cats mate frequently but do usually have a non-breeding period of 2–4 months in the autumn; some toms in breeding catteries do not have this rest, hence the number of queens should be controlled.

Although capable of siring kittens earlier, male cats are best allowed to mature fully before starting a stud career, at between 10 to 18 months. They should not be allowed too many queens during the first few months. Stud cats require a highly nutritious diet to ensure physical fitness during the main breeding season.

Experimental Breeding Breeding to establish new varieties in the cat world should only be undertaken by breeders with a wide knowledge of the species and with a good grounding in genetical principles.

Introducing a stud to the queen so that they become acquainted before mating

The resultant offspring of such experiments should be carefully examined at each generation for the detection of undesirable characteristics which may prove detrimental to the cat. This examination should be carried out by a veterinary surgeon and, if possible, representative post mortem examinations undertaken. In this way it should be possible to avoid the perpetuation of congenital abnormalities which are proving such a trial to dog breeders.

In-breeding In-breeding is the practice of mating together closely related animals with the aim of duplicating good points of both parents. The core of in-breeding is relationship, the closer the better, so that parent-offspring or brother-sister matings are often used. The term is sometimes expanded to include less close relationships such as half-sister, half-brother, etc. Strict weeding-out or culling of kittens showing undesirable features is essential for successful in-breeding, certainly in the early stages of the breeding programme and possibly for many generations.

Advantages of in-breeding are that it fixes type quicker than any other technique, it fixes desirable characters thereby increasing the prepotency of individual animals, it tends towards the formation of distinct families within a breed and family-based selection of breeding stock is better than selection based on individuals.

Disadvantages of in-breeding are that it fixes undesirable characters just as much as desirable traits. It may easily give rise to a line of mediocre animals which may prove extremely difficult to improve, and the severe culling required is not easy for the true cat lover.

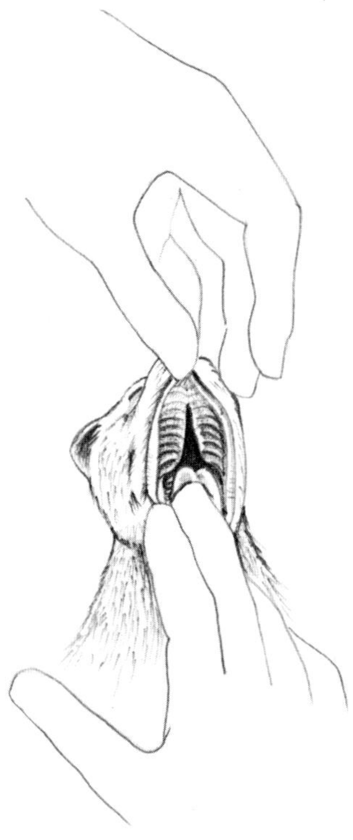

Cleft palate

Line-breeding Line-breeding may be defined as the mating of individuals within a particular line of descent, in an attempt to keep the offspring as closely related as possible to an outstanding forebear. Like in-breeding, this technique is no method for the novice as it requires a knowledge of pedigrees and the actual cats in them as well as of their ancestors and their progeny. Where possible the selected ancestor should be recognized whilst he is still alive, so that direct matings to him are possible. If matings have to be made to his descendants, then his desirable features will be rather diluted.

Out-breeding Out-breeding is really the opposite of in-breeding and denotes the mating of individuals less closely related than average. It is the only way in which new genes can be introduced into an inbred strain. This method may produce a show winner, due to the 'hybrid vigour', but tends to diminish breeding worth.

Breeding Abnormalities Congenital abnormalities, i.e. abnormalities which are present at birth, are not very common in the cat. This is probably due to the fact that the cat has remained true to its ancestral type, and there has not been the same degree of deliberate breeding of animals with exaggerated differences in form as has occurred in the dog world. Thus the cat of any breed still has the basic shape and size of a cat. Congenital abnormalities may or may not be hereditary in nature.

Bent and Shortened Tails These are quite common defects in the cat and some are believed to be hereditary in origin. Undoubtedly many cases of kinked or bent tails are due to injury, either at the time of birth or later. Certain strains of Siamese show either a shortened or a kinked tail but the fault has been almost eliminated in those animals bred for show purposes. Shortened tails have been shown to be due to a simple recessive gene but the kinked tail pattern of inheritance is a much more complicated matter and there are probably different manifestations of the same genetic entity, differences in the degree of expression of the defect being due to differences in the strain.

Cleft Palate and Harelip As these conditions are usually associated they can be considered together. The defects are due to failure of the two halves of the embryonic hard palate and the upper lip to fuse together. It is not thought that the anomaly is hereditary but the actual cause is unknown. An increased incidence is seen in certain geographical locations, so environmental factors may be involved. The defects have been produced experimentally by the administration of certain drugs, at certain times during pregnancy.

Cryptorchidism The term cryptorchidism means literally 'hidden testicle' and as the name implies it describes a condition in which one or both of the testicles fail to descend from the abdomen into their normal position in the scrotum. There are different degrees of the defect, in some cases the retained testicle is within the abdomen, in others it is situated within the inguinal canal, whilst in some cases it is actually outside the abdomen but held close to the inguinal ring. If both testicles are within the abdomen, the temperature there precludes the formation of spermatozoa and the cat is sterile although it will remain sexually active. If one testicle has descended however – a monorchid – the cat is fertile, but should not be used for breeding purposes as the condition is thought to be hereditary.

Flattened Chest This is a fairly common condition in the cat and is usually associated with a deficiency of vitamin A in the diet of the queen. The deformity is a flattening of the rib cage from above to below, leading to difficulties in normal expansion of the lungs. The condition is often combined with other skeletal abnormalities. Administration of vitamin A halfway through pregnancy is said to considerably reduce the incidence of the deformity.

See also Vitamin A Deficiency under NUTRITION.

Flop or Folded Ears Normally the ears of the cat are carried in an upright or pricked manner, but in this condition the ears are folded forwards. Until about one month of age, the kittens appear normal, but then the ear tips turn forwards and downwards to form the fully developed fold by the age of three months. The condition is inherited. Sadly attempts to establish a new breed of these flop-eared cats are being made at the present time.

Hydrocephalus Hydrocephalus, the so-called 'Water on the Brain', is uncommon in the cat. The condition may be hereditary in nature. The condition may also occur as a developmental anomaly. The whole head may be involved and appear enlarged and dropsical, this type often being associated with oedematous swollen limbs. In other cases only the skull is enlarged and dome-shaped due to swelling of the brain. Affected animals are usually mentally abnormal and should be put to sleep at birth.

Meningo- and Encephalo-coele Failures of the bones of the roof of the cranium to fuse, so that a portion of the meningeal covering of the brain or the brain itself protrudes through the top of the skull. Affected kittens are usually still-born or should be destroyed at birth.

Microphthalmos and Anophthalmos These conditions are rare in the cat. Anophthalmos is a complete absence of the eyes whilst microphthalmos is a condition in which the eye remains small and may become cystic. The defect may affect one or both eyes.

Polydactylia The presence of extra toes on the foot is quite a common abnormality in the cat. Usually the front feet are affected, the number of extra toes varying between a more prominent development of the inside, or dew, claw up to three supernumerary well-developed toes. The number of extra toes may vary between different feet on the same cat. The hindfeet are rarely, if ever, abnormal unless the front feet are affected. The abnormality is thought to be hereditary.

Split-foot In this condition there is a central cleft on either one or both of the front feet caused by abnormalities of the carpal and metacarpal bones. There may be associated anomalies such as fusion of toes to form double claws, absence of toes or abnormal pads to the toes. The defect is inherited as a dominant trait.

Strabismus or Squint Squint occurs quite frequently in some strains of the Siamese breed. Usually the eyes are turned inwards – cross-eyed – but the squint may be outwards. The condition appears to be hereditary.

Umbilical Hernia Umbilical hernia is relatively common in the cat and is due to a failure of the umbilical ring to close after birth. In the smaller herniae the sac contains a small pocket of fat, but the larger herniae contain loops of bowel, omentum and mesentery. An hereditary form of the abnormality has been described in Abyssinian cats in Sweden. Usually the smaller herniae can be left untreated but the larger ones require surgical repair of the defect in the ventral abdominal wall.

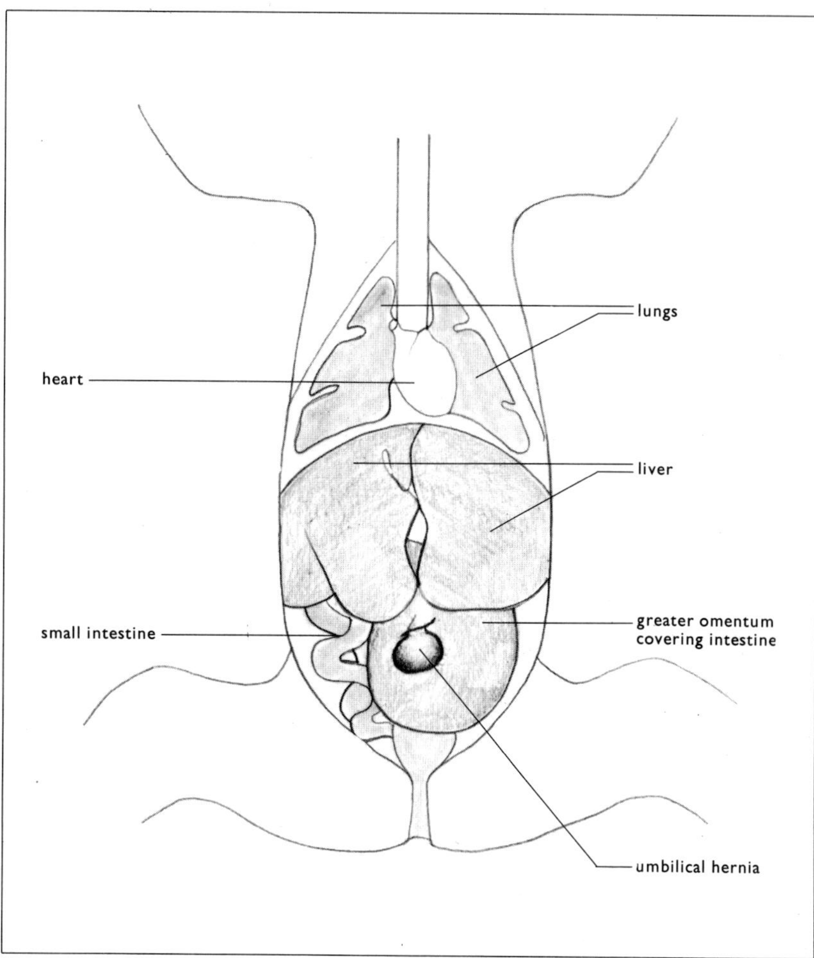

Position of Umbilical hernia; muscle wall removed

See also GENETICS and MONGREL LITTERS.

British Blue The most popular of the British Short-hairs and probably the one that comes closest to the set standards.

In the early days of the Cat Fancy in Britain cats with self-coloured blue coats were shown under various names, such as the Archangel, the Russian, the Spanish, the Chartreux and the American Blue. Some had British type and others had the longer slim bodies and long heads, now known as Foreign type. The classes at the shows were for short-haired Blues, and as some judges preferred one type and some the other, there was a great deal of argument as to what was really required. Eventually, it was decided that there should be two classes, and before

left British Blue; *right* British Blue Cream

long, by using only carefully selected cats with the right characteristics, breeders managed to produce the British Blue as we know it today. A beautifully balanced cat with body of medium length on strong legs, with a good head with full cheeks, and big round orange or copper eyes – 25 points are allowed for these – it is typically British. The colour of the fur, for which 25 points is given in the standard, may be a light to medium blue, but should be the same right down to the roots, with no white hairs or any tabby markings.

A British Blue male mated to a Cream female may sire Cream males and Blue Cream females, while a British Blue female mated to a Cream male may have Blue Cream females and Blue males. A Blue male mated to a Blue Cream may result in Blue and Cream males, and Blue and Blue Cream females.

Although frowned on by some, an occasional out-cross to a Blue Long-hair is liked by many breeders to ensure that there is no loss of type.

The British Blues are renowned for their placid and affectionate nature and their high intelligence.

Neutered they make excellent pets, while the females have the reputation for being good mothers.

The Chartreux in Europe are now considered to be the same as the British Blues in Britain, while the nearest in North America would be an Exotic Short-hair with blue fur.
See colour plate 12, *page 47*.

British Cream see CREAM SHORT-HAIR

British Short-hairs In Britain there are two types of recognized short-haired cats, the British Short-hairs and the Foreign Short-hairs. The latter are slim-bodied cats, with long fine heads, almond-shaped eyes, big ears, and long thin tails, while the British are very much the reverse. Descendants of the first domestic cats thought to have been introduced into Britain by the Romans, careful breeding over the last century has produced attractive pedigree short-coated cats with characteristics conforming to the set standard, in a variety of colours and coat patterns.

The standard generally calls for cats with well knit, powerful looking cobby bodies, with full broad chests. The legs should be of good substance, with well rounded feet, and the shortish tails should be thick at the base, slightly tapering at the tip. The broad, apple-shaped heads should have well-developed cheeks, big expressive round eyes, shortish broad noses, and small slightly rounded ears. Sturdy muscular cats, with short plushy coats, very independent but extremely affectionate, they make ideal pets, being exceedingly easy to groom.

The general characteristics required are much the same for all the British varieties, but probably the British Blue, one of the most popular, comes closest to the recognized standard.

It has been found necessary in order to keep the type as required in the standard, to outcross with an outstanding Long-hair every five or six generations. The first of such crosses may have fur that is too long and fluffy and should be neutered, but the second generation by a mating to Short-hair should have very good coats. The fur texture is very important. There should be no woolliness, and it should be firm, short and fine, without any harshness. Points are given for the general characteristics, as follows:

10	Body and tail
5	Legs and Feet
10	Head and neck
10	Ears
10	Coat
5	Condition
50	

Another 50 points are apportioned for colour and eyes in the individual varieties.

Grooming For the British Short-hairs, grooming is fairly simple as, unlike the Long-hairs, the fur does not tangle into knots. A few minutes daily grooming is all that is necessary to keep the cat's coat looking beautiful. It should be brushed and combed very lightly to remove any old hairs, dirt and dust. Over-use of the comb should be avoided, as it does tend to leave track marks in the fur and may cause it to appear too open. Hard hand grooming is good and is usually much appreciated by the cat. Finally, to produce a beautiful sheen, the coat should be polished all over with chamois leather or a piece of silk or velvet.

The ears must be inspected daily to make sure that there are no signs of ear mites, and any dirt in the corner of the eyes should be wiped away gently with a small piece of cotton wool. It is as well to go through the fur occasionally with a fine tooth comb to ensure that there are no fleas present. They may be detected by flea dirt, tiny black shining specks in the coat, with the cat constantly scratching.

Showing If daily grooming is carried out and the cat is given a good mixed diet, he should always be in first class condition, and if to be exhibited, will need very little extra attention. It should be remembered that dirty ears and fleas in the fur may mean the cat being turned down by the veterinary surgeon and not being permitted to enter the show, with the loss of the entry fees.

An outstanding British Short-hair always stands a good chance of winning at the shows, as competition is not so fierce as for all the other varieties.

Bronchi see RESPIRATORY ORGANS

Bronze Mau see EGYPTIAN MAU

Brown Burmese see BURMESE

Brown Tabby see TABBY LONG-HAIR and TABBY SHORT-HAIR

Bruises Bruises, or contusions, are closed wounds involving rupture of small blood vessels below the skin. A certain amount of swelling, heat and tenderness can usually be detected in association with bruising. Cold compresses will often help to relieve the pain, but bruises usually heal satisfactorily without complication.

Bruises occur as a result of road-accidents, falls, fights or objects falling on the patient.

Burmese *Brown Burmese* The majority of the different varieties of pedigree cats throughout the world have originated in Britain, usually through selective breeding, but one exception is the Brown Burmese, known as Zibelines in France, which was introduced into the U.S.A. in 1930, having been brought there by a Dr J. Thompson. Recognition was granted in the States in 1936, but it was not until after the 1939–45 War that they were seen in Britain. It took several years for them to become established, a provisional standard being finally granted in 1952,

Blue Burmese

which was approved after two years with very slight amendment.

The Brown Burmese is foreign in type, but in comparison with the Siamese, the wedge-shaped heads are not quite so long, and the pointed ears not quite so large. The graceful bodies are medium in size, on slim legs, with small oval feet; the tails being long and tapering. The colour should be a rich dark seal-brown, with no white hairs in the coat. The ears, mask and points may be very slightly darker than the body colouring, giving only an impression of contrast; this may be more definite in kittens and younger cats. The kittens when young may be coffee in colour with some shadow markings, but the fur does darken with age. The almond-shape eyes should be intense golden yellow, but most Brown Burmese have eyes which are chartreuse yellow. Green eyes are definitely frowned on.

In North America, the standard requires the heads to be more rounded and the bodies shorter, presenting a more compact cat.

Since their introduction the Brown Burmese have rapidly increased in numbers, being second only to the Siamese and have become much favoured as house pets.

There are a number of Brown Burmese on the Continent, but the rise in popularity has not been so spectacular as in Britain.

See colour plate 15, *page 48.*

Blue Burmese Following the introduction of the very popular Brown Burmese, in certain litters it was noticed that some kittens were appearing with coats that were more fawn than coffee coloured, and when adult, the fur was a bluish grey, with a silver sheen. Several breeders became interested in these Blue Burmese, which were eventually recognized in 1960. The characteristics required were the same as those of the Brown Burmese, with the fur being predominantly a bluish-grey, slightly darker on the back. The kittens when young are usually lighter in colour, and may have some tabby markings which fade with growth. The eyes may be yellow to yellowish green in colour, but must never be a definite green.

The Blue Burmese has proved very popular in Britain and is now seen on the Continent too, but until comparatively recently was practically unknown in North America.

See colour plate 14, *page 48.*

New Colours During recent years through careful planned breeding, a number of now pure-bred colour variations have appeared in the Burmese. Having the same type and characteristics as that given for the Brown and Blue, the colours are: *Cream,* with fur of a rich cream colour, becoming darker on the face and back and a paler hue on the chest and belly; *Blue-Cream,* the fur to be cream coloured as above, but mixed with blue. This is a female-only variety; *Red,* the fur to be a rich golden red shading to a lighter colouring on the chest and belly; *Tortie*, another female-only variety, with the fur a mixture of red, brown and cream.

Following the importation in 1968 from the U.S.A. of six Burmese, four being Chocolate and two Brown, but all carrying the necessary genes, both Lilac and Chocolate Burmese are being bred in Britain. Of pure breeding, the Lilacs have coats of pinkish dove grey, with an overall frosted sheen appearance, while the Chocolate have fur pale milk chocolate in colour, with both having the type and characteristics as given for the other Burmese.
See colour plate 16, *page 48.*

Burns see ACCIDENTS

Bush Cat see AFRICAN WILD CAT

Butt ended kitten see BIRTH

Buying a Cat This requires a great deal of forethought and patience, particularly if you are buying a cat which you intend breeding.

Buying a Pedigree Cat If you are not experienced in the breed you are going to buy, read all you can about this breed, visit a few cat-shows, and, if possible, enlist the help of an established expert. Look at as many kittens as possible, so that you become familiar with the characteristics and conformation to aim for. Having selected a kitten, you are perfectly justified in asking the breeder to have her veterinary surgeon examine it for soundness and fitness, and issue a certificate. Be sure to find out what foods the kitten has been accustomed to, whether it is house-trained, and if it has been vaccinated against feline infectious enteritis for which a certificate should be obtained.

Buying a Mongrel Cat In this case, you are looking for a healthy, attractive looking cat that will grow up with a pleasant temperament. A strong, fit kitten is alert and playful, with a fairly solid body, well-knit limbs and dense, shiny coat. The eyes should be clear and free from discharge, and the nose, ears and skin should be clean. The anus should be clean and free from any signs of diarrhoea. By buying a sickly kitten, you will be letting yourself in for a lot of nursing, which may only end in heartbreak. If you cannot resist some pitiful little cat 'flu patient, make sure it has veterinary attention promptly, and be prepared to force-feed it and keep the eyes and nose clean day and night. It is always better to buy mongrel kittens direct from a private house than from a pet shop, since the latter tends to be a source of infected stock.

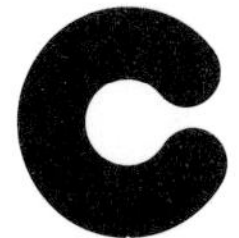

Caesarean Birth Caesarean birth is the delivery of a foetus by incision of the abdominal and uterine walls, and is performed when birth through the natural passages is considered impossible or dangerous to the mother or the offspring. The method was included in the codification of the Roman law (lex caesarea) in 715 BC, from which the name is derived, as a means of salvaging a child, if living, or of providing for its separate burial in the event of its mother's death.

In the cat, almost any difficulty in kittening is usually treated by Caesarean section, as the birth canal is too small to permit manual correction of any malpresentation of the kitten. The operation is usually performed under inhalation anaesthesia, as the barbiturates tend to depress the respiration of the kittens and may cause death. The site of incision is normally in the flank region so as to avoid interference with the mammary glands and subsequent suckling of the litter. If it is the cat's first litter, the maternal instinct may not be too well developed and the kittens may have to be reared by hand or on a foster-mother.

Caffre Cat *Felis ocreata* – also referred to as Kaffir, Caffre or Egyptian cat – is not generally accepted now by zoologists as a separate species but is considered to come under the classification of the African Wild Cat.

Calcium see ECLAMPSIA and NUTRITION

Calico see TORTOISESHELL AND WHITE LONG-HAIR and TORTOISESHELL AND WHITE SHORT-HAIR

Calling see BEHAVIOUR, SEXUAL

Calorie A calorie may be defined as the amount of heat required to raise the temperature of one kilogram of water from 14°C to 15°C. When foodstuffs are oxidised in the body after their digestion and absorption, they give out heat, and it has been found convenient by dieticians to qualify foods on the basis of the calorific value, that is how much heat a certain food will produce when oxidized in the body. It has been found that fats have the highest calorific value and proteins the lowest, with carbohydrates coming between the two.
See also NUTRITION.

Cameo Tabby see TABBY LONG-HAIR and TABBY SHORT-HAIR

Cameos Cameos are given as colour variations listed for the Persians in the U.S.A. and comparatively recently they have been seen at shows in Europe. Several breeders in Britain are now endeavouring to produce these attractive Long-hairs. They may be produced in various colours, and the following are recognized in the U.S.A.: *Shell Cameo*, similar to the Chinchilla, with white undercoat, but the tippings to be red. Eyes copper; *Shaded Cameo*, having a white undercoat and red tippings forming shadings down the sides, face and tail. The whole appearance being redder than that of the Shell. Eyes copper; *Cameo Smoke or Red Smoke*, undercoat to be white, deeply tipped with red, forming a contrast as in the Smoke and Blue Smokes, with the coat having a red appearance, and the white undercoat only appearing as the cat moves. Eyes copper; *Cameo Tabby*, the ground colour off-white, with red markings. Eyes copper.

The type for the Cameos should be as for other long-hairs and is usually good.

Several have been shown in Britain in the 'Any Other Colour' classes, still being in the experimental stage, produced in the first place from the crossing of Chinchillas or Smokes with various other colour Long-hairs.
See colour plates 17 *and* 18, *page 73.*

Canker Canker is a lay term which has no specific meaning in feline medicine. It is used by the public as a term to describe a serious ear condition. The fear it usually engenders may result from the similar sound to cancer. See also EAR DISORDERS.

Cannibalism This is the term used to describe the killing of the newborn kittens by the mother cat. It usually occurs when she is emotionally upset during kittening – for example by excessive noise, unnecessary interference or attempts to handle the kittens. Some queens, however, have an innate tendency to destroy their young. Cannibalism usually involves biting off the head, which is then eaten. The body may be left untouched. Alternatively one leg or tail may be chewed off. Cats that show a tendency toward cannibalism are best not bred again.

Capsules The term used to denote a gelatinous envelope containing a drug which may be in a powder form or liquid form. For example, antibiotics are frequently presented as capsules. Cod-liver oil may be similarly obtained although most cats will take it readily enough on food or in a spoon. Medicinal capsules have two advantages – they are relatively tasteless and they do not stick in the throat. Capsules are administered in the same way as tablets – see DOSING.

Car Sickness Car sickness or distress can occur in animals unused to travel. Anxiety will make cats salivate and eventually vomit. The motion can also produce nausea. Fortunately the promazine group of drugs which are tranquillizers will remove anxiety and prevent vomiting. These are easily obtained from veterinary surgeons who will give advice about dosage.
See also TRANSPORTATION.

Caracal Lynx *Felis caracal* is easily recognized by its pointed ears with their long black tufts, short tail and rather oriental eye placement. Its colouring blends well with the surroundings and can vary from yellowish-grey to a rich reddish-yellow. The coat is uniform in colour, the chin and underparts white, and there is a dark patch above the eyes and at the side of the whisker pads.

This lithe and extremely elegant cat gives the impression of great strength although it only measures from about 26–30 in. from head to the base of the tail which is a further 9–10 in.; it often bursts from cover and hurls itself towards its prey; it can also leap into the air to grab a bird which attempts to get away. Like the Cheetah, Caracals can be trained to hunt, and the Gaekwar of Baroda used to keep a pack with which to hunt peafowl, hares and other game. They have been known to kill the tawny and martial eagles and can also attack and kill animals as large as the impala and reedbuck.

Caracal used to be found in a wide area which ranged from the deserts of southern Russia to northern and central India, the Middle East, Arabia and many parts of Africa, but now it is quickly disappearing.

Carbohydrates see NUTRITION

Cardboard collars see ELIZABETHAN COLLARS

Careers with Cats A number of careers are open to cat-lovers:

1. *Cattery Manager or Assistant* This could be pursued in a large breeding or boarding cattery, and would involve such tasks as feeding, cleaning, grooming, exercising, showing; caring for sick and nursing cats; selecting stock and planning breeding programmes; house training; and keeping records. A genuine affection for cats is required for success in this field. Since many catteries are small and run by family teams, there are few posts for assistant cattery managers. To establish one's own cattery, considerable capital is required, and the venture should be soundly backed by an insurance policy. When setting up a cattery, get as much advice as possible from proven cattery owners and veterinary surgeons, since the enterprise can very easily founder, with heartbreaking rapidity, and economic disaster.

2. *Registered Animal Nursing Auxiliary* This job is definitely not for the squeamish, but is very suitable for those who love cats, are practical and scientifically-inclined. Veterinary practices vary considerably, but a number of them cater exclusively for cats and dogs, and some of those in larger cities tend to consist almost entirely of cat-owning clients.

3. *Animal Technician* Animal technicians care for laboratory animals. Contrary to popular opinion, the vast majority of laboratory cats are used for harmless purposes. Large numbers of cats are for example kept in superb conditions for palatability tests by the petfood manufacturers. In fact, some of the beautiful cats shown in television commercials are experimental animals. Such cats, kept in the peak of their condition, and handled with kindness from birth, are a delight to work with.

4. *Zoological Gardens Assistant* Most zoo curators are reluctant to employ women for working with any but the smaller species, so the job of caring for the large cats is confined mainly to men. A good deal of patience and perseverance is required to reach a satisfactory standard in the handling of the large, wild cats, but success brings ample rewards.

Caries see TEETH CARE

Carrier Baskets A carrier basket is essential if you wish to transport a cat. It is also advisable to use a carrier for a cat in a car unless the driver has nerves of steel, all the windows are kept tight shut, and the cat is truly relaxed. There are several types of carrier.

1. *Wicker basket*. This is airy, comfortable (newspaper or a blanket should be placed inside), relatively light, and, if soundly constructed, secure. The disadvantages are that it can only be disinfected by total immersion and subsequent drying, and that it tends to leak if the cat passes urine or diarrhoea.

2. *Plastic box*. This is very hygienic, tough, light,

A comfortable basket carrier though a determined cat may escape. Disinfection of this type is difficult

above A perspex and polythene carrier – light, durable, escape-proof and easily disinfected; *far right* An excellent carrier made of strong wire coated with plastic

secure and comfortable. Air holes are provided. The box usually has a handle and two clipfasteners, and it may have a lid on the top or a door at one end.

3. *Plasticized wire basket*. This is easier to disinfect than a wicker basket, but also tends to leak. The cat can be seen clearly without raising the lid, which is a great advantage if it needs to be observed in illness or emergency.

4. *Shopping basket*. Provided a piece of really strong fabric is securely placed over the top, and tied around the edge, a shopping basket is perfectly adequate for transporting a cat. Likewise Ali Baba or laundry baskets may be used.

5. *Picnic hamper*. This is also quite suitable if strong and with secure fasteners.
See also TRANSPORTING.

Carrots The old adage about being able to see at night better for eating carrots is perfectly true. Carrots do, in fact, contain carotene, or vitamin A precusor, which is converted to vitamin A in the tissues, and this helps form 'visual purple' in the retina of the eye. But egg-yolk and milk (particularly Channel Islands milk) are much better sources of vitamin A for the cat. Fish liver oils are also useful. It is doubtful if cats can convert carotene to vitamin A, as we can. If your cat happens to enjoy a little raw, grated carrot on his food, by all means give it to him. Cooked carrots are, like potatoes, a useful source of carbohydrates. Carrot tops probably contain a certain amount of water soluble vitamins.

Caspian Tiger see TIGER

Castration Castration is the term used for the removal of the testicles.

Testicles are the two organs situated beneath the penis in the male. They are responsible for the production of the male sex hormone which produces male sexual behaviour and for the sperm producing semen.

Castration is a simple operation performed under anaesthetic and relatively free from risk. Although castration is possible at any age it is best performed before the animal reaches sexual maturity. Four to five months is a satisfactory age. See also BEHAVIOUR.

Cat Clubs There are a number of cat clubs throughout Britain which cater for people with a mutual love of cats. Whilst the majority are interested in all breeds, a few are specialist societies looking after the interests of particular breeds, and nominating judges to judge them, subject to the approval of the Governing Council (see BREED CLUBS). Many of the larger clubs, such as the National Cat Club, run an annual show. All countries have similar cat clubs – with the Cat Fanciers' Association in the U.S.A. alone having nearly 400 associated clubs.

Each club is an independent body, financed by the members' yearly subscriptions, whose business is conducted by a chairman, committee, an honorary secretary and honorary treasurer. When a club has been in existence for three years, and its membership is 100 or more, it may apply for affiliation to the Governing Council of the Cat Fancy. If this is granted, and if the club wishes, it may request representation and may elect a delegate to represent the club on the Council to look after its interests.

In Britain many clubs guarantee classes at the shows for their members and give special prizes or rosettes to the prize-winners. A number of the clubs have special funds to assist members to care for their cats, should the need arise; to pay for the cats to be looked after until homes can be found should a member die; and to donate monies each year to Animal Welfare societies.

Cat Doors or Flaps Cat doors are small flaps fixed to a hole cut in a suitable door in the house. It allows cats to come and go as they please without allowing the entry of unwanted humans. It does however have the disadvantage that local stray cats can also gain entry and if a female on heat lives with you the neighbouring toms will come calling accompanied by their characteristic odour.

Cat Fancy This is a general term used when referring to pedigree cats, cat clubs and the cat fanciers collectively.

In Britain it is included in the title of the registering body that looks after the interests of all varieties of pedigree cats, that is the Governing Council of the Cat Fancy.

This is a democratic body composed of delegates selected annually by the members of the affiliated cat clubs and societies. Registrations and transfers are dealt with by two paid registrars, and a secretary deals with the general business. All the delegates give their services free, attending meetings of the full council a number of times each year, and many also serving on sub-committees, such as the Executive and Cat Care.

The Governing Council grants breed numbers, approves standards, issues stud lists and a stud book, grants licences for cat shows and gives challenge and premier certificates at the appropriate shows. The various Cat Fancies throughout the world all have their own governing bodies whose functions are much the same as those of the Governing Council in Britain.

Cat Fancy in Northern Ireland The Cat Fancy in Northern Ireland, though relatively small, is increasing steadily and expanding its range of breeds beyond the already established Long-haired and Siamese cats.

There is reliable information that a pair of Sealpoint Siamese were brought from Hong Kong to Co. Londonderry during the early part of the century but unfortunately, there are no records to suggest that they were bred from, and it would seem that a high percentage of the present day Siamese owe their existence to their English ancestry. On the other hand, the Irish strain of the new and elegant Foreign White cats, was originated in Bangor, Co. Down.

The Burmese are becoming popular and there are prospects of Ulster-bred Abyssinians, Chinchillas and Colourpoints in the near future.

Apart from Manx cats, the British Short-haired cats, as far as one can ascertain, seem conspicuous by their absence but it is hoped that their advent together with that of such breeds as Turkish, Birman, Rex, will not be long delayed.

The two clubs, the Ulster Siamese Cat Club, formed in 1961, and the Northern Ireland Cat Club (all breeds), formed in 1970, each hold annual shows under the auspices of the Governing Council of the Cat Fancy. By virtue of a small Fancy and the geographical position of Northern Ireland, Championship Shows have not yet been possible but it is hoped that time will rectify this.

Cat Fancy in the Republic of Ireland With the foundation of the Siamese Cat Club of Ireland in the early nineteen-fifties, the Cat Fancy in the Republic of Ireland had its beginning. This club started a register of Siamese cats which was maintained until the founding of the Governing Council of the Cat Fancy of Ireland in 1968. It was then entrusted to the new Governing Body which appointed a Registrar and expanded the register to include all breeds of pedigree cats.

In the mid-sixties Burmese cats made their first appearance at the shows and are probably next in popularity to Siamese but still numerically a long way behind. Also popular are the long-haired varieties and latest additions include the Rex cat, Birmans and Colourpoints. With the advent of bigger shows, classes for non-pedigree pet cats are popular and are well supported, especially by young exhibitors.

Each year in Dublin there are two Championship cat shows, both promoted by the Siamese Cat Club, but catering for all breeds. These shows represent the only opportunities to win challenge certificates and despite the obvious difficulties a considerable number of cats have managed to win three and attain the status of 'Champion'.

Interest in the Cat Fancy, previously confined almost entirely to the capital, is now spreading to the Provinces with the recent formation of clubs in Waterford and Cork.

Cat Flea see FLEAS

Cat Flu see FLU

Cat Lore Perhaps because of its unique behaviour – a bland acceptance of some of the benefits of domestication but the retention of a large degree of social and psychological independence – the cat has been endowed with a wide variety of mystical characteristics. Man has at different times regarded the cat both as a god and the personification of evil; as a benefactor and a purveyor of bad luck; to have the ability to cure illness or the power to inflict disease and death.

Although a male cat deity, Ai Apaec, was worshipped by Mochicas in Peru, perhaps the best known culture which venerated the cat was the early Egyptian civilization. Several lesser feline gods of varying significance existed throughout the long period of their cat worship, which covered over 2000 years, but the most important was the female cat god Pasht, daughter of Isis and Osiris. Herodotus, writing in the 5th century BC, tells of a splendid temple, which contained a shrine to the goddess, at Bubastis. Pasht controlled the fertility of humans, animals and crops; had the power to heal the sick and protected the souls of the dead. As a result of this deification, cats were treated with great respect and love by the Egyptians. They were constantly adorned and pampered. On their death they were embalmed and treated with all the respect accorded a human demise.

Later religious cultures have in general been less sympathetic to the cat. Buddhism is in general hostile but Chinese and Japanese Buddhist sects have treated it less harshly and sometimes elevated its image to the deities. Peasant farmers worshipped the cat-god Li-Shou and made sacrifices to it after the harvest, in thanks for the protection it afforded from rodents. In Japan the 18th-century temple of Gotokuji in Tokyo was consecrated to the cat. The altar is decorated with their effigies and it is surrounded with cat burials.

As a consequence of the religious connotations, healing, benefaction and fertility have become common benefits thought to ensue from cat worship. In Japan it was believed to cure fits, melancholy and epilepsy. English folklore accredited the cat with the power to cure blindness and other eye complaints. In particular in Cornwall the hair from a black cat's tail was considered efficacious for eye disease. The tail also had the ability to alleviate skin irritation and to remove warts. In Holland the freshly removed skin of a cat applied to the human skin was believed to cure skin disease.

Since its rise to fame in ancient Egypt, the cat has had associations with fertility rites both for human beings and for crops. Although some of these beliefs were advantageous to the cat leading to gross over indulgence, the ability to produce fertility was equally believed by some to ensue from burying the wretched creatures alive in the soil. Such a tradition is known to have existed in Russia. Perhaps a lingering pagan belief in its relationship to fertility accounts for the legend that a cat gave birth to kittens in the stable as Christ was born. Consequently Italians have in general been sympathetic to the cat. Various saints, including St Jerome, St Martha and St Francis have been linked with feline fancy.

In many countries as a result of its connection with good, the cat has been used as a protection or to ensure good luck. Japanese sailors sailed with tortoiseshell cats to protect them from ghosts and to give warning of storms. In China cats were believed to have the power to drive away evil spirits and were kept in houses for that purpose. Bretons believed every black cat had in its tail a pure white hair which was regarded highly as a talisman. In South East Asia cats are believed to have the power to bring rain. For this to be achieved immersion in water is critical.

A drawing of an ancient Egyptian cat artifact

Recognition of the cat's apparent bravery and savage ferocity has been secured in some folklore. Celtic warriors for example decorated their helmets with cat-heads, while the Dutch in their struggle for freedom from Spain used the cat as a symbol because of its fierceness and independence of spirit.

Even the Japanese however, who worshipped the cat with some enthusiasm, believed that without care it could become evil. Severing its tail was thought to prevent this unfortunate transformation. In general Buddhism and Christianity concentrated on this power of evil rather than its beneficence. This may have resulted from the cat's inclination for night wandering, silent movement and reflective eyes which were thought to have sinister implications, or because of its unfortunate connections with previous pagan religions. Buddhist legend records that the cat's presence was forbidden at Buddha's funeral because it had killed the rat which had been sent to fetch life saving medicine for him and had added insult to injury by failing to weep when Buddha died. Indian Buddhists as a result preached love for all creatures except the cat.

Because of its evil connections it has been subjected to extremes of torture. It seems often to have been used as a scapegoat for guilt complexes surrounding the Christian religion. In Shropshire cats were whipped at Shrovetide and in France were hurled from a steeple during Lent. More sinister are the burnings to which it seems to have been subjected at times of religious festivity throughout the world. Hungarians thought that old cats could become witches and that this could be prevented by making a cruciform incision in the skin.

In association with its evil connections the cat has often been accused of the ability to interfere with the souls of the dead. In China they were believed to have a soul-recalling ability which could resurrect a corpse and turn it into a zombie. Cats were therefore kept away from unburied bodies. Elsewhere it is believed to bode ill for the dead person's soul if a cat jumps over the coffin unless the unfortunate feline is killed immediately. In Scotland a cat could acquire second sight by eating the eyes of a dead person and could inflict blindness on the first person over whom it jumped. Cats approaching corpses were therefore destroyed.

Scottish cat lore abounds with horrific tales of evil cats. Agnes Sampson in 1590 was said to have used cats in the rites in which she attempted to call up a storm at sea to drown King James VI and Queen Anne. In 1662 Isobel Gowdie confessed that her coven became cats during devil devotions. Slavs believed that cats became devils during thunderstorms.

The dubious advantages of acquiring second sight was believed to have been bestowed in various ways by feline intervention. The cat killing ceremonies of Taigheirm which enacted over four days the slow roasting of huge numbers of black cats were perpetrated to this end.

Perhaps as a consequence of its evil associations or because of the ferocity it produces during adversity, cats have been used as an adjunct to punishment. Unfaithful wives in Iceland and throughout the Ottoman Empire were trussed in a sack together with a cat and thrown into a drowning pool. The French have on more than one occasion placed murderers in an iron cage and roasted them to death together with several innocent cats.

Various societies, particularly more primitive cultures, have identified closely with animal life, and associate their own characteristics and abilities with those of the chosen beast. The power of the lion, speed of deer, bravery, ferocity and strength of the bull, are just a few examples of an endless list, but perhaps the cat alone can claim such a wide diversity of human following.
See also DOMESTICATION HISTORY.

Cat Protection League This is a British institution which aims in particular to rescue and find homes for strays and to encourage the neutering of cats, in order to reduce the number of unwanted kittens. The League has homes in London and the major cities, where strays can be housed until owners are found for them. The neutering is performed by private veterinary surgeons and the League bears some, or all, of the cost.

Cat Scratch Fever A systemic (generalized) infection probably of viral origin, suffered by humans after disease organisms have been introduced by a cat scratch. Some people appear to be particularly susceptible to the condition. It is always wise to apply antiseptic to any cat scratch and then irrigate it with plenty of cold water. This is particularly important if the skin is dirty when the scratch is received. In an emergency, apply a magnesium sulphate paste poultice (cold), to help draw the infection until medical attention may be given.

Cat Worship see CAT LORE

Cataract see BLINDNESS and EYE AND EYELID DISORDERS

Catarrh Catarrh or Snuffles is a popular name for the condition of Chronic Rhinitis/Sinusitis of the cat. This is a distressing disease encountered quite frequently in the cat where it appears as a sequel to infection with one of the feline respiratory viruses. The condition is bacterial in nature although as mentioned above, there seems to be little doubt that viral infection paves the way for the bacterial invasion of the affected tissues. The disease consists of a chronic inflammation of the nasal passage, giving rise to a chronic catarrhal nasal discharge. Extension of the infection up the lachrymal duct may lead to an associated chronic conjunctivitis. Common organisms isolated from the nasal discharges include streptococci, staphylococci.

The main symptom of catarrh is a thick, catarrhal discharge from the nose, usually affecting both nostrils. There are frequent attacks of sneezing, often of an explosive nature, in which quite large quantities of discharge may be sprayed around. There may be pain at the angle of the jaw. The cat has a rather capricious appetite probably due to a diminution in its sense of smell. Ulceration of the inflamed mucous membrane may occur and give rise to flecks of blood in the nasal discharge.

Treatment is difficult although there is usually a temporary response to the antibiotics, the corticosteroids and the antihistamines. The most lasting relief of the condition appears to follow opening into the frontal sinuses by drilling a small hole through the overlying bone (trephining). Antibiotic and corticosteroid solutions can then be used to irrigate the sinuses, which are often the seat of the chronic infection. This trephining may have to be repeated on several occasions before a permanent cure can be obtained.

Cattery see ACCOMMODATION

Cattery Names see AFFIXES AND PREFIXES

Central American Jaguar see JAGUAR

Cerebellar Hypoplasia see under PANLEUCOPAENIA

Challenge Certificates Once a registered pedigree cat, in Britain, reaches the age of nine months, it may be entered in the Open Breed classes at the Championship shows held under the jurisdiction of the Governing Council of the Cat Fancy in Britain.

At these shows, challenge certificates may be awarded to the winners of the adult open classes, provided they are considered by the officiating judges to be worthy of such an honour.

The winning of such a challenge certificate is the first step towards a cat becoming a champion, as three such wins at three separate shows under three different judges is necessary to achieve this.

Certificates may be awarded to both the male and the female of each recognized variety, but should the number of exhibits in the two classes be less than seven, only one certificate may be given. If, however, the winner of the opposite sex is of high standard, a judge may give a second certificate provided another judge agrees to this.

Neuters are not eligible for challenge certificates, but may compete in their own classes for Premier certificates on similar terms.

On the Continent such certificates are known as the Certificat d'Aptitude au Championnat. The term is not used in North America. See CHAMPION.

Champion In Britain a Champion is a cat that has won three challenge certificates at three different shows run according to the rules laid down by the Governing Council of the Cat Fancy (see CHALLENGE CERTIFICATES).

The title of Champion has to be approved by the Governing Council, and on the winning of the third certificate, the owner should submit details of such wins to the Secretary of the Council for verification.

To own a cat, or especially to have bred one that becomes a Champion, adds considerably to the prestige of the breeder and the value of the stock.

In North America for a cat to become a Champion it has to win four Winners ribbons, that is to win the open class at least four times under three judges or more and to have been granted a certificate to say that the title has been awarded by the appropriate Association. A cat that has won a Championship certificate in more than one country may by winning the classes for such cats eventually become an International Champion. Working on a points system, which may vary from one Association to another, it is possible for a cat to become a Grand Champion. This entails a number of wins over other Champions, and an International Champion may also become an International Grand Champion under similar conditions. The term challenge certificate is not used.

On the Continent a cat has to win three open classes under three judges to become a Champion. The winner of the open class is given a CAC, otherwise a Certificat d'Aptitude au Championnat. On winning three such certificates, the cat may become a Champion and may then be entered in the class for Champions only. A winner in such a class may be given a CACIB, or a Certificate d'Aptitude de Beauté. The winner of three CACIBs at three shows under three judges may compete in the class for Grand International Champion. The winner of this class may be given a CAGCI, or Certificate d'Aptitude au Grand Championnat International, with three such wins entitling the cat to bear the title Grand Championnat International, which is the highest award. In Europe, as there is no quarantine between the countries, apart from Britain, cats may be exhibited freely at the various shows.

Chartreux Said to have been taken to France from South Africa by the Carthusian monks, hence the name, the Chartreux is an attractive Short-haired blue cat, thought by many to be the same as the British Blue.

Originally there were certain differences with the fur being more greyish than blue and the chest if anything even broader. Of recent years, however, judges agree that the coat colouring and the build has become the same as that of the standard required for the British Blues.

It is a sturdy well-muscled cat, with a round head, with powerful jaws, and well developed cheeks. The medium sized ears are slightly rounded and the large eyes are orange or golden yellow. The fur should be of the same even colour throughout, with no white hairs.

Gentle, intelligent cats, they make most affectionate pets, but are also said to be very efficient mice and rat catchers, if necessary.

Cheetah *Acinonyx jubatus jubatus* and *A. jubatus venaticus* are the African and Asian forms respectively, but there is no really marked difference between the two. Both are very long and slim measuring about 4½ ft with the tail another 2½ ft. At the shoulders it is sometimes 3 ft in height. The head is small and there are two heavy black tear-stripes running on either side of the nose from the corners of the eyes to the corners of the mouth, which gives it a sad yet beautiful and regal expression and distinguishes it from all other cats. The colouring is tawny with small solid black spots evenly distributed; underparts, chin and whisker-pads are pale creamy-white.

The adult Cheetah's claws are permanently extended and the pads are ridged rather than rounded, this feature enables it to grip the ground firmly and together with the unique arching of the back and the swing of the powerful back legs very high speeds are attained. They take less than two seconds to attain forty-five miles per hour, and speeds of up to sixty-five miles per hour are usual; this cannot be maintained for many hundreds of yards as stamina is not good enough. The fastest mammal on earth, they have the ability to out-run and catch gazelle and blackbuck.

These exquisite dog-like cats appear to be domesticated by instinct. They are not as easily trained as some report, but adapt more easily than any other wild cat and become very attached to their human owner if treated with intelligence.

The Cheetah's original distribution was all parts of Africa where conditions were suitable, and also the Middle East and a large area of Asia as far eastwards as India. Few remain now in Asia, and possibly a mere remnant in Persia and the area immediately to the north in Afghanistan; they have not been seen in Israel for over a hundred years, and none have been seen in India for some twenty years. In Africa, particularly in the north, they have become very rare and are doomed to extinction unless the recent Government legislation is immediately effective.

They inhabit sandy plains and areas of stunted bushes which provide sufficient cover; they avoid thick cover and mountainous areas. Besides gazelle and blackbuck, their prey includes small game such as hares. When they were numerous they kept the baboon population under control.

Chestnut Brown Foreign see HAVANA FOREIGN and FOREIGN SHORT-HAIR

Cheyletiella parasitivorax and ***C. yasguri*** see DANDRUFF and MITES

Children and Cats Cats and children can benefit greatly from one another's companionship. Cats make just as suitable pets as dogs do, but it is important that children are taught not to tease the cat, restrain it when it wants to be free, or handle it roughly. It is best to buy a kitten when the youngest child in the family is about two. Cats belonging to families to which a child is born are sometimes jealous of the attention the new arrival receives. It is unwise to leave a small baby and a cat together, lest the cat should be provoked into attack – as might occur if the baby tumbled over it, or persistently grabbed at it. Cats often show a tendency to snuggle into the blankets of a pram left outdoors on a sunny day, and there have been instances of babies being suffocated by cats lying on their faces. Cat nets can be bought which prevent this. Encouraging older children to feed and groom a cat, and to consider its comfort and needs, can form a valuable part of their education. It may be important to explain the basic psychological differences between cats and dogs to children. For example, cats are individualists and therefore do not obey commands or benefit from punishment. Nor do they readily accept petting and fuss unless in the mood for it. Cats like their dignity and privacy respected, and should not

The Cheetah, *Acinonyx jubatus*

be disturbed when going about their duties, such as washing and feeding.

Chinchilla One of the loveliest of the Long-haired varieties, with fur of pure white delicately tipped with black on the back, sides, head, ears and tail, giving the coat a sparkling appearance. The characteristics required are as for the other long-haired varieties, but the Chinchilla does tend to be lighter in bone, although it is in no way as delicate as the fairy-like appearance might imply. The tip of the nose should be brick red, and the large round eyes, a deep emerald or blue-green in colour. They are frequent Best in Show winners.

Heavy tickings are bad faults, and any yellow patches also.

When first born the kittens are dark, often with tabby markings, but as the fur grows these vanish, and in a very few weeks they look most decorative, and are frequently featured in television advertisements.

In North America, Chinchillas are recognized in both the Exotic and American Short-hairs (see TYPES), but these are unknown in Britain. The standard is the same as given for the Long-hairs, but, of course, the fur is short, and type is as for the Short-hairs.
See colour plate 19, page 73.

Chinese Desert Cat *Felis bieti* was not discovered until the latter part of the nineteenth century, and still very little is known about its origin and habits. The size is approximately that of the domestic cat, or perhaps a little larger; the colouring is greyish-yellow which blends in well with the surroundings. Its head has slight ghost markings, the body is not spotted or striped but there are dark guard-hairs. The underparts are white and the tail has several dark rings with a dark tip.

Its habitat is Mongolia and the Chinese provinces of Katsu and Szechuan and there is one report of it being seen in the mountains east of Sungpan. With regard to diet, very little is known but as it mostly inhabits dry grasslands and semi-desert, food would undoubtedly be similar to other small wild cats and consist of small mammals, reptiles and birds.

Such an interesting species undoubtedly requires further study and documentation.

Chinese Tiger see TIGER

Chocolate Burmese see BURMESE, NEW COLOURS

Chocolate Cream Point see SIAMESE, ANY OTHER COLOUR

Chocolate Point see HIMALAYAN, SIAMESE and BIRMAN

Chocolate Self see LILAC SELF

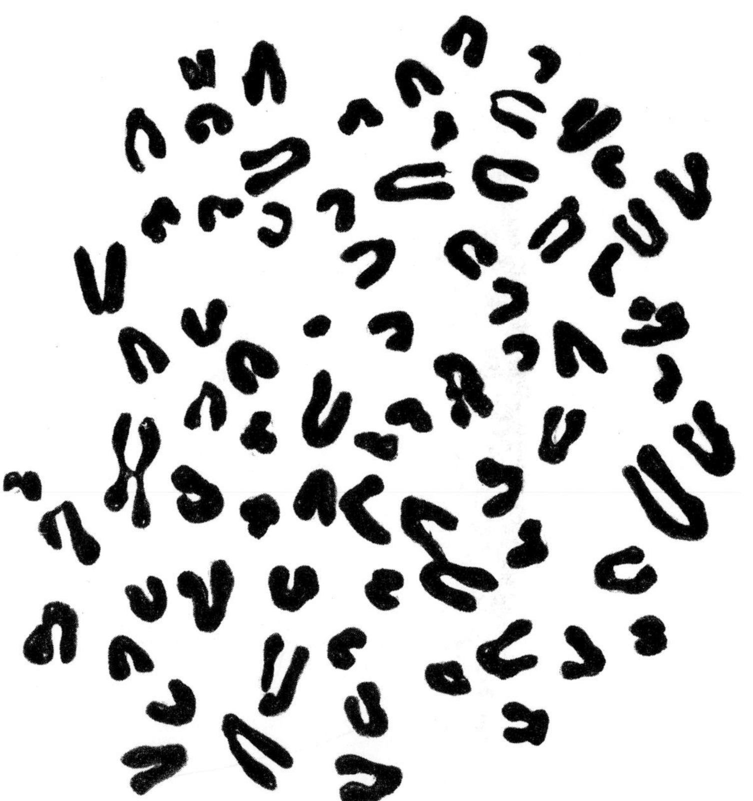

17

19

Chocolate Tortie Point see SIAMESE, ANY OTHER COLOUR

Choking Cats as a consequence of their fastidious ingestive behaviour rarely if ever swallow objects large enough to cause obstruction and consequent choking.

Occasionally fish bones or needles become lodged in the mouth causing profuse salivation and distress to the animal. Veterinary attention is often necessary as general anaesthesia is sometimes required to remove it. Antibiotics are usually given to prevent secondary infection.

Chromosomes Chromosomes are rod-shaped structures which arise from the nuclear network of the cell during the process of cell-division. These structures carry the hereditable material as genes at various sites (loci) throughout their length. Each species of animal has a characteristic fixed number of chromosomes, in the case of the cat this being 38. This number is made up of 19 pairs of chromosomes, in 18 pairs of which, (the autosomes), each member of the pair is identical with the other, and one pair, (the sex chromosomes), which are identical in the female and dissimilar in the male. The 38 chromosomes are found in all the cells of the cat's body with the exception of the germ cells and make up the Diploid number of the animal. In the germ cells, the sperm and the egg, this number is halved

above left Chromosomes of a male cat as seen under the microscope just before the cell divides – 76 chromosomes are therefore shown

colour 17 Cameo, Shaded
18 Cameo kittens, Shaded, Red and Shell
19 Chinchilla
20 Cornish Rex

to form the Haploid number. When fertilization takes place, the fertilized egg receives 19 chromosomes from the father and 19 chromosomes from the mother to make up the diploid number of the new individual. Obviously at the same time it receives the genes carried on the father's and mother's chromosome and thus the inherited characters of both parents.

The dissimilar sex chromosome of the male is small compared to the other chromosomes and is known as the Y-chromosome. This chromosome is responsible for the determination of the sex of an individual – if present the offspring will be a male, if absent, a female. The female chromosome is called the X-chromosome and if two of these are present, in the absence of a Y-chromosome, the offspring will be a female. See also GENETICS.

Classes at Shows *Britain* All the classes are listed in the show schedule. The first and most important are the Open breed classes for each recognized variety, adult and kitten. There are also a number of miscellaneous classes, such as:

Senior For cats 2 years old or over
Junior For cats under two years old
Breeders For cats and kittens bred by Exhibitor
Novice For cats and kittens that have not won a 1st prize under G.C.C.F. rules
Limit For cats that have not won more than four 1st prizes
Special Limit For cats that have not won more than two 1st prizes
Debutante For cats and kittens that have never been exhibited at a show held under G.C.C.F. rules
Maiden For exhibits that have not won a 1st, 2nd or 3rd prize at any show held under G.C.C.F. rules
Novice Exhibitors For cats and kittens whose owners have never won a money prize at any show held under G.C.C.F. rules, although the exhibits themselves may be prize-winners
Radius For exhibitors living within a certain distance of the hall
Champion of Champions Class For full champions only
Premier of Premier Class For full Premiers only

In addition to the above classes, there are the many classes guaranteed by the various clubs.

The kitten classes are for kittens up to the age of nine months, and the adult classes for cats over that age. Challenge certificates may be awarded to the winners of the Open breed adult classes. Neuters have their own classes and may not be entered in the same classes as other exhibits.

North America The classes are listed in the premium list (schedule) and include, for each Breed and Colour recognized:

Kitten Class For kittens four months and over but under eight months
Novice Class For cats that have never won a 1st award
Open Class For cats that have won a 1st award
Champion Class For cats which have become champions, and hold the required certificate
International Champion Class For cats that are champions in more than one country
Grand Champion For cats that are Grand champions
International Grand Champion Class For cats that are International Grand Champions

Continent

Grand Champion International As above
Champion As for British
Open As for British
Kittens 3–10 months
Couples For two cats of the same variety
Breeder For cats bred by the same person

In both North America and on the Continent there are classes for neuters very much the same as for the unneutered cats, the Champion equivalent being Premier.

Classification of the Wild Cats In 1758 Carolus Linnaeus originated a system of classifying living things and placed cats in a single group or genus called *Felis*. Now in 1972, zoologists classify cats into four such groups namely: *Panthera, Acinonyx, Neofelis* and *Felis*.

This classification is due mainly to anatomical differences. For example, the structure of the larynx of the great cats which results in their ability to roar; the non-retractile claws, except when young, and ridged pads which enables the Cheetah to grip the ground and gain speeds of up to 65 mph, and the intermediate species, the Clouded Leopard.

As will be appreciated, the descriptions are subject to slight variations in background colour; intensity and distribution of striping; whether or not the striping is breaking into spots or the evanescence of striping or spotting. Further, through man's encroachment of natural habitat some cats are showing marked decrease in size as well as geographical disturbance.

The study of the wild cats of the world still leaves much scope for further investigation and observation to provide detailed reports – but time is running short, as the majority of these exquisite animals are in grave danger of becoming extinct through exploitation for skins, and devastation of their habitat.

Claws Cats' claws are retractable; they are withdrawn when not in use into a protective sheath. The purpose of this adaptation is to ensure their sharpness at all times. When worn the cat scratches on branches, pulling off the worn outer layer of the claw leaving the new sharper layer beneath. If this is understood the futility of cutting cats' claws will be recognized since on realizing its claws are blunt the cat will be stimulated to increase its scratching in an attempt to resharpen them.

colour 21 Cream Long-hair
22 Cream Long-hair kitten

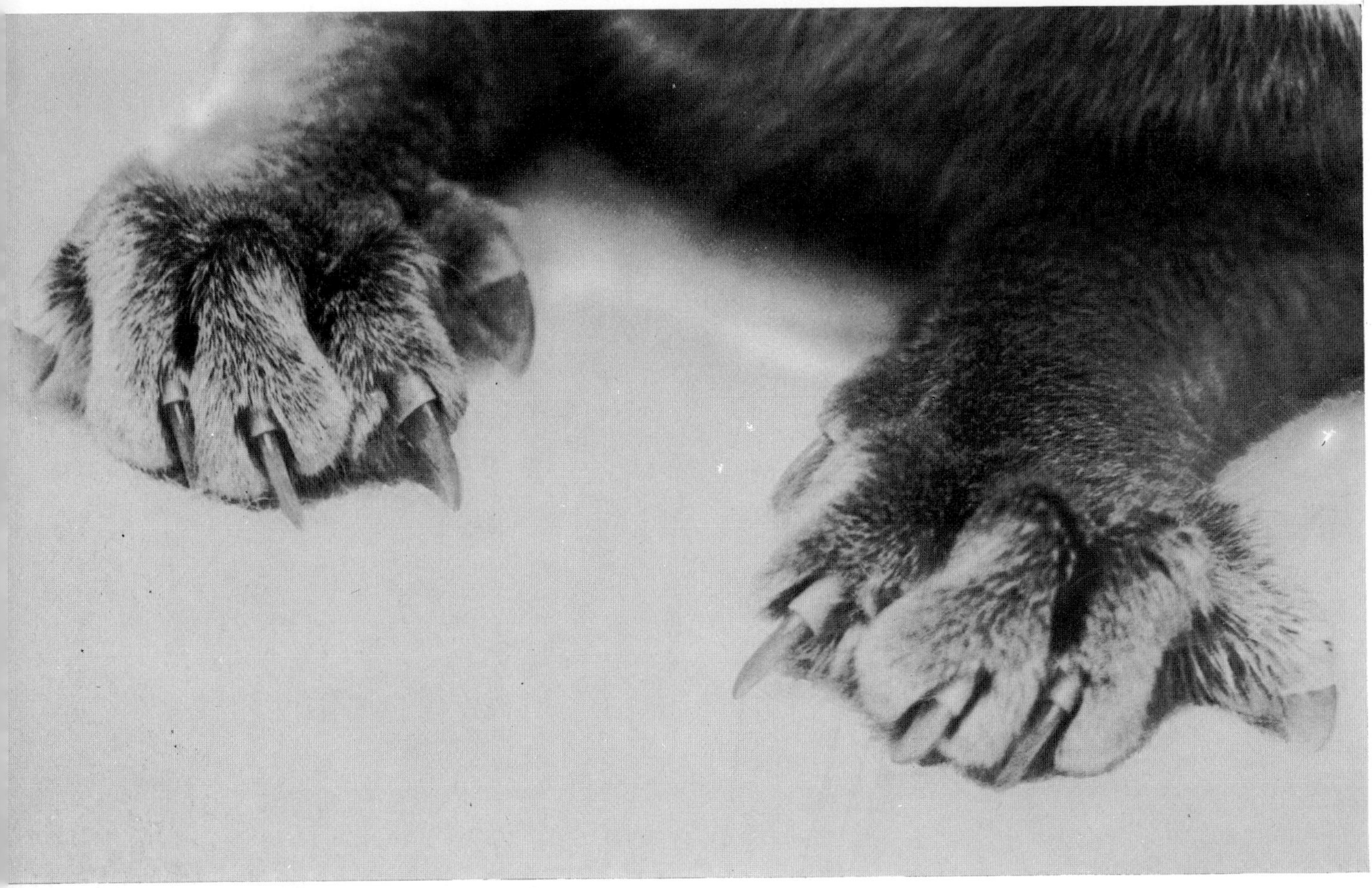

Cats use claws for climbing both in hunting and to escape enemies. They also use them for protection when cornered.

Dewclaws Dewclaws are claws that are found lying flat against the inside aspect of the leg a short distance above the foot. Unlike the claws of the foot, the dewclaws cannot be retracted and extended at will. Their main function is to assist in activities such as climbing and to a lesser extent, in self-defence. Double dewclaws are occasionally encountered.

De-clawing Also known as onychectomy, this operation has recently found favour among some cat owners who object to their pets damaging items of furniture during 'claw-sharpening' activity. Although articles published in British veterinary journals have proved that, correctly carried out, the operation causes the very minimum of discomfort to the patient, and that subsequent adjustment of the cat to his state of clawlessness seems adequate, the practice is generally frowned upon in veterinary circles in the U.K. It is felt that a far more satisfactory answer to the problem is to train young kittens to use scratching boards of the type widely available from petshops. This is not hard to achieve, particularly if breeding queens are previously introduced to a scratching board, and their offspring will then learn by imitation.

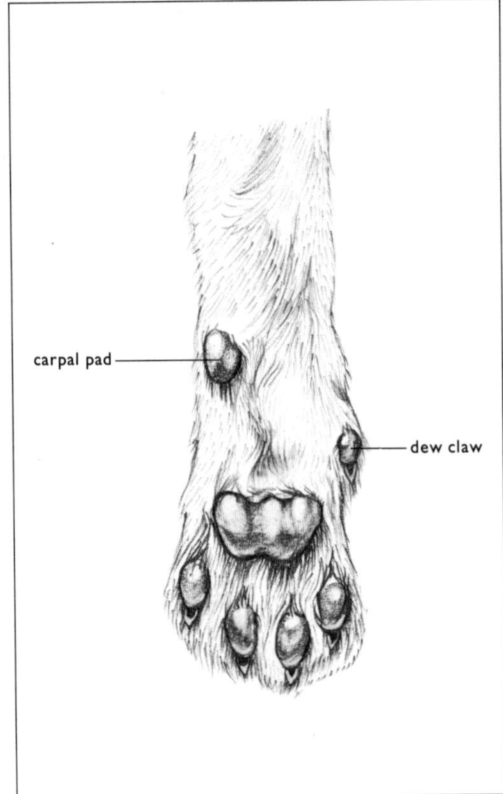

CLAWS *above* Claws extended provide a good grip; *left* a cat's paw showing the position of the dewclaw and carpal pad; *right* claws retracted and extended

The operation of de-clawing is carried out under general anaesthesia; each claw is cut back individually to its point of attachment to the distal bone of the phalanx. Provided this is done carefully, no re-growth of the claws should occur.

Systemic antibiotic coverage is also normally given. Normal locomotion is generally resumed upon removal of the bandages. The major effect of the operation is to reduce the animal's tree climbing ability. It is, of course, also important to ensure that a de-clawed cat does not fall prey to aggressive dogs, since, armed only with its teeth, it will be at a grave disadvantage.

Cats which have been de-clawed may not be entered in cat shows in the U.S.A. See also PAWS.

Cleft Palate see BREEDING ABNORMALITIES

Clerks see STEWARDS

Clipping Normal cats are never clipped. Occasionally neglected animals become hopelessly matted and require general anaesthesia for the situation to be rectified.

Clostridium septium see GAS GANGRENE

Clouded Leopard *Neofelis nebulosa* is the largest member of the Asian purring cats so that most zoologists agree to it being placed in a genus of its own – *Neofelis*. Recorded measurements are somewhat contradictory but large males are stated as measuring from 3 to 3½ ft from head to tail base, with a 2½–3 ft tail; females are smaller and total lengths are given as 5–5½ ft. Weight is recorded for males as up to 49 lb. and 37 lb. for females. Slender in build they become less graceful and appear thicker set in captivity.

The background colour of the coat is variable and may be greyish, brownish or yellowish and the underparts are almost white. The beautiful blotches run vertically and are partly etched in dark brown with clouded centres. In size they extend almost up to three-quarters of the depth of the body becoming smaller on the flanks and on the legs where they diminish into spots. Two bands, with narrower bands in between, run down the back and there are dark rings on the tail. The head and face are marked with streaks and spots of rather uneven pattern; the whisker pads and chin are pale. The small ears are black with a buff spot.

Their habitat is of eastern distribution being found in Sikkim, Bhutan and Assam, Burma, Siam, the Malay peninsula, Borneo, Sumatra, Taiwan, Hainan and parts of the mainland of China, but with the advance of civilization and wars they are becoming extremely rare and have now been placed on the list of endangered species.

Clouded Leopards are usually found in the thick jungles and are expert tree climbers spending much time concealed lying up in the branches of leafy trees. There are reports that they also inhabit secondary woodland and may be more diurnal than nocturnal as is stated by some authorities.

Their prey as far as is known is similar to those of other related species, although they have been seen to attack domestic livestock including dogs. They are reported as being less aggressive than the Marbled cat, and are tameable but present difficulties by refusing to eat 'dead' meat.

Coats Coats and overalls are an essential item of cattery equipment in breeding, boarding and quarantine establishments, or even when dealing with a single cat in the home if the animal is a valuable breeding queen, stud or one which is sick. Coats should be provided for visiting Veterinary Surgeons, Public Health Inspectors or prospective purchasers of stock in order to prevent the introduction or spread of infection.

They are best purchased from suppliers of veterinary protective clothing as the design as well as materials are carefully selected. Especially useful are shrunk white Drill as these can be boiled. Other materials include Terylene/cotton and Nylon.

Clinical coats are also available in waterproof materials and these are useful when hosing down cattery runs or for work in wet weather and for winter.

Cheap plastic raincoats may be purchased from the majority of clothing stores and are ideal for the infrequent visitor but will not be serviceable for general purposes.

Coccidiosis Infection with protozoan parasites, the Coccidia, is not common in the cat but does occur where the standard of hygiene in a cattery is low. The life cycle of the parasite is direct and infection is contracted by the cat swallowing an infective egg. This hatches in the intestines and liberates spores which develop into sporozooites. These invade the intestinal cells and feed on the contents. The sporozooites develop into trophozooites which in turn divide to form merozooites. These then leave the cell and enter other cells where they again form trophozooites. It is this cycle of cell damage which causes the symptoms of the disease, namely diarrhoea with faeces which may be bloody and slimy, anaemia, progressive weakness and emaciation, depression and dehydration. After a time the asexual reproduction ceases and the merozooites develop into male and female gametes which fuse to form an oocyst. The latter is passed out in the faeces and its contents develop to become spores (sporulation). Under conditions of indifferent hygiene, the cat will often re-infect itself by eating infective oocysts. Treatment is by the administration of gut active sulphonamides. It may be necessary to treat the dehydration by the infusion of suitable fluids and the anaemia by blood transfusions in severe cases. Improvement in the hygiene of the cattery is essential for the prevention of re-infection.

Cod Liver Oil Cod liver oil is a rich source of vitamins A and D. It can be administered as liquid in food or as capsules. Kittens, nursing queens and old cats may benefit from added vitamins but normal healthy cats on varied diets should not need such supplements. Veterinary advice should always be sought before giving vitamin additives to any animal. See also Vitamins under NUTRITION.

Codeine Being a morphine derivative, this drug should never be employed in the cat. Felines differ from other species in their reaction to morphine and allied compounds in that they are stimulated by them to the point of hypersensitivity and convulsions.

Colds The cat is not affected by the virus which causes human colds. Several conditions which resemble the human cold symptomatically, producing running nose, sneezing and watery eyes exist, however. See also CATARRH and FLU.

Collars Most cat-lovers come down heavily either in favour of, or against collars. There are two types. Those made of chain, plastic or unelasticated leather are definitely 'out'. A cat wearing one of these collars may get caught on the spike of a railing or the handle of a cooker, and throttle himself in his effort to escape. The only type of collar suitable for pet cats is an elasticated leather collar or simply a length of elastic. An identity disc or tube may be attached to this or a small 'Noddy bell', if you dislike your cat hunting birds – see BELLS.

Insecticidal collars that keep the cats permanently free of fleas are now available at some petshops. It is best, however, to use these only on veterinary advice, since they have not been on the market long enough for any side-effects to be reported.
See also ELIZABETHAN COLLARS.

Colostrum Colostrum, or first milk, is a specially rich milk produced by the mother cat, soon after kittening. As well as having a high food value, colostrum contains antibodies which confer immunity against diseases. Antibodies consist of protein, and in the normal way, protein substances are treated by the body as food – they are digested. Kittens under the age of about three days, however, do not digest proteins, they simply absorb them, and this means that the colostral antibodies pass through the gut and into the bloodstream unchanged. Since the mother only produces colostrum for a limited period, and the kitten can only absorb antibodies up to a certain age, it is essential that newborn kittens receive colostrum from a newly-kittened queen – either their mother, or another cat which has just given birth. See also FOSTER MOTHER.

Colourpoint see HIMALAYAN

Colourpoint Short-hair see AMERICAN SHORT-HAIR

Commercial Catfoods Modern research suggests that it is possible to put together all the ingredients (fats, proteins, carbohydrates, minerals and vitamins) required to maintain a cat in top condition, and to present them, in the correct proportions, in a prepared food. Commercial canned, dried, frozen or dehydrated foods should be fed according to the manufacturers' instructions. The types of food are:

Canned. This falls into three main categories – the chunky type with lumps of meat or fish in gravy or jelly; the loaf of finely minced, mixed meat (loaf products often also contain cereals, so it is wiser to read the label); and the intermediate product, which is not as stiff as the loaf and with smaller meat pieces than the chunky type.

Biscuit Meal Made up of fragments of broken biscuits, which are baked in the same way as biscuits for human consumption, biscuit meal for cats and dogs is usually wheat-based, with added vitamins and minerals, and often with extra protein or meat flavour. Available in a number of sizes, the smallest ones being suitable for kittens, it may be offered either soaked in milk, raw egg, gravy, or by itself as a crunchy dinner. Biscuit meals for dogs are perfectly suitable for cats, although care is needed to ensure that the very coarse lumps are removed when the large sizes are purchased. Some cats never take to

Elasticated collars are the best

biscuit meal, and should be offered rice, cornflakes, bread or mashed potatoes occasionally, as a source of carbohydrates.

Dehydrated Meat Just like the dehydrated meat in foods produced for human consumption, the meat is reconstituted by the addition of hot or boiling water.

Complete Dried Foods Made of meat, carbohydrates and fats, they are in the form of crunchy lumps about the size of a broadbean. Some doubt has recently been expressed concerning the use of these dried foods. It has been suggested that they predispose cats to urethral obstruction.

Frozen and deep-frozen meats. It is important to realize that only some of the canned and complete dried foods will supply all the nutritional requirements. If the other foods are used, they should form only part of the diet. The aim should be to supply meat (containing protein and fat) as well as carbohydrate (as biscuit).

Concussion see BRAIN DISORDERS

Conditioners They are usually patent medicines composed of minerals and vitamins. Healthy cats do not require constant conditioning. Such additives to normal diet should only be given under veterinary supervision.

Conformation Conformation refers to the shape and proportion of the cat's body. The cat demonstrates nature producing an animal whose conformation is perfectly adapted to its way of life. The shape of its skeleton and the development of its muscles provide its extreme agility. Conformation is maintained in the wild by selection for survival.

Conformation can be altered by selective breeding. The results can be seen in modern pedigree cats in the heavy bone and cobby shape of the British Long-hair and Short-hair compared to the fine bone and long body of the Siamese.

Unless such breeding is carefully controlled such alterations to conformation may become exaggerated to the detriment of the breed.

In all breeds of animals a 'sport' showing an alteration in shape may be born, but in view of the splendid conformation of the cat it would be foolish to perpetuate nature's mistakes by breeding from it.

Conjunctivitis see EYE AND EYELID DISORDERS

Constipation This is not an uncommon condition in the cat. Mild cases should be treated with liquid paraffin or one of the preparatory bulk food additives available as granules from most chemists. If no success is obtained in 24–48 hours veterinary attention is essential.

It is often necessary to administer a general anaesthetic in order to manipulate the bowel by palpating it from outside the abdomen in order to break down the faecal mass. In addition enemas may be required. Rare cases require surgery to obtain relief.

Some old cats suffer from a condition where the bowel loses the ability to function normally. This may have similarities to a similar condition in children where nerve supply to the lower bowel has been lost.

COLLARS Ornamental collars should be loose-fitting

Cooked Food see NUTRITION

Cornish Rex The first known Rex was born in 1950 in a litter of kittens from two ordinary short-coated cats in Cornwall, England. The coat differed from all others in that it was curly, without guard hairs. Mating the first kitten back to his mother resulted in further curly-coated kittens, later to be known as Rex, after the rabbits of that name. Fanciers were intrigued with these kittens, realizing that it was not a new variety but a mutation affecting the coat, and that it would be possible eventually to produce such fur in any coat colour. In 1960, in Devon, England (see DEVON REX) a similar coated kitten appeared and at first it was thought that this strain would prove a useful outcross for the already established Cornish, but it proved to be a different gene, and the resulting kittens were all straight-coated.

The standard for the Cornish Rex calls for animals with foreign type, having medium wedge-shaped heads, with straight profiles, large ears, oval shaped eyes, the eye colouring being in keeping with the coat. The bodies should be slender, but muscular, on long straight legs, and the tail long and tapering. The all-important and distinctive coat should be short, thick and plushy, curly and wavy, particularly on the back, with the tail being well covered. Bare patches are looked on as bad faults. Any coat colour is permitted, but any white markings except in the Tortoiseshell and White should conform to a pattern.

The Cornish Rex has proved to be most prolific and their distinctive appearance has found many admirers.
See colour plate 20, *page 73.*

Cougar see PUMA

Coughs Coughs occur as a sequel to a variety of conditions of the respiratory tract, and they may be acute or chronic in nature. Possible causes are: lungworm infestation; the ingestion of hair, commonest in Long-hairs and cats that are losing excessive quantities of coat but are not being groomed sufficiently; foreign bodies in the upper respiratory tract, stimulating reflex coughing which is likely to be fairly dramatic in nature, but should subside fairly quickly after removal of the foreign body unless damage to the throat has occurred; inhalation of irritant substances, causing immediate coughing and

CORNISH REX *left* Rex kittens; *right* Cornish Rex Brown

with a more persistent cough possibly supervening caused by laryngitis; neoplasia of the larynx (see LARYNX); laryngitis (see LARYNX); and haemorrhage or excessive mucus production in the respiratory tract.

Cream Abyssinian see ABYSSINIAN

Cream Burmese see BURMESE, NEW COLOURS

Cream Long-hair A very popular variety, with fur the colour of Devonshire cream, with no whiteness on the tail or stomach, or tabby markings. Once referred to as 'Fawns', they are said to have resulted from crosses between Blue and Reds in the early days of the Cat Fancy, and took many years to establish themselves. Selective breeding has resulted in outstanding Creams, with very good type and beautiful large round copper eyes. The fur must not be harsh in texture, nor reddish in colour. The latter, known as 'hot' is considered a bad fault. It does seem to happen when Creams are mated to Creams indefinitely, and a Blue Cream mating may help to correct this. The fur may tend to darken just before moulting, and daily grooming will be necessary to remove this to keep the pale cream coat looking immaculate.

The Cream is useful for mating to a Blue male and this may produce Cream male kittens and Blue Cream females. A Blue female mated to a Cream may have Blue male kittens and Blue Cream females. For the kittens which may result in the mating of a Blue Cream by a Cream male see Blue Cream Long-hairs. It is also a useful mate for Blacks, Tortoiseshells, and Tortoiseshells and Whites.
See colour plates 21 *and* 22, *page 74.*

Cream Point see SIAMESE, ANY OTHER COLOUR

Cream Short-hair A comparatively rare British variety and difficult to produce without markings, as required in the standard. The self-coloured coat should be a rich cream, even in colour, with no signs of tabby markings. Unfortunately, although cats are seen with the correct coat colouring, many have some bars and stripes; the most common fault being the ringed tail. In Britain 35 points are allowed in the standard for the colour, and 15 for the eyes, which should be deep copper or orange in colour. The type is frequently very good.

Creams are used to produce the short-haired Blue Creams, also the Tortoiseshells and the Tortoiseshells and Whites.

A Cream mated to a Blue Cream may have Blue males, Blue Cream females, and both male and female Creams. A Cream female mated to a British Blue could produce Blue Cream females and Cream males, but a Cream male mated to a British Blue female may result in Blue Cream females and Blue males. A good specimen does well at the shows, as there are so few about, but even those with markings make delightful pets, always being much admired.
See colour plate 13, *page 48.*

Cream Long-hair

Cream Tabby *see* TABBY LONG-HAIR and TABBY SHORT-HAIR

Cream Tabby Point see SIAMESE, ANY OTHER COLOUR

Creosote see Dangerous Liquids under ACCIDENTS

Cruelty see A.S.P.C.A., BLUE CROSS, P.D.S.A., R.S.P.C.A., and VIVISECTION

Cryptorchidism see BREEDING ABNORMALITIES

Crystal Palace Shows The first official cat show was held at the Crystal Palace in July 1871, when approximately one hundred and sixty cats and kittens were exhibited. The show which was under the management of Mr F. Wilson and organised by Mr Harrison Weir, later President of the National Cat Club, proved to be the forerunner of all cat shows throughout the world today.

At the 1871 show, the judges were Mr Harrison Weir, his brother and the Rev. J. Macdona, and the cats were judged according to 'Points of Excellence' prepared by Mr Weir. These 'Points' with some revisions formed the basis for today's 'Standard of Points'.

The show proved to be such a success that it very soon became an annual event until the Crystal Palace was burnt down in 1936, the day before the Cat Show was due to be held there.

At the early shows, the classes were not very numerous, being mostly for the various colours, limits, novices, braces and teams. There were special classes for working men or working women with reduced entry fees.

Crystal Violet see GENTIAN VIOLET

Ctenocephalides canis and ***C. felis*** see FLEAS

Cymric Developed from long-haired kittens without tails which appeared from time to time in litters of the short-haired Manx in the U.S.A. in the late 1960s, this variety is now being bred by several fanciers. The type and characteristics required are as for the Manx, the important features being the rounded rump and complete taillessness. All colours and coat patterns are possible. Championship status has not yet been granted.

Although occasional kittens have been seen in Britain, they are not being bred as a variety there or on the Continent yet.

Cystic Calculi and **Cystitis** see BLADDER DISORDERS

Dandruff Dandruff is a generalized, excessive scurfiness of the coat. Normally dead skin cells are shed continually and replaced by growth of new cells, but in dandruff the rate of loss is accelerated and the masses of dead cells become noticeable in the hair. The usual causes of the condition in the cat are infestation with the mite, *Cheyletiella parasitivorax* or *C. yasguri*, vitamin A deficiency, or seborrhoea. Treatment of the first two of these is straightforward, but seborrhoea has a multifactorial causation and it may be difficult to correct.

DDT Also known as dicophane, this is a powerful insecticidal compound which should never be applied directly to the body of a cat. Cases of poisoning may occur accidentally when DDT is used to reduce insects in houses especially where large quantities of DDT powder are present in the atmosphere in a confined space, or aerosols are used, and the cat cannot avoid inhaling it. It is safest to exclude cats from the room until it has filled with fresh air again.

Symptoms of DDT poisoning are hyperexcitability, convulsions and paralysis, followed by death in severe cases. Sedation with barbiturates is used as a method of controlling nervous symptoms.

Deafness Deafness may result from severe ear diseases (see Otitis Media under EAR DISORDERS) and, very occasionally, from damage to the nerves carrying impulses from the ear to the brain. Deafness may be complete or only partial. The range of audio frequencies perceived by any one species is often different from that perceived by another species, and therefore deafness trials in cats should include a number of sounds that, although above the human audio frequency range, would normally be perceptible to a cat. Should it turn out that the cat being tested can hear certain sounds, these may be used as a means of communication by the owner – for example a 'silent' dog-whistle may be used to call a cat indoors. Partial deafness, slowly deteriorating to total deafness, is seen in ageing cats, and there is no cure for this condition.

Temporary deafness may accompany acute ear infections. Deafness can be hereditary. See also ALBINO.

Devon Rex kitten

De-clawing see CLAWS

Deficiency Diseases see NUTRITION

Dehydrated Meat see COMMERCIAL CATFOODS

Dermatitis Strictly translated dermatitis means inflammation of the skin. It is not a specific condition, has no specific cause and is purely descriptive. The diagnosis of the cause is the important factor for successful treatment of skin conditions but can be extremely difficult. See SKIN DISEASES.

Dermatomycosis see RINGWORM

Desert Cat, Chinese see CHINESE DESERT CAT

Desert Cat, Indian see INDIAN DESERT CAT

Devon Rex First found in Devon in 1960 it was thought to be a similar gene to that of the Cornish Rex, but events proved that it was entirely different, and eventually the Devon Rex were given a separate breed number. The coats were found to be thinner than those of the Cornish, and are still inclined to be so. The coat should be very short and fine, wavy and soft with no guard hairs, and the whiskers and eyebrows should be crinkled. It has been found possible to produce the coat in many colours, even reproducing the Siamese coat pattern, as in the Si-Rex. Any colour is recognized, with the exception of white markings, although Tortoiseshell and White is permitted. The wedge-shaped heads should be full cheeked, and unlike that of the Cornish, the nose should have a strongly marked stop, with the forehead curving back to a flat skull. The ears should be large, the medium length body hard and muscular on long slim legs, with the tail long, fine and tapering. The eye colour should be in keeping with the coat.

The Devon Rex is noted for its good temperament and character, and makes an excellent pet, particularly for flat dwellers, having a very quiet voice.
See colour plate 23, *page 91*.

Dewclaws see CLAWS

Diabetes Diabetes may occur in the cat in one of two forms; 1. Diabetes mellitus – which is due to deficient secretion of insulin by the pancreas causing interference with carbohydrate metabolism and the excretion of glucose in the urine, 2. Diabetes insipidus – which is due to deficient secretion of antidiuretic hormone by the pituitary gland in the brain causing excessive thirst and the passage of large volumes of very dilute urine.

1. *Diabetes mellitus* Diabetes mellitus or Sugar Diabetes is not uncommon in the older, neutered male cat. The symptoms of the disease are mainly those of increased thirst and more frequent urination. There is loss of weight and lack of energy, followed by loss of appetite, extreme emaciation and often the development of a foul mouth with soft deposits of tartar on the teeth. Cataracts may develop in the lens of the eye. Diagnosis can be made by the demonstration of glucose in the urine or by a fasting blood sugar level which is raised above 120mg/100ml. Treatment is usually very effective and consists of the daily injection under the skin of a dose of between 5 and 10 units of Protamine Zinc Insulin.

Insulin Insulin is the hormone produced by the beta cells of the Islets of Langerhans in the pancreas. It is secreted into the bloodstream where it regulates the metabolism of sugar and other carbohydrates. The Insulin used for the treatment of Diabetes mellitus is produced commercially from ox or pig pancreas. Being of a protein nature, insulin is rapidly destroyed by the action of the digestive juices and for this reason must be given by injection. Usually the subcutaneous (under the skin) route is used although the injection may be made into a vein in cases of emergency. To minimize the frequency of injections, the insulin is usually combined with zinc protamine which slows down the rate of absorption.

For economic reasons it is usually necessary for the owner to perform these injections, but this seldom presents difficulties. There does not appear to be any benefit to be derived from changes in the cat's diet. Any infection must be treated strenuously with antibiotics, as diabetic cats are very prone to bacterial infections and wounds heal rather slowly.

2. *Diabetes insipidus* This is a rare condition in the cat but presents somewhat similar symptoms to those seen in Diabetes mellitus. With the deficiency of the anti-diuretic hormone, the animal is unable to concentrate the urine and this leads to excessive thirst and the passage of large volumes of urine with a specific gravity approaching that of the water imbibed. Treatment involves the intramuscular injection of the hormone, pitressin, at intervals of from one to three days.

Diagnosis Diagnosis is the procedure undertaken by clinicians to identify the cause of a disease. It relies on observation of the patient, symptoms related to the clinician and the use of the scientific laboratory tests. It is without doubt the most difficult and complicated part of a clinicians function, requiring a great deal of background knowledge and years of experience. It cannot be undertaken by amateurs.

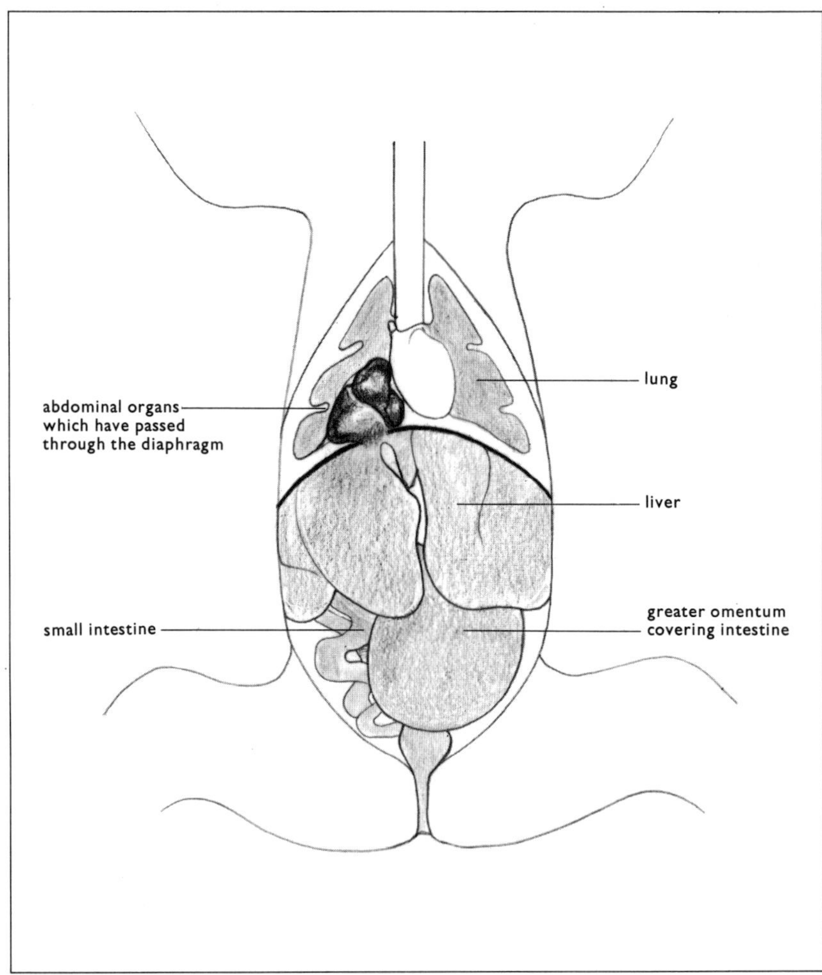

above Diaphragmatic hernia

Diaphragmatic Hernia This term means the entry into the thoracic (chest) cavity of organs normally situated in the abdominal cavity, following rupture of the diaphragm. In the sound healthy cat, the only structures found in the thoracic cavity are the lungs, heart, thymus and oesophagus. The structures most commonly involved in diaphragmatic hernia are the liver and stomach, but occasionally, if the damage to the diaphragm is extensive, a portion of the duodenum may also enter the chest. Since the lungs are compressed by the weight of the abdominal organs, breathing becomes laboured, but this can usually be eased by raising the chest above the lower half of the body.

Very occasionally, diaphragmatic hernia occurs without any detectable cause. Some individuals are probably born with the condition. These cases are usually mild. By far the commonest cause is a heavy impact on the body of the cat leading to bursting of the diaphragm, as may occur in traffic accidents. Surgical treatment of diaphragmatic hernia is complicated by the fact that 'positive pressure' methods of ventilation are required to prevent the lungs from collapsing during the operation. Radiography is almost always carried out beforehand to give the surgeon an accurate idea of the extent of the herniation.

Diarrhoea This is the passage of watery faeces. Its immediate cause is that the bowel contents move too rapidly through the colon to permit water resorption to take place there. Persistent diarrhoea results in considerable loss of body fluids and a consequent state of dehydration, characterized by listlessness or collapse, a staring coat, thirst, cold extremities and increased pulse. Soreness of the perineal area is frequently encountered in diarrhoea cases. It can be alleviated to some extent by the application of bland creams after cleansing. Pure talc or baby talcums are also helpful in keeping the area dry.

Diarrhoea is a symptom of several different conditions. Diarrhoea accompanied by haemorrhage is known as dysentery.

Veterinary attention should be sought early in all cases of diarrhoea that do not respond to simple measures, such as the withholding of food for a few hours, followed by the feeding of raw beaten egg, arrowroot gruel and other binding substances.

Dicophane see DDT

Diet see NUTRITION

Digitalis This is a drug produced from the foxglove, *Digitalis purpurea*. When administered by mouth it slows and strengthens the heartbeat and is therefore useful in the treatment of valvular abnormalities. Unfortunately one of its side-effects is to cause vomiting, although an allied substance, digoxin, has been administered by injection with better results.

Dipylidium caninum see PARASITES and Tapeworms under WORMS

Disease Prevention Many diseases occur in spite of any precautions taken. There are however basic rules which will minimize the risk to cats.

The provision of an adequate well-balanced diet in correct quantities is essential. Exercise facilities ensure physical health maintaining muscular tone. Hygienic surrounding with particular attention to bedding and feeding dishes will prevent the build up of infectious agents.

Careful grooming particularly of long-haired cats is essential for health and hygiene.

Regular visits to the veterinary surgeon particularly as middle age is reached will help to identify disease in its early stages and thereby the chance of successful treatment.

Dishes Feeding dishes should be hygienic, light, durable, quiet in use and easy to stack and store. No single type of dish fulfils all these criteria. Metal dishes are very hygienic, since they can be sterilized by boiling or scalding, but they are noisy in use and expensive. Polythene dishes are cheap, light and 'quiet', but they can only be disinfected by the use of chemicals. Some cattery owners prefer to use dis-

below A selection of dishes

DISHES *above* A dish made of hygienic, unbreakable plastic. Feeding shelves are an excellent idea especially in catteries

posable dishes of the type used by supermarkets for the display of fruit. For the owner of a small number of pet cats a plastic or enamel dish, shaped so that they do not tip over easily is probably the best buy. Dishes should be washed in hot water and detergent and then rinsed thoroughly between meals – cats are fastidious about cleanliness.

Dislocations The term 'dislocation' indicates the loss of articulation of a bone. Dislocation may be partial – when loss of articulation is not total – or complete – when it is. The commonest sites of dislocation in the cat are the hip-joint, the elbow joint, and the jaw. Following the infliction of the injury, extensive swelling generally occurs, which makes reduction of the dislocation difficult, but also facilitates the transport of fluids that promote healing to the area. The correction of dislocation is a painful procedure and is nearly always carried out under general anaesthesia. It involves the application of traction to the limb until the two bones come into apposition and articulation is restored. Sometimes the effect is only temporary – the bones showing a tendency to redislocate readily – and this is termed a chronic or recurrent dislocation.

After a dislocation has been corrected, it is wise to restrict the animal's exercise, and adhesive strapping may be applied to immobilize the limb until the damaged ligaments have healed – particularly in the case of elbow dislocation.

Dislocation of the toe is fortunately very unusual in the cat since the condition is difficult to correct and the affected toe might have to be amputated. Patients normally compensate very quickly and easily for the loss of a toe, and normal locomotion is soon regained.

Fortunately, dislocation of the elbow is rare in the cat. Considerable force is required to effect loss of articulation. The cause is usually impact of the type sustained in a traffic accident. The condition is an extremely painful one, and the affected leg is not used at all by the cat. There is usually considerable

colour 23 Devon Rex

colour 24 Egyptian Mau

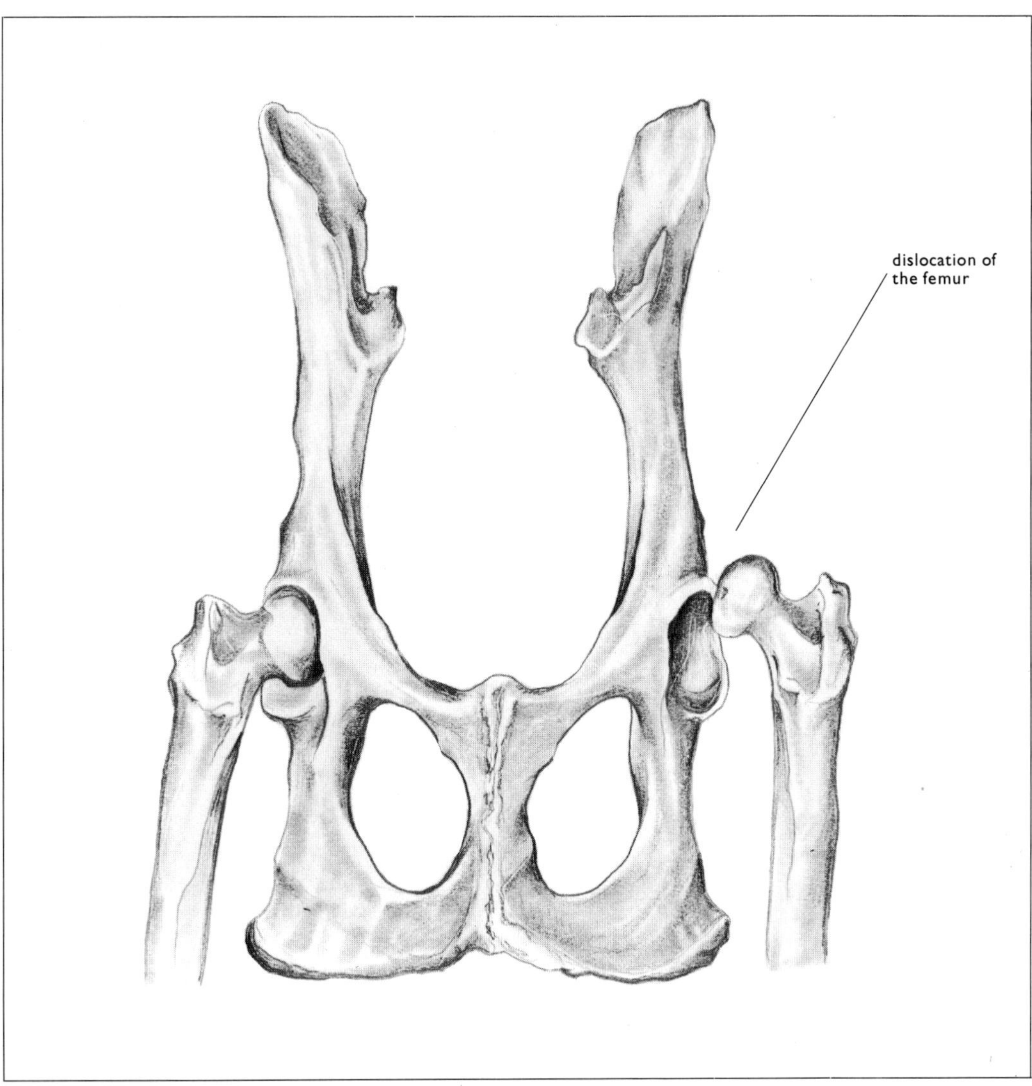

right Dislocation of the femur

swelling. Treatment involves a general anaesthetic to correct the dislocation. A supporting bandage is usually applied to help immobilize the limb. The cat should be encouraged to rest as much as possible following correction. See also ACCIDENTS.

Diuretics Diuretics increase the amount of urine produced. They are mainly used to treat conditions where abnormal quantities of fluid build up in the body. Examples include heart disease, ascites (dropsy), lung diseases. They also have a place in kidney disease to increase the flow of urine thus flushing out infective organisms. A wide range of diuretics are available.

Docking This is not normally required for cosmetic reasons in the cat. Manx are the only short-tailed cats, and they are born that way. But docking may be necessary if a cat damages its lower tail severely and there is a danger of the injured part becoming necrotic. Infective organisms may invade the area and eventually cause general infection. A general anaesthetic is normally given, and a tourniquet applied to the upper tail. The skin and muscle are incised, and the veterinary surgeon cuts through the ligaments and between two vertebrae, leaving plenty of skin to cover the severed end of the tail. The skin flaps are then sutured, and superficial healing is usually complete in 10 days. There should be little or no bleeding after the operation, as the tail vessels are ligated ('tied off').

Dog Flea see FLEAS

Dogs Despite the tradition that the dog and the cat are arch enemies, they will co-exist very happily provided they are brought up to tolerate one another. Young puppies may be discouraged from chasing cats.

Cat owners should not worry unduly about their cats being attacked and injured by dogs. Only the most tenacious of terriers ever manages to make much impression on a cat. As a rule, the cat escapes. If cornered, he may be attacked, but usually the dog emerges with far worse wounds than the cat. It seems that cats rarely reach the stage of biting dogs if it comes to an encounter, because a few scratches on the nose and eyes are enough to make most dogs turn tail.

Rearing a pup and a kitten together is the most satisfactory way of keeping a pet of both species.

Dogs will often act as foster-mothers to orphan kittens.

Domestic see AMERICAN SHORT-HAIR and EXOTIC SHORT-HAIR

Domestication History Unlike dogs, the cat came late to share the comforts of man's hearth. Fossil remains of cats in archaeological sites belonging to the Neolithic, Bronze and Iron Age periods are almost certainly of wild felines.

There can be little doubt that domestication of the cat occurred in ancient Egypt. The term 'Puss' is assumed to come from the Egyptian goddess Pasht. The actual period of domestication is difficult to establish. The Egyptians made use of great variety of animals in the early part of their civilization around 3000 BC, and it is possible that the cat was so subjected, but no firm evidence exists. There is, however, no doubt that it was established as a domestic animal in Egypt by 1800 BC.

Originally the wild forms may have chosen to associate with man in order to avail themselves of the ready supply of rodents inhabiting the granaries, but with time it became fully accepted and elevated to the religious import of a deity, associated with the goddess Budastis.

Cats enjoyed considerable privileges in Egypt until the coming of outside pressures. They were fully protected by the law. Even the accidental killing of a cat was punishable by death. When a cat died its owners entered mourning and the remains were mummified and buried in sacred ground. Such veneration was the main factor in its slow spread from Egypt, since for a long time, exportation was prohibited. The reason for the removal of exportation restrictions or the manner in which they were instigated, is unknown. Pottery decorations indicate that it was well known to the Greeks as rather a curiosity until it was eventually imported from Egypt in small numbers around 1000 BC confirming the existence of trading and cultural links between the two countries.

Some rather doubtful evidence suggests it may have been kept in domesticity by the Etruscans as early as the 4th century BC.

From Egypt it also spread to Babylonia in the 2nd century BC, and then on to India, where it has been known for 2000 years.

Certainly by early Christian times cats were kept in large numbers by the Romans and marched with the Imperial legions to all parts of the Empire. Several remains of domesticated cats have been found in Roman archaeological sites in Britain, and footprints impressed on Roman tiles during their manufacture support the fossil evidence that they were domesticated. By this time cats had lost their religious significance and were used by the Romans to replace polecats as a means of rodent control.

Far from the exultation afforded it by the Egyptians, in the Middle Ages in Britain it was associated with evil. Black cats symbolized witches connections with Satan. During this period it was subjected to extremes of cruelty, being used as an adjunct to religious festivities and holy days. In an attempt to drive out evil spirits it was variously burnt alive, tortured and sacrificed, showing how closely superstition, ancient religions and Christianity were inter-related.

The variety of breeds available today are the result of selective breeding and genetic mutations rather than separate acts of domestication in the various parts of the world after which they were often named.

Having been variously of utilitarian use, a deity and the personification of evil, the function of modern pet cats is to interact with the owners psychology to counteract inadequacies in the environment. Thus the function of domestic pets can be seen as dynamic, evolving with human society.
See also CAT LORE.

Dosing The cat-owner is likely to want to dose his cat for a number of reasons during its lifetime: to eradicate intestinal parasites; to give antibiotics, tonics, etc., prescribed during illness; to give travel-sickness pills and pre-firework sedatives; to give emetics if the cat is thought to have swallowed poison. The dosing technique is also used when force-feeding is required. Solid preparations given to cats include powders, pills, pastes, and tablets. The powders are best mixed with water, butter or honey. The technique is as follows:

Get an assistant to hold the patient's front legs and support its hindquarters to stop it moving backwards. Then hold the cat's skull in the same way as a bowler holds a cricket ball, with the fingers spread wide and roughly at right-angles to the spine, and bend the wrist so the skull moves upwards and the jaw drops, opening the mouth. To give a tablet or pill, throw it on the back of the tongue, poke it gently with your finger or a smooth, blunt object, and hold the mouth shut, simultaneously stroking the throat. To give a paste or powder, smear it on to the back of the tongue. If the cat is very intractable, the 'scruff' can be held high up behind the ears instead of the whole skull.

When giving liquids, great care must be taken to ensure the cat does not choke, so it is best to give small amounts very gently. A teaspoon or long-necked bottle may be employed. The mouth is opened as described above, and the liquid introduced on to the back of the tongue.

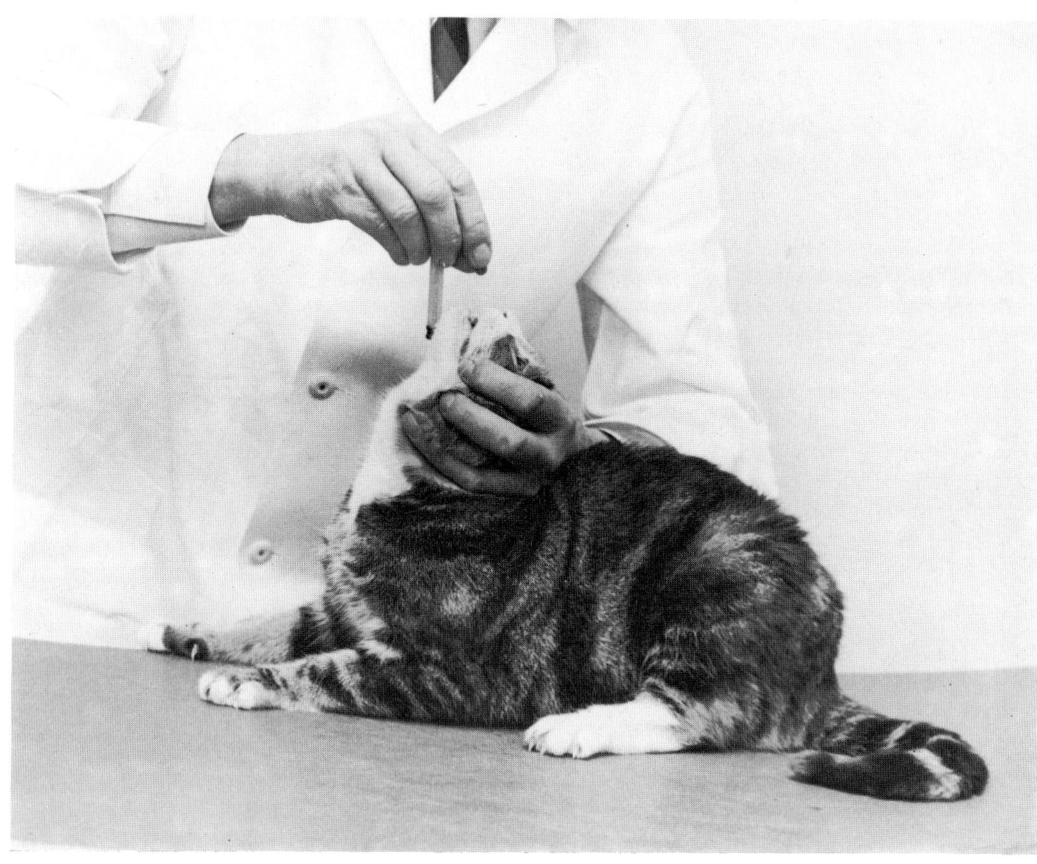

DOSING How to give a cat a pill. Note the prodder – in this case the plunger of a disposable syringe

Dribbling Dribbling, or salivation, may occur both in health and disease. Copious saliva is produced in response to stimuli such as the smell or sight of food that is relished by the animal, and the saliva is frequently allowed to escape from the mouth.

Dribbling may be stimulated by irritant vapours if these are inhaled. Cats receiving ether anaesthesia are frequently treated with special drugs that reduce saliva secretion before the induction of this anaesthesia, so abundant is the saliva produced by inhalation of this agent.

Dribbling also occurs if the mouth cannot be closed or if excess saliva cannot be swallowed, as in cases of foreign bodies of the mouth or pharynx. Likewise heavy tartar deposits may initiate dribbling.

Fear may sometimes cause dribbling, particularly in cats that dislike travelling. On removal from its transport box at a journey's end, such an animal will be found to have extremely damp chin, chest and fore-paws.

Cats suffering from fits often dribble quite heavily, and the saliva is usually mixed up with air, hence the description 'foaming at the mouth' used of animals undergoing fits.

Dried Foods see COMMERCIAL CATFOODS

Drink Requirements Like nearly all mammals, with the exception of a few aquatic or desert-inhabiting species, the cat requires adequate supplies of fresh water to be available to it all the time. This is particularly important in the case of old cats suffering from nephritis, and conditions when the fluid balance is upset, for example, gastroenteritis and diabetes. Water is normally only rationed if a cat shows a tendency to drink large volumes of it and then vomit. If clean cold water is not available to a healthy cat, he will find water elsewhere, perhaps dripping from a tap, standing in a gutter or drain, or even in the WC. Many cat owners who supply their cats only with milk would be horrified if they knew where their cats obtained water.

Boiled water is sometimes given to cats with a history of urinary calculi (bladder stones).

Dropsy see ASCITES

Drowning, First Aid for Contrary to popular belief, cats swim fairly efficiently and cases of drowning are only likely to occur where the cat is unable to climb out of the water, where turbulence causes him to swallow a lot of water.

The first-aider should first rescue the victim by grasping him by the scruff – a drowning cat will tend to panic, like any other species, and there is a danger of getting scratched if any other approach is taken.

The animal should then be taken ashore as speedily as possible. Unless he is struggling dangerously, do not hold him by the scruff a minute longer than is necessary, since this may hamper breathing.

If the cat is semiconscious, hold him firmly above the hocks, and, standing with the feet apart, swing him (either between your legs or from left to right in front of you). This should cause any water, weed or mucus to fall from the trachea or pharynx. Then apply artificial respiration.

If he is sufficiently conscious to cough and splutter do not swing him, but proceed at once to apply artificial respiration (see ARTIFICIAL RESPIRATION). Afterwards, the patient should be treated for shock, as follows:

1. Dry him, preferably with a hair dryer.

2. Wrap him up with a towel or light blanket and put him somewhere comfortably warm. Hot water bottles, electric blankets etc., are not advisable. It is much better to conserve the heat produced by the cat's body than to heat him artificially. If heat is really necessary an infra-red lamp is best.

3. Give glucose and water mixture by mouth *if* the patient is able to swallow without choking.

4. Keep the patient quiet, turn off bright lights and encourage him to rest.

5. Do not give food or stimulants (e.g. brandy, tea) unless advised to by the veterinarian. It is, of course, wise to summon the latter at the earliest possible opportunity.

See also EUTHANASIA.

Drug Sensitivity The cat shows an unusual degree of sensitivity to many of the drugs used in modern veterinary medicine. This extra sensitivity is especially marked in the phenol group of disinfectants, e.g. Lysol, Jeyes Fluid, carbolic acid, etc., in morphine and its derivatives, and in aspirin. Whether the sensitivity to the phenols is due to some inherent species idiosyncracy or to the well-known habit of the cat of licking substances from the coat, is still a matter for conjecture. Apart from these marked sensitivities, the cat also shows untoward reactions to the administration of certain of the antibiotics, notably Streptomycin, which may produce loss of balance and permanent deafness, and Neomycin, which again may cause deafness and also kidney damage. The pesticides, such as benzylbenzoate (used for the control of mange mites), the chlorinated hydrocarbons, e.g. DDT, Gammexane, etc., and the organophosphorous compounds, e.g. Malathion, Ectoral, etc., have all provoked severe side-effects when applied to cats. Finally vitamin A, when given in excessive amounts, may cause a crippling overgrowth of bone in the spine in the neck region. Drug manufacturers tend to transpose the results of toxicity trials in laboratory animals to dogs and cats and this can lead to unfortunate drug reactions.

Dual Mating The mechanism in the cat during the period in which she will allow the male to mate her is such that the act of copulation stimulates ovulation. This means that spermatozoa introduced have an excellent chance of meeting and penetrating the ova, which are shed at the same time. Having once been mated, a female cat will often accept other male cats at various stages during pregnancy. But ova are normally shed only at the first mating. Therefore conception will only take place at the second mating if it occurs a short time after the first one. Any matings that occur once the shed ova have died will not result in conception. Dual mating may be carried out using one tom only or two different toms. The disadvantage of the latter procedure, is that it is impossible to identify the progeny of either one with accuracy. See also BREEDING, BEHAVIOUR and SUPERFOETATION.

Dyspnoea Dyspnoea may be defined as difficult or laboured breathing. The condition is quite frequently encountered in the cat and presents the veterinarian with difficult problems in differential diagnosis. This is due to the fact that many different factors may be involved in the causation of dyspnoea. These factors can be loosely grouped into five main categories:

1. Infection by living organisms. This group includes bacterial, and mycotic infections. These infections may produce pneumonia or pleurisy.

2. Mechanical agents. These agents are mainly those of injury, such as diaphragmatic hernia, fractures of the ribs, and lung haemorrhage.

3. Tumours of the lungs.

4. Circulatory disturbances. Disturbances of the circulatory system may result from heart disease, anaemia or haemorrhage.

5. Miscellaneous. This is a wide group and includes all the conditions such as fear, shock and pain, which can produce dyspnoea but which are not included in the previous groups.

The symptoms of dyspnoea are that the cat usually adopts a prone position, crouched down on its chest with elbows held away from the chest wall to allow free movement, the head and neck are extended, and the animal may breathe through its mouth, sometimes puffing out the cheeks with each expiration. Any movement tends to accentuate the difficult breathing. The inside of the mouth and the tongue may be a livid, bluish colour (cyanosis) due to deficient oxygenation of the blood. Unless relieved the cat will die from lack of oxygen or from heart failure.

Treatment can be very difficult even if a diagnosis of a specific cause can be made. Any attempts at medication may be strongly resisted by the cat and provoke a fatal aggravation of the dyspnoea.

E

Ear Anatomy and Function Hearing is the special sense whereby sounds are communicated through the ear to the brain. To appreciate the mechanism of hearing it is necessary to have some understanding of the anatomy of the ear. The ear can be divided into three main portions: 1. The Auricle or External Ear. This is the visible portion of the ear and in the cat is fairly mobile, being capable of movement in the direction of the sounds. The external ear forms a funnel leading down to the tympanic membrane or ear drum, which is stretched across the ear canal. 2. The Middle Ear. This is made up of three small bones, the auditory ossicles, which extend from the tympanic membrane to an opening in the wall of the inner ear, the oval window. 3. The Inner Ear. This consists of a vestibular apparatus, which is concerned with balance, and a cochlea. The latter is in the form of a spiral tube, the cochlear duct, encased in bone and surrounded by and containing a fluid, the perilymph. In the cochlear duct is found a highly complex sensory structure, the organ of Corti, which contains the endings of the eighth cranial or acoustic nerve.

Sound waves are picked up by the auricle and directed to the tympanic membrane which is thrown into vibrations. These vibrations are transmitted mechanically through the auditory ossicles to the cochlear duct and thence hydraulically to the organ of Corti. Here they generate nerve impulses which pass up the acoustic nerve to the brain where they are 'decoded' into recognizable sounds.

Deafness in the cat is usually of a hereditary nature associated with white coat colour (see ALBINO). Deafness in old age is usually due to bony changes occurring in the auditory ossicles which limit their mobility.
See DEAFNESS.

Ear Cleaning Normally ears remain clean and require no attention. In some cases of ear disease cleaning is essential. It is however a task for skilled hands and should only be carried out by the veterinarian or on explicit instructions. The lining of the ear is very delicate and sensitive. Inexpert probing and cleaning can exacerbate a mild ear condition, and cause it to become serious.

The most satisfactory agents for removing excessive wax are cerumenolytics – agents which dissolve wax.

Ear Disorders *Otitis* Otitis means inflammation of the ear. Otitis is of three types – otitis interna, affecting the internal ear, otitis media, affecting the middle ear, and otitis externa, affecting the external auditory meatus. Otitis externa is much the commonest condition. Possible causes are infection by bacteria, yeasts and moulds, entry of a foreign body, and infestation of ear-mites (*Otodectes cynotis*). The disease is characterized by irritation of the external ear, often accompanied by the production of an evil smelling discharge. Treatment varies depending on the severity of the condition. Syringeing of the ear with detergent antiseptics to free it of wax and discharge may be necessary. See also MITES.

Otitis Media and Interna Middle ear disease or Otitis media is a term applied to an inflammatory process within the middle ear and which is almost always associated with inflammation of the inner ear, Otitis interna. Infection may spread to the middle and thence to the inner ear from the external ear canal through the ear drum, or via the Eustachian tube from the throat region. Symptoms suggest that the cat is in obvious pain, the head is rotated ventrally and there are varying degrees of ataxia (staggering gait). In severe cases, the head may be twisted almost upside down. The ataxia may vary from a slight swaying gait to a progression in a drunken, lurching manner with the cat tending to fall over when walking. These symptoms are due to inflammation of the vestibular apparatus which is intimately concerned with the maintenance of balance. Treatment is by incision of the ear drum to promote drainage coupled with the administration of the broad spectrum antibiotics to control the bacterial infection. The corticosteroids may be helpful in hastening the return of normal equilibrium. The Eustachian tube may be opened by blowing air through the opened ear drum in order to improve drainage of the infection. Recovery may take several weeks and some cases remain permanently ataxic.

EAR DISORDERS Haematoma of the ear

Haematoma Haematoma of the ear (aural haematoma) is the result of numerous small blood vessels within the pinna or flap of the ear rupturing. The escaping blood fills the space between the walls of the ear flap, causing the flap to balloon out. Rupture of the blood vessels is usually the result of head-shaking, as a result of irritation in the ear. The formation of the haematoma itself adds to the pain and discomfort experienced by the patient, and tends to stimulate further bouts of head-shaking. If aural haematoma is not treated, the blood will eventually clot, fluid will be resorbed, and fibrosis will occur in the pinna, so that the ear becomes thickened and acquires a crumpled appearance. Surgery relieves the discomfort and restores the earflap to very nearly its original appearance. Under general anaesthesia an ellipse-shaped section is cut out of one wall of the earflap. This releases the blood, and any blood clots can be removed. Sutures are inserted to prevent reformation. The causal ear condition must be treated concurrently.
See also DEAFNESS.

Eclampsia Eclampsia, also known as Lactational Tetany or Milk Fever, is a rare condition in the cat in which nervous symptoms occur during the period of lactation. Usually the cat is nursing a fairly large litter of five or six kittens, and the time of onset varies between three to eight weeks after kittening. The symptoms vary, but are essentially nervous in character comprising inco-ordination, especially of the forelimbs, ataxia (staggering gait), muscular twitchings and tonic spasms of the limbs, paralysis, collapse and coma. Other symptoms sometimes seen are vomiting, a very high temperature (up to 109°F), dry mouth, dilatation of the pupils and rapid, panting type respirations. Treatment consists of the administration of calcium, preferably intravenously. The kittens should either be removed entirely and reared by hand, or reduced in number and augmented feeding instituted. Cats which have suffered an attack of eclampsia should not be allowed to rear more than four kittens in any subsequent litter.

Ectropion see EYE AND EYELID DISORDERS

Eczema see SKIN DISEASES

Egyptian Cat see CAFFRE CAT

Egyptian Mau Said to closely resemble those cats featured in wall paintings by the ancient Egyptians, the Egyptian Mau was developed in the U.S.A. from cats brought from Cairo, Egypt in 1953. Siamese in type, they are graceful long lithe cats with wedge-shaped heads and oriental eyes. There are two varieties, one having black spotting on a silver ground coat, and the other bronze spotting on tawny coloured fur. They are known respectively as the Silver and Bronze Mau.

A few years ago they were seen in America and

Egyptian Mau

much liked by a British breeder who realized that the quarantine restrictions and the cost would make it exceedingly expensive to bring some breeding pairs to Britain. She decided to try to produce similar cats by scientific breeding and has now succeeded.

The type and coat pattern is very much the same, but the British Egyptian Maus have a most distinctive mark on their foreheads closely resembling the shape of a scarab beetle. Cat statuettes made at the time of the Pharaohs, which may be seen in some museums such as the Louvre in Paris and the British Museum in London, frequently have such markings on their heads.

The Mau is recognized by some Associations in America, but at the moment is registered as Any Other Variety in Britain.

See colour plate 24, *page 92.*

Elastic Bands Occasionally as a result of children playing with elastic bands and cats concurrently, the bands are placed over a leg, around the neck or tail of the cat. As the band contracts continually in diameter it causes a wound encircling the affected appendage. Frequently the bands become well buried before the damage is observed. Surgery is sometimes required to find and remove them.

Electric Shock Patients suffering with electric shock are usually encountered in private households, although a number of cases are on record of cats that have sustained electric shock following contact with live rails and other such sources of current in the outdoor environment. The commonest causes of electric shock are faulty insulation and cats chewing a live flex in play. It is a wise precaution to turn off all electricity at mains sockets before shutting a kitten in a room.

When the animal receives an electric shock, it may remain in contact with the source of the current, being unable to move away. The best way to detach a cat from the cable or appliance to which it is stuck is to place Wellington boots or rubber gloves over the hands and gently pull the animal. On no account should persons attempt to remove the animal from a current source with bare hands unless they are wearing rubber-soled shoes and have only their feet in contact with the floor. Having once removed the patient, artificial respiration may be required, but there is also some danger of heart failure so that urgent veterinary treatment may be needed. Ideally one person should administer artificial respiration while another drives both the patient and the first-aider to a veterinary establishment.

Elizabethan Collars Elizabethan collars may be necessary for two reasons: the cat has a wound on its head, and shows a tendency to scratch at it with the hind legs; or it has a wound or patch of eczema or toxic powder on its body, and you wish to prevent it from biting and licking itself. Some people bandage the hindpaws to cushion the claws in the former instance, but an Elizabethan collar is probably more effective.

These may be fashioned out of leather, plastic or cardboard, or they may be improvised using flower pots or bowls made of plastic. In the latter case, the bottom of the vessel must first be removed by cutting it out with old scissors and holes are then drilled around the perimeter of the hole left. Tape is looped through these holes and used to attach a leather cat collar to the bowl or pot, and elastic adhesive tape is used to prevent the edges of the pot from rubbing against the cat's neck. The Elizabethan collar is then placed over the cat's head and the leather collar fastened.

A cardboard collar may easily be made from a rigid piece of cardboard about 14 in. square, such as from the side of a grocery box. This is cut to make a disc about 10 in. in diameter and a round hole, the diameter of the cat's neck, is cut from the centre. About 1/6th of this ring is cut away to make a 'C' shape and the two ends of the 'C' are joined together by staples overlaid with adhesive tape. Adhesive tape may also be used to strengthen the outer and inner edges. Holes are then punched around, near the inner perimeter, and tape is laced through then. A leather cat collar is threaded through the loops of tape which is then pulled tight and the whole collar placed over the cat's head and the leather collar fastened around its neck.

The collar must, of course, be removed at intervals to allow the cat to feed, drink and wash. Some cats simply will not tolerate a cardboard collar, but many soon learn to live with it. It should be remembered that the collar restricts vision to some extent, and it is therefore best not to let the cat wander outdoors. See also COLLARS.

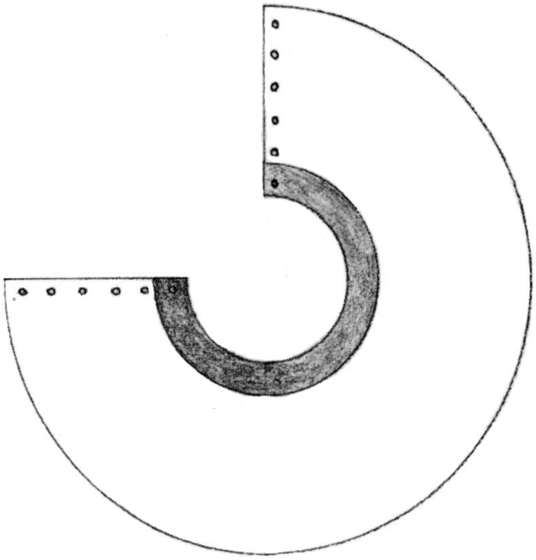

Encephalitis see BRAIN DISORDERS

Encephalo-coele see BREEDING ABNORMALITIES

Entire The word entire is used to describe a male cat which has not been castrated and which has both testicles descended and in the normal position in the scrotum, and is capable of reproduction.

Entropion see EYE AND EYELID DISORDERS

Eosinophilic Granuloma see RODENT ULCER

Eperythrozoon felis see ANAEMIA and FELINE INFECTIOUS ANAEMIA

Epilepsy The condition is fortunately rare in the cat. Epilepsy is still little understood. Electrical changes occur during an attack which can be recorded on suitable machines but the precipitating cause remains a mystery. Drugs can help epileptic patients but successful control depends on the severity and frequency of attacks. See also BRAIN DISORDERS.

European Type see TYPES, BRITISH

European Wild Cat *Felis silvestris silvestris* at first glance is not unlike the domestic tabby, but on closer scrutiny a number of different features will be noticed and identification simplified. The typical tabby pattern of this species is the mackerel type and

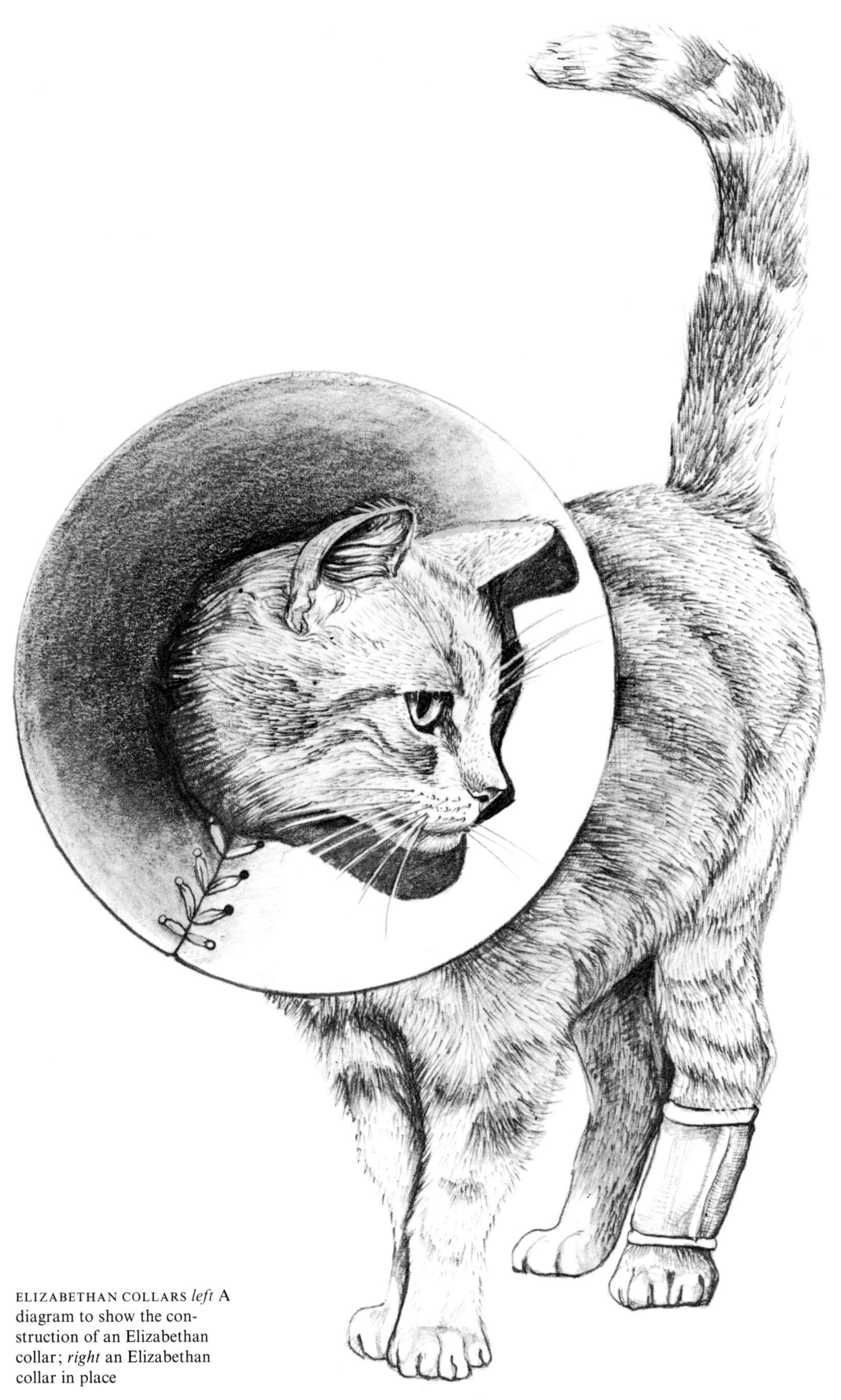

ELIZABETHAN COLLARS *left* A diagram to show the construction of an Elizabethan collar; *right* an Elizabethan collar in place

for this reason it is customary to refer to this form of pattern as the 'wild type' and colouring is stone-grey with black stripes and buff underparts. The full bushy tail is heavily ringed and has a very blunt tip unlike hybrids with the domestic which have pointed tips. The skull and teeth of European Wild Cats are larger and the head is flat. The leg bones are longer, and the intestines considerably shorter so it is relatively simple to identify a dead animal. According to most authorities there is little variation if any between their size and the domestic cat; measurements given are up to 2 ft from nose tip to base of tail, which may be a foot long. Males are generally bigger than females, though their weights over-lap, males ranging from a minimum of 6½ to 15 lb. and females from 7 to 10 lb. One Scottish specimen is recorded as reaching 15 lb. 10 oz.

Distribution extends today from Scotland, as *F. silvestris grampia* throughout Europe, as *F. silvestris silvestris* into Asia, excluding Scandinavia, and before 1850 it extended throughout Britain. The latest survey shows that in Scotland it has decreased in the north-west, but increased in the eastern Highlands and has emerged as far south as within forty miles of Edinburgh. It is reported as probably more numerous in Scotland now than at any time in human memory. Recent reports that some have been seen in the wilder parts of Wales await definite confirmation but many feel them to be reliable. A member of the National Museum in Cardiff measured the leg bones of a cat from Pembrokeshire and they were as long as those of a Scottish Wild Cat and considerably longer than a domestic cat. He considered it possible that a wild cat strain still existed amongst the feral cats there. Other reports substantiate this claim.

Normally hunting at dawn and dusk in Scotland, the European Wild Cat is reported to be more diurnal in Europe. They largely subsist on rabbits, hares, rodents and birds, but if hard pressed they will attack game birds, young lambs and raid poultry yards and have also been known to attack and kill small roe deer fawn. Wild cats may be traced by their black droppings which, unlike the domestic cat, are left exposed, or by paw marks, typically in a straight line.

The species is virtually impossible to tame – kittens taken at a very tender age of two to three weeks remain spitting bundles of fury, and an adult can be extremely ferocious. However, some attachment has on occasion been claimed between cat and owner, in as much as it recognizes the human owner as a provider of food, but most attempts to cage and keep them as pets usually result in very great suffering and death. Fortunately, Germany has now given protection to this species and it is to be hoped the British Government will follow their lead.
See also AFRICAN WILD CAT, INDIAN DESERT CAT and SWISS MOUNTAIN CAT.

Euthanasia Euthanasia means putting to death in a painless manner, and is carried out when the cat is suffering from an incurable illness; to prevent further suffering in a painful condition with a doubtful outcome, when the cat is gravely injured in an accident and has little or no prospect of leading an active life thereafter; in old age when life has become a burden; in the case of unwanted kittens immediately after birth.

There are various methods of euthanasia, and the veterinary surgeon who is to carry it out must be the one to decide which is best for the particular cat. This will partly depend on the disposition of the cat. The best method is a massive overdose of barbiturate though electrocution, shooting and lethal chambers are also used.

Drowning Unwanted Cats This is a barbaric practice, and should never be used. It is always possible to have unwanted pets euthanitized humanely.

left and below The European Wild Cat, *Felis silvestris*

Exercise Most cats will take as much exercise as they require, if allowed the freedom of the house and garden.

Exercise is beneficial because it tones up the alimentary canal, preventing constipation, and stimulates the circulation: prevents the feet from becoming soft, and improves the state of the skeletal muscles. Moreover, it provides the cat with an added interest in life.

Exercise of Kittens Kittens will get as much exercise as they need from scampering about in play. Over-exercise of kittens could result in bone deformities.

Exhibiting see SHOWING

Exotic Short-hair In North America apart from the Short-hairs with Foreign type, as seen in the Abyssinians, Siamese and so on, there was originally one short-haired variety only, then known as the Domestic, but now referred to as the American Short-hair. It was found at the shows that those with shorter noses and smaller ears invariably won, so in an endeavour to improve the type and to produce more winners, there was some cross-breeding between the Domestic and the Persian varieties, resulting frequently in attractive sturdy cats with short fur but with definite Persian type. More often than not these cats won over the Americans, and there was much dissatisfaction, and it was certainly most confusing. Eventually the Cat Fanciers' Association decided that it was only fair that there should be two standards and two classes, one for the American Short-hairs and the other for the Exotic.

The colours recognized are the same as for the Persians, and the type is similar, that is the heads should be broad and round, with short, snub broad noses, full cheeks, small rounded ears, and large round eyes. The bodies should be cobby on short thick legs, with short tails but in proportion to the body, while the soft fur should be of medium length.

The points awarded are:

30 Head
20 Type
10 Coat
10 Condition
20 Colour
10 Eye colour

Experimental see ANY OTHER COLOUR and ANY OTHER VARIETY

Exportation Exportation of cats to foreign countries is surrounded by complex legal requirements. Difficulties arise since each country has its own legal stipulation for importation. It is therefore essential to apply to the embassy of the country concerned in plenty of time to establish what is required. Several companies exist which will arrange transportation of animals. Veterinary certificates indicating freedom from infections or contagious diseases, external

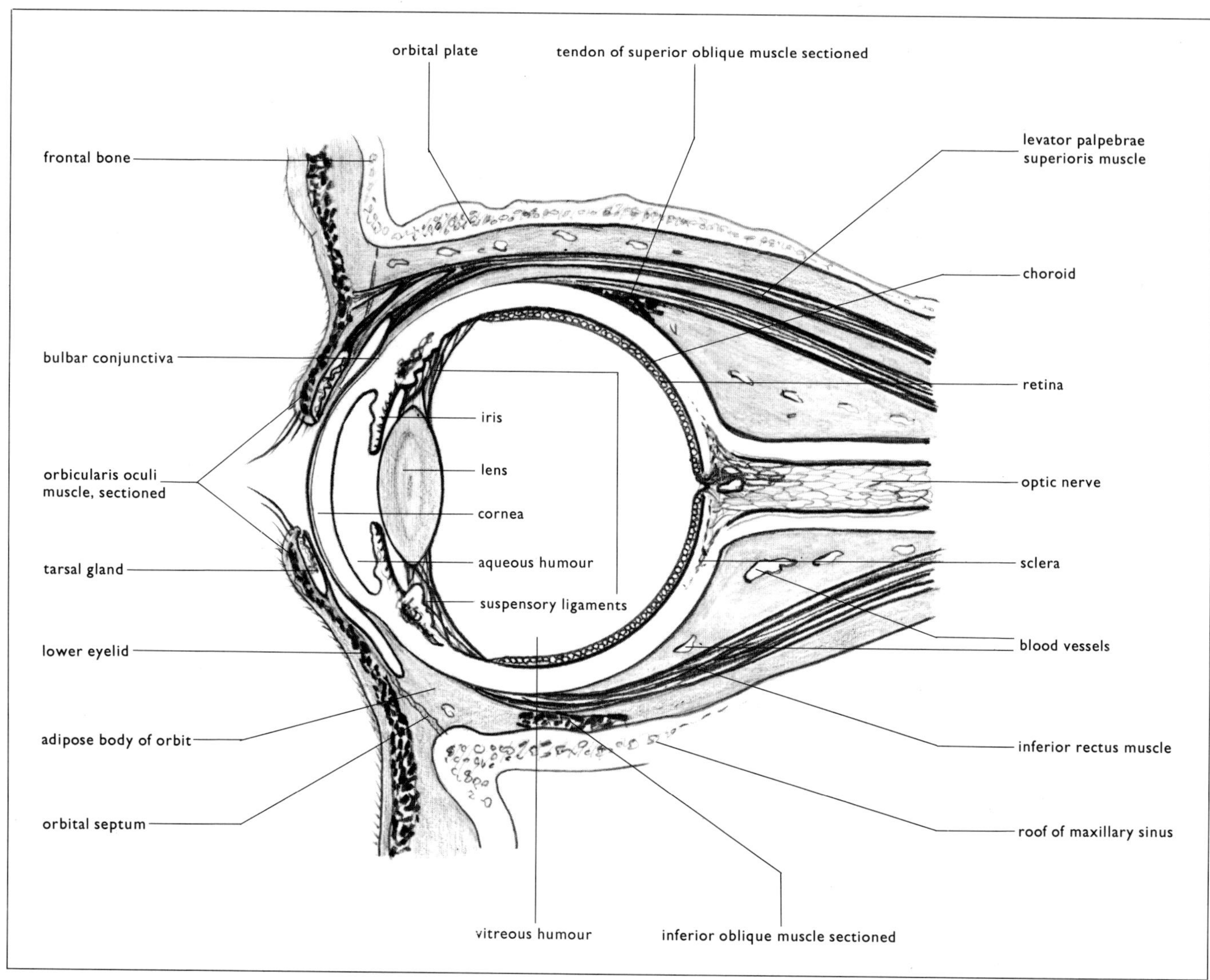

above Anatomy of the eye

parasites and fitness to travel are almost universally required. These should be given within 24 hours of travel.

Exudative Pleurisy see RESPIRATORY DISEASES

Eye Anatomy The eye is a spherical structure situated in a bony socket, the orbit, that serves to protect it. Within the eye are two chambers, the anterior one containing a relatively watery substance, aqueous humour, the other behind the lens a jelly-like material, vitreous humour. The front surface of the eyeball is transparent, and is known as the cornea. The cornea is protected both by the movable eyelids and the third eyelid (nictitating membrane). The conjunctiva, a delicate membrane covers the eye and inner surface of the lids. Behind the cornea can be seen a septum known as the iris. The hole in the middle of it is called the pupil. Through the pupil can be seen the lens. The latter is a transparent body which serves to focus light-rays that enter the pupil on to the retina, the light-sensitive surface at the back of the eyeball. The eye is rotated by means of muscles attached to the eyeball. The cornea is kept moist by means of tears produced by the lacrimal gland. Blinking serves to spread this secretion over the cornea. See also LACRIMAL APPARATUS.

Eye and Eyelid Disorders *Cataract* A cataract is a change in the transparency of the lens. The normal lens is a clear structure, freely permitting the passage of light. Cataracts occur when the lens becomes opaque, reducing vision. Cats rarely suffer from cataract formation. Near-normal vision can also be restored by surgical removal of an opaque lens. Given careful nursing and supportive treatment, cats undergoing this operation frequently show gratifying results. The commoner causes of cataracts are diabetes mellitus and inflammatory and degenerative diseases of the eye. Some cats are born with cataracts.

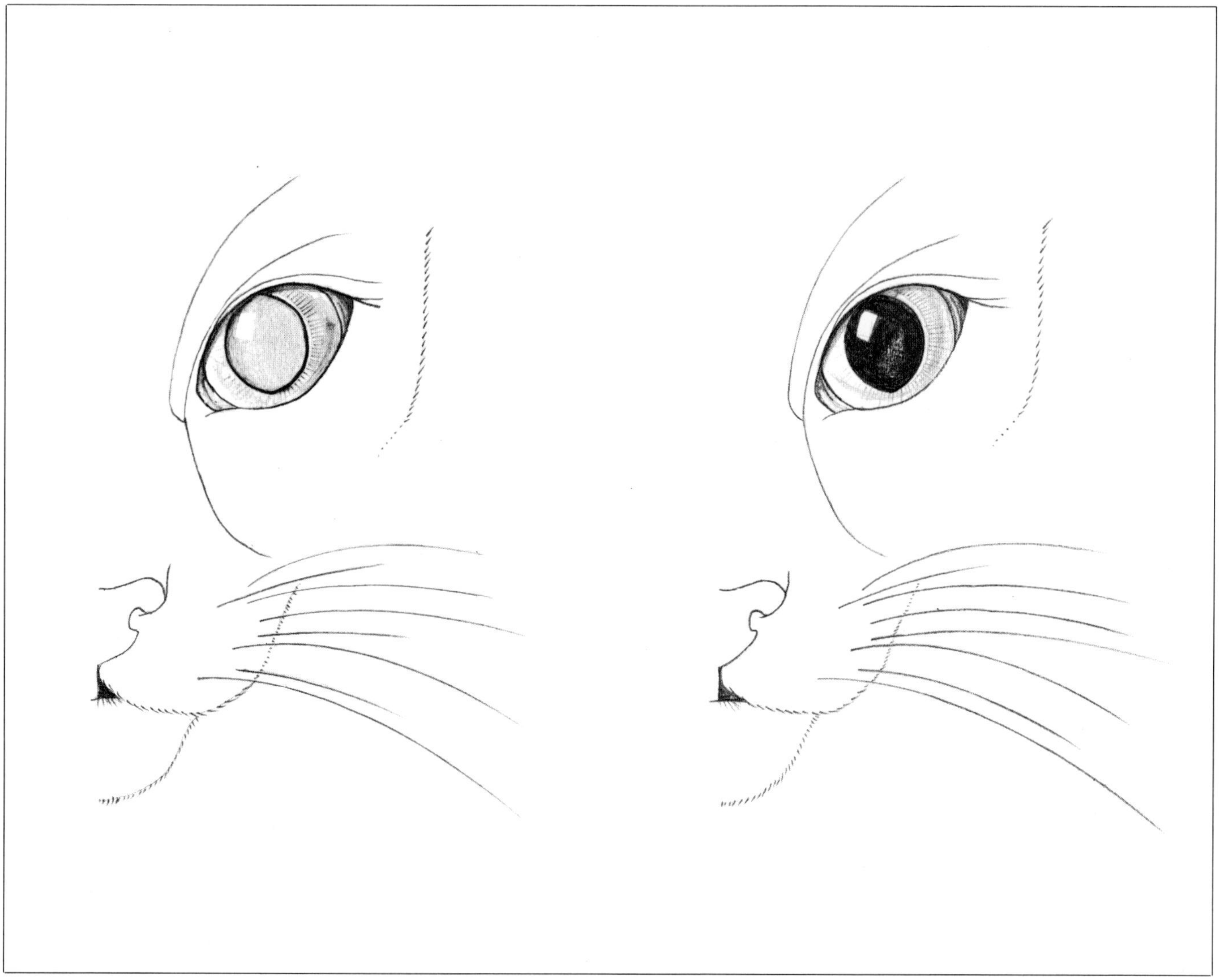

above left Cataract; *above right* a normal eye

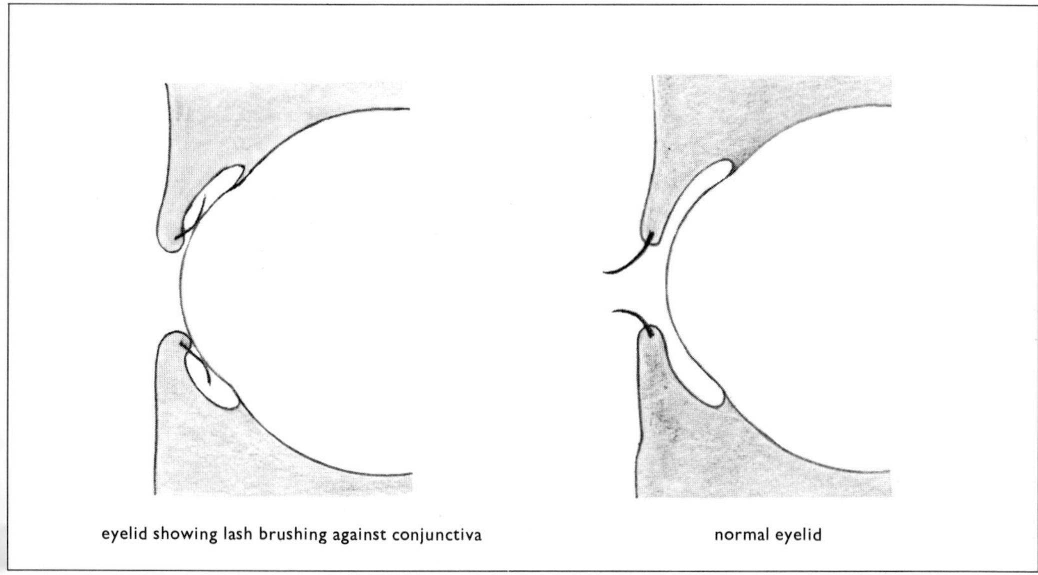

EYE AND EYELID DISORDERS
far left Entropion, *left* a normal eye

above left Haw; *above right* a normal eye

Conjunctivitis This term means inflammation of the conjunctiva, the delicate membrane protecting the eye. The signs include redness and puffiness of the conjunctiva, often accompanied by a thickish, mucous discharge, which tends to collect in the corner of the eye, causes of the condition include: mechanical damage, such as foreign bodies, dust and grit; bacteria; chemicals, and in particular the respiratory virus of cat 'flu', which often results in a chronic conjunctivitis.

Ectropion Eversion of the eyelids is extremely rare in cats.

Entropion Inversion of the eyelids, is known as entropion. It is comparatively uncommon in the cat, but is seen in cases of microphthalmia (very small eyes), a condition present at birth. It may also occur following a bite wound on the eyelid, when subsequent healing results in a deformity. Results of the condition are irritation of the surface of the cornea. The cat shows a tendency to rub the eye and blink. In severe, protracted cases, corneal ulcers may result, so that early treatment is essential. The treatment for entropion is an operation to re-construct the eyelids and relieve mechanical irritation of the eyeball.

Glaucoma Glaucoma is an increase in the pressure of the fluid within the eyeball. It may be due to excessive production of the fluid or to interference with its drainage. The condition may be divided into those cases which cannot be attributed to any disease within the eye – primary glaucoma, and those that follow a specific eye disease – secondary glaucoma. It is very doubtful whether primary glaucoma ever occurs in the cat, the disease being almost invariably secondary to some pre-existing eye disease or some damage to the eye. Most of the feline cases result from dislocation of the lens into the anterior chamber of the eye thus interfering with drainage of the fluid. Usually the condition has reached the stage of gross distension of the eyeball before veterinary advice is sought. The pupil is distended and does not

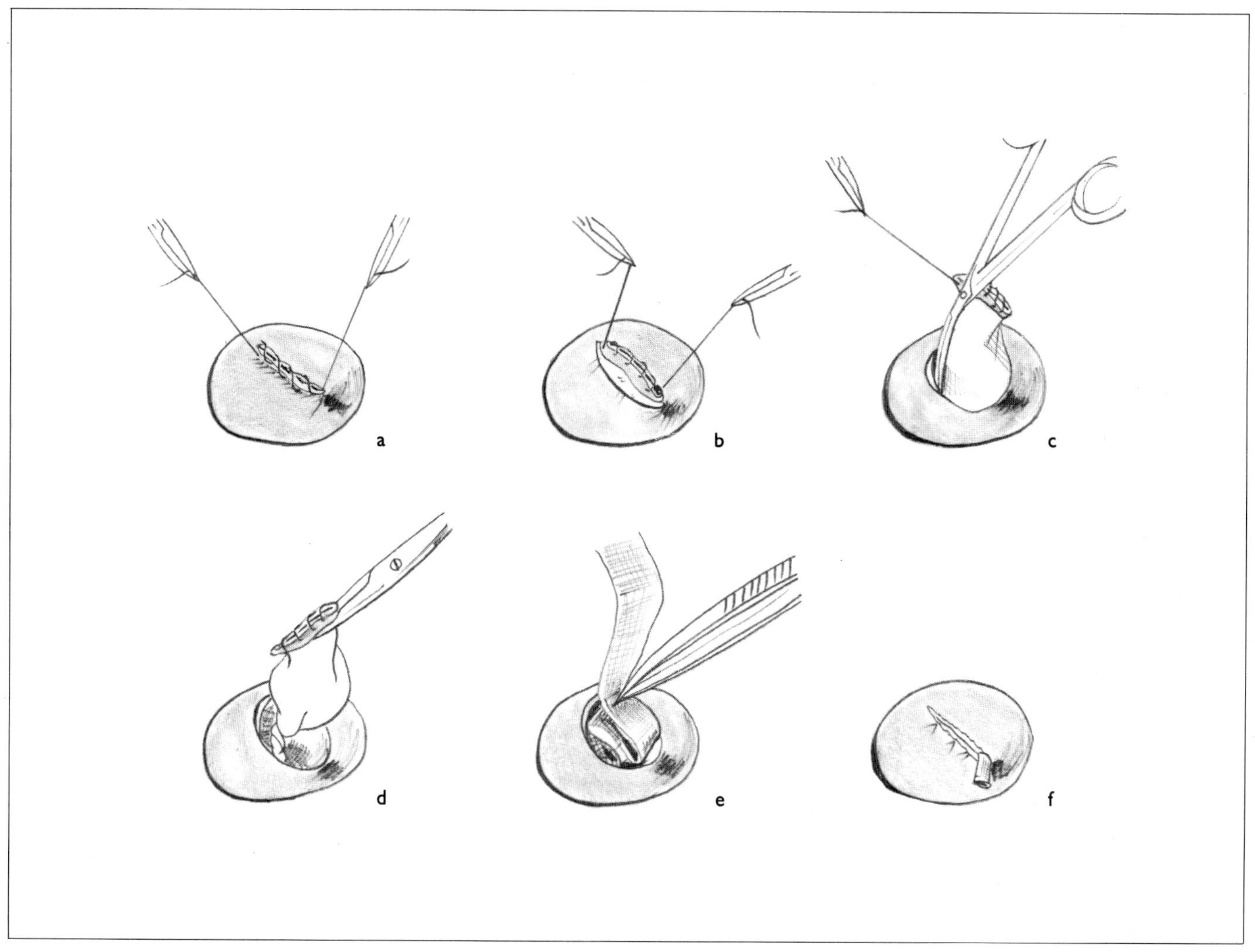

above Excision of the eyeball: *a* the palpebral fissure is closed by a continuous suture; *b* an elliptical incision is carried around the sutured tarsal rims; *c* the globe, within its conjunctival sac, is dissected free; *d* torsion is used to sever the optic stalk; *e* gauze ribbon is packed into the cavity; *f* the wound is closed with a short tag of gauze protruding at the inner canthus

respond to light, the cornea often becomes opaque, but there appears to be little pain involved. Treatment is difficult and depends upon the cause. Where dislocation of the lens is diagnosed, removal of the lens will usually prevent the development of glaucoma, but, cases are rarely seen before irreversible enlargement has occurred.

Haw The third eyelid may appear and the cat should be taken to a veterinary surgeon as it sometimes indicates disease. At other times there is no apparent cause for the haw eye and the condition rectifies spontaneously.

Keratitis Keratitis is inflammation of the cornea. Keratitis may be produced by many different factors and is often secondary to an infection of the conjunctiva (the lining membrane of the eye socket). Injury of the eye from wounds, burns, foreign bodies, irritating chemicals, or from the cat rubbing the eye, may all result in keratitis. Infections may produce inflammation of the cornea as may glaucoma (see above) and vitamin A deficiency (see Deficiency Diseases under NUTRITION).

Symptoms of keratitis are usually a loss of the transparency of the cornea, congestion of the blood vessels of the white of the eye (sclera). These changes are accompanied by signs of pain, photophobia (the cat avoids light and keeps the eye closed) and an excessive flow of tears (lachrymation).

Treatment should be directed towards removal of the cause of the inflammation. In the case of bacterial infections, antibiotics should be applied to the eye.

Eye Removal Excision of the eyeball is necessary in cases of gross damage, gross infection and primary or secondary glaucoma. The latter commonly occurs following dislocation of the lens.

Eyelid Disorders see also ANKYLOBLEPHARON

Eye Teeth This is a common lay name given to the canine teeth. See TEETH.

F

Facial Paralysis Facial paralysis, or Bell's Palsy, occurs where there is damage to the 7th cranial or Facial nerve. As the nerve supplies all the muscles of facial expression, the forehead and the ear, paralysis leads to one sided flaccid paralysis of the face. The affected side of the face looks smooth, the eye is held open with the lower lid sagging and some drooping of the upper lid, the cheek is paralysed so that saliva tends to drip from between the lips and food may accumulate between the teeth and the flaccid cheek. The ear on the affected side may also droop. The condition is rather rare in the cat, but may result from pressure on the nerve within the skull from a brain tumour, or from damage to the nerve from abscesses, blows, or wounds, along its course outside the skull. The paralysis may be temporary or permanent. Treatment mainly consists of keeping the animal as comfortable and as clean as possible. Massage of the paralysed muscles is said to assist in maintaining their tone until the nerve function is restored.

Faeces The faeces are the unrequired remains voided at the end of the alimentary tract. Useful substances in the food are first digested and then absorbed through the gut walls. The indigestible portions of the food go to make up the faeces together with waste products. Other substances present are bacteria from the gut, pigments formed by the breakdown of blood cells, and a certain amount of mucus. The blood pigments make the faeces, brownish in colour, while the bacteria are responsible for the characteristic odour. Cat's faeces, in common with those of most carnivores, are particularly strong-smelling. Water is resorbed from the foodstuffs in the lower gut, which means the faeces are semi-solid. When for some reason foodstuffs pass extra-rapidly through the gut, the faeces remain liquid and the condition known as diarrhoea. If the faeces are withheld for a period instead of being voided, they become hard, due to continuous water extraction, and constipation ensues.

Sometimes a veterinary surgeon may request a faecal sample. If asked for a sample, the owner should take care to produce a fresh uncontaminated one, and to bring it in a clean well-sealed container with a wide mouth. See also MELAENA.

Fats see NUTRITION

Fatty Acids see NUTRITION

Feeding see NUTRITION

Felicola subrostrata see LICE

Feline Acne see SUB-MENTAL ORGAN INFECTION

Feline Infectious Anaemia Feline infectious anaemia is an acute or chronic haemolytic anaemia caused by a blood parasite, *Eperythrozoon felis (Haemobartonella felis)*, which infests the red blood corpuscles (see ANAEMIA). The disease is usually subclinical, i.e. symptomless, but clinical disease in the form of anaemia associated with a high fever (104°–105°F) and accompanied by loss of appetite, lassitude, depression, weakness and a considerable loss of condition, develops whenever the cat is subjected to stress or intercurrent disease. It is probable that a large percentage of the cat population are symptomless carriers of the organism. The parasite appears in a stained blood smear as tiny microorganisms of variable form attached to the surface of the red blood cells. The life cycle and the mode of transmission of the parasite is not yet known. It has been suggested that the disease may be transmitted by the bite of an infected cat or of a blood-sucking insect, e.g. fleas. Infection of kittens within the uterus has been shown to occur and the parasites may be responsible for deaths in newborn kittens. Treatment is by the administration of antibiotics, or by the intravenous injection of arsenical compounds supported by blood transfusions in severely affected cases. Iron and vitamins of the B complex should also be given to stimulate new blood cell and haemoglobin formation.

Feline Infectious Enteritis see PANLEUCOPAENIA

Feline Infectious Peritonitis see PERITONITIS

Feline Picornavirus Infection see FLU

Feline Viral Rhinotracheitis see FLU

Felinophile Cats can inspire almost limitless affection. They cast their spell not only over people who are of a gentle or loving disposition, but also over those who are quite the opposite. Cardinal Thomas Wolsey, Henry VIII's callous minister, regularly took his pet cat to state functions, and Cardinal Richelieu, the Machiavellian French minister of the 17th century, was a fanatic cat-lover. He had dozens of cats at court, the cynosure of sycophants, and his will included provision for 14 of his pets; alas, Swiss mercenaries butchered them all for a gargantuan stew. Under Louis XV cats enjoyed renewed popularity because his queen adored them.

Dr Johnson venerated his cat Hodge and spoon-fed it oysters in its decline. Sir Walter Scott cherished Hinx, Thomas Southey kept a succession of oddly-named cats, Pope Leo XIII had Micetto and Queen Victoria was devoted to White Heather which outlived her to bask in the affection of Edward VII. H. G. Wells called his last cat Mr Peter Wells, and Samual Butler's correspondence is full of references to cats. Other cat enthusiasts, to varying degrees, have been Einstein, Dr Schweitzer, Bernard Shaw, Thomas Hardy, Chateaubriand, Balzac, Gautier, Colette and Zola.

General Eliott who commanded the Rock of Gibraltar during the epic siege of 1779–1780, was always accompanied on his daily tour of inspection by a pet cat which was impervious to the artillery fire. During World War Two Sir Winston Churchill's ginger tom was present at many cabinet meetings. See also AILUROPHOBIA.

Felis bengalensis see LEOPARD CAT; ***F. bieti*** see CHINESE DESERT CAT; ***F. caracal*** see CARACAL LYNX; ***F. chaus*** see JUNGLE CAT; ***F. colocolo*** see PAMPAS CAT; ***F. concolor*** see PUMA; ***F. geoffroyi*** GEOFFROY'S CAT; ***F. guigna*** see KODKOD; ***F. jacobita*** see MOUNTAIN CAT; ***F. libyca*** see AFRICAN WILD CAT; ***F. lynx*** see NORTHERN LYNX; ***F. manul*** see PALLAS'S CAT; ***F. margarita*** see SAND CAT; ***F. marmorata*** see MARBLED CAT; ***F. nigripes*** see BLACK-FOOTED CAT; ***F. ocreata*** see CAFFRE CAT; ***F. ornata*** see INDIAN DESERT CAT; ***F. pardalis*** see OCELOT; ***F. planiceps*** see FLAT-HEADED CAT; ***F. rubiginosa*** see RUSTY-SPOTTED CAT; ***F. rufa*** see BOBCAT; ***F. serval*** see SERVAL; ***F. silvestris*** see AFRICAN WILD CAT, EUROPEAN WILD CAT, INDIAN DESERT CAT, SWISS MOUNTAIN CAT; ***F. silvestris grampia*** see EUROPEAN WILD CAT; ***F. silvestris libyca*** see AFRICAN WILD CAT; ***F. silvestris ornata*** see INDIAN DESERT CAT; ***F. temmincki*** see TEMMINCK'S GOLDEN CAT; ***F. tigrina*** see TIGER CAT; ***F. viverrina*** see FISHING CAT; ***F. wiedi*** see MARGAY CAT; ***F. yagouaroundi*** see JAGUARONDI

Fighting Fighting occurs among cats to protect their territories or as a result of sexual activity. The result of combat is often large painful debilitating abscesses.

The amount of fighting is exacerbated under domestic conditions since the size of a cat's territory is artificially reduced. See also BEHAVIOUR and ABSCESS.

Fire Precautions Fire precautions at catteries are essential and regulations must be strictly observed at all times. Specific equipment will depend on the type and size of the cattery, as well as its situation.

The requirements of local planning authorities should be sought before new buildings are commenced and also those of insurance companies who often insist on the provision of a certain minimum of appliances before they will give the necessary cover. It is advisable to consult the local Fire Precautions Officer who will be able to advise in detail.

Normally equipment will include fire extinguishers, hose and reel equipment, buckets of dry sand, all of which must be readily to hand.

Cats will usually become quite frantic should a fire break out and endeavour to escape, or run back into a blazing building to hide. It is necessary therefore to keep wire carrying baskets handy in which to safely secure cats and take them to safety. Cats are particularly sensitive to smoke and to the chemical fumes from fire extinguishers.

In the case of fire involving electrical apparatus the first essential is to try to render the circuit dead, but where it is not possible to switch off the current, the appropriate non-conducting extinguisher must be used.

Electric wiring and all apparatus should be expertly installed and also expertly inspected for deterioration at frequent intervals. Wiring should always be at a height where it cannot be clawed or chewed by cats. In no circumstances should electric tubular heaters be secured to painted wood or hardboard walls which are inflammable. Careful checking is necessary to see that the circuit is never overloaded which can easily occur if further extensions are made.

Every breeding and boarding establishment should compile their own fire drill, and assistants be carefully instructed.

First Aid see ACCIDENTS

Fish see NUTRITION

Fish Eczema see SKIN DISEASES

Fishing Cat Easily distinguished from other spotted cats, *Felis viverrina,* is of thicker build with rather a short neck and short legs. The head and body measure about 24–32 in. and the narrowly ringed tail measures a further 10–12 in. An average specimen may weigh from 17 to nearly 25 lb. Its colouring is earthy-grey to tawny-grey and patterned with small dark spots and broken lines with narrow streaks over the head and face. The ears are relatively small and widely set and the toes are slightly webbed. Its coat is short and very coarse and so has no commercial value.

The Fishing Cats' habitat is quite wide and includes India – where its distribution is rather patchy – Ceylon, Indo-China, Thailand, Malaya, Burma, Sumatra and Taiwan. Haunting low-lying swampy forestland it may be found very often near water, which has given rise to the theory that it catches fish. A bold hunter, it has been known to attack goats, sheep and calves and is even reputed to carry off human babies. These feats have led to the assumption that it is untameable, but an early naturalist (Blyth) kept several males. An interesting species it warrants further study.

Fistula see ABSCESS

Fits see BRAIN DISORDERS

Flat Dwelling Sadly as more people are forced to live in tower blocks, cats are expected to live a life of total confinement. Such a situation is deplorable since cats enjoy freedom to determine the extent of their environment.

Where the situation is unavoidable cats should be given adequate provision of toys and as much freedom as possible. Scratching posts and if possible branches to climb, are much appreciated. Great care should be taken to avoid obesity since this is common in flat dwelling cats.

Two kittens purchased instead of one will do much to remove the disadvantages of life in a flat for a cat. See also GRASS.

Flat-headed Cat *Felis planiceps* is very small, weighing about 3–4½ lb. and measuring about 12–20 in. from nose to tail base with a 6–8 in. tail. The legs are very short. Coat colour varies from brown to a dark reddish-brown and graduates to white underparts, throat and chin. Many of the guard-hairs are white tipped. The flat head with its widely placed small oval ears has rather unusual and attractive markings; white stripes run from the corners of the eyes up over the forehead, and there are white rings under the eyes and white whisker pads.

Distribution is through Borneo, Sumatra and Malaya where it is now extremely rare. Reputed to be nocturnal, it hunts chiefly on the river banks, fish, frogs and small birds forming its diet. It is also reputed to be tameable.

Flattened Chest see BREEDING ABNORMALITIES

Flatulence Flatulence is the abnormal accumulation of gas in the stomach or intestines, popularly known as 'wind'. In the cat the condition is uncommon. Where gas does accumulate in the stomach, the cat is obviously uncomfortable, finding difficulty in settling in one position, breathing shallowly, and actual distension of the left side of the abdomen may be detectable in severe cases. In the intestines, distension of the bowels may give rise to attacks of colicky pain with loose motions and the frequent passage of offensive gas through the anus. Treatment depends to a large extent upon the cause of the excessive gas production. Stomach flatulence will often respond to the feeding of frequent small finely chopped meals, plus the administration of an antacid such as milk of magnesia. Sometimes drugs which lower surface tension may be effective. The intestinal form is mainly caused by bacterial fermentation of the intestinal contents, so the administration of a wide-spectrum antibiotic will often change the bowel bacterial flora and clear the trouble.

Fleas Fleas are frequent parasites of the cat, particularly of the long-haired varieties, and they may cause a good deal of skin irritation, sometimes out of all proportion to their actual numbers. Three species of flea commonly infest the cat, *Ctenocephalides felis* – the cat flea, *Ctenocephalides canis* – the dog flea, and *Pulex irritans* – the human flea. The symptoms of flea infestation vary considerably from cat to cat and this is probably due to the fact that some cats are allergic to an antigen contained in flea saliva. Generally there will be varying degrees of itchiness (pruritus), the cat scratching or biting itself and twitching its skin. There may be a reflex licking response in which the cat will lick the front of the chest and the forepaws when the back is lightly stroked. Fat cats may have convulsion-like attacks in which, in attempting to turn and bite or lick the irritable areas, the animal falls over on its side where it remains for a variable period of time in this contorted attitude. The skin becomes covered by a brownish deposit and there may be raw, moist areas due to the cat's licking and biting activities. It may be difficult to detect the actual fleas in a light infestation, especially in long-haired cats, but the appearance of blackish or dark brown, pin-head sized granules in the coat is diagnostic of flea infestation. These are the faeces of the flea and have a high haemoglobin content derived from the blood of the cat. If placed on a sheet of moistened blotting paper, the blood pigment leaches out to form a red circular patch around the granule of excreta.

The life cycle of the flea takes place off the body of the cat in most cases. In some long-haired cats, however, the eggs may be laid in the coat and hatch there. Usually the eggs fall out of the coat and in favourable conditions they hatch into maggot-like larvae. These feed on micro-organisms and other protein material in dust and dirt and pass through a pupal stage before emerging as adult fleas. The pupal stage is very resistant and may last for several months especially at low temperatures. The longevity of adult fleas depends upon whether they are fed and

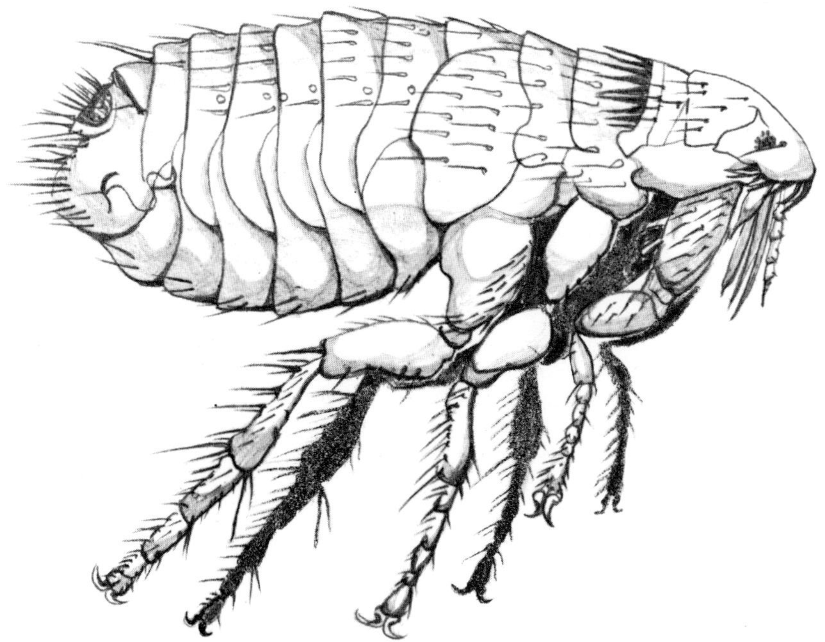

The cat flea, *Ctenocephalides felis*

on the moisture content of their environment. The cat flea lives for about 58 days when fed, and up to 234 days unfed in air which is nearly saturated with moisture. If fed intermittently, the maximum life span is around two years.

Treatment is by the application of parasiticidal powders or shampoos to kill off the adult fleas in the coat. The safest of these preparations are derris and pyrethrum, other substances sometimes causing toxic reactions in the cat. Beds and bedding should be of the disposable type and destroyed weekly, and a good vacuum cleaning performed on upholstery and the undersurfaces of mats and carpets at least twice weekly, particularly in humid weather. These cleaning measures will do much to break the life-cycle by eliminating flea eggs, larvae and pupae, and by denying food supplies to any surviving larvae.

Flop Ears see BREEDING ABNORMALITIES

Flu Cat 'Flu' is the popular name for the disease syndrome produced by infection with the feline respiratory viruses plus secondary bacterial infection. The term is a misnomer as the viruses involved bear no relationship to the influenza viruses of man. There are two main groups of viruses concerned with the production of respiratory disease in the cat: 1. Herpes virus – causing Feline Viral Rhinotracheitis (FVR), and 2. Feline Picornavirus Infection (FPI).

Cat Flu is a very common disease of cats especially those gathered together in groups as in catteries. The disease commences with a rise in body temperature which persists for two or three days before returning almost to normal. Thereafter there are mild temperature fluctuations throughout the course of the illness. There is frequent sneezing and usually dribbling of saliva from the mouth, which soaks the hair on the undersurface of the neck and the front of the chest. The eyes and nose commence to water and with secondary bacterial infection occurring, the discharges from eyes and nose tend to become more catarrhal and muco-purulent in nature. The eyelids may become gummed together with discharge and the conjunctiva is reddened and swollen, sometimes sufficiently to obscure the eye. There may be coughing, which is more common with FVR infection, and the cat loses its appetite and condition and becomes depressed and dehydrated. Sometimes the dribbling from the mouth becomes more pronounced and the saliva may become blood-tinged or foul-smelling. Examination of the mouth in these cases will reveal the presence of ulcers on the tongue, the pharynx and the hard palate. The ulcers in FVR infection are said to be more extensive and ragged in outline compared to the rather 'punched-out' ulcers of FPI. Pneumonia may supervene and this complication is more often seen in FVR infection than in FPI. The pneumonia is usually bacterial in nature but recent evidence suggests that a true viral pneumonia may occur with FVR infection. The severity of the actual illness appears to depend upon the dose of virus received and also upon the type of organism making up the normal bacterial flora of the affected cat's nose and throat at the time of infection. The more severe illnesses are associated with the presence of streptococci, staphylococci and *Pasteurella multocida (septica)*.

Treatment of Cat Flu is largely a question of careful nursing of the affected cats. The animals should be nursed in sunny, warm, airy but draught-free quarters. The eyes and nose should be kept clean by careful wiping away of all discharges and a little petroleum jelly smeared around the eyes and nose to obviate cracking and chapping of the skin. Cats which can be kept feeding rarely become severely ill, so all efforts should be made to encourage voluntary feeding. Much of the loss of appetite can probably be attributed to loss of the sense of smell, so highly-scented foods, such as kippers, game, tinned salmon, should be offered. One prominent veterinarian recommends that the owner should cuddle the cat fairly frequently as this serves as a great morale booster for both animal and owner. Usually the veterinarian will prescribe the broad-spectrum antibiotics to control the secondary bacterial infection.

Prevention of Cat Flu is difficult as no effective vaccine is yet available or seems likely to be so in the foreseeable future. Unfortunately the immunity produced by either a natural attack of the disease or by vaccination is relatively short-lived, lasting only for from one to three months. There are many symptomless carrier animals which means that infected cats may be difficult, if not impossible, to recognize. This phenomenon implies that quarantine and isolation procedures are not practicable means of preventing infection entering a cattery. Careful thought should be given to disease prevention when constructing a new cattery or adapting a room for use by cats. The important thing is to provide a controlled environment, as any stress, such as sudden changes of temperature, will markedly lower the resistance of the cat to infection. The rooms should be kept at a relatively non-fluctuating temperature of between 50°–78°F with a controlled airflow providing approximately 10–12 air changes per hour. An alternative measurement of the airflow is an air-exchange rate of around 88 cubic feet per hour, and this can be achieved by allowing roughly one square inch of air inlet and slightly more air outlet per cat. Installation of an electric extractor fan of suitable capacity for the size of room is probably the most effective way of meeting the desired criteria. Good ventilation is an essential in a cattery as it serves as an agency for the dilution of airborne organisms, both bacterial and viral, and thus tends to reduce the dose of infection received by any individual cat below the threshold necessary for the manifestation of clinical disease. The rooms should be kept as dry as possible, as the viruses are much more resistant to external influences in moist surroundings. This means that if walls and floors are being washed and disinfected, then they should be dried off as quickly as possible after completion of the cleansing. Frequent cleansing and disinfection of the cattery is advisable as this again will lower the bacterial and viral content of the surroundings and thus the dose to the cats. Feed adequate balanced diets, as well-nourished cats are much more resistant to infection.

Folded Ears see BREEDING ABNORMALITIES

Food Poisoning This term is generally interpreted as a digestive disease caused by the ingestion of food containing pathogenic bacteria. Salmonella organisms are often incriminated in cases of food poisoning. As a rule, food containing sufficient numbers of bacteria to cause food poisoning will have an odour that renders it unpalatable to cats. This fastidiousness frequently saves them from suffering the effects of food poisoning. Any food suspected of gross bacterial contamination should be rejected. High standards of meat inspection make an invaluable contribution to the quality of meats offered for sale. See also SALMONELLOSIS.

Forced Feeding Forcing animals to take food causes more problems than it solves. There are considerable dangers to pushing food down an unwilling throat. It may cause choking or inhalation pneumonia and will certainly weaken a sick patient.

The gentle introduction of very small drops of broth or glucose water may be of value but should only be attempted on the instructions of the veterinarian.

It is often simpler and safer for fluids or foods to be injected and this will be done by the veterinarian, if they are considered necessary.

Foreign Bodies This term is used to describe an unusual object that enters the body tissues and lodges there. A splinter of wood or glass in the pad of the foot, a fishbone in the oesophagus, a grass-seed in the eye or ear and an air-gun pellet in the muscle of the trunk are all examples of foreign bodies. Foreign bodies may travel within the tissues and cause trouble at a site far removed from their original point of entry.

For instance, a grass-seed, being sharp, may penetrate the soft skin between the pads and work its way up the leg, to emerge again at the hock. Very small foreign bodies may enter the bloodstream and get carried round with the blood until they reach the heart, often with fatal consequences. Foreign bodies taken into the mouth do not generally cause an obstruction until they reach the small intestine.

Needles are quite often seen in the cat. Kittens playing with thread or wool swallow some of it, find they cannot regurgitate it, and so make an attempt to swallow the rest, accidentally taking in the needle at the same time. The needle may stick in the mouth, from which it is removed with relative ease, or it may be carried further down the alimentary canal and then penetrate the muscle of the neck, chest or abdomen. Modern X-ray techniques have a valuable contribution to make in the locating of needles, which greatly facilitates their removal.

Small splinters in the feet may offer more of a problem, so that gradual removal by poulticing may be more practical than immediate extraction by surgical techniques.

Provided they do not interfere with the functions of the tissues, and do not act as a source of infection or irritation, foreign bodies may remain in place without any adverse effects. The body responds by encapsulating them – isolating them by means of a wall of specialized tissue.

Foreign Lilac see FOREIGN SHORT-HAIR

Foreign Short-hair A number of short-haired varieties are known as Foreign, but this title refers solely to their type and has nothing to do with the country of origin. The Siamese do come under this category (see SIAMESE) but usually it is taken to refer to the Abyssinians, Burmese, Havanas, Devon and Cornish Rex, Foreign Whites, Foreign Lilacs, Russian Blues and the Korats.

The general characteristics of all those mentioned are much the same. They have wedge-shaped heads, with large pricked ears, slanting eyes, slim bodies on slender legs and long tapering tails. Apart from colour, there are also certain differences in some cases between the head shape, tail length and so on. One hundred points are allocated in the standard for the required characteristics, with, for example, 50 being awarded for the body colour and ticking of the Abyssinian, and 30 for the coat of the Havanas. Full details of the various standards may be obtained from the appropriate registering bodies.

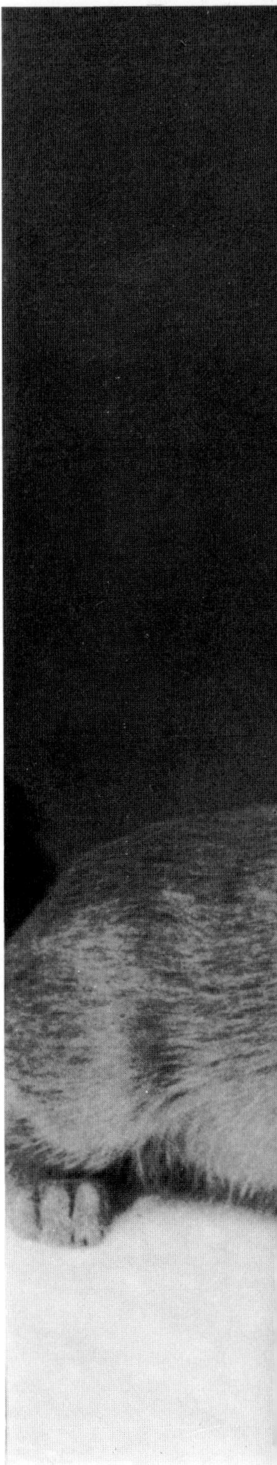

Two Foreign Lilac kittens and a Havana

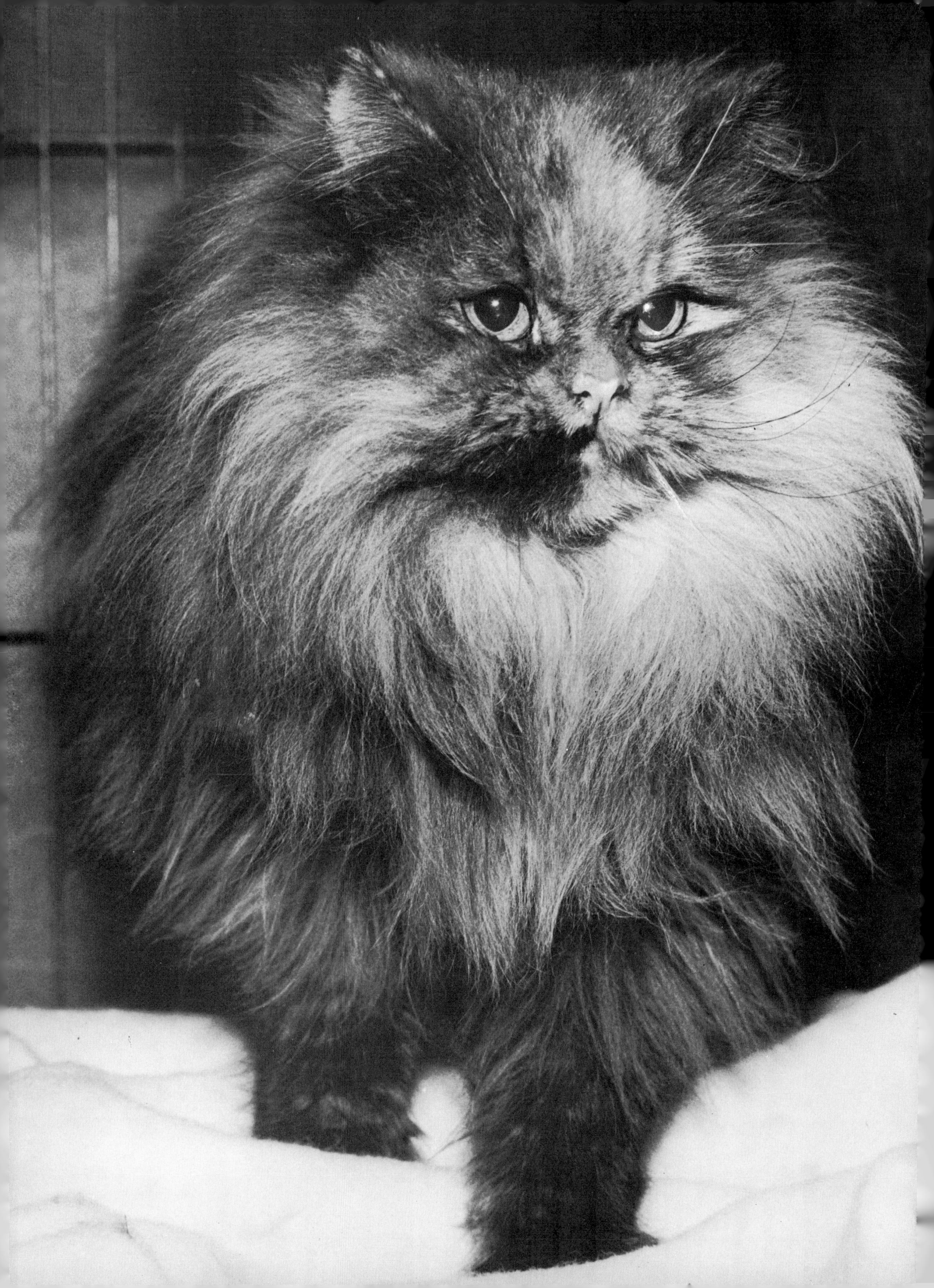

The frill on a Tortoiseshell Long-hair

The Foreign Short-hairs' characters differ from one variety to another, but in the main, with most, companionship is essential, whether that of another cat or of a human being.

Compared with the Long-hairs grooming is simple. They all appreciate hand-grooming which gives the coats a wonderful sheen, although some breeders do use a short-bristled brush, polishing afterwards with a chamois leather. A wide-toothed comb should not be used, as it may leave track marks in the fur, but a steel close-toothed comb could be run through the coat at least once a week to make sure that there are no fleas. The ears must never be poked inside, but any dust may be wiped away with a little slightly dampened cotton wool. Should there be any signs of dark matter, a sign of ear mites, a veterinary surgeon should be consulted.

Like the Siamese, the Foreign Short-hairs mature at an early age, with the females calling when only six months old sometimes. The males too may be fully developed when not much older. If not required for breeding, the females should be spayed and the males castrated when they are old enough.
See colour plate 25, *page 117 and plate* 26, *page 118.*

Foreign White see FOREIGN SHORT-HAIR

Foster Mothers If a queen should die shortly after giving birth, it is much better to find a foster mother for the kittens than to attempt to hand-rear them yourself. There are two reasons for this: it is difficult to mix and administer formula milk to orphan kittens, as well as being somewhat exhausting. They have to be fed every 2–3 hours and it has been found that kittens reared by a human fail to socialize adequately with other cats when adult.

Great gentleness and patience is required in the early stages of introducing kittens to a foster mother, and the queen should be watched carefully to begin with, in case she attacks the litter.

If possible, the foster mother should have kittened at about the same time as the mother-cat that has died. You should consult your veterinary surgeon if your kittens have not had colostrum at the time when you introduce them to the foster mother. Your veterinary surgeon may be able to help locate a foster mother. If no cats with milk are available, you might like to consider asking someone who has a lactating bitch to adopt your kittens. Bitches with false pregnancy, as well as those which have lost their puppies, will often successfully rear kittens.

Fractures see Broken under BONE DISORDERS

Fresh Air Beneficial to cats, fresh air is invigorating and reduces the risk of respiratory infection associated with poor ventilation. Flat-dwelling cats enjoy having access to a balcony or a well fenced flat roof.

Cats are sensitive to air pollution. Paint fumes and aerosols can upset their digestion; carbon monoxide from coal gas or coke boilers can cause asphyxiation or temporary deafness, even in comparatively small quantities; even dust can cause extreme respiratory discomfort.

Frill This is the name given to the long fur which grows around the neck of the long-haired cats and which, right from kittenhood, should be trained to stand up around the head forming a frame for the face. If it is encouraged to grow this way from an early age, three weeks not being too soon, by the time the adult coat is through, there will be a full frill framing the head, enhancing the cat's appearance.

If a cat is to be shown, the frill will need special attention. Care must be taken not to over-groom pulling the fur out and after feeding the frill may need to be wiped so that it is not stained. In the U.S.A. the 'frill' is usually called the 'ruff'.

Frost Point see Lilac Point under SIAMESE

Frozen Foods see COMMERCIAL CATFOODS

Fur Ball Fur ball is an infrequent condition in the cat in which there is an abnormal accumulation of fur or hair in the stomach. The condition is more common in the long-haired varieties of cats as they swallow more hair during their routine grooming activities. Most cats regurgitate pellets of matted hair at fairly frequent intervals of about 10 days but occasionally this process does not occur at the time of moulting or coat change when there are excessive quantities of loose hair available for ingestion by the cat. An affected cat becomes somewhat dull and although eager for food usually only eats a small quantity before leaving its dish. This lack of appetite results in a progressive loss of condition amounting to emaciation in some severe cases. Treatment may be surgical, involving opening into the stomach and removing the matted fur, or medical. Prevention is aided by frequent grooming to remove as much loose hair as possible from the coat.

Fur loss see ALOPECIA, BALDNESS and MOULT

G

Gait see MOVEMENT

Gamma Benzene Hexachloride Gamma Benzene Hexachloride is a white, tasteless crystalline powder with a slightly musty odour. It is a member of the organo-chlorine, or chlorinated hydrocarbon group of insecticides. Gammexane is reasonably safe for use on cats in powder form, but poisoning by absorption through the skin may occur if cats are washed in this substance. When the powder form is used, poisoning may occur through the cat ingesting the drug after licking it from the coat. An obvious precaution is to brush the powder from the coat after allowing time for it to have the desired effect. Symptoms of poisoning include twitching of the facial muscles followed by similar spasms of the muscles of the neck, the shoulders and forelegs, and finally the hindquarters. There is excessive salivation with champing of the jaws and the cat may become quite frenzied and incoordinate in its movements. Later convulsions may occur and in fatal cases the animal dies from respiratory failure during one of these. First aid treatment consists in keeping the cat in a quiet darkened room until veterinary assistance can be obtained.

Gas Gangrene Wounds infected with *Clostridium septicum* may occur and give rise to gas gangrene. The affected tissues die and bubbles of gas are produced in the depths of the wound. This complication is more likely to occur with deep puncture wounds such as those inflicted by cat teeth. Untreated the condition is often fatal.

Gastritis see GASTRO-ENTERITIS

Gastro-enteritis Gastritis is inflammation of the stomach, enteritis inflammation of the small intestine and gastro-enteritis inflammation of both.

Gastritis Gastritis, alone is not common in the cat but can result from the ingestion of irritant substances licked from the coat. A mild form of the condition occurs in which the irritant material is usually hair which has been swallowed during grooming activities. The main symptom of gastritis is vomiting. The cat may show signs of abdominal discomfort by adopting a tucked-up, crouched posture and is evidently reluctant to move. Often the animal will lie on a cold surface, sometimes even in a sink or drain. There may be considerable thirst, especially for stagnant or dirty water which may be consumed in quite large quantities and often aggravates the vomiting. In the mild form of the disease, the cat is apparently hungry and eats food ravenously, only to regurgitate the meal within a short space of time. Sometimes the meal is returned before the cat has finished feeding, even before it has moved away from its plate.

Treatment of gastritis depends upon diagnosis and removal of the cause. In the case of irritant material on the coat, any remaining should be removed by washing with soap and water, or, if necessary, clipping the hair. Gastric sedatives, such as demulcent substances like white of egg or bismuth, are useful first aid treatments. Persistent vomiting may be controlled by the administration of centrally-acting anti-emetics which depress the vomiting centre in the brain. The mild form of the condition is best treated by dieting – the feeding of small meals frequently, starting with as little as half a teaspoonful of finely chopped food and gradually increasing the amount until normal sized meals can be retained.

Enteritis The main symptom of enteritis is diarrhoea. The precipitating causes of enteritis are many and varied and require examination by qualified veterinary personnel in order to determine the cause. It may be due to bacterial, viral, protozoal or parasite infection; dietary change; ingestion of irritant or poisonous substances; or as part of a more general body condition.

First aid treatment should be instituted until veterinary advice can be obtained. This includes complete starvation and the offering of frequent small drinks of cold boiled water.

Gastro-enteritis The implication of both the stomach and the intestine simultaneously is commonly seen. The causes are identical to those for gastritis and enteritis as are the treatments.

Immediate veterinary attention is essential.

colour 25 Foreign Lilac

overleaf 26 Foreign White
27 Havana Foreign
28 Himalayan (Colourpoint) Chocolate Point
29 Himalayan (Colourpoint) Blue Point
30 Himalayan (Colourpoint) Lilac Point

26 27
28 29

31 32
33 34

Feline Infections enteritis or Panleucopaenia is a specific and very serious condition which is considered more fully under PANLEUCOPAENIA.

Gene see GENETICS

Genetics Genetics is the study of heredity. Gregor Mendel, an Austrian monk, first propounded the laws of genetics in 1866, following his work on the breeding of pea plants. These principles still hold good today although it is now known that the whole situation is much more complicated than was first thought. Mendel's theory was that certain factors are inherited in related pairs, one member of each pair from each parent and these come together in the fertilized egg and by their interaction with each other control the characters or attributes of the new individual. The factors of Mendel are now known as Genes, hence the name Genetics, and are minute portions of a chromosome (see CHROMOSOMES), each chromosome consisting of thousands of genes. The chromosomes can be visualized as strings of beads, each bead being a gene and the chromosome the whole string. Each gene occupies a specific position on the chromosome.

In each cell of the cat's body, apart from the germ cells, there are 19 pairs of chromosomes, one pair being the sex chromosomes. During the formation of the germ cells, i.e. the egg and the sperm, each chromosome divides into two, each half carrying one member of each pair of genes, and these separate and pass into the two new germ cells. At fertilization the pairs of genes are recombined, but at this union, one of each pair is derived from the father and one from the mother. The characteristics of the offspring will depend upon the interaction of these recombined gene pairs.

The basic principles of heredity therefore depend upon two main laws: 1. the law of separation of the genes and 2. the law of independent assortment of the separated genes in various combinations and crosses at fertilization.

During cell division the genes duplicate themselves to produce exact copies. Rarely an inexact copy is made and this is termed mutation, the different gene being known as a mutant. Genes may be dominant or recessive. A dominant gene is one which suppresses the effects of its partner in the gene pair. A recessive gene is one which is masked by the presence of its dominant partner unless it is inherited from both parents and is thus present in a double dose or homozygous. Dominance is denoted by the gene symbol being written as a capital letter, whilst the recessive gene symbol is shown as a small letter, e.g. the agouti gene is shown A for dominant and a for recessive, the homozygous being AA or aa whilst the heterozygous is Aa. Dominance may not always be complete with the result that intermediate forms between the two parental characters occur in varying degrees.

The outward appearance of the animal is known as the phenotype, whilst its genetic make-up is termed the genotype. The phenotype may give little or no indication of the genotype.

We can now consider the genetic mechanism of one or two simple crosses. If a short-haired female is crossed with a long-haired male where the gene symbol for hair length is S for the dominant short-hair and s for the recessive long-hair, the sperms will all carry the gene s whilst the eggs carry the gene S. The resulting kitten will have the phenotype of short-hair but its heterozygous for short- and long-hair Ss. The dominance of the short-hair gene S ensures that the animal will be short-haired. The cross here is known as the Parental or P generation whilst the resulting kitten is termed the First Filial or F^1 generation. If we now cross two of the heterozygous Ss F^1 generation kittens, the eggs will carry either S or s as do the sperms. The egg carrying S has an equal chance therefore of being fertilized by a sperm bearing S or s giving rise to the Second Filial or F^2 generation kittens SS or Ss. Similarly the egg bearing s may be fertilized by either sperm carrying S or s producing F^2 kittens with genotypes Ss or ss. Thus in the F^2 generation we will get one SS (homozygous short-hair), two Ss (heterozygous short-hair) and one ss (homozygous long-hair). The latter has the phenotype of long-hair as the recessive gene s is derived from both parents and is thus present in a double dose. Such a cat will produce only long-haired cats when mated to a long-haired animal which must also have the genotype ss.

These examples form the basis of the understanding of the genetic mechanism. Naturally the genes chosen for illustration purposes are very simple examples where there is plain dominance and recessiveness with full expression of gene action. Unfortunately it is not so simple to apply these basic rules as characters such as coat colour may be the result of the interaction of many different genes and gene action itself may be modified by the presence of complementary genes, modifying genes, incomplete dominance, mimic genes, incomplete penetrance, masking genes, etc., the exposition of which is beyond the scope of this short discourse.

Due to the confines of space, the foregoing can only be a very brief introduction to the subject of genetics and the enquiring reader would be well advised to consult one of the numerous textbooks available which are entirely devoted to the subject.

Gentian Violet Also known as crystal violet, this is a dye of the rosaniline group, and it has an anti-bacterial effect. As it is brightly coloured, and stains the tissues, it is used in conjunction with other agents when it is desirable to see exactly where a substance has been applied. Gentian violet may be used to spray on operation sites or areas of dermatitis. Solution of gentian violet in water may be used as a wash for wounds of the abrasion type and for burns. Gentian violet is also used as a staining agent in bacteriology.

colour 31 Himalayan (Colourpoint) Red Point kittens
32 Himalayan (Colourpoint) Seal Point
33 Himalayan (Colourpoint) Tortie Point
34 Korat

Geoffroy's Cat *Felis geoffroyi* somewhat resembles the domestic spotted tabby. In size it may measure over 3 ft which includes a tail length of 15 in.; the head is relatively large, the ears are black with a brown patch. Both grey and brown forms occur.

Distribution extends from the Rio Grande do Sul in Brazil to Santa Cruz in Patagonia and into south-west Bolivia. An excellent climber with habits not unlike those of the Jaguar, it uses branches of trees for rest and ambush, in both mountainous regions as well as the foothills and scrubland. Avoiding human habitation it subsists on birds and small mammals but on occasion may raid an outlying ranch.

Geriatrics see AGEING

Gestation The term is used synonymously with Pregnancy and denotes the period of development of the foetus of viviparous (bearing live young) animals from the time of conception until parturition (birth). In the cat, the average length of the period of gestation is 65 days but may extend up to 71 days. It is unlikely that kittens born before the 56th day of gestation will survive. Ovulation (egg shedding) occurs approximately 24 hours after mating. Fertilization of the eggs takes place 24–36 hours after mating and the implantation of the embryos into the lining of the womb occurs about two weeks later. Pregnancy can be diagnosed by palpation of the abdomen from the 21st to 35th day and then from the 49th day onwards. Radiography can be used for pregnancy diagnosis by the detection of the enlarged uterus from the 25th day, but the skeleton of the developing kitten does not begin to be visible until the 38th day. Abdominal distension occurs in cats carrying several kittens from between the 5th and 6th weeks. In cats carrying their first litter, the nipples become more prominent and pink after the first two weeks. The mammary glands become enlarged mainly during the last two weeks of gestation.

Gestation table Kittening dates for even dates of mating can be estimated by direct interposition.

DATE OF MATING	DATE DUE TO KITTEN	DATE OF MATING	DATE DUE TO KITTEN
Jan. 1st	Mar. 6th	Jan. 17th	Mar. 22nd
" 3rd	" 8th	" 19th	" 24th
" 5th	" 10th	" 21st	" 26th
" 7th	" 12th	" 23rd	" 28th
" 9th	" 14th	" 25th	" 30th
" 11th	" 16th	" 27th	Apr. 1st
" 13th	" 18th	" 29th	" 3rd
" 15th	" 20th	" 31st	" 5th
Feb. 1st	Apr. 6th	Feb. 17th	Apr. 22nd
" 3rd	" 8th	" 19th	" 24th
" 5th	" 10th	" 21st	" 26th
" 7th	" 12th	" 23rd	" 28th
" 9th	" 14th	" 25th	" 30th
" 11th	" 16th	" 27th	May 2nd
" 13th	" 18th	" 28th–29th	" 3rd–4th
" 15th	" 20th		
Mar. 1st	May 5th	Mar. 17th	May 21st
" 3rd	" 7th	" 19th	" 23rd
" 5th	" 9th	" 21st	" 25th
" 7th	" 11th	" 23rd	" 27th
" 9th	" 13th	" 25th	" 29th
" 11th	" 15th	" 27th	" 31st
" 13th	" 17th	" 29th	June 2nd
" 15th	" 19th	" 31st	" 4th
Apr. 1st	June 5th	Apr. 17th	June 21st
" 3rd	" 7th	" 19th	" 23rd
" 5th	" 9th	" 21st	" 25th
" 7th	" 11th	" 23rd	" 27th
" 9th	" 13th	" 25th	" 29th
" 11th	" 15th	" 27th	July 1st
" 13th	" 17th	" 29th	" 3rd
" 15th	" 19th	" 30th	" 4th
May 1st	July 5th	May 17th	July 21st
" 3rd	" 7th	" 19th	" 23rd
" 5th	" 9th	" 21st	" 25th
" 7th	" 11th	" 23rd	" 27th
" 9th	" 13th	" 25th	" 29th
" 11th	" 15th	" 27th	" 31st
" 13th	" 17th	" 29th	Aug. 2nd
" 15th	" 19th	" 31st	" 4th
June 1st	Aug. 5th	June 17th	Aug. 21st
" 3rd	" 7th	" 19th	" 23rd
" 5th	" 9th	" 21st	" 25th
" 7th	" 11th	" 23rd	" 27th
" 9th	" 13th	" 25th	" 29th
" 11th	" 15th	" 27th	" 31st
" 13th	" 17th	" 29th	Sept. 2nd
" 15th	" 19th	" 30th	" 3rd
July 1st	Sept. 4th	July 17th	Sept. 20th
" 3rd	" 6th	" 19th	" 22nd
" 5th	" 8th	" 21st	" 24th
" 7th	" 10th	" 23rd	" 26th
" 9th	" 12th	" 25th	" 28th
" 11th	" 14th	" 27th	" 30th
" 13th	" 16th	" 29th	Oct. 2nd
" 15th	" 18th	" 31st	" 4th

DATE OF MATING	DATE DUE TO KITTEN	DATE OF MATING	DATE DUE TO KITTEN
Aug. 1st	Oct. 5th	Aug. 17th	Oct. 21st
,, 3rd	,, 7th	,, 19th	,, 23rd
,, 5th	,, 9th	,, 21st	,, 25th
,, 7th	,, 11th	,, 23rd	,, 27th
,, 9th	,, 13th	,, 25th	,, 29th
,, 11th	,, 15th	,, 27th	,, 31st
,, 13th	,, 17th	,, 29th	Nov. 2nd
,, 15th	,, 19th	,, 31st	,, 4th
Sept. 1st	Nov. 5th	Sept. 17th	Nov. 21st
,, 3rd	,, 7th	,, 19th	,, 23rd
,, 5th	,, 9th	,, 21st	,, 25th
,, 7th	,, 11th	,, 23rd	,, 27th
,, 9th	,, 13th	,, 25th	,, 29th
,, 11th	,, 15th	,, 27th	Dec. 1st
,, 13th	,, 17th	,, 29th	,, 3rd
,, 15th	,, 19th	,, 30th	,, 4th
Oct. 1st	Dec. 5th	Oct. 17th	Dec. 21st
,, 3rd	,, 7th	,, 19th	,, 23rd
,, 5th	,, 9th	,, 21st	,, 25th
,, 7th	,, 11th	,, 23rd	,, 27th
,, 9th	,, 13th	,, 25th	,, 29th
,, 11th	,, 15th	,, 27th	,, 31st
,, 13th	,, 17th	,, 29th	Jan. 2nd
,, 15th	,, 19th	,, 31st	,, 4th
Nov. 1st	Jan. 5th	Nov. 17th	Jan. 21st
,, 3rd	,, 7th	,, 19th	,, 23rd
,, 5th	,, 9th	,, 21st	,, 25th
,, 7th	,, 11th	,, 23rd	,, 27th
,, 9th	,, 13th	,, 25th	,, 29th
,, 11th	,, 15th	,, 27th	,, 31st
,, 13th	,, 17th	,, 29th	Feb. 2nd
,, 15th	,, 19th	,, 30th	,, 3rd
Dec. 1st	Feb. 4th	Dec. 21st	Feb. 24th
,, 3rd	,, 6th	,, 23rd	,, 26th
,, 5th	,, 8th	,, 25th	,, 28th
,, 7th	,, 10th	,, 27th	Mar. 1st
,, 9th	,, 12th		or 2nd
,, 11th	,, 14th	,, 29th	,, 3rd
,, 13th	,, 16th		or 4th
,, 15th	,, 18th	,, 31st	,, 5th
,, 17th	,, 20th		or 6th
,, 19th	,, 22nd		

Gestation periods of some wild cats

DAYS	ANIMAL
109	Lion
108	Tiger
92	Leopard
92	Puma

Gingivitis Gingivitis is the inflammation of the gums. It may occur as a symptom of a systemic disease or, more frequently, in response to conditions of the mouth.

Commonly gingivitis results from the accumulation of tartar on the teeth. This forms a hard crust on the crowns of the teeth, and presses on the gums, which become bright red in colour at the junction of the tooth crowns and roots. Infection of the gums may supervene in bad cases.

Trench mouth, which is tartar formation accompanied by invasion of fusiform and spirochaete bacteria, also results in gingivitis, the inflammation often being severe enough for bleeding of the gums to be a feature. Gingivitis is often very difficult to treat successfully.

Glaucoma see EYE AND EYELID DISORDERS

Golden Cat, Temminck's see TEMMINCK'S GOLDEN CAT

Granuloma A granuloma is a tumour-like mass which arises in response to chronic (long-standing) inflammation or irritation. In the cat the condition is seen most frequently in the Eosinophilic Granuloma of the lip and the mouth, but also occurs in Cat Leprosy, Tuberculosis and Lickers' Skin. See also RODENT ULCER, TUBERCULOSIS.

Grass Cats occasionally eat grass. The purpose of this is still poorly understood. It may be to provide some mineral or vitamin which the diet lacks or to add fibrous bulk. Grass eating increases in frequency in cats which are ill particularly with digestive upsets. Here it may cause vomition to empty stomach contents or be an instinctive attempt to cure constipation.

Whatever the purpose of grass eating, flat dwelling cats should be provided with a flower pot or seed box of growing grass to fulfil their needs.

Grooming The state of the coat reflects the general health of the cat, and is an excellent barometer of the animal's condition. While conformation and temperament are important in the eyes of the judge, a coat that is abundant, of a good texture, shining and well cared for, makes a very important contribution to the appearance of a show-bench cat. The skin should be soft, clean and supple, and free from signs of external parasites. The hair itself should be clean and resilient, without excessive moulting.

Factors that contribute greatly to the appearance of the coat are a well balanced diet and it is thought that long hairs may have a higher aminoacid requirement than short hairs and an environment of the correct temperature and relative humidity.

Systemic diseases, have a detrimental effect on the coat and cause general acceleration of hair loss.

Though healthy cats groom themselves most efficiently, they all benefit from extra grooming by the

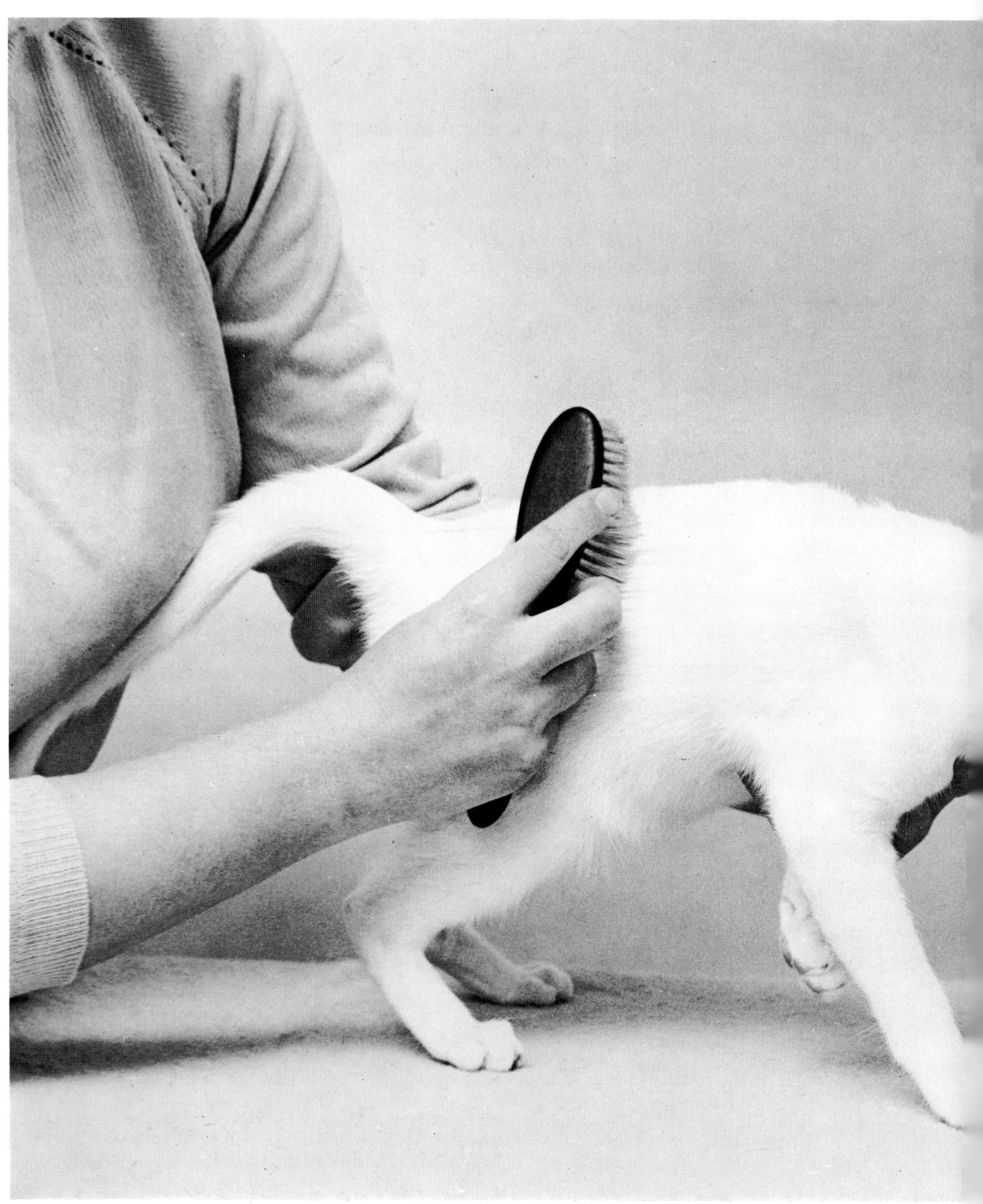

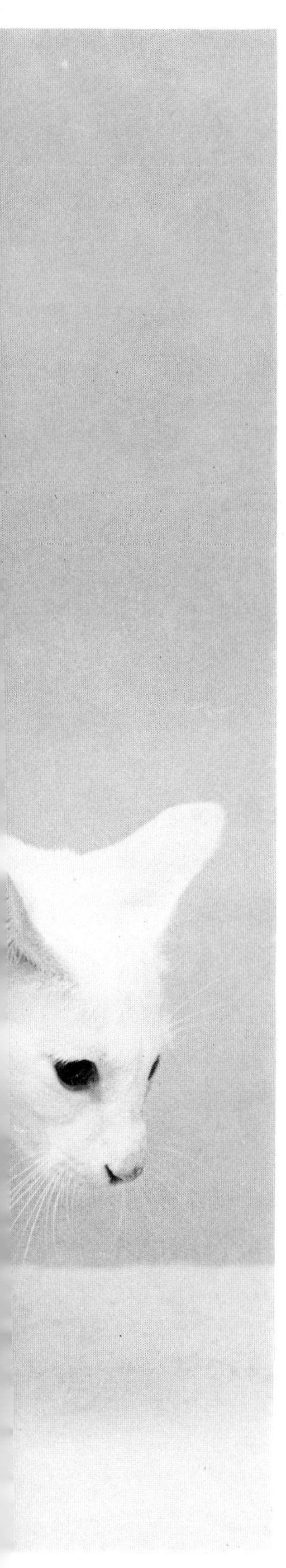

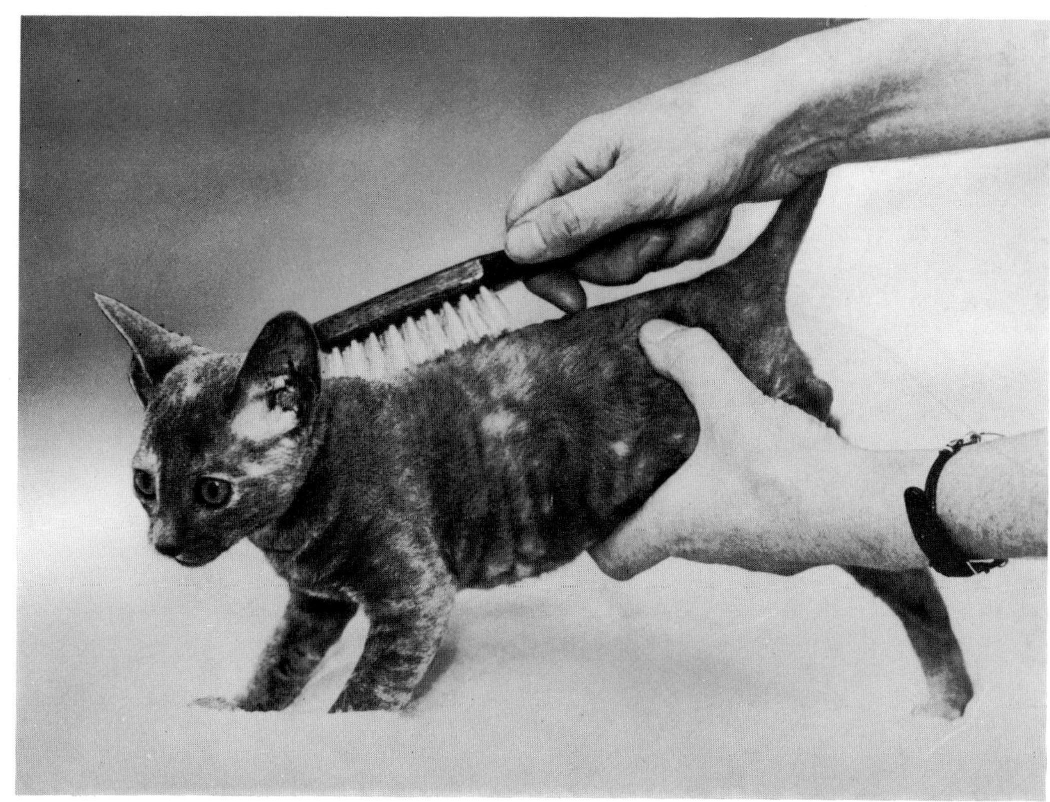

GROOMING *left* Baby brushes are excellent for short-haired cats; *above right* a very soft brush is needed for rex cats as they have no guard hairs; *right* a daily requirement for long-haired cats

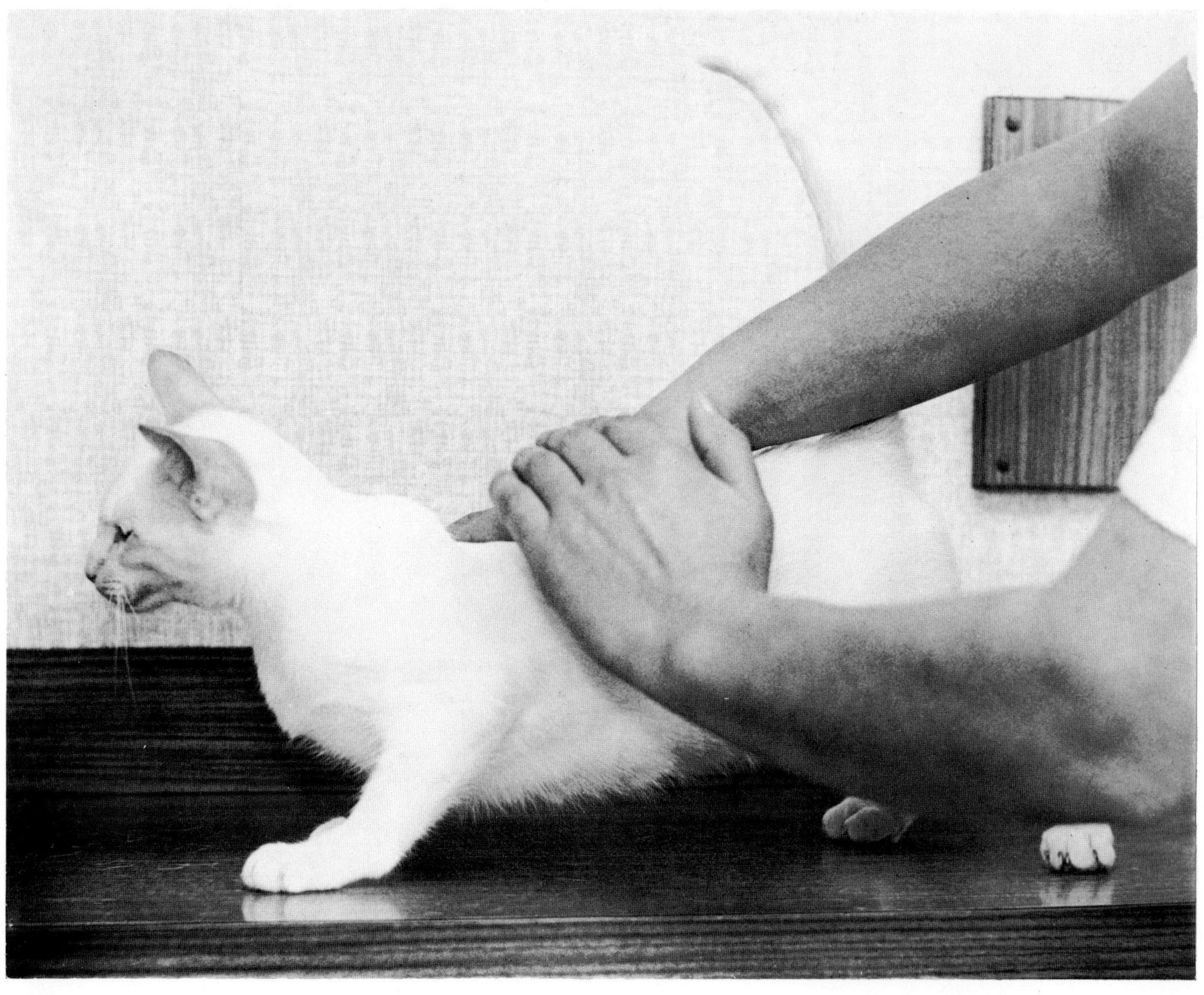

GROOMING Polishing the coat of a Siamese type with the palms of the hands

owner. During illness however a sick cat often stops cleaning, even its face and grooming must be more extensive. Keeping the face and paws clean contributes a great deal towards the well being of the patient.

Brushing stimulates the circulation, removes tangles, exposes parasites and scurf, cleans the coat and removes dead hair. It is advisable to begin brushing at an early age, so that the cat grows up to enjoy it, and to accept it as part of his routine.

When combing take care to comb very gently and to avoid pulling the skin when tangles are encountered.

For polishing an old nylon stocking, chiffon scarf or chamois leather are suitable. They may be wrapped around the hand or the head of the cat's brush. Firm strokes in the direction of the 'lie' of the coat remove minute specks of dust and give the body a sheen.

A brush with a rubber cushion and nylon bristles is best, except for very short-haired cats for which a baby's hairbrush is more suitable.

Hand grooming is particularly enjoyed by Siamese. Good for toning up circulation, it is really a kind of vigorous caressing of the body in a head-rump direction, with the fingers flexed and held apart and almost rigid. Dead hair is brought to the surface and collects around the rump, it can be removed later. See also Grooming under BRITISH SHORT-HAIRS and under LONG-HAIRS.

Growth Growth is the process whereby the body of an animal increases in size. It begins when male and female gametes fuse to form a zygote within the body of the female cat, progresses very fast indeed during the life of the foetus, continues considerably more slowly during kittenhood and finally ceases when the cat reaches the age of 10–12 months. In the case of female cats, a small amount of extra growth may be noted after the birth of the first litter, and in all adults some growth due to obesity may occur, but dimensions of body structures do not generally increase appreciably after 10 months of age.

Growth is due to the preponderance of anabolic ('building') processes over catabolic ('breaking down') processes. It is governed to a large extent by the thyroid gland. Abnormalities in growth may occur as a result of incorrect feeding, too much or too little exercise, endocrine dysfunction or hereditary defects. It is most important that kittens should receive a good diet at every stage of their development, as it is not possible to pay off a 'nutritional debt' later in life. Neutering the cat at an early age does not have a marked effect on growth, although entire tomcats often develop larger cheeks and thicker skins than male neuters.

Growths see NEOPLASIA

Guard Cats Legend has it that cats were used by the ancient civilizations to guard their temples and warehouses from marauders. It is rather difficult to believe that the presence of cats could deter the professional criminals of the ancient days but possibly the veneration with which cats were treated kept them, and thus the buildings they guarded, free from molestation. It seems more likely that cats were kept to guard the temples against the evil eye.

In modern times, cats have frequently very successfully guarded their homes by warning their sleeping owners of approaching fire.

See also SACRED CATS.

Gum inflammation see GINGIVITIS

Haematoma This is the name given to the swelling which occurs when a number of blood vessels burst within the tissues and bleed into a cavity between the tissues layers, commonly called a blood-blister. It is most commonly seen in the ear (see EAR DISORDERS), although haematomas will also form after an operation, a road accident or a fall from a height. Until veterinary treatment is available, the application of cold swabs or icepacks to haematomas will help to relieve the pain and swelling.

Haematuria This is a descriptive term for the presence of blood in the urine. It is a symptom of a variety of diseases and should always be regarded as serious. Veterinary attention should be sought immediately. See also BLADDER DISORDERS.

Haemobartonella felis see ANAEMIA and *Eperythrozoon felis* under FELINE INFECTIOUS ANAEMIA

Haemolytic Anaemia see ANAEMIA

Haemorrhage This is the scientific term for bleeding. Haemorrhage may be classified as follows: arterial, when the blood is bright red (oxygenated) and escapes in rhythmic spurts from the wound; venous, darker red blood which is emitted steadily; capillary, where there is a slow ooze of blood. Bleeding may also be classified as external – when blood is visible, either on the body surface, or escaping from a natural orifice, such as the mouth, nose, ears, anus or external genitalia, or internal – when the blood leaves the ruptured vessels to enter a body cavity such as the chest or abdomen. In the latter case, there are no obvious external signs of blood loss. Paling of the lips and gums will indicate severe internal haemorrhage. Because it is impossible to prevent haemorrhage from a large vessel from continuing except by operating to expose the vessel and placing a ligature around, internal haemorrhage constitutes a very serious condition. See also ACCIDENTS and ARTERIAL BLEEDING.

Haemothorax Haemothorax denotes the presence of free blood within the thoracic or chest cavity. The condition is rather rare in the cat but may result from injury whereby a fractured rib may damage a blood vessel in the chest wall or the lung. Haemorrhage into the chest cavity may also occur following breakdown of a blood vessel wall due to pressure from a tumour or from the extension of an inflammatory process within the chest. Symptoms depend upon the amount of blood accumulating in the thoracic cavity. If the haemorrhage is severe there will be restlessness, distressed breathing due to the pressure of the blood on the lungs, anaemia due to blood loss, and possibly signs of shock. The cat will tend to adopt the prone, sternal posture with head and neck extended and the elbows held away from the chest wall. There may be periods of mouth breathing with the cheeks being puffed out with each expiration. Treatment consists of rest and measures to arrest the haemorrhage and counter shock, coupled with aspiration of the chest to remove the accumulated blood. See also ACCIDENTS.

Hairloss see ALOPECIA, BALDNESS and MOULT

Halibut Oil A useful source of vitamins A and D. This oil is basically very similar to Cod Liver Oil (see COD LIVER OIL), except that it is prepared from the whole fish and not just the liver.

Hand Feeding see FORCED FEEDING

Handling Like all other domestic species, cats benefit both psychologically and physically from firm, gentle handling. On the other hand, a cat that dislikes being restrained will probably put up more of a fight than almost any other animal.

The only reliable way to hold and restrain a cat is by its scruff. Even then it may manage to scratch the handler with its hind feet. But to hold a panicking cat by the neck, trunk, tail or one limb is to invite attack. Once the scruff is secured, the trunk can be supported with the other hand, unless the legs are flailing, in which case, the cat should be held at arm's length by the scruff until a secure box is available. Many people object to 'scruffing', but, mother cats carry their young by the scruff.

If the cat is not angry or terrified, it should be possible to pick him up by the shoulders and transfer

colour 35 Lilac Self

35

colour 36 Manx

right The correct way to carry a peaceful cat

him to the crook of your arm for carrying. Pet cats often ride quite happily on their owner's necks or shoulders.

If you need to make a cat lie down, in order to look at his belly or paws, ask an assistant to hold his neck or scruff, lay him on his side and hold the two legs nearest the surface he is on (i.e. one front leg, one hind). Cats dislike lying on their backs, so do not hold them in this position unless it can be avoided.

A well-behaved cat can be held in the arms, or restrained on a table by placing the hand under his chin or breast-bone.

Harelip This deformity of the lip often accompanies cleft palate. It is a congenital deformity possibly of hereditary origin. Animals with this condition should not be bred from. Surgery can correct the condition physically. See also BREEDING ABNORMALITIES.

Harness Harnesses are really only necessary for cats that are led. The harness should be of soft leather or nylon and should be padded inside if studs are used to join the straps. Harnesses are less likely to get caught on things than are collars, but it is, nevertheless, advisable either to ensure they are slightly loose, or to have an elastic section in the main strap. See also COLLARS and LEASH TRAINING.

Harvester Infestation see MITES

Hate for cats see AILUROPHOBIA

Havana Brown see HAVANA FOREIGN

Havana Foreign Once known in Britain as the Chestnut Brown Foreign, but now in keeping with most other countries, referred to as the Havana

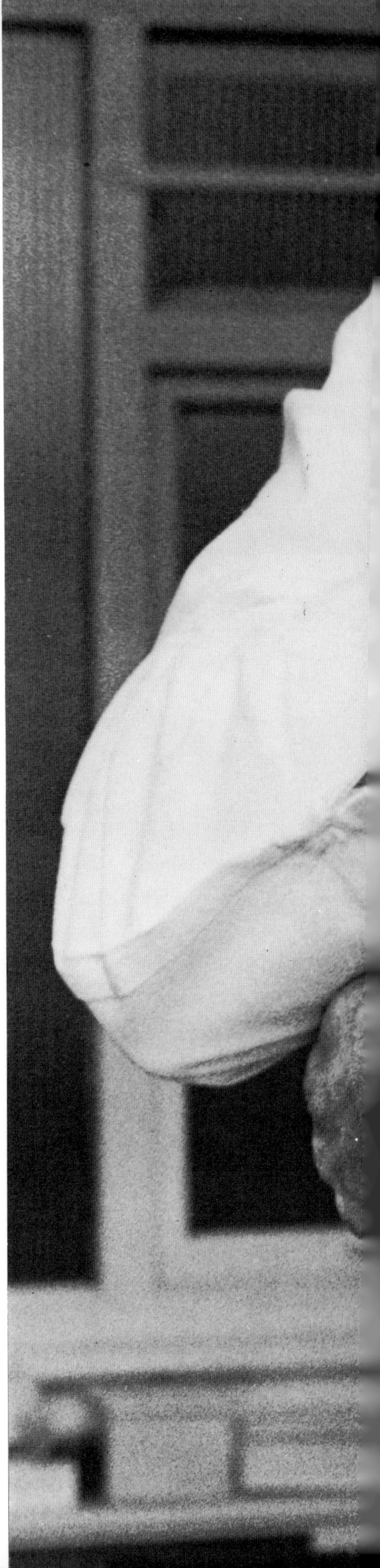

HANDLING *top left* The correct way to carry a cat requiring some restraint; *bottom left* restraining a cat; *right* carrying or lifting a nervous or bad tempered cat

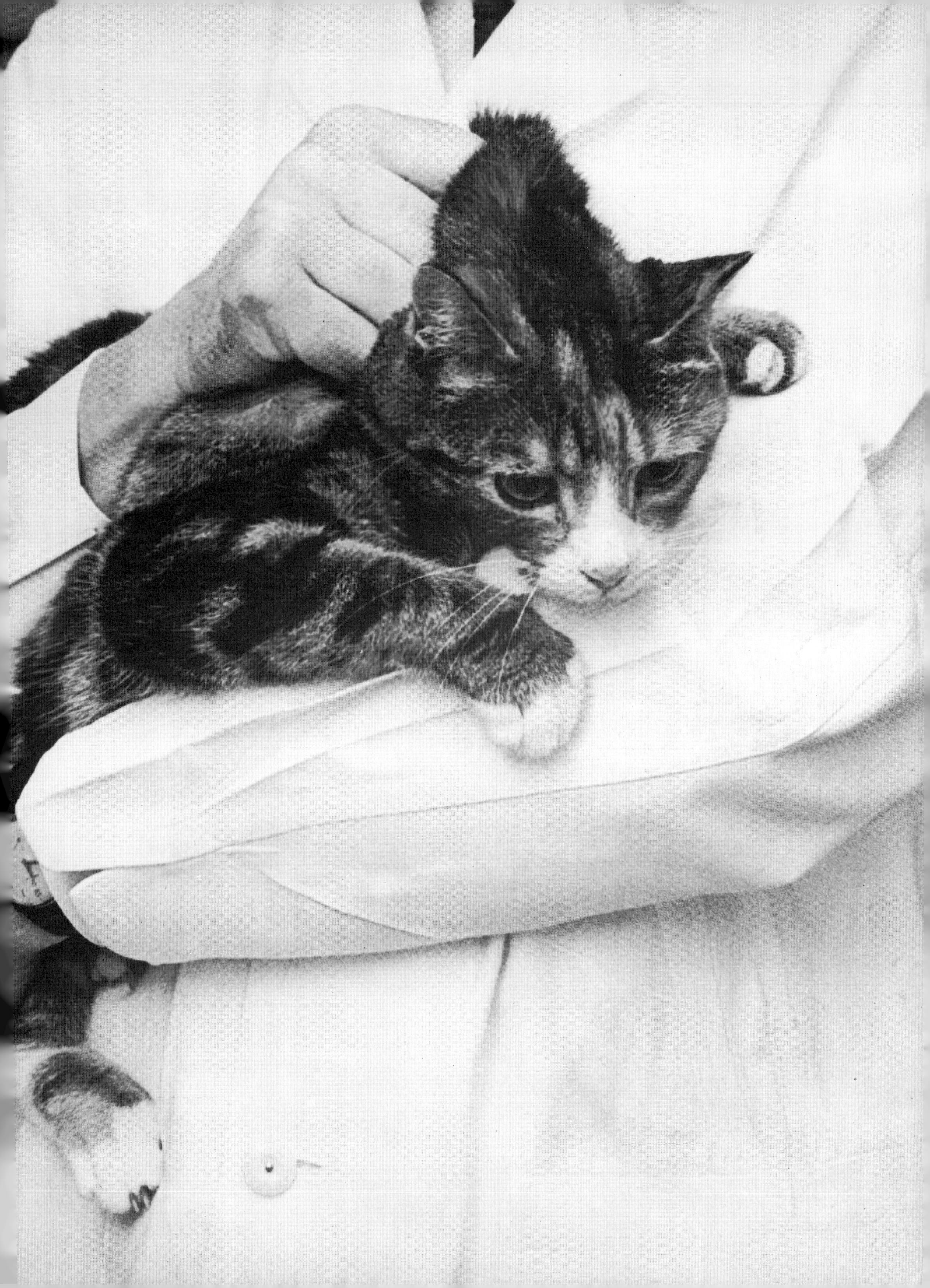

HANDLING *left* Even with a fence between, male studs showing animosity; *above* one contestant subdued by a thick towel thrown over – if necessary he may be then rolled up in it

Foreign, this attractive variety has foreign type and fur of a rich chestnut brown colour.

At first glance it may have the look of the Brown Burmese, but the colour is a decidedly richer brown, the eyes a definite green, and there are no ghost markings, as sometimes seen in Burmese kittens.

The graceful body should be long, lithe, but well muscled, and the whip-like tail should be long, with no suspicion of a kink. The head should be long and well proportioned, with large pricked ears, and the slanting almond-shaped eyes a decided green in colour. A distinctive feature is the pink pads to the feet. The fur should be short, glossy and even in colour.

Quiet, affectionate and home-loving, the Havanas make delightful pets, but are comparatively few in

Havana

number as yet. They are becoming increasingly popular in the U.S.A. where they are called the Havana Brown rather than the Havana Foreign. *See colour plate* 27, *page 118*.

Haw see under EYE AND EYELID DISORDERS

Head Mange see Notoedric Mange under MITES

Hearing see EAR ANATOMY

Heart and Blood System The heart is a muscular pump that serves to circulate blood around the body. The muscle of the heart is highly specialized and is found nowhere else in the body. It has an inherent tendency to 'beat' continuously, indeed the heart begins beating as soon as it forms in the embryo, and continues doing so until death. Around the heart is a strong membrane called the pericardium, and the space between the heart and this membrane is filled with pericardial fluid. Four chambers make up the heart, two thick-walled chambers, the right and left ventricles, and two relatively thin-walled chambers, the right and left auricles (sometimes called atria). The left sided chambers are larger than those on the right. Blood containing carbon dioxide is collected from the body tissues into tubes called veins, all of which eventually lead to the right atrium of the heart. The blood then passes into the right ventricle. From here it passes via the pulmonary artery to the lungs. Here the blood gives up carbon dioxide and absorbs oxygen. It becomes reoxygenated. It returns to the left auricle of the heart by the pulmonary vein. Muscular contractions now drive the blood into the left ventricle and thence around the body by a very large artery, called the aorta. This gives off many smaller branches which carry oxygenated blood to all parts of the body where the oxygen is used. Carbon dioxide is removed from the tissues by the blood and the whole cycle begins again.

The arteries are thick-walled, muscular tubes, built to withstand the considerable pressure produced by the pumping action of the heart. The arteries connected to the heart are large but become finer as they branch. The smallest ones are called arterioles. These vessels link up with arterial capillaries. These hairlike blood vessels are so narrow that the red blood cells can only move inside them 'in single file'. The arterial capillaries link up with venous capillaries, which are connected to small veins called venules, and these carry the blood back to the veins. The veins are thin-walled tubes. See also ANAEMIA, ANATOMY and LEUKAEMIA.

Heart Disease Heart disease in the cat is so rare that discussion here would be superfluous. Occasionally inherited or congenital conditions occur in the kitten and surgery can be performed to obtain relief.

Aortic thrombosis A condition of the circulatory system which is seen sometimes is a clot of blood in the aorta where it divides to supply the hind limbs. It causes pain, paralysis and the legs feel cold. Surgery can sometimes effect a cure.

Heat see BEHAVIOUR and OESTRUS

Heat Exhaustion Heat Exhaustion occurs when the temperature of the environment is high and the animal is unable to main his body-temperature at normal levels.

Mild heat exhaustion is manifested by the prostration of the patient and a rise in body temperature of 2° or 3°F. Placing the animal in a cool spot and bathing the head and feet with iced water should soon effect recovery. The rectal temperature should be checked at intervals. A very severe case may show a temperature rise of up to 5½°F. Immersion in a cold bath or the application of icepacks all over the body are the means used to lower the body temperature. Cold enemas (injections into the rectum) are sometimes also employed. If the temperature of an animal affected with heat exhaustion should exceed 107°F, irreversible brain damage may occur, with possibly fatal consequences.

Heat exhaustion may be prevented by ensuring that catteries are well ventilated and humidity controlled; inmates should always have access to shade. Pet cats should not be left in small rooms or cars in hot weather.

Heating of Catteries The type of heating used in catteries depends on the construction, as well as the breed of cat as coats vary from the almost hairless Rex to the thick coat of the Long-hair.

Underfloor heating is not usually recommended except possibly for laboratories where the animals are housed in cages off the ground. Hot water circulation is ideally suited to large buildings, but both types must be used in conjunction with the appropriate air humidifiers if animals are to remain healthy. Research has shown that, in normal conditions, there is a very thin, moist film covering the surfaces of the nasal passage, throat and lungs which in dry conditions dries out, allowing dust and bacteria to collect and so increase the risk of respiratory disorders.

Tubular heating is also drying if used in a high wattage and care must be taken to provide adequate ventilation.

It is generally agreed that for the smaller individual cat house, and also for use over cages in which sick cats are being nursed that infra-red heaters are preferable. If used correctly, a warm bed is guaranteed while the ambient air remains healthy; the cat is warm while at rest but not over-warm when at play or moving around.

Where a higher temperature is required for rearing kittens, infra-red can be boosted by the addition of tubular heaters as generally catteries are not of sufficient height to take higher watt infra-red heaters. A thermometer should be used to record bed level temperature.

It is also necessary to fix thermostats, but again the reader is reminded that temperature will depend greatly on the breed of cat. Generally 65° to 72°F is considered average for an average coated cat. The geriatric cat requires more warmth than a younger one or hypothermia may be a cause of death.

It is important that extractor fans are not overlooked in the building and heating of catteries. Some authorities consider that 8 to 10 changes of air per hour is sufficient, but recent opinion suggests that 16 may be necessary to keep stock healthy.

Heights Heights rarely present problems to a cat, since the righting reflex ensures that a feet first landing occurs.

Many small kittens, however, reach the top of trees and decide they dare not descend, or fall from scaffoldings and windowsills.

Although the self-righting mechanism enables them to fall on their feet, the chin often acts as the fifth impact-absorber. Thus, fracture of the mandibles, ruptured soft palate and fracture of the femur are the commonest major injuries associated with falls.

Survival after falls is frequent; cats falling from the fifth, sixth and seventh storeys being known to have been unscathed. See also ACCIDENTS and BONES, Broken.

Hemiplegia see PARALYSIS

Hepatitis see LIVER INFLAMMATION

Hermaphrodite This word is applied to an animal possessing some or all of the external and internal genitalia of both sexes. Often an hermaphrodite has a normal scrotal sac complete with testicles, but has a vulva with penis projecting from its centre. Alternatively the testicles may remain in the abdominal cavity. Although abnormal, the external genitalia generally function satisfactorily, so they do not require any surgical treatment.

Hernia A hernia is the abnormal passage of body tissues or organs through natural openings. The commonest are inguinal and umbilical hernias.

Inguinal Hernia This appears as a soft swelling in the groin which can vary in size from time to time. Inguinal hernias are formed when the inguinal canal is larger than normal allowing abdominal organs to pass through contained in a sac of peritoneum. Normally they cause little trouble but can become strangulated. This results when the blood supply to the organs in the hernial sac is cut off, often due to gas in a loop of bowel within the hernia. If neglected the tissue and organs with the sac die for want of a blood supply and infection follows.

Hernias are readily corrected by surgery.

Umbilical Hernia This results from incomplete closure after birth of the opening in the body, which allows passage of the umbilical cord during gestation. See also BREEDING ABNORMALITIES.

Normally the contents of the hernial sac are small amounts of fat. Rarely large holes are left allowing the passage of larger organs. The danger of hernication is again strangulation. Large hernias are better repaired but smaller ones are often left as they cause little trouble normally.

Diaphragmatic hernia see DIAPHRAGMATIC HERNIA.

Himalayan Known as the Colourpoint in Great Britain and the Himalayan in other parts of the world, this variety is a perfect example of a 'made' breed. Produced after many years of experimental breeding, involving the use of long-haired Blacks and Blues and Siamese, this striking cat with typical long-haired type, but having a Siamese coat pattern was given a breed number in 1955 in Britain, 1957 in the U.S.A., and has since become most popular.

The characteristics required are as given for the long-hairs, but the colour of the long thick fur should be as for the Siamese, cream for the Seal-pointed, glacial white for the Blue, and ivory for the Chocolate, with the appropriate point colouring. The eyes should be large, round and a bright blue. Lilac, Red and Tortie points are now being bred. A kink in the short full tail would be considered a defect, and any similarity to Siamese in type would also be faulted.

The Colourpoints are pale all over when first born, with the points appearing as the kittens grow, and deepening in colour until the adult stage is reached.

See colour plates 28 *and* 29, *page 118; plate* 30, *page 119, and plates* 31, 32 *and* 33, *page 120.*

History see DOMESTICATION

Holidays Holidays present problems for cat owners. Since cats are so orientated to their own territory

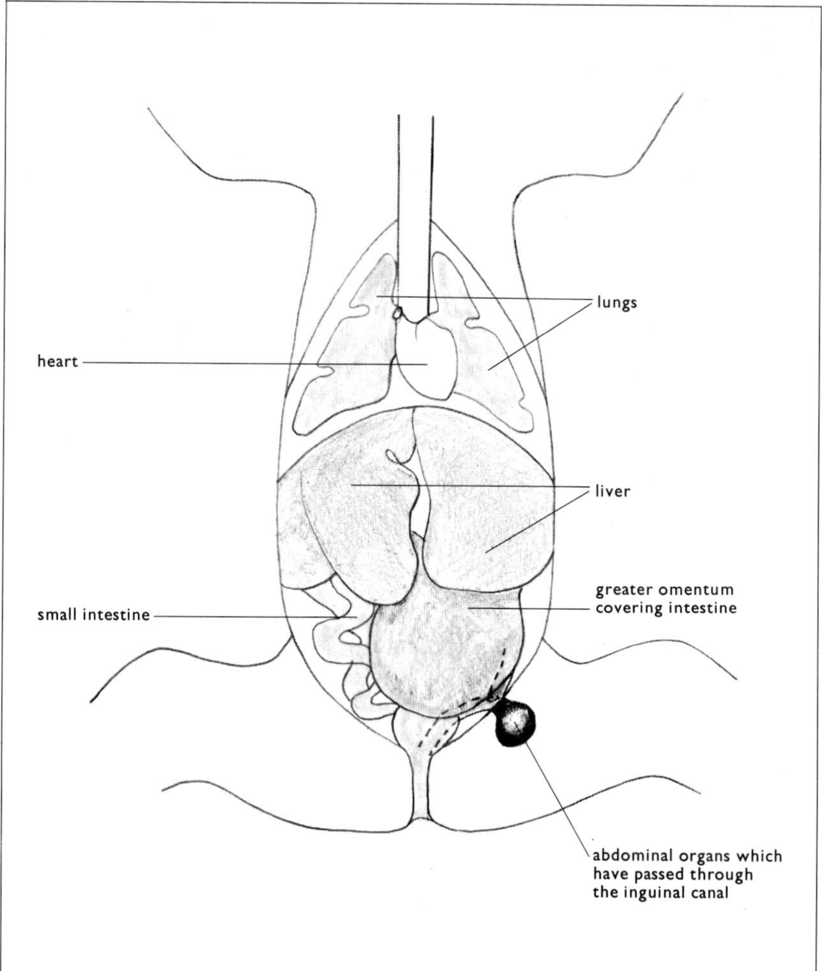

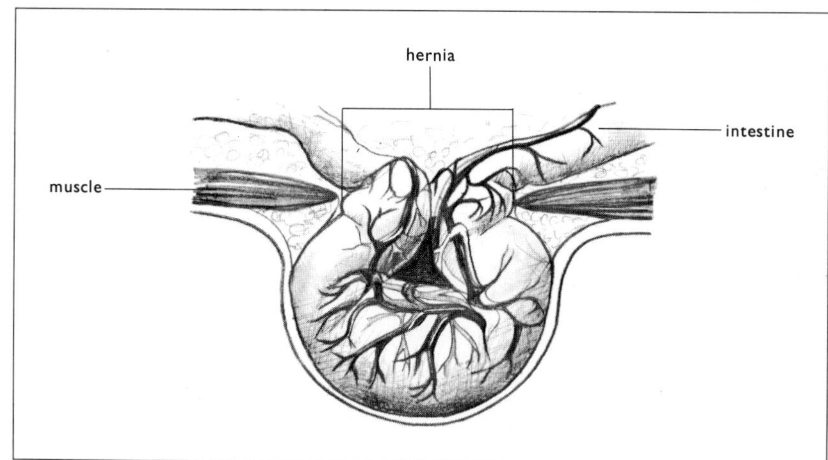

HERNIA *above top* Inguinal hernia; *above bottom* a schematic representation of an inguinal hernia

right Himalayan (Colourpoint) Blue Point

it is much the best arrangement to leave the cat in its own home and arrange for reliable neighbours to feed and water your pet.

Cats do not respond well to boarding but when necessity demands very good catteries are available which will cater adequately to the animals' needs. Inspect the cattery before agreeing to leave your cat there and ensure that it is fully orientated. The best boarding catteries will not accept cats which are not accompanied by up-to-date vaccination certificates.

Remember vaccination against cat flu is not a practical proposition and this condition remains a scourge of catteries. It is difficult to detect in the early stages. Once in a cattery it spreads very rapidly. Be understanding if your cat contracts this disease while you are away. The cattery owner will be as distressed as you are. See also ACCOMMODATION and BOARDING.

Homeopathic Treatment This is the application of herbal remedies. It is not wholly based on lore and tradition, since homeopathologists often receive basic training in accepted medical principles and go on to study homeopathy.

A few members of the veterinary profession employ homeopathic techniques, apparently with some success.

Homing It is difficult to make definite statements on the subject of feline homing since impressive stories abound, but it is not always possible to substantiate them. One thing is certain, and this is that cats vary greatly in their ability to find their way home. Thus a Siamese cat was said to have been found wandering up and down a lane only a couple of hundred yards from home, after being missing for nearly a week; while there are also reports of cats that have travelled thirty or forty miles to return to their old homes after the owners have moved house. Motivation has also to be considered. A cat may be missing from his home for months before it is discovered that he has moved in with someone else in the vicinity. In this case, it is clearly not due to a faulty homing instinct, but to the fact that the cat finds the second household more to his taste. On the whole, cats that travel away from their homes on foot have a better chance of finding their way back than do those which are taken, purposely or accidentally, by motor transport.

Hookworms see WORMS

Hot Climates Cats can live and thrive in hot climates because they are homothermic, warm-blooded animals, with the faculty of regulating their body temperature in a changing environmental temperature.

Obviously short coated cats are more suited to hot climates than are long-hairs. This is so not only because of the amount of fur coat that long-hairs carry but also because it is simpler in a short coat for the owner to find and remove the ticks which are prevalent in hot countries.

Owners must be on the look-out for diseases occurring in these countries, and especially for hookworms which are much more common than in temperate regions. Cats must have access to shade and to drinking water. Long-haired cats will not grow such heavy coats as in cold climates and many people clip them all over in the hottest weather.

If cats are to be kept in a cattery there must be adequate ventilation and shade. See also HEAT EXHAUSTION and WORMS.

House Cat This term is used to describe a cat kept as a pet in the home, as opposed to a farmyard cat or a cat housed in a cattery or breeding unit. Most cats adapt very well to the life in a house – indeed many are kept indoors all their life, and appear to thrive on it. It is desirable to allow house cats access to the garden, however, particularly in summer.

House Training see MANNERS IN THE HOUSE

Human Flea see FLEAS

Hunting see BEHAVIOUR

Hydrocephalus see BREEDING ABNORMALITIES

Hydrogen Peroxide Classified chemically as an oxidizing agent, this has a tendency to destroy bacteria by oxidizing them, making it a useful antiseptic agent.

The correct hydrogen peroxide to purchase for use as an antiseptic is known as '20 volume' hydrogen peroxide. One part of solution should be diluted with nine parts of water, giving a 'one in ten' solution. It is now ready for use in the cleansing of wounds. It is particularly valuable where shallow wounds of the abrasion type are encountered, since the fizzing action of the hydrogen peroxide helps to float small particles of grit out of the wound. It is also sometimes employed as a cleansing agent in the ears, and for the irrigation of established wounds.

Hydrothorax see PLEURA DISORDERS

Hygiene Hygiene relates to the care and cleanliness of both the animal and its surroundings necessary to prevent disease.

The cat should be kept free of external and internal parasites which may not only cause disease themselves but may also transmit disease.

Regular grooming is necessary for the well-being of cats, and in long-hairs it is essential. A matted coat cannot properly fulfil its function of insulation and causes discomfort to the cat.

The ears should be inspected regularly for the presence of any discharge indicating infection with ear mites, and the mouth looked at for formation of tartar on the teeth or inflammation of the gums.

The cat's sleeping quarters should be kept clean and dry and the bedding changed frequently. The cat, like all fur-bearing animals, can withstand successfully cold dry conditions but its resistance is soon lowered when exposed to damp. Changes of bedding and the cleansing and disinfection of sleeping boxes help to prevent fleas.

The sanitary tray should be kept as clean as possible and disinfected daily. Cats dislike strong smells. Do not therefore use too pungent a disinfectant. Some cats will not set foot in a tray which has already been used and will squat on the floor near it instead. In such cases, either provide two trays or attend to the tray as soon as it is soiled.

If the food is not finished at mealtimes, remove the dish immediately. Flies contaminate the food and in warm weather bacteria will multiply rapidly, increasing the risk of gastro-enteritis. Food dishes should be washed carefully and well rinsed. The water dish must be washed.

Hypoplasia, Cerebellar see under PANLEUCOPAENIA.

Hypothermia Hypothermia is the condition when the body temperature drops appreciably below normal and may be caused in various ways. It may occur when the heat regulating centre in the brain stops functioning during general anaesthesia or when the cat is unconscious or shocked as the result of an accident. It is therefore essential to keep surgical and accident patients warm.

Hypothermia can also result if the cat is immersed in water. Its woolly undercoat gets soaked and loses its property of insulation.

Most significant to cat breeders is the hypothermia which affects newly-born kittens. Here it may be due to an inexperienced queen failing to dry and lick the kittens; or by kittens being born in quick succession, when the mother is unable to cope with them all at once. The temperature in the room where the cat is kittening should not be below 70°F (21°C), and if any kittens are cold and damp they should be removed from the queen, dried, and kept warm in a blanket on a hot water bottle until the dam can attend to them.

Hysterectomy Hysterectomy is defined as the surgical removal of the uterus or womb from the female. In fact, hysterectomy proper is very rarely carried out in the cat. It is far more usual to perform ovario-hysterectomy – removal of uterus, ovaries and fallopian tubes, known as spaying, for social reasons. If only the uterus is removed, the animal will continue to come into season and even permit the male to mate her, so that most of the problems associated with keeping an entire female will remain. See also SPAYING.

I

Icterus Icterus or Jaundice is a symptom not a specific condition in which there is excess bile pigment in the blood. This is deposited in the tissues imparting a yellow colour to the affected animal. Icterus is not very common in the cat and when it does occur it is usually a sign of fairly severe liver damage.

The symptoms of icterus are that the skin and mucous membranes of the mouth and eyes become a yellow colour which is more easily observed in daylight. Allied to this yellow colouration are the more general signs resulting from the condition producing the jaundice. These are usually signs of liver failure. See also LIVER INFLAMMATION.

Immunity Immunity refers to a variety of mechanisms used by animal life to resist attack by disease organisms.

Innate Immunity This form is due to the inherent characteristics of the individual. Examples are species immunity – the cat is immune to canine distemper and human measles – and sex immunity, males being immune to diseases of the female genital tract.

Acquired Immunity This form of immunity is conferred by the presence in the bloodstream of antibodies, which may be thought of as soldiers. Each group is specially trained to attack a specific disease. Thus a cat that is immune to feline panleucopaenia possesses antibodies capable of combating feline panleucopaenia viruses only. If, as is more often the case, the animal is immune to a variety of diseases, it will possess antibodies of different types, each one designated to attack specific disease organisms. Acquired immunity may be of the following kinds.

1. Natural Passive acquired immunity. This is found in young kittens, which have received antibodies in the colostrum from their mothers during the first few days of life. Such antibodies persist in the bloodstream of kittens until they are about 6–10 weeks old, protecting them from disease. The number and type of antibodies will depend upon the immunological status of the mother – if she is immune to a number of different diseases, she will pass this on to her offspring.

2. Natural Active acquired immunity. This is developed by an animal that has been exposed to disease organisms. If exposed to small numbers only, immunity develops without contracting the disease. Alternatively, if exposed to a large number of organisms, the disease may be precipitated and recovery follow, again immunity develops.

Artificial Acquired Immunity This is conferred upon the animal by the administration of biological agents produced by man. The most important of these are vaccines and immune sera.

Active Artificial Acquired Immunity This is effected by the administration of a vaccine which consists of the disease organism which has been rendered harmless. It normally takes about a fortnight for antibodies to be formed, but the animal is then able to resist most exposure to the disease organisms. This sort of immunity is long-lasting, comparable with the natural active acquired form. 'Booster' vaccinations may be necessary at intervals.

Passive Artificial Acquired Immunity This is conferred by the administration of serum which, like the mother's colostrum, contains antibodies. This form of immunity takes effect as soon as the serum is given, but it does not persist for very long.

Thus serum is often given to an animal either just before or after it is exposed to a disease, in contrast to a vaccine which is given to an animal that *may* be exposed to a disease later on, when its immunity has fully developed.

The need for brevity has necessitated some oversimplification in the foregoing account. It should be noted that both natural and artificial antitoxins – substances that neutralize toxic substances produced by some disease bacteria – also play an important role in the immunity to disease. See also VACCINATION.

Impotence Impotence may be defined as inability to perform the act of mating in the male, a lack of virility. The condition is rare in the cat but can occur where there is a deficiency of vitamin A in the diet. This results in changes in the cells of the testicles concerned with the production of the male sex hormone, testosterone. A psychic type of impotence may arise where the male is moved into unfamiliar surroundings for mating purposes. For this reason the queen should always be brought to the stud cat for mating as it appears that the latter must demarcate his territory by such activities as urine spraying, before the right psychological environment for mating can be created. See also BEHAVIOUR and APHRODISIACS.

Inbreeding see BREEDING

Incisors see TEETH

Incubation Period The incubation period of a disease is the period of time between the moment of entry of a disease-producing organism into the body and the first appearance of the symptoms of the disease. Incubation periods can only be accurately determined by experimental study where the actual time of infection is known. There is a good deal of variation in the incubation period of any one disease. Factors such as: the resistance of the animal; the size of the infecting dose; have an effect on the time of appearance of the symptoms. A knowledge of incubation periods is essential for the determination of rational quarantine or isolation periods. Incubation periods for the important virus diseases of the cat are as follows:

Feline Panleucopaenia 4–10 days
Feline Viral Rhinotracheitis 2–5 days
Feline Picornavirus Infection 3–6 days
Rabies usually up to 6 months

Indian Desert Cat *Felis ornata* is not generally recognized as a separate species but is considered by some authorities to be *F. silvestris ornata*. There has been a great deal of confusion about these small cats and zoologists have not yet reached any definite agreement as to their relationships. Inhabiting the drier parts of the north-west it subsists on the usual small rodents and birds, and mode of living would undoubtedly be similar. Certainly it is an animal which is in need of study.

Indian Lion see LION

Indo-Chinese Tiger see TIGER

Infection Infection may be defined as the invasion of the body by bacteria, viruses, protozoa or parasites, and the reaction of the tissues to their presence and to the toxic products produced by them. In general the term is used to denote invasion of the body by harmful bacteria, viruses or protozoa, the word infestation being reserved for invasion by parasites.

Infertility see APHRODISIACS and IMPOTENCE

Influenza see FLU.

Inguinal Hernia see HERNIA

Inherited Character Inherited Character is an attribute, characteristic, quality or trait, which is passed from parent to offspring. A character is present in an individual animal as a result of the action and interaction of genes. Genes are not the same as characters but are responsible for them. Inherited characters include such things as coat colour, hair length, size, shape of head, etc. See also BREEDING and GENETICS.

Injections Injections are a way of introducing drugs into the body. The advantages of giving drugs by injection are that it is possible to ensure very accurate dosage and that it is often simpler than any other method for very fractious patients; furthermore, the rate of absorption of the drug is predictable. Injections may be designed to take effect locally – for example, intra-conjunctival injection for the treatment of infection of the eye, and intra-articular injection, for relief of inflammation of the joint – or to be absorbed into the whole system, being thus effective all around the body. The three injection techniques most commonly employed for general systemic use are subcutaneous, intramuscular and intravenous.

Subcutaneous Injections A subcutaneous injection is made into the soft connective tissue lying between the skin and the muscle. It is gradually absorbed by the blood vessels supplying the area, and carried by the bloodstream around the body. The great advantage of this gradual absorption is that antibiotics administered in this way enter the bloodstream at a fairly steady rate over a period of about 24 hours, and thus only one injection per day is necessary.

Intramuscular Injections Intramuscular injections may be made into any convenient pad of muscle, those of the hind legs being most favoured in the cat. A few drugs are irritant when given subcutaneously, but do not harm when given by injection into the muscle. The muscle has a rather better blood supply than the subcutaneous tissues, so that absorption of the drug into the system is more rapid.

Intravenous Injections Intravenous injections are usually made directly into the veins of the fore or hind legs, although the jugular (neck) vein may be used. For reasons of hygiene, the hair is usually clipped away first, and then the area is swabbed with antiseptic, the needle slipped into the vein and the drug gently injected. This technique is used when it is desirable for a high blood concentration of an agent such as an antibiotic or vitamin preparation to be attained or for the administration of anaesthetics.

Because they do not usually become tense with anticipation, as do humans, the majority of cats tolerate injections remarkably well.

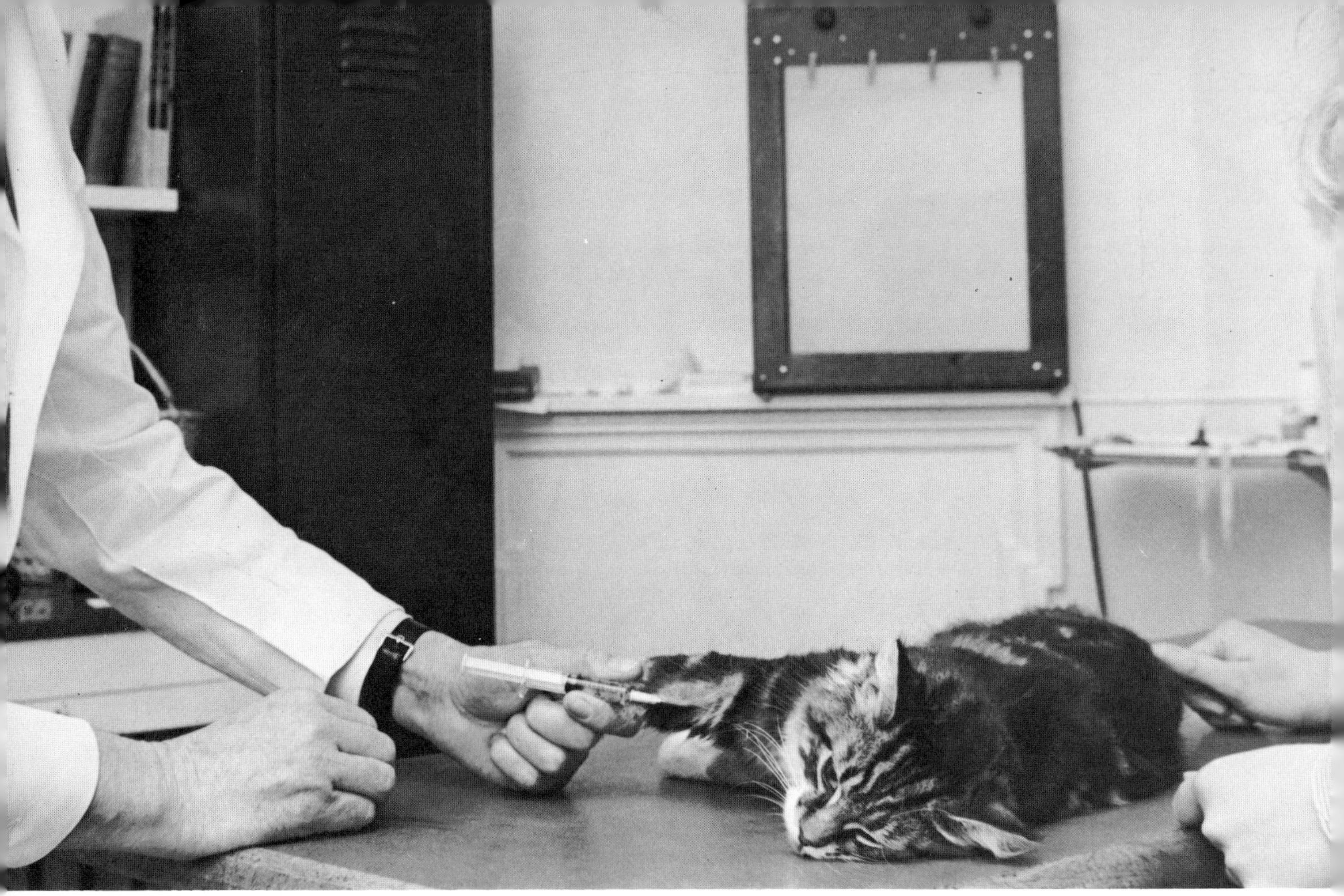

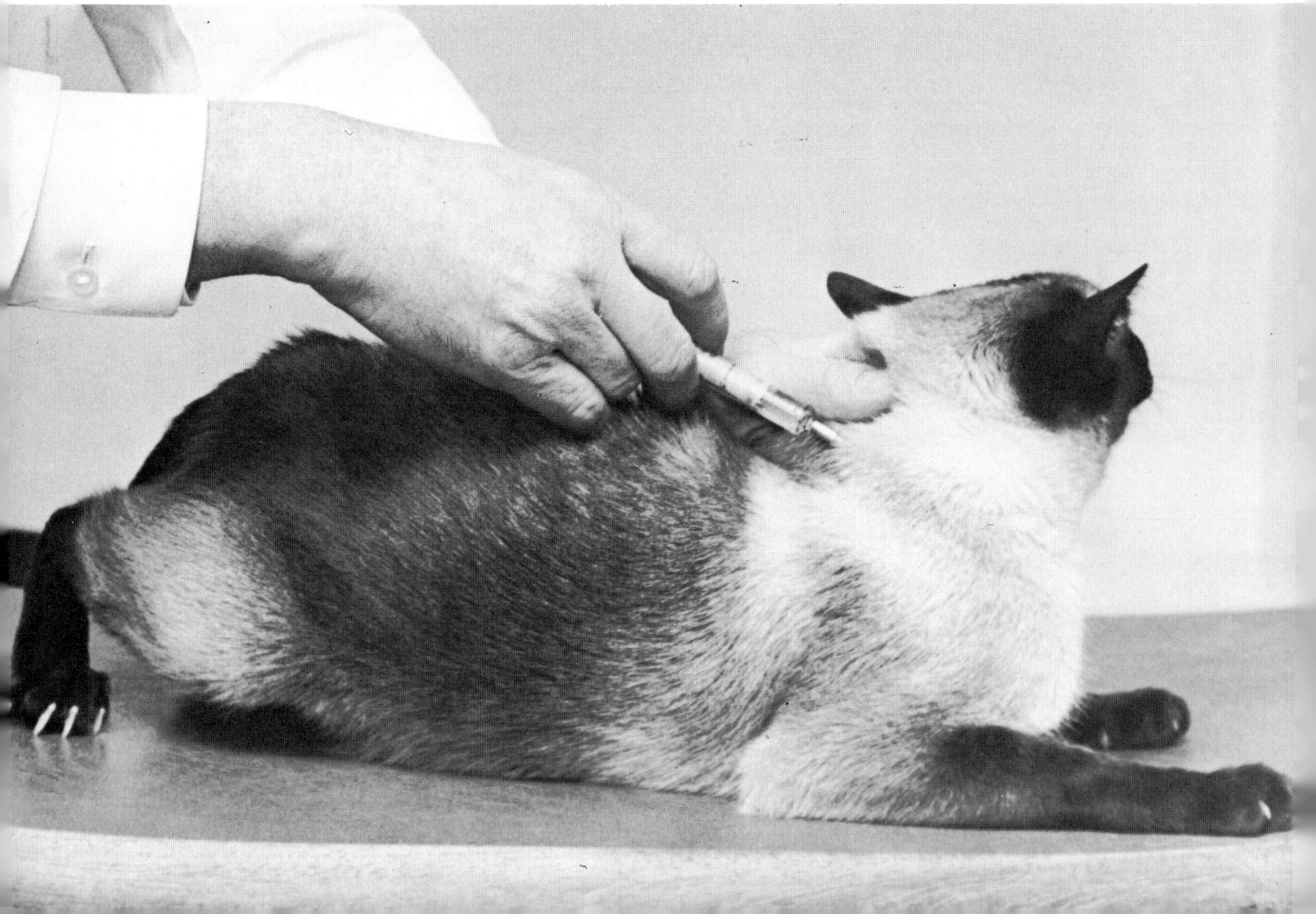

INJECTIONS *top left* Intravenous injection – the hair above the point of puncture is clipped away; *bottom left* subcutaneous injection – most cats scarcely feel this

Insulin see DIABETES

Intelligence Intelligence is often wrongly considered to denote learning ability. It is extremely difficult for humans to judge objectively the intelligence of any other species. Only a cat can apply an accurate criterion to feline intelligence, so any statements made on the subject by a mere homo sapiens must be taken in context.

Many people consider that because cats are less easily trained than dogs, they are less intelligent. This is fallacious in two respects: professional cat-trainers achieve results that compare very favourably with those of professional dog-trainers; and, because a cat does not obey its owner's commands, one should not infer that he does not understand them. It is far more likely that he understands them perfectly but does not concur. It should be remembered that dogs in the wild are highly social, with a pack-leader and a definite 'pecking order'. Cats, by contrast, tend to be individualists, and do not take kindly to domination, be it feline or human. See BEHAVIOUR.

In behaviour experiments, cats show that their learning ability is excellent, e.g. they quickly learn how to operate a latch in order to open a door and reach their food, or to walk through a maze. They can also distinguish between left and right, and remember information they acquire. It remains extremely difficult to make meaningful comparisons of intelligence between species.

Invalid Diet see NUTRITION

Invalids The basic principles of home nursing apply and an invalid cat should be cared for in a clean, cheerful room with an easily washable floor, good ventilation without draughts, good heating system and no superfluous furniture. For choice, a lino or tile-floored room should be allocated, but, failing that, thick newspapers may be used to cover a carpet. Although the room should be well-lit for inspection and treatment, it is helpful if it can be easily darkened to allow the patient to rest.

The attendant should ensure that the bedding is warm, hygienic and comfortable. The patient's face and coat should be kept clean unless he is so ill that handling causes him discomfort. It is important to strike a happy medium between over fussing and neglect. All observations should be reported to the veterinary surgeon.

The owner should learn how to take the cat's temperature and how to give medicines correctly. See THERMOMETER and DOSING.

Iodine This is a non-metallic element that occurs as brownish-black shiny crystals. It dissolves readily in alcohol to which potassium iodide has been added to form the well-known tincture of iodine. It may also be dissolved in water, in which case the solution is known as Lugol's Iodine, or aqueous solution of iodine. Both the tincture and the aqueous solution are good antiseptic agents, and repeated applications of the tincture are fungicidal, and may therefore be used to control fungous skin diseases. In general, the aqueous solution is used as a wash for fairly deep wounds or for vaginal douching (0·2% strength), and the tincture for application to the more shallow wounds, such as scratches, and to superficial skin lesions.

Ixodes sp. see TICK INFESTATION

Jackets Cats object to wearing coats and jackets, since these impede their movement and their ablution procedures. In general, jackets should not be used unless it is considered necessary by a veterinary surgeon to keep the chest covered during disease.

Jaguar *Panthera onca,* the Jaguar, and *Panthera onca centralis,* the Central American Jaguar, resemble the Leopard very closely being descended from a common ancestor. The difference being that the Jaguars' rosettes are fewer and larger and there are one or two black spots in the centre; the black or dark brown rosettes become solid on the flanks and legs and extend in rings around the lower part of the tail which is black tipped. It is unstriped except for black bars along the spine, chest and throat. The coat colour varies from almost white, clear yellow and tawny and there are black melanistic forms on which the rosettes are scarcely visible. The Jaguar is not such a svelte animal as the Leopard, in fact some authorities have described it as being almost clumsy in appearance; the head is larger, the top more rounded and the backs of the ears are black. The largest of the cats of the New World, a male can weigh up to 290 lb. although there are some records of 350 lb.; weights varying according to the region. The females are smaller and may weigh between 160 and 200 lb. Measurements vary between $5\frac{1}{2}$–9 ft of which 2–$2\frac{1}{2}$ ft may be tail. The Central American Jaguar, *P. onca centralis,* is said to be smaller than average. However, 1972 reports state that all are showing a marked decrease in size due to the disturbance of their habitat and exploitation for their skins.

Distribution extends from the south of the U.S.A. southwards to Central America and South America as far as northern Patagonia. Habitat, like the Leopards' is thick cover; it is a good climber and so prefers jungles and swamps although it roams into open grassy plains and deserts in the north and south

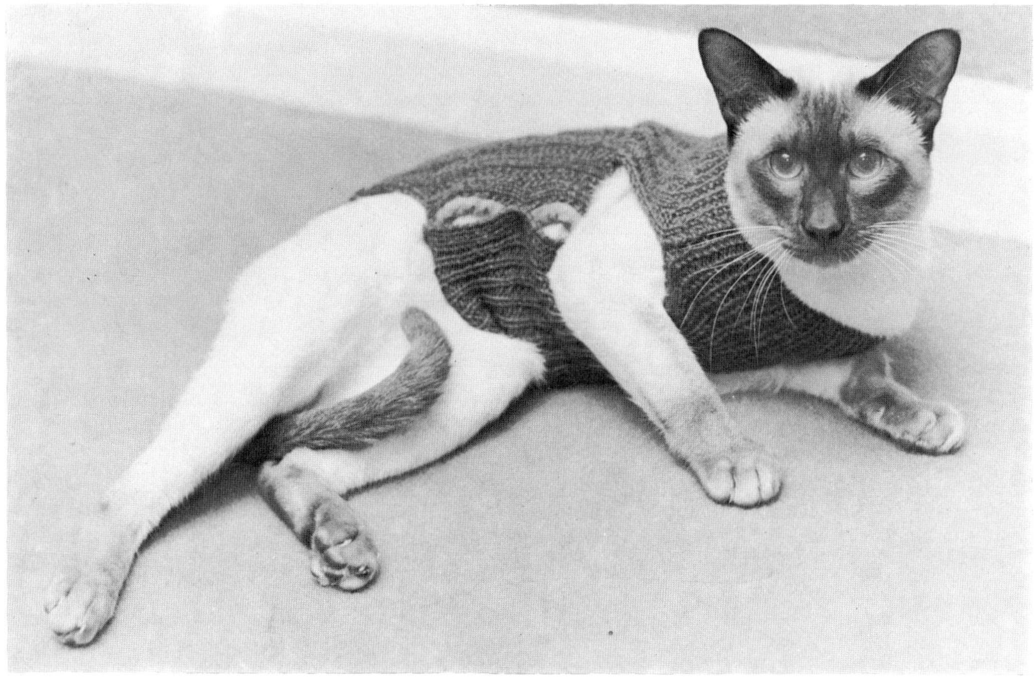

JACKETS *left* Jackets should only be used on the advice of a veterinary surgeon

colour 37 Red Self, Premier and female Champion

of its range. In Columbia it sometimes dwells in the mountains; having no fear of water it swims well and can be seen relaxing in the branches of trees overhanging rivers. Prey includes deer, feral cattle, tapirs, capybaras, agoutis, sloths, wild turkeys and birds, and the pig-like peccaries. Fish also forms part of its diet and it is reputed to kill small alligators and crocodiles. If the opportunity occurs it will attack domestic stock but it rarely attacks man and so it is not greatly feared.

The Jaguar is a most magnificent cat and in need of preservation. Fortunately some states have already banned its hunting and export, and have pleaded with the World Wildlife Fund to use their influence in bringing about an import ban in Europe.

Jaguarondi *Felis yagouaroundi* is a most unusual cat; despite its name it looks nothing like the Jaguar but shows remarkable resemblance to the mustelids – the family which includes the badgers, martens, weasels and otters. Its head is very like the otter's – long and low with small ears and typical otter 'expression'; the body is very long and graceful with fairly short legs. Total length might vary from slightly under 3 to over 4 ft of which the long tail may be a further $1\frac{1}{2}$ ft or sometimes even more; the shoulder height is low, perhaps only as much as 10–12 in. Weight of this species varies from 10–20 lb.

There are two colours, one grey or grey-black, and the other a light brown which may deepen to dark chestnut. At one time it was thought that two species existed, but this has now been discounted. Both colours may appear in the same litter, the brown variety being known as 'eyras'. They are unspotted and unstriped.

Distribution extends from the Argentine and Paraguay in South America, to Mexico and southern Texas in the U.S.A. but are becoming rare since the clearance of the thickets in the delta of the Rio Grande. Equally active by day as by night, they frequent open as well as bush country and also forest. Due to extreme suppleness of body, they are able to travel great distances entirely by way of branches and on the ground move at considerable speed. Very solitary animals they only contact other members of their species at mating time. They subsist on a variety of small mammals, birds and perhaps frogs and fish and have been observed to eat figs – this is very unusual in a carnivorous animal although the domestic cat will sometimes eat fruit and cucumber.

Japanese Bobtail Cats with short tails, very like those of the Stumpies often found in Manx litters, have been known in Japan for centuries. Frequently featured in Japanese art, they were unknown elsewhere until in 1969 in the U.S.A. kittens were born from stock imported direct from Japan.

A provisional standard has been granted and the numbers now are steadily on the increase. The colours may be black and red in the form of patches on a white ground, with each patch being entirely distinct from the other. It is also possible to have self-coloured cats with coats of black, red or white, also Bi-colours in black and white, or red and white, and Tortoiseshells, with patched coats of black, red and cream.

colour 38 Russian Blue

The heads are longish, with large ears, the bodies being medium in length, with the hind legs higher than the forelegs. The distinctive feature is the tail which may be from about one to four inches long.

Although similar in appearance this variety has no connection with the Stumpies produced from Manx, and is unknown in Britain and on the Continent at the moment.

Jaundice see ICTERUS

Javan Tiger see TIGER

Jaws The jaws are the bones comprising the skeleton of the mouth. The upper jaw or maxilla is composed of the maxilla and the premaxilla bones which carry the upper set of teeth. The lower jaw or mandible is hinged to the under surface of the skull by the mandibular joint. The lower jaw consists of a pair of mandible bones, which are fused together at the chin in the mandibular symphysis, and which carry the lower set of teeth. Movements of the jaws are effected by the muscles of mastication, notably the masseter and temporal muscles, which stretch between the skull and the mandible.

Jealousy Cats may exhibit what appears to be jealousy towards other cats or towards other species. Usually jealousy is occasioned by a human being giving his attention to something or someone other than the cat in question. Manifestations of jealousy include sulking, furious washing, growling and dramatic protests, such as leaping on the human's shoulder and displaying affection. Siamese in particular are renowned for this last form of behaviour. Sometimes a jealous cat will attack the animal or object receiving his master's attention.

Most cat lovers are rather flattered by shows of jealousy on the part of their pets, since they indicate that the owners' attention is highly valued by the cats.

Joint A joint is formed at the union of two bones. It includes the surfaces of the bones which are in direct contact and their cartilage coverings, the fluid between, which acts as a lubricant, and the capsular ligament which encloses the joint. Damage to joints results in arthritis and is always potentially serious. See also ARTHRITIS and BONE DISORDERS.

Judging The method of appointing judges differs between the various countries and the different cat organizations. In Britain judges do not have to take examinations, being nominated by specialist clubs as being able persons to judge a certain variety. Before anyone can be considered as suitable, it is

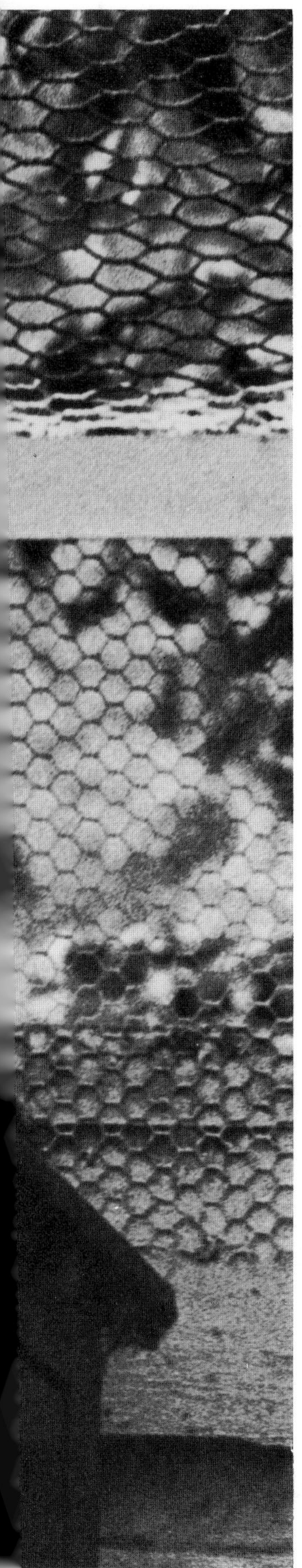

necessary to have stewarded a number of times for a judge judging a particular variety and also to have bred that variety. In Britain, the Siamese cat clubs have a joint committee which consider applications from those who have stewarded twelve times for six judges or more. The committee discuss the capabilities of the applicant and lack of experience, or some such reason, may mean an application being refused, but the candidate may apply again.

Other clubs do not have the same procedure, would-be judges being selected and voted on by the committee from nominations previously received. Whatever the method used, the names of all successful applicants are submitted to the Governing Council of the Cat Fancy for ratification before they may start judging.

It is usual for the judges to be on a probationers list at first, that is they must judge kittens in the open classes at least three times, before being permitted to judge the adults and award challenge certificates. This rule does not apply to all specialists clubs.

In Europe the method is entirely different, with would-be judges having to steward for at least four shows and to have been student judges at six. A student judge has to sit beside a qualified judge and to watch the way the cats are judged, and be able to comment on them when asked. Both for stewarding and student judging, letters of approval must be given by the judges in question. Finally, the applicant has to be examined both orally and in writing by two senior international judges. There are different examinations for the long-hairs and the short-hairs, so that it takes a considerable time to become an all-round judge.

In the U.S.A. the procedure is most complex. To begin with the greatest difference is that judges are paid so much for each cat judged, and also that there is no stewarding as in Europe. Before even being considered as a judge, the applicant must be of good standing and have exhibited and shown cats for a number of years. If acceptable, it is compulsory for him to attend a clerking school; to be a clerk at several shows, eventually serving as Master clerk. After this it will be necessary to attend a judging school, and to act as an apprentice judge where specified, and to complete successfully a most intensive written examination. As may be imagined, all this may take several years, before one emerges as a fully-fledged licenced judge.

Jungle Cat *Felis chaus* is widely dispersed and can be found in Egypt, the Middle East and Asia Minor, Russia just east of the Caspian Sea, India, Ceylon, Nepal, Burma, Indo-China and Thailand. Jungle cats frequent dry grassland, scrub and reed beds and often roam near to villages where they will sometimes snatch chicken; their main diet consists of birds and small mammals but they have been known to kill birds as big as peacocks.

Somewhat larger than the average domestic cat, they weigh up to 20 lb. and measure some 2½ ft from nose tip to the base of tail, which might add a further 10 in. The body colour varies but is usually grey-brown with faintly striped markings which are more broken than the African Wild Cat. The underparts and chin are white, the ears have small tufts and may be dark rimmed; the tail is ringed with a dark tip.

Less nocturnal than many cats, they can be tamed but remain suspicious of strangers.

The Jungle Cat, *Felis chaus*

K, L

Kaffir Cat see CAFFRE CAT

Kaolin Kaolin is a compound extracted from kaolin clay. Once purified, kaolin may be used both externally and internally in the treatment of disease.

'Heavy' Kaolin is used as the main constituent of kaolin poultice. It has the two very useful properties of combining with toxic substances produced in a wound and of acting as an insulation material, helping the dressing to remain hot for longer periods. This prolonged application of heat to a wound helps to speed up inflammatory processes and reduce the total healing time. Kaolin poultices are applied to abscesses, superficial infected wounds, sprains and strains.

Another use of 'heavy' kaolin is as the base of dusting powders such as insecticidal and skin-sedative agents. The kaolin and a powdered form of the active ingredient, are well mixed, and the powder dusted into the animal's coat.

'Light' Kaolin is used as a liquid mixture in the treatment of infections of the alimentary canal. As the kaolin passes through the gut, bacteria and bacterial products become attached to the particles and are thus carried out of the system. Kaolin may be used alone or mixed with a number of other agents.

Keratitis see EYE AND EYELID DISORDERS

Kerosene see Dangerous Liquids under ACCIDENTS

Kidney The kidneys main function is to filter the waste products from the blood. These highly poisonous substances are continually produced and very soon cause severe illness if not removed from the body. The kidneys thus receive a very large proportion of the blood through them to maintain health. The structure itself is very delicate and very complex. A large number of substances will damage it irretrievably.

Kidney Disease see NEPHRITIS

Killing Instinct see BEHAVIOUR

Kink This expression, used in cat parlance, usually refers to the sharp bend present in the end of the tail of many Siamese. It is an hereditary phenomenon, and it is surrounded by legend. See also BREEDING ABNORMALITIES.

Kodkod *Felis guigna* is a most distinctively patterned cat of greyish-brown with lines of small spots along the back and flanks; the tail is heavily ringed with black; there are lines running from the eyes to the ears and two lines running up the head. The underparts and chin are light, and some observers state that there is a prominent blackish-brown band across the throat.

Not a large cat, the total length may be about 27 in. of which 9 in. may be tail. It is becoming very rare and nothing is known about the weight.

Distribution is the foothills of the Andes in Chile, but it does not extend as far as Patagonia. Subsisting mainly on small mammals such as rodents, the Kodkod has been known to raid domestic poultry runs in parties but it is not known whether this cat is more social than other wild cats, or whether these raids have been made by the female and her growing kittens.

Korat The Korat is a self-coloured cat with a short blue coat having a distinctive silver sheen. It is said to have originated in Thailand, although apparently it is quite rare there. As long ago as 1896, a blue cat from Thailand was exhibited at one of the London shows, but there were arguments as to what the variety was, and it was referred to by one judge as a Blue Siamese, much to the owner's disgust. Nothing else is known about this particular cat. Again similar cats from Thailand were seen in the U.S.A. in 1934, but unfortunately there seem to be no details about them. It was not until 1959 that a breeding pair was imported into the U.S.A. with further importations following and these proving to breed true, were accepted as a distinct variety in 1966. They are just beginning to make an appearance in Britain having been imported from the U.S.A.

The Korat is admired for its heart-shaped face and brilliant green-gold eyes. The ears are large, with rounded tips, the head broad, curving softly to a

well-developed, but not sharply pointed muzzle, and the medium sized body is strong and muscular while the tail is of medium length, tapering to a rounded tip. Both in the U.S.A. and Canada, these quiet, intelligent cats are appearing in greater numbers at the shows.
See colour plate 34, *page 120.*

Lacrimal Apparatus The term 'lacrimal apparatus' is used to describe the anatomical structures responsible for the production of tears which constantly bathe the eye. It is essential that the eyeball should be kept moist throughout life if it is to function properly. The film of tears, which is regularly renewed by the act of blinking, acting both as a lubricant and a mild, natural antiseptic. Tears are also responsible for the removal of dust particles and tiny insects. When these enter the eye, tear production is increased, so that they are gently floated across the cornea and into the corner of the eye and onto the skin. Tears produced in response to exposure of the eyes to irritant substances, such as paint fumes, insecticidal sprays, and other atmospheric pollutants are attempting to protect the eye from the harmful effects of such agents.

There are a number of lacrimal glands, responsible for producing tears. Within a sac formed by the conjunctiva is the lacrimal lake, which collects tears preparatory to their flowing away down the lacrimal duct and out onto the surface of the eye. Any excess of tears produced drains across the eye and into the lacrimal sac, situated at the inner corner of the eye. Tears finally drain away from the lacrimal sac and into the nose. If copious tears are produced – as, for example, in response to irritant fumes – they may spill over from the eye onto the face. A heavy throughput of tears from the eyes to the nose will similarly cause discharge of a watery substance from the nostrils.

Diseases of the lacrimal apparatus are not common in the cat. See also EYE ANATOMY.

Lactation Lactation is a term which is applied to the formation or secretion of milk or sometimes to the period of suckling of the young. In the cat, lactation averages seven weeks in duration and weaning commences during the fourth or fifth week after birth. In full lactation, the food requirements of the cat often exceed her ability to consume and digest sufficient food and she then draws upon her reserves of fat and muscle protein with consequent loss of weight and condition. It is important to remember this increased need for food at the height of lactation and also the increased calcium requirements (see Deficiency Diseases under NUTRITION). Kittens should feed almost as soon as they are born, they consume about 5 gm of milk at each feed, and should gain weight at the rate of 10 gm daily. The average percentage composition of cat's milk is: Water 82·4%, Total protein 7·0%, Fat 4·8%, Lactose 4·8%, Ash 1·0%.

Lactational Tetany see ECLAMPSIA

Lameness This word is used to describe the abnormality in gait of an animal that either puts no weight on a limb or places a reduced amount of weight on it. The limb not used normally in locomotion is described as the lame leg.

Lameness can be a sign of a number of conditions, including fractures, dislocations, bites, foreign bodies and arthritis. The cure of lameness involves diagnosing and treating the cause. See also ABSCESSES, ACCIDENTS and ARTHRITIS.

Laparotomy This term describes the surgical operation to open the abdominal cavity. Because the peritoneum – the membrane lining the abdomen and covering all its organs – is very susceptible to infection resulting in peritonitis, the operation is always performed using instruments, swabs and operating drapes that have been carefully sterilized, and great care is taken of the patient during the recovery period.

Larynx see RESPIRATORY ORGANS

Larynx Disorders *Laryngitis* This is inflammation of the larynx and, like many inflammatory conditions, it may take an acute form – sudden in onset, dramatic in effect, but subsiding comparatively readily – or a chronic form – gradual in onset, persistent in nature and very resistant to treatment. Neglected the acute form may recur and eventually become chronic. Laryngitis may be caused by bacteria or viruses. Often these are associated with infections of other parts of the respiratory tract, so that laryngitis often occurs concurrently with other conditions. Signs of the condition are pain in the Adam's apple area, on swallowing, and a change of voice. Coughing occurs when pressure is gently applied to the larynx. The temperature may be raised, particularly if laryngitis has set in as a sequel to some other infection. The condition is treated by antibiotics to combat bacterial infection, and, in some cases, by the use of anti-inflammatory drugs. If exudate is present inhalation infusions such as are used for nasal congestion in humans may help. This may best be done by placing a cat in an openwork basket or cage and standing it over a steaming dish containing the inhalation infusion. Great care should be taken in giving medicines by mouth to cats suffering from laryngitis, because swallowing is usually painful. The patient should be kept warm and protected from draughts.

Oedema of the Larynx Severe swelling of the mucous membranes covering the surfaces of the larynx can occur as a sequel to laryngitis, or by irritation due to foreign bodies or insect stings. Laryngeal oedema is very serious in that even a small amount of swelling greatly reduces the internal diameter of the respiratory tube, causing breathing difficulties or if severe, asphyxia. It is important to avoid exciting the patient or to allow it to make any exertion which will increase the oxygen requirement. The membranes of the gums and lips may turn a bluish-purple colour, indicative of a shortage of oxygen. Artificial respiration is of no assistance unless it is of the mechanical type, using a ventilator and oxygen supply. In very severe cases, tracheotomy (opening of the windpipe at a point below the larynx to permit the entry of air) may be required. If, however, the condition is recognized and treated in its early stages, the patient should not reach the point where emergency measures are necessary.

Neoplasia of the Larynx Tumours of the malignant type sometimes form in the walls of the larynx. The larger growths cause respiratory embarrassment, similar to that seen with laryngeal oedema. A change in the character of the voice and the purring mechanism is, however, usually observed long before breathing is embarrassed.

Leash Training This requires a good deal of patience. Kittens should wear a light collar for a few days before the leash is introduced. It may be helpful to use a piece of strong nylon or light string instead of the proper leash to begin with. If the kitten pulls backwards, do not pull strongly against him, but slacken the leash and make encouraging noises to persuade him to walk in the same direction as you. Most cats are sensible enough to prefer the slack, comfortable leash that results from their co-operation, and soon co-operate. If the cat dashes ahead, increase your pace, but check him gently at the same time. Initial training sessions should be kept very short. Titbits and caresses should be used to reward good behaviour.

Leopard *Panthera pardus* and *P. pardus japonensis* are forms of a species where the spots are clustered together to form rosettes. Unlike the Jaguar (*P. onca*) there are no spots in the centre of the rosettes and they are smaller and more evenly distributed over the whole body, only becoming true spots on the head and legs. Coat colour is tawny-brown varying in hue with light underparts and chin, with prominent markings on the back of the ears. There is a dark brown melanistic form which is called by its alternative name 'Panther' (Black Panther), and both colours may be found in the same litter. The Leopard is altogether a more finely proportioned cat than the Jaguar. An average length is about 7½ ft of which 3 ft may be tail; there is a variation in individual size according to locality and some can measure more; the record being some 9 ft. Weight may be from 100–180 lb., exceptionally up to 200 lb.; females are lighter. The most variable Leopards, *P. pardus japonensis* considered a sub-species, are those of northern China. They are large and have longer and thicker fur which is no doubt an adaptation to the cooler climate; markings are larger.

General distribution of the Leopard is from Africa to southern Asia, although they are almost extinct in Morocco and adjoining areas as well as parts of South Africa. Naturally keeping to the cover of thick plant growth where possible they are most agile climbers and move about in trees, often in very thin branches where they lie up and are well camouflaged and so go unseen. They are very secretive cats. Usually hunting at dusk they are swift killers, killing by biting through the jugular vein or crushing the vertebrae of the neck. Prey consists of a very great variety of animals such as antelopes – Impala and Waterbuck, baboons, other monkeys and large rodents. After consuming the more tempting parts, the remainder is removed into branches of trees away from non-climbers such as jackals and hyaenas. Leopards will attack domestic animals and children, but adults are not quite so likely to be attacked. They are good swimmers.

One of the world's most beautiful cats, the Leopard has now been placed on the list of endangered species.

Leopard Cat *Felis bengalensis* is one of the spotted varieties which is in very grave danger of extinction due to exploitation for its skin as well as for 'exotic' pets. As pets they are ferocious and as difficult to tame as the European Wild Cat and very much misery and cruelty results from attempts to tame them by anyone other than a zoologist. In size they are larger than the domestic cat ranging from 1½–2½ ft with a tail of 9–14 in.

They have the superficial resemblance to a very small leopard, but the spots are not grouped into rosettes. Colouring is variable according to the area in which it is found, and may be yellowish or greyish with white underparts, there are streaks on the head and neck, and the rounded ears – well placed – are black with a white spot. The tail spots tend to form bands towards the end which is black tipped.

Distribution is from south-eastern Asia, where it is found in Burma, the Malay peninsular, Sumatra, Java, Borneo and some of the Philippines and extends to northern India, Tibet, China and eastern Siberia. Inhabiting hilly areas and secondary jungle and avoiding the thickest forest it can climb actively and its prey consists of large birds and small mammals including hares, and even mouse-deer, dropping on them from a tree like a leopard. It is usually nocturnal.

Leopard, Clouded see CLOUDED LEOPARD

Leopard, Snow see SNOW LEOPARD

Leprosy The disease known as cat leprosy has been recorded in New Zealand, the U.K. and the U.S. and it is probably world-wide in its distribution. It should not be confused with the human condition.

The lesions take the form of fairly rapidly developing, painless skin nodules in various sites of the

The Leopard Cat, *Felis bengalensis*

body, mainly on the head and limbs. The nodules may be single or multiple and range in size from 1–3 cm in diameter. In some cases, the skin overlying the lesions remains intact but others show quite extensive ulceration with the formation of raw areas. The cat appears to be in good health otherwise, and if the nodules are removed surgically, they show no tendency to recur at the same site. In some cases, however, similar nodules occur in the internal organs, particularly in the liver and the spleen. The causal organism has been tentatively named *Mycobacterium lepraemurium*. It seems probably that infection of cats takes place as a result of the bites from infected rats. This would also account for the frequent distribution of the lesions on the head and limbs.

Treatment consists of surgical removal, or since the organism is sensitive to streptomycin, antibiotic therapy.

Leukaemia Leukaemia is a term derived from the Greek meaning 'white blood'. It is used to denote a condition in which there is a malignant or cancerous proliferation of the white blood cells. This proliferation leads to enlargement of the sites of production of these cells, the lymph nodes and the spleen, and eventually of other organs which become infiltrated with white blood cells. This leads to interference with the affected organs' functions. There is an associated loss of condition and finally death. Leukaemia is by far the most common cancer of the cat. Most of the affected animals die within three months of the diagnosis being made.

Feline leukaemia has been shown to be due to infection with virus FLV, which is very similar in appearance to the viruses causing leukaemia in the fowl and the mouse. This virus has been isolated and purified in the laboratory and can be grown by tissue culture outside the body, in cells derived from healthy cats. The virus will also grow readily in other mammalian cells, but there is no evidence at present to suggest that FLV can cause leukaemia in man. The virus is transmitted from mother to kittens whilst they are still within the uterus, or immediately after birth via the milk. There is some controversy as to whether transmission from cat to cat can occur.

The disease is inevitably fatal and it is advisable to have affected animals put to sleep as soon as the condition is diagnosed. No effective treatment is available at present and despite the negative findings reported in the survey the disease remains a hazard, especially where children are in close contact with affected cats.

Lice Lice infestation is not very common in the cat, but may occur in young kittens or in adults which are debilitated in condition. Two types of louse may infest the cat, the biting lice, *Trichodectes canis* and *Felicola subrostrata,* and the sucking louse, *Linognathus setosus*. The predilection sites for infestation are the head and the flexures of the elbows, but the parasites may be found anywhere on the body. Itching is not so apparent as in flea infestation, so self-inflicted damage does not occur to the same extent. There is usually a scurfy condition of the skin in the affected areas and the lice can be seen either moving about slowly or stationary attached at right angles to the skin surface. They appear as pinhead sized, bluish-grey, oval bodies, easily visible to the naked eye. The life cycle is completed on the host animal, the eggs or nits being laid cemented to the hair and hatching out into nymphs which are similar to the adult lice in appearance. Treatment is similar to that used in flea infestation, but it is important to repeat the applications of insecticidal powder at fairly frequent intervals to catch the nymphs as they hatch out of the resistant eggs.

LICE A biting louse, *Felicola subrostrata*

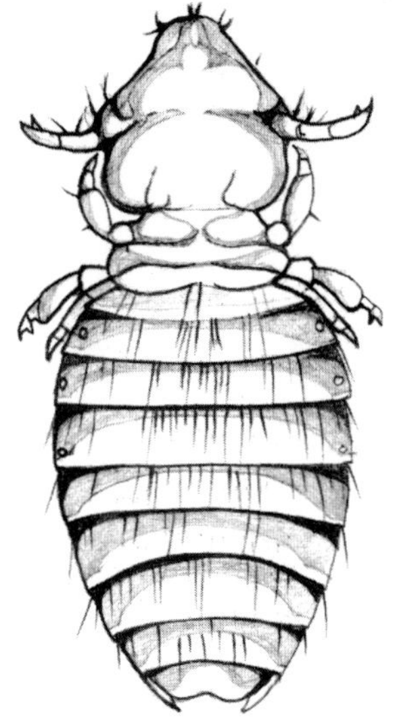

Licking The cat's tongue is adapted for grooming. Licking is also used for drying newborn kittens and stimulating their respiration and circulation.

Licking can work against the cat's interests when used to remove sutures, ointments, dressings or insecticidal powders. Here it is best to prevent licking by use of an Elizabethan collar. See ELIZABETHAN COLLARS.

Life Expectancy The life expectancy of an animal is the probable number of years of survival for an individual of a given age. The average life span of the cat is probably around 14 years but there is little statistical evidence to confirm this. Cats have been said to be the longest-lived of the small domestic mammals, living in exceptional cases for 25–30 years. See also AGEING.

Lights The term used to describe lungs which are sold for meat. Sometimes the heart and trachea and bronchii are also attached. Lights are not very nourishing, as they contain a high proportion of air, but they appear palatable and easily digested.

Lilac Cream Point see SIAMESE

Lilac Point see HIMALAYAN and SIAMESE

Lilac Self Long-hairs Produced in the first place as off-shoots when breeders were endeavouring to breed Lilac Colourpoints, one or two have been exhibited at shows in recent years. The lilac colouring is most attractive, but the type is not as good as yet as of the other long-hairs. At the moment the big round eyes are yellow in colour. By selective breeding Chocolate Self Long-hairs are also being produced. The coat should be the colour of milk chocolate with eyes of deep copper. As the colours are not yet recognized there can be no set standards and they are entered in the 'Any Other Colour' classes. *See colour plate 35, page 129.*

Lilac Tortie Point see SIAMESE, ANY OTHER COLOUR

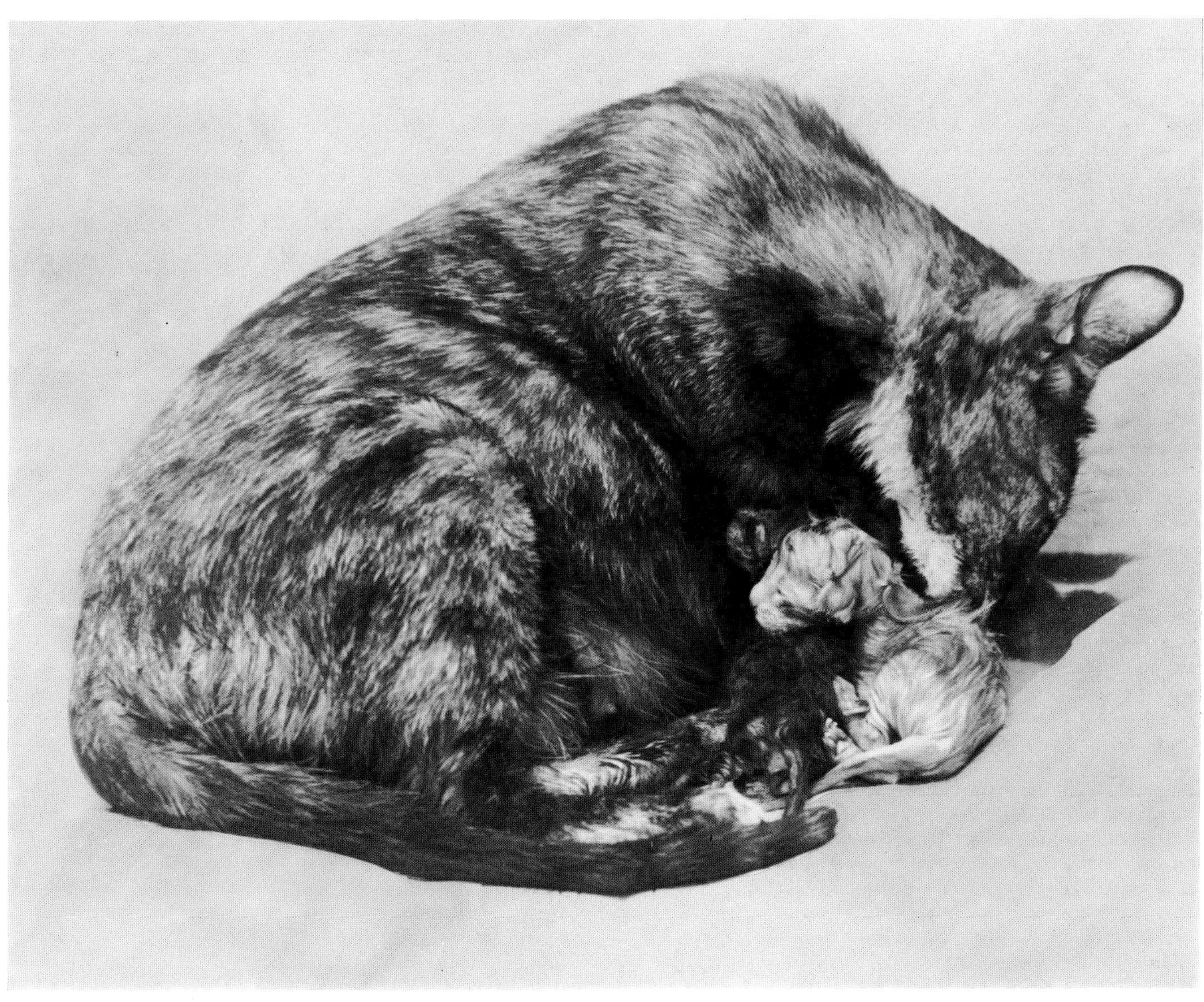

LICKING Licking to dry a new born kitten

Line Breeding see BREEDING

Linognathus setosus see LICE

Lion *Panthera leo* is more variable than is generally accepted. The African lion has thick hair on the mane, shoulders, head, chest and elbows, while the Indian, regarded now as a sub-species, has much less hair on the head and mane, but it is thicker on the chest, elbows and tail. Both species, and both sexes have a thick tuft on the end of their tails. The body colour of both African and Indian lions varies from a pale brownish-fawn to a tawny blue, and the mane varies from tawny brown to black; it may also be intermingled with paler streaks. The cubs are spotted – the Indian ones less so – but this gradually fades with maturity except for some slight spotting on the legs and underparts, the ground colour which is paler than the body. A few very faint lines may be seen on the face and head, and there are dark patches on the lower parts of the back of the ears, which are small and rounded. The head is long and the profile straight. The average male measures about 9 ft long, but may vary from 8–9½, 10 ft being exceptional. It is said by some authorities that the Indian lion is slightly stockier than the African, but both are cats of great beauty and elegance although they vary in weight from 300–400 lb.

In former times the range was continuous from Europe, the Middle East, and through India and Africa, but due to man's relentless persecution it is now found only in 'pockets'; in Africa, south of the Sahara, in western Africa as far west as Liberia, and in eastern Africa. In India, they are now found only in the Gir Forest, a small area near the north-western coast, and at the last counts gave about 290 (Denis 1964) and 280 (Boorer 1969). There do not appear to be any recent counts for Africa.

As the habitat includes much open country they fall easy prey to the hunter.

Their prey is varied and they have been known to kill animals as small as rats but they kill large herbivores such as antelope, gnu, zebra, goats, and they will also feed on carrion.

Panthera leo is the only social cat, and up to thirty may be found living in prides, the study of which is particularly absorbing.

Litter Boxes Litter boxes – or sanitary trays, should be available at all times, even for pet cats which have the use of gardens because when they are boarded out and have to use a tray they are liable to hold back from defecation and urination which can lead to stress and ill-health. A pet cat shut indoors for the night should always be provided with a tray. Allowing breeding stock to foul their runs can lead to serious infection of endemic nature in a cattery.

Sanitary trays are preferably made of polypropylene which can be steam sterilized and which also stands up well to the action of urine and disinfectants. Disposable ones may be used if preferred and are useful for quarantine and boarding establishments, and also for Cat Shows. Suitable trays of either kind may be purchased from most pet stores and cats' accessory agents. In case of emergency a good sized washing-up bowl may be used.

Material for use in trays should be a proprietary brand litter, whitewood shavings, sand or peat moss. Sawdust is ill-advised as it can be ingested causing stomach and intestinal upsets; it also clings to the coats of long-hairs causing matting. In the U.S.A. heat dried clay is the most common product used for the litter tray.

Trays should at all times be kept in the same secluded place and should be changed whenever necessary as after each defecation, or at least morning and night, with thorough cleaning and disinfecting and rinsing once daily. During illness this procedure will of necessity be more frequent.

Little Spotted Cat see TIGER CAT

Liver Inflammation Hepatitis is inflammation of the liver and this condition is always serious as the liver constitutes one of the vital organs of the body. The greater proportion of hepatitis in the cat is of toxic origin. Certain drugs can produce gross inflammatory and degenerative changes in the liver, but a more frequent chronic form of the disease may result from the ingestion of toxic substances from the cat's coat during grooming activities. Parasites may produce hepatitis by their presence within the liver tissue. Viruses and bacteria also affect liver tissue.

Symptoms do not arise unless the greater portion of the liver is affected, as this organ possesses considerable functional reserves. There is usually general dullness, nausea, and there may be digestive upsets with diarrhoea and constipation alternating. The cat is usually intensely depressed and there may be obvious signs of jaundice. There may be spontaneous haemorrhages due to interference with the clotting mechanism of the blood, and occasionally excitement and nervous tremors as a result of failure of the detoxicating powers of the liver.

Treatment depends upon the cause of the condition but in general it is directed towards assisting the liver's own considerable powers of regeneration. Where possible the cause should be removed, glucose added to the diet coupled with the judicious use of drugs such as the corticosteroids, choline, and the amino acid, methionine.

In the chronic cases, the liver cells may be destroyed and replaced by fibrous tissue resulting in cirrhosis or fibrosis of the liver. In these cases, due to the obstruction of the blood flow through the liver, fluid accumulates in the abdominal cavity (see ASCITES) and this symptom together with jaundice is characteristic of cirrhosis. No effective treatment of this condition is available at the present time.

Lockjaw see TETANUS

Longevity see AGEING

Long-haired Cats The first domesticated cats in Great Britain were those with the short fur, and, as far as can be ascertained, it was not until the end of the sixteenth century that cats with long coats were seen in Europe, having been taken there by travellers from Angora, in Turkey, and also later from Persia. These early long-hairs were looked on as great rarities and much prized, but it was not until after the Crystal Palace Cat Show in 1871 that fanciers really became interested in the possibilities of breeding cats to order, and pedigrees were started. The resident short coated cats were not so much favoured as those with the long fur, which rapidly increased in number. The Persians too were preferred to the Angoras (see ANGORA and PERSIAN).

Through selective breeding, the type was improved and more colours were introduced until today in Britain, there are twenty recognized long-haired varieties, basically much the same in type, but varying considerably in the fur colours and the coat patterns.

The Birmans and the Turkish differ slightly in head and body shape, otherwise the standard is much the same for all other varieties. The heads should be round and broad, with space between the small neat ears, the noses short, the cheeks full and the eyes large and round. The bodies should be cobby, massive and low on the leg; the coats long and flowing, with full frills, and the tails short and full. One hundred points are allocated for the required characteristics as set out in the recognized standards. The number of points vary slightly, such as 20 being allowed for the head in the Black, 25 for the Blue and 25 points are allowed for coat colour for the Black, 30 for the Cream, and so on.

LONG-HAIRED CATS Cream Long-hair

Grooming Grooming is all-important for the longhairs and if a cat is always to look at its best, it must be done daily, with time being allowed for this.

Good condition is vital, so that the fur stands up and responds to the brushing and combing. A cat in poor health will have lank, close clinging fur, lacking in lustre.

Grooming varies according to the coat colours. Talcum powder may be used on the lighter coated cats to remove the grease, but is unsuitable for the Blacks and patterned coats. It is best to start when the kitten is about three weeks old, to get it used to being handled, and to encourage the fur to grow the way it should. Only a few minutes a day will be necessary at this age, but at least 15 minutes or longer should be allowed for an adult cat.

If talcum powder is used, it should be sprinkled well into the roots of the fur and brushed and combed right out, with the fur around the head being brushed up to form a frame for the face. The ears and eyes should be inspected daily, with any dirt being carefully wiped away with a little dampened cotton wool. The coat should be inspected for fleas, and if seen, a little insecticide (one recommended as being suitable for cats) should be rubbed into the coat and then brushed out.

The correct brush is important, it should never have harsh or wire bristles that will tear the fur out, but if possible should be of hair. A steel comb with wide teeth is also necessary, and one with narrow teeth to catch the occasional flea.

Some breeders believe in bathing their cats, partilarly the Whites, a few days before a show especially. If this is done, it is best to use a baby shampoo or a shampoo made for cats, never anything too strong. This must be rinsed out completely and the cat kept in the warm, away from draughts until the fur is completely dry, as cats do catch cold very quickly.

Showing Good feeding, first class condition and proper grooming are essential for any cat that is to be shown, but extra attention will be essential for a week or more prior to the show. Over-grooming must be guarded against, particularly of the frill which may be easily pulled out. If the cat is to be bathed, this should be done several days beforehand, to allow the natural grease to return to the coat.

Each cat has a thorough examination by a veterinary surgeon before being allowed into the show hall and may be disqualified should the ears be dirty, if there are signs of fleas in the coat, or if the cat shows the slightest symptoms of any kind. This is not only a safeguard for the other exhibits, but also for the cat, as if it should be a little below par, it may easily pick up some infection.

For a long-haired cat to win at the shows, as well as being as close as possible to the set standard, it should be presented looking as beautiful as possible.

Lore see CAT LORE

Love for Cats see FELINOPHILE

Lucilia sericata see MYIASIS

Lungs see RESPIRATORY ORGANS

Lungworms see Roundworms under WORMS

Luxation, Bilateral see BLINDNESS

Lynx, Bay see BOBCAT

Lynx, Caracal see CARACAL LYNX

Lynx, Northern see NORTHERN LYNX

Lynx Point see SIAMESE, TABBY POINT

Mackerel Striped see TABBY SHORT-HAIR

Mad Itch see PSEUDORABIES

Magpie see BI-COLOURED

Maine Coon The story of the Maine Coon cats of the U.S.A. goes back more than a hundred years when unusual looking cats with long coats were taken by sailors from Turkey to Maine.

These cats mated freely with the resident domestic ones, the result being exceedingly sturdy and powerful-looking animals with thick shaggy coats. Frequently from this mixed breeding, the fur resembled that of the racoon, and so the legend grew, biologically impossible, that they were the result of matings between cats and racoons.

For many years, these highly intelligent cats were much favoured, and still are as neutered pets, with the result that there was little increase in numbers. Comparatively recently, however, more fanciers have taken up this variety, and more and more are appearing at the shows. They now have their own standard, which says that the heads should be medium in width, with longish noses, more like original Angora type. The ears should be big and the large eyes slightly oval in shape. The bodies should be long and muscular and the tails long, full and tapering, but blunt ended. The fine textured coats are not as long as those of most long-hairs and ruffs not so full. The colours are various, ranging from most self-colours to tabby.

Since 1953, in May, at Skowhegan, Maine, a special exhibition is held for these cats, including neuters, when the Maine State Champion Cat of the Year is chosen.

These cats are not yet known in Britain but on the Continent an attempt is being made to breed them.

Maltese The Maltese, also known as the American cat, was a short-haired blue. It was also referred to as the Blue Russian or Archangel cat, but according to some authorities these were entirely different cats. See RUSSIAN BLUE.

In *The Book of the Cat* by Frances Simpson (1903), it was said that 'the Maltese cat has been one of the institutions of the American continent, and there seems to be some grounds for believing the original tradition connected with the name Maltese – that the Maltese cat came from the East and was treasured as something out of the common.'

The colours were light or dark blue, and some cats had white spots on the chest. Apparently the kittens were pure coloured at birth, with no sign of tabby markings, as were seen in the newly-born Russian kittens.

Some had small heads and cobby bodies, but the larger heads and larger bodies were preferred. The fur was not so glossy and lighter in colour than the Blues seen in England at that time.

The name stuck for a great many years, and as recently as 1955 a writer said that the Maltese cat in America was the same as the British Blue in Britain. It is not listed in the standards under that name, but blue is one of the colours given for the American Short-hair, whose type is somewhat similar to that of the British Blue.

Mammary Glands The mammary glands lie in pairs on the underside of the cat's chest and abdomen. They develop in size during pregnancy and, following the birth of kittens, produce milk throughout the period of lactation.

Mange see SKIN DISEASES

Mange, Head see Notoedric Mange under MITES

Mange, Notoedric see MITES

Manners in the House It is more difficult to train cattery reared cats and kittens than those born and reared in the home. Fortunately many breeders now realize this and bring their kittens in daily in order to accustom them to the home environment which is so different from the cattery.

Healthy kittens are naturally clean by instinct, their mothers often guide them to the sanitary tray so this is one of the lesser problems of house manners.

It is advisable to start with the routine that is meant to become the permanent one as an animal can become a mentally disturbed adult if this rule is not strictly observed. If a kitten is allowed to sleep on the bed only when it is small, and banished to another room when it becomes large and adult it can become most unstable.

Cats and kittens should always be fed before the main household mealtimes in order that they do not become a nuisance through begging and crying.

Essential items of equipment for a cat or kitten are a bed, a sanitary tray, a scratching block or post, suitable toys, a travelling basket or box. These items should be kept in the same place so that the kitten knows where to find them and does not become bewildered.

After suitable equipment, a set of suitable training words is necessary. A name should be chosen immediately and quietly spoken while the kitten is being petted. The next words used should be *come here.* Other words – command words – should be *No*!, *Ah*! *Go back*!, *Down*! These should be used in a firm sharp tone. A cat has extremely acute hearing so that shouting should never under any circumstances be resorted to as this will disturb it mentally and it will never make an ideal pet.

Another word which is useful is *Out*? This assists in ascertaining requirements when it cries and it is not known what it wants. The word should be used every time it is let out and it will quickly recognize and connect it with outdoors. The more a cat is talked to the more knowing it will become.

When training a new kitten it should not be allowed to climb up an arm or trousered leg onto a shoulder as it will want to continue when it is adult with disastrous results to clothes and also to its nervous system if suddenly rebuked.

Correctly trained, beautiful cats and beautiful furnishings are complimentary, but a badly trained cat can be a great nuisance.

Manx Unique among all cats is the Manx with its complete lack of tail. A true Manx must be absolutely tailless, with no suspicion of a stump. There should be a decided hollow where in other cats the tail would be. There are many legends concerning their arrival on the Isle of Man, one dating back to the Spanish Armada when, it is said, tailless cats swam ashore from one of the wrecked Spanish vessels at a point now known as Spanish Head. In all probability the taillessness originated as the result of a mutation which was perpetuated through inbreeding in the confined area of a small island.

It is not always possible to breed Manx to order. Two Manx mated together will not necessarily produce tailless kittens, while in the same litter it is possible to have kittens with tails, some with stumps, often referred to as stumpies, and some with no signs of tails, sometimes called rumpies. It is also possible for cats with tails to produce the occasional Manx, providing they carry the necessary gene.

The Manx are usually included in the British

classification, but the heads are slightly larger, the noses a little longer than those of the Britishers and the cheeks very prominent. The ears, which are wide at the base, taper off to points. The eye colouring varies with the coat colours, but in a first class specimen should conform to the colouring of the fur, as given for the British varieties. The coat is all important, in that it should be double, soft and open like that of a rabbit and with a soft thick undercoat. Other important features are the complete taillessness, with the rump being as round as an orange; the height of the hind-quarters and the shortness of the back, with the depth of the flank combining to give the Manx its true rabbity or hopping gait.

In the set standards the points allocated are:

Britain and Europe		*U.S.A.*
15	Taillessness	10
15	Height of hindquarters	—
—	Body	25
15	Shortness of back	5
10	Roundness of rump	—
—	Legs and feet	15
10	Depth of flank	5
10	Double coat	15
10	Head and ears	10
5	Colours and markings	5
5	Eyes	5
5	Condition	5
100		100

The lack of tail appears to have little effect on their capabilities, Manx are still able to climb and jump; their balance seemingly being unaffected.

Care must be taken during the weaning period not to overdo the milk feeds, but once this stage is past, Manx are usually very healthy, most playful, and need no special attention.

There is a steady demand for kittens, and the Isle of Man has now established a breeding cattery, sending kittens all over the world to owners wishing to have one of these delightful and unusual pets. *See colour plate* 36, *page 130*.

Marbled Cat *Felis marmorata* could be described as a smaller edition of the Clouded Leopard. It is a most beautiful cat and as its name suggests it has a 'marbled' coat of very soft texture. The body markings which are large on the back decrease gradually in size until they are seen as spots on the legs; the spots form rings on a long tail which is thicker than in many species. The head has lines running from the eyes to the ears and the top of the head is spotted. The ears are larger than those of the Clouded Leopard, and it has a comparatively finer muzzle. In size it is a little larger than the domestic cat.

Although little is known of this species because of its rarity, it has been found to inhabit the area from Nepal and the slopes of the Himalayas, through Burma and the Malay Peninsula, to Sumatra and Borneo.

MANX *far left* A stumpy; *left* a rumpy

It is thought to feed mainly along river banks and in clearings on the ground although it is a good climber and may easily hunt birds amongst the branches thus avoiding attention.

Margay Cat *Felis wiedi* is very similar to the Ocelot and to the Tiger Cat. An average specimen is about 2 ft in length with a tail of approximately 1 ft. However, the biggest males are said to compare with the Ocelot (Denis 1964) and have a weight of 35 lb. and measure as much as 4 ft in length, of which 20 in. may be tail; females have been recorded up to 3½ ft but they are usually slimmer, with a relatively longer tail. Conversely, a three-year-old Margay may weigh only 3 lb. (Baldwin 1968) and it is stated (Merrell 1963) that an adult is usually no heavier than 13 lb. Clearly, there is much variation in weight and no doubt this makes for confusion in identification.

In colouring it varies also, and may be greyish or tawny ground colour with underparts ranging from white to yellowish. The black markings are well defined and occasionally encircle patches of ground colour. There are horizontal lines across the chest and neck; spotting continues down the legs and paws. The eyes are large, very dark and expressive; there is a conspicuous white streak at the side of the nose – but this does not continue over the eyes – and also under the eyes; the striping from nose to forehead tends to be pear-shaped thus helping to distinguish it from the Ocelot and the Tiger Cat. The ears are more rounded and they have a faint fine dark rim inside but not quite at the edge. Towards the tip of the tail the spots merge together to form wide rings.

As its habitat overlaps that of the other South American spotted cats its habits have been difficult to record, but it is thought to be a good climber and because of its long tail, to feed chiefly on birds taken from the trees.

While there are many recorded stories of it as a pet, there are also very many recorded tragedies and most zoologists strongly advise against people obtaining them for pets.

Marmalade Many of the pet cats seen around with sandy or reddish coloured coats are referred to as 'marmalade cats'. Although most attractive, their colouring and type seldom resembles that of the pure bred pedigree cats with coats of a rich red, mahogany colour.

The marmalade pet cats usually have some form of tabby markings, with bars and stripes, and kittens with this colouring and markings are much liked. When neutered, they make sturdy, strong, home-loving pets.

It is stated quite frequently that all marmalade cats are males. This is often the case but only because they are of very mixed breeding and in the mongrel litters, it is very possible that any marmalade kittens will all be males. In pedigree breeding, with both parents having pure red colouring, both males and females may result.

The Margay Cat, *Felis weidi*

Mastitis This term means inflammation of the mammary glands and, like many inflammatory conditions, it may be acute or chronic in nature. It is almost invariably seen in the breeding queen during lactation. Retention of the milk, following death of offspring during the lactation, often results in mastitis. Mechanical damage to the teat may induce mastitis, since bruising and laceration of the tissues render them extremely susceptible to invasion by disease organisms.

Mastitis is characterized by a rise in temperature, with accompanying symptoms of fever, i.e. loss of appetite, thirst, vomiting and depression. The mammary glands are tense and often very painful. The female resents the kittens sucking. The application of hot fomentations to the mammary glands relieves the discomfort; and the use of antibiotics combats the infection. It is usually necessary to feed the kittens by hand while the mastitis is being cleared unless they have reached the age of 5–6 weeks, when they can conveniently be weaned. If it is hoped that the mother will continue suckling the litter when she has recovered, the glands should be gently stimulated by regularly drawing off some milk – otherwise the secretion may dry up.

Mating see BEHAVIOUR and DUAL MATING

Mau see EGYPTIAN MAU

Meal Frequency In common with many carnivorous species, cats do not require frequent meals, one main meal usually proving sufficient for an adult, healthy cat.

Newly-weaned kittens should have four, small meals per day, as their stomachs are small and large quantities of food are needed to satisfy growth requirements. Two of these should consist of meat or fish and the other two of balanced baby cereals made with milk.

Meat see NUTRITION

Meat, Dehydrated see COMMERCIAL CAT-FOODS

Melaena This is the term used to describe blackened faeces which results from bleeding in the anterior part of the gut.

Mendelism see GENETICS

Meninges, Meningitis Meningitis describes inflammation, of the meninges, the membranes which surround and protect the brain and spinal cord. The disease is serious. It often results in fits, and may necessitate destruction of the animal.

Most cases of meningitis are caused by disease

bacteria gaining access to the meninges. This may occur as a result of serious bite wounds over the spinal cord or by the spread of infectious conditions from tissues adjacent to the central nervous system. For example, severe rhinitis (infection of the nasal chambers) may spread eventually into the anterior part of the brain, and middle ear infection may extend along the auditory nerve to the meniges.

Meningo-coele see BREEDING ABNORMALITIES

Metoestrus see OESTRUS

Mexican Hairless In 1902, a certain Mr Shinick, living in New Mexico, owned a pair of unusual cats with no fur, a brother and sister, which he had obtained from the Indians. He was told that they were the last of the Aztec breed known only in New Mexico. They were valued at 1,000 dollars each.

Pictures show the two cats, completely hairless, with wedge-shaped heads, big ears, long bodies and long whip-like tails. Their bodies were mouse-coloured on the backs and flesh tinted on the stomach and legs. They were said to have very short fur on the back and along the tail in winter, which fell off in warmer weather. Their eyes were amber in colour and their whiskers long. They were never bred, and unfortunately the male was killed by a dog, while still quite young.

Over the years there have been other cats born without fur, but there are no records of their producing similar kittens. In Canada and the U.S.A., however, there is now a variety known as the Sphynx, which is practically hairless except for a faint fuzz and appears to be very like those Mexican cats of long ago. They have now been given a proposed standard, and their appearance at shows attracts a great deal of attention.

Microphthalmia see BLINDNESS and BREEDING ABNORMALITIES

Microsporon canis see RINGWORM

Micturition see URINATION

Milk Cows' milk makes a useful foodstuff for cats, and many of them are fond of cream, which they digest readily. Milk is not, however, essential to a cat's health, as is commonly thought. Some individuals tend to suffer from diarrhoea after drinking milk, and it should not be offered in place of water. Cats given milk but no water tend to drink out of puddles, drains, etc.

Milk may be given by itself or diluted with water. Evaporated, condensed or powdered milk is also generally acceptable. Proprietary lactols, whose formulation comes closer to that of cat's milk than any other product, are particularly useful for lactating queens and growing litters. See also LACTATION and ACID MILK.

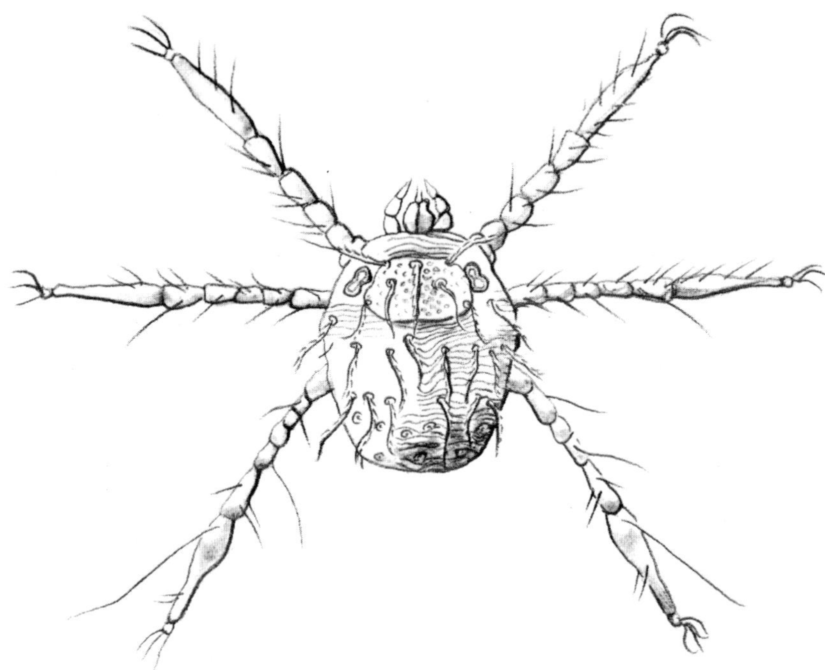

MITES *above* The harvest mite, *Trombicula autumnalis*, infects during the late summer; *far right* a mite, *Otodectes cynotis*, often affecting the ear.

Milliary Dermatitis and **Milliary Eczema** see SKIN DISEASES

Mineral Salts see NUTRITION

Mites Mites belong to the same group of arthropods as spiders, having four pairs of legs in adult life. Several mites affect the skin of the cat.

Cheyletiella Two mites of this genus, *Cheyletiella parasitivorax* and *Cheyletiella yasguri*, are known to infest cats. The infestation appears to cause little discomfort to the affected animal although it may show signs of skin irritation. There is, however, usually a considerable amount of dandruff or scurf in the coat (see DANDRUFF). The mites can infest human contacts where they cause an irritant, papular rash on the inside of the forearms, the chest and the abdomen. The life cycle of the mites appears to be a direct one, the eggs being laid in the depths of the coat, hatching into nymphs and then developing into adults on the affected cat. The mites are sufficiently large to be seen with the naked eye and move about quite actively among the dandruff scales. Treatment is best accomplished by the use of a suitable parasiticidal shampoo. The natural host of the mite is thought to be the rabbit, so contact with rabbits or rabbit infested areas should be eliminated as far as possible to prevent re-infection.

Harvester Infestation Infestation with the Harvest Mite, *Trombicula autumnalis*, occurs quite frequently in cats in certain geographical areas during late summer and autumn. The Harvest Mite is the six-legged larval stage of a Trombiculid mite and is just

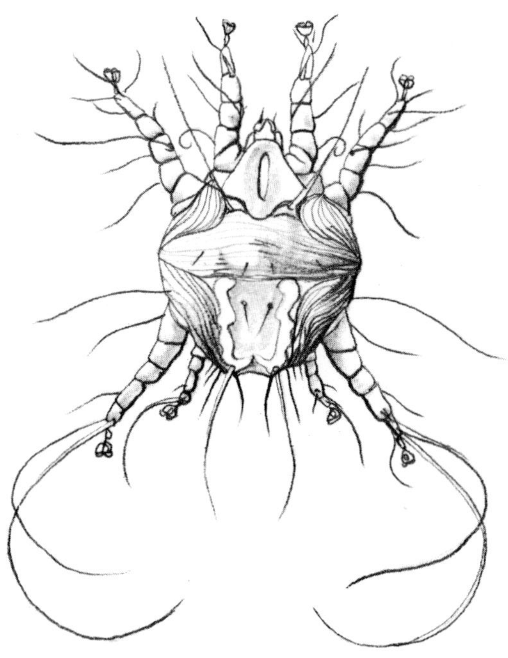

visible to the naked eye, being usually orange-red in colour. The larvae congregate on small clods of earth and on matted vegetation and will attach themselves to any warm-blooded animal with which they come into contact. In the cat the favourite sites are those where the skin is relatively thin and hairless, e.g. between the toes, on the abdomen. The mite feeds by inserting small hooked fangs into the skin. This produces irritation which is often complicated by the reaction of the affected cat in the form of licking and biting of the infected areas. Symptoms of infection are the appearance of raw, moist areas usually surmounted by a hard scab, which are obviously irritable to the cat and in which the mites appear as orange-red bodies. Predilection sites are the head, especially around the ears and the lips, the armpits, the abdomen, the groins and between the toes. Infection occurs during July, August and September and is limited to these months. The treatment is to apply a non-toxic insecticide, such as pyrethrum, derris or sulphur.

Notoedric Mange Notoedric or Head Mange of the cat is caused by a microscopic mite, *Notoedres cati,* which burrows into the skin producing a good deal of skin irritation and inflammation. As the name, Head Mange, implies, the affected areas of skin are usually confined to the head and neck, but the condition may spread from there to involve the remainder of the cat's body. The infection usually commences at the base of the ear where the hair is normally rather sparse. There is loss of hair and the formation of small brownish scales or scabs on the surface of the skin. The irritation produced by the activities of the mites causes the cat to scratch, wash, or rub the head vigorously, giving rise to self-inflicted injury to the skin of the area. Secondary bacterial infection may occur with the formation of pustules and small abscesses. In chronic cases the inflammation causes the skin to become thickened and thrown into corrugations and often a typical mousey odour develops. In a severe case with spread to the rest of the body, the cat can become quite emaciated or even die, probably as the result of toxaemia from the septic skin condition. Treatment is usually effective in the localized form of the disease and consists of the application of a suitable parasiticidal dressing. Dressing usually require repeating at twice weekly intervals on three or four occasions.

Otodectes cynotis Infection of the external ear by the ear mite *Otodectes cynotis* causes a dark brown discharge.

The ear mites can be transmitted from cat to cat or from cat to dog and vice versa. Kittens become infected from the dam, who may herself have only a mild infestation. The mite causes intense irritation and the cat will be seen to flick its ears, shake its head and scratch frenziedly with a hind foot, thereby damaging the ear and allowing the entrance of the pus forming bacteria.

Treatment consists of cleaning out the discharge, which may be softened by a cerumenalytic agent. When the ear has been cleansed the inflammation is treated by soothing antiseptic ointments or lotions and the mites killed by an appropriate parasiticide. Prolonged treatment is usually necessary to clear up the condition, and recurrence is common.

Mongrel Litters The word 'mongrel' comes from the old English, 'monger', to mix. Generally speaking, if two pure-bred animals are mated, the offspring is termed a 'first-cross', 'half breed' or 'cross-bred'. A mongrel is thus: the offspring of a pure-bred and a first-cross' (assuming neither of the latter's parents are of the same breed as the pure-bred); or the offspring of two mongrels; or the offspring of a mongrel and a pure-bred. Occasionally, the offspring of two first-crosses is termed a 'quarter-bred' animal, but it is commoner to call it a mongrel.

One of the constant characteristics of mongrels is that they do not breed 'true', because of their mixed ancestry. Thus if two mongrel cats of similar appearance were mated, it is unlikely that all the members of the first litter would bear a strong resemblance to the parents, and some members may be totally unlike either parent. Even if the offspring of the first litter disobeyed this rule, those of subsequent litters would be likely to give proof of it. Pure-bred cats, on the other hand, produce young which tend to resemble their parents, grandparents and great-grandparents. See also GENETICS.

Mongrel litters are often more difficult to find homes for than are pedigree litters. But in many areas, a notice in the local paper or petshop or post office will bring a number of enquiries. Would-be owners of kittens should be carefully screened to ensure that they will look after their pets carefully. In some places veterinary surgeons, welfare societies or Animal Rescue organizations undertake to help find suitable homes for unwanted mongrel kittens. Despite the fact that mongrel kittens are far easier to place than mongrel pups, it is advisable for owners of mongrel cats to think twice before allowing them to breed. Likewise, owners of pedigree cats should take precautions to ensure that their pets are not mated by the local mongrel tom.

Morphine Morphine, a product manufactured from the opium poppy, is used in man and a number of domestic species as a painkiller and a narcotic. It should, however, never be used in cats, because it has a stimulant, rather than a quiescent effect on them. It is important that human medicines, such as cough mixtures and 'stomach mixtures' should not be given to cats, lest they contain morphine or one of its derivatives.

Moss see PEAT MOSS

Mothering see BEHAVIOUR

Moult In the cat normal fur loss is referred to as a moult. Moulting usually occurs once a year, the coat being shed usually in the spring or autumn, the hair loss taking place in a mosaic pattern as in man, i.e. hair loss takes place indiscriminately from various parts of the body at the same time. Kittens have their first moult at about the age of one year irrespective of the season of the year. Where a moult is excessive, the new coat may be darker in colour, due to temperature changes in the more exposed skin leading to excessive pigment deposition in the skin and the new hair. See also ALOPECIA and BALDNESS.

Mountain Cat *Felis jacobita* is also sometimes referred to as the Andean Cat. Very little is known about it except that it inhabits the mountainous areas of Chile, Peru, Bolivia and Argentina hunting medium-sized rodents, including chinchillas and vizcachas.

The coat colour is greyish-brown with darker markings of streaks and bars down its flanks, it has bands round a rather bushy tail, which can be as long as 1½ ft; the body from nose to the base of the tail can measure 2½ ft.

Mountain Lion see PUMA

Movement Cats are among the most graceful of animal movers. Their numerous gaits vary from a sedate walk to a casual canter which can so rapidly develop into an explosive movement forward if their prey is near. The ability of cats to climb depends in part to the tremendous momentum they achieve on the horizontal plane before changing to the vertical and in part on the sharply curved retractable claws.

When stalking their prey cats become the personification of power controlled. Each movement is slow and flowing while the fur appears to flow like fluid across the surface. Such controlled movement can in an instant be transformed into a terrifying projectile as the prey is seized. Horrifying yet fascinating is the hunting cat.

Muscles Muscles are composed of specialized fibres which possess the power to contract in length in response to a nervous stimulus. There are three types of muscle tissue found in the body:

1. Voluntary, striped, striated muscle which is under the voluntary control of the animal.

2. Involuntary, smooth or unstriated muscle which carries out functions not under voluntary control, e.g. muscle of the intestinal and blood vessel walls.

3. Cardiac muscle which is specialized for the functions of the heart and is unique in possessing an inherent power of rhythmic contraction.

The term muscles is usually employed to denote the skeletal muscles which afford the animal the power of movement by their contraction and relaxation. These muscles clothe the skeleton and play an important part in the determination of the form and contours of the animal. They are under voluntary control and are usually attached to the two bones forming a joint. The muscles that straighten or extend a joint are known as Extensors, whilst those that bend or flex joints are Flexors. Muscles that move the limb away from the body are Abductors and those that move the limb towards the body Adductors. For descriptive purposes the muscle attachments are divided into Origins and Insertions. The origin is fairly fixed and is usually the attachment nearest the midline of the body. The insertion is movable and is usually furthest away from the midline. Muscles arise from their origin by a fibrous attachment but are secured at their point of insertion by a specialized cord of fibrous tissue, the tendon. A muscle may have more than one origin and insertion.

Mutton Mutton contains considerably more fat than does lamb, but cats can tolerate very high levels of fat in the diet and still maintain health, so that mutton is a useful food, except in some disease conditions. If mutton is purchased specifically for consumption by the household cat, it is best boiled, but the remains of roast leg of mutton are very acceptable and quite suitable. In cases where cats have dermatitis thought to be associated with a diet of beef, a changeover to mutton and lamb sometimes effects a cure. It should, however, be remembered that not all skin abnormalities are caused by dietary factors.

Mycobacterium lepraemurium see LEPROSY

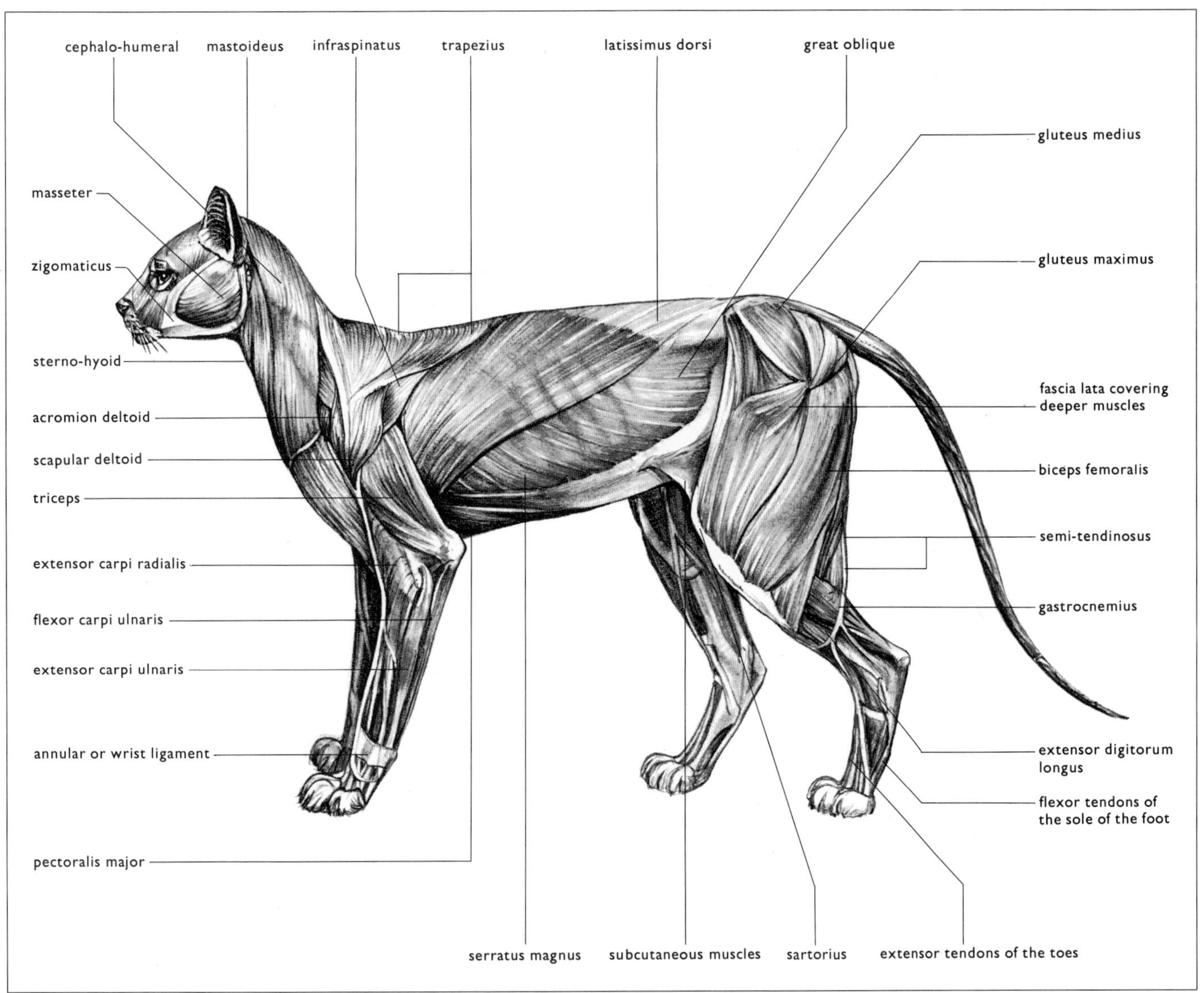

Muscles of the cat

Mycobacterium tuberculosis see TUBERCULOSIS and Tubercular Peritonitis under PERITONITIS.

Myiasis Myiasis or Blow-fly Strike is a condition in which the blow-fly (*Lucilia sericata*) lays its eggs on the fur and skin of the cat. This usually occurs in the older cat, which is not very active, or in areas which are badly soiled with urine or faeces. The usual sites are around the anus, infected wounds or abscesses, and occasionally the conjunctival sac of the eye, particularly where there has been a chronic discharge from the eye. The larvae or maggots which hatch from the eggs feed initially from the skin surface but later burrow their way into the tissues causing severe inflammation and an eating away of the flesh. Symptoms of the condition depend to some extent upon the site of infection but usually the cat is restless, shows discomfort or even pain, and there is a characteristic odour emanating from the sites of maggot activity. Often the affected cat will rapidly become quite seriously ill and even after the maggots have been removed the damaged skin areas take a considerable time to heal. This is probably due to the action of the digestive enzymes secreted by the larvae during feeding. In the case of eye infection, there is obvious irritation with a fairly profuse occular discharge and the maggots can easily be seen moving about in the conjunctival sac. Treatment is to remove the larvae and this may necessitate general anaesthesia. The affected skin should be clipped over a wide area, thoroughly cleansed and all maggots searched for and removed with forceps. Antibacterial cream containing the parasiticide, gamma benzene hexachloride, are useful in preventing further fly-strike and help to kill any larvae which may have escaped removal. Once the maggots are removed from the eye the irritation soon clears.

Nailbed The nailbed is the name given to the tissues in which the upper end of the claw is inserted. It consists of hairless skin which lines the depression in which the claw is situated, and is continuous with the wall of the claw at the point where the latter originates from the digit. It is somewhat elastic, enabling the claw to be retracted and extended by voluntary muscular action. Because it has a folded surface, the nailbed is prone to fungal infections, and these can sometimes be quite hard to clear, because of the problems of penetrating the nailbed with topical antifungal agents.

Needles Needles may become lodged in the skin and feet of a cat, or they may sometimes be swallowed, and penetrate structures in the mouth, pharynx or oesophagus. Removal of needles from the superficial tissues is relatively straight-forward, since it involves restraining the patient and withdrawing the needle as smoothly and quickly as possible. It is best to seek veterinary advice after the event as antibiotics may be indicated. There is not usually much haemorrhage associated with these cases, even the perforation of large vessels causing little bleeding because of the shape of the needle and a natural tendency for the hole in the blood vessel wall to seal. Withdrawal of a needle from the mouth or pharynx is a more skilled procedure, although cat-owners may well be able to accomplish it provided the patient is reasonably tractable. The cat's mouth should be held open in the same way as for the administration of a tablet, and the needle pulled out gently, using pliers, eyebrow tweezers or similar gripping instruments, or even the fingers. Antibiotic treatment is again indicated, and if extensive laceration has occurred, the patient should be kept on soft foods for a few days. The usual reason for needles lodging in the alimentary tract is that cats chew pieces of cotton, silk and wool in play, start to swallow them and the needle attached at the end is pulled into the mouth. Needles that lodge in the deeper tissues and lower down in the alimentary canal, should, of course, be extracted by veterinarians, since general anaesthesia and full surgical techniques are often required, as well as the use of X-ray to locate the needle.

Neofelis nebulosa see CLOUDED LEOPARD

Neonatal This term describes the period immediately after birth. A neonatal kitten is a new born kitten. Neonatal disease includes the failing kitten syndrome in which kittens begin to fail, appearing sick and weakly and eventually die. Several causes of the problem have been identified. Veterinary attention is essential.

Neoplasia Neoplasia literally means the formation of new tissue but is generally used to denote tumour or cancer formation. A neoplasm may be benign or malignant. A benign neoplasm is one which grows slowly and does not spread from its original site of growth. A malignant neoplasm grows rapidly, infiltrates neighbouring tissues, and spreads to other parts of the body via the blood stream.

Neoplasia is quite common in cats. Unfortunately about three-quarters of the neoplasms of the cat are malignant in nature. Five of the body systems comprise the origin of almost 90% of feline neoplasms, namely the alimentary system, the skin, the lymphoid system, the female reproductive system and the bones, over half the tumours originating in the alimentary system and the skin.

In the alimentary system, neoplasia is almost always malignant in type. The upper alimentary tract, i.e. the mouth and its contents, and the oesophagus, is affected almost entirely by carcinomas (tumours of epithelial tissue), whilst in the intestine the majority of tumours are lymphosarcomas (see LEUKAEMIA). Neoplasia of the stomach is exceedingly rare in the cat unlike man. In the skin the important tumours are the carcinoma and the sarcoma. The lymphoid system is the site of origin of the lymphosarcoma, whilst the female reproductive system is mainly represented by the mammary gland, which is a frequent site of carcinoma formation. The bones are mainly affected with sarcomas and these tumours originate chiefly in the bones of the forelimbs, the hindlimbs and the remainder of the skeleton in about equal numbers.

Symptoms of neoplasia will obviously vary a great deal depending upon the site of and type of tumour.

Treatment of neoplasia in the cat is mainly confined to surgical removal where practicable. A little work has been done on X-ray therapy, but this type of treatment is not yet widely available chiefly because of economic reasons. Cytotoxic therapy has also been used in a restricted number of cases.

Neoplasia of the bone see BONE DISORDERS

Neoplasia of the larynx see LARYNX

Nephritis The type of nephritis most commonly encountered is Chronic Interstitial Nephritis, to which this account is confined.

The disease is seen in ageing cats. Signs of chronic interstitial nephritis are weight loss, which is spread over a period of time, staring and sparse coat, excessive thirst, increased urinary frequency, and fluctuations in appetite. Ulceration of the mouth may also occur. In severe cases, digestive disturbances such as vomiting and diarrhoea, changes in the appearance of the eye and halitosis (bad breath) will also be observed.

Treatment of the condition is aimed at a general improvement in the state of the patient and slowing of the course of the disease; cure is impossible. The owner of the cat has an important part to play in the day-to-day therapy, which includes the provision of sufficient water (except in cases where drinking provokes bouts of vomiting), and the feeding of a special diet that contains just enough high-quality protein to replace that broken down by normal body processes. Control of the environmental temperature and ensuring that the patient lives an undisturbed existence and receives plenty of affection are also extremely helpful. In some cases, dental attention is also required.

In spite of treatment nephritis is often the terminal condition of many pet cats.

Nervousness Cats vary considerably in temperament: a great deal depends on their early upbringing. Animals which have been brought up away from human beings tend to be apprehensive in their company. Careful and gentle patient handling can considerably improve the situation, but can rarely completely cure nervousness.

The most successful pets are produced by the constant company of several human beings who show constant affection.

Nictitating Membrane see EYE ANATOMY

Neoplasms of the mammary glands

NURSING *left* A kitten should be firmly held when feeding it by hand

Nipples see TEATS

Northern Lynx *Felis lynx* is a most exotic animal and consequently it is ruthlessly exploited for its beautiful, soft, long fur, which is a mixture of tawny yellow shading to cream on the underparts. The spotting is often evanescent and together with the long guard hairs of silvery-white, its appearance is almost ethereal. The ears are long and buff-brown with white spots and slender black tufts. The tip of the tail is black – unlike the Bobcats'. There are also some very rare blue 'dilute' specimens. The total length is about 3–4 ft, and the largest is reputed to weigh about 40 lb.

Distribution originally included all the temperate forests of the Northern Hemisphere, but the advance of civilization, the destruction of its natural cover and the exploitation has resulted in its disappearance from many of its former haunts. It is still relatively common in Alaska, and a few still exist in Northern New England, the Adirondack Mountains, N.Y. and on the U.S. side of the Great Lakes. A few also may be found in Spain and Portugal and parts of Scandinavia, Poland, the Balkans and Sardinia, but they are rapidly diminishing.

A nocturnal animal found in dense forest or thick bush on mountain-sides its prey consists of animals varying in size from roe deer to mice also skunks, foxes and game birds.

Nose The nose consists of the nasal cavities, which link the nostrils and the pharynx. It acts during respiration as a passage for air as well as constantly monitoring the air passing through it for odours. Furthermore, the nose acts as a bacterial filter, helping to protect the lower respiratory tract from infection. The nostrils are two small apertures situated on the end of the muzzle. The nasal chambers contain special delicate, scroll shaped bones, covered by a fine moist layer of tissue known as the nasal mucous membranes. Small hairlike structures or cilia situated on these membranes beat continuously to keep a layer of mucous moving across them. The mucous helps to trap bacteria. The membranes also serve to warm and moisten incoming air before it enters the lungs. See also RESPIRATORY ORGANS.

Notoedres cati see Notoedric Mange under MITES

Notoedric Mange see MITES

Novice see ANY OTHER COLOUR

Nursing Nursing is, in spite of modern drugs, still a very important adjunct to therapy. Nursing requirements vary considerably with different disease conditions and these will be prescribed by the

colour 39 Scottish Fold, fath
and daughter
overleaf 40 Siamese Blue Point
41 Siamese Chocolate Point
42 Siamese Lilac Poin

veterinarian. There are, however, general principles which can be applied to all cases. Cats should be kept warm and given soft clean comfortable beds. They should be kept clean and groomed. Eyes and nose should be kept free from discharge and the mouth wiped when necessary. Food should be varied and nutritious with particularly tempting items on the menu, but it should never be forced into animals. Careful observations should be made by the persons responsible for nursing, recorded and communicated to the veterinarian. Temperature recordings made twice daily are extremely useful in judging progress. See also INVALIDS.

Nursing Queen Diet see under NUTRITION

Nutrition Food of plant or animal origin is composed of varying proportions of proteins, fats, carbohydrates, vitamins and mineral salts with amounts of water varying from 10% in dry foods (biscuit meal etc.) to 90% in liquid milk. Food provides a definite amount of energy (calories) when utilized in the body.

The food of herbivores consists of the whole or parts of plants, while the food of carnivores consists of the whole or parts of animals. Omnivores consume both plants and animals. The cat is a true carnivore, adapted to eating whole carcasses of small rodents, birds and their eggs, young herbivores, lizards, frogs, fish, grasshoppers and other insects as and when available.

Proteins are manufactured from amino acids. Like the letters in a word and the words in a sentence, the amino acids are arranged in a definite pattern which gives the protein its characteristic features, peculiar to each species and even to each individual organism. To utilize food proteins the cat must break them down by means of enzymes secreted in the digestive tract, so that the liberated amino acids can be absorbed by the cells lining the small intestine. This is highly efficient in the healthy cat on a good diet, only 5% of the protein consumed being lost in the faeces. Normally the cells lining the intestine are replaced every three to five days. Amino acids from digested proteins are carried in the blood stream to the liver and to other organs of the body, where they pass into the cells and are rebuilt into proteins characteristic of the individual cat. Breakdown products of nitrogen (protein) metabolism (urea, creatinine, uric acid) are excreted via the kidney, dissolved in the urine. This obligatory daily loss, and the loss of skin, hair, cells lining the alimentary canal etc., must be made good from the proteins supplied in the food, otherwise the cat will lose weight.

Carbohydrates These comprise sugars, starches, celluloses and glycogens, and form a large group of important structural and reserve materials in plants. Cooked starches and some sugars are converted by the digestive enzymes of the cat into simpler sugars, mainly glucose. Under the influence of insulin, glucose is stored in the liver and muscles and is used to provide energy. Consequently blood sugar falls, insulin output is reduced and fresh supplies of glucose are released from the liver glycogen store, keeping the blood sugar around 0·1%.

colour 43 Siamese Red Point

Fats Fats or lipids are esters of fatty acids which form structural, reserve and messenger substances in the cat's body. Digestion of fats involves emulsification with bile salts, hydrolysis by pancreatic enzymes and active absorption by the cells lining the small intestine. Digestion of fat is very efficient in the cat, 95% of the fat in food being absorbed. Failure to absorb fat is evidenced by pale, bulky, evil smelling stools, and is the result of malfunction of either liver, pancreas or small intestine. Some adipose tissue is essential to the cat, cushioning vulnerable organs such as the kidney from vibration, and forming a blanket insulator beneath the skin. But excessive adipose tissue is a burden, the extra weight having to be supported by the skeleton and moved from one place to another by the same muscles that produce locomotion in a normal sized cat. Damage to the walls of blood vessels (atherosclerosis) is associated with excessive fat, and a strain is placed on the heart, which has to pump additional blood to supply the extra tissue.

Vitamins Vitamins are an unrelated group of organic compounds conveniently divided into fat-soluble A, D, E and F, and water soluble B complex and C and K. They are accessory food factors essential for metabolic processes, which the animal is unable to manufacture for itself. If vitamins are lacking in food, deficiency diseases appear. However, vitamins are only needed in very small quantities and excess can, in some cases, be as damaging as deficiency. The individual requirements for particular vitamins vary between species, between varieties, between individuals and even at different stages in the life history of one individual. The casual addition of vitamins to the diet is to be deplored, whether by owners or by pet-food manufacturers. Proper fortification of compounded foods requires considerable technical knowledge.

Mineral Salts These are relatively simple chemical substances, consisting of fairly small molecules, and usually being made up of two or three elements. A number of them are present in foodstuffs, and are essential to health. Metallic elements, which are present in the form of salts such as phosphates and chlorides, include sodium, potassium, calcium, magnesium and iron. Non-metals include chlorine, phosphorus, carbon and sulphur. 'Trace' elements – i.e. those needed only in very small quantities – are copper, cobalt, zinc, manganese, iodine and fluorine. Certain foodstuffs are renowned for being rich in specific minerals, for example, milk and bones (calcium and phosphorus), fish (magnesium), liver and red meat (iron), salt (sodium, chlorine). Where mineral deficiency is suspected, a good vitamin/mineral supplement may be added to the diet on veterinary advice. Any excess or disproportion in the amounts of minerals fed can cause disease conditions.

Deficiency Diseases Deficiency diseases are those in which the cause is a deficiency of some constituent of the diet. Total deficiency of food, i.e. starvation, is the most severe deficiency disease and results in emaciation, lack of growth, weakness and eventual death. Less severe deficiency diseases include:

Protein Deficiency Protein deficiency can easily occur in the young kitten which requires a relatively high protein diet. Symptoms of deficiency are cessation of growth, loss of weight, oedematous swelling of the limbs and ascites due to the low serum protein levels. In the adult cat, protein deficiency leads to loss of weight chiefly due to muscle wastage, although affected animals often have quite appreciable reserves of fat.

Calcium Deficiency Calcium deficiency is quite often seen mainly in the growing kitten, because of the prevalent habit of owners feeding such kittens on meat or fish from which all the bones have been removed. Such deficiency occurs especially in the Siamese breed where the defect is compounded by the kitten preferring water to milk. Affected kittens grow well at first and have good, thick coats. After a time, however, they become quiet, cease to play preferring to lie in a dark corner or in their bed, and resent being moved about. The bones become very thin and fragile and fractures may occur following a minor fall. Fractures of the spine may produce paralysis and there may be convulsion due to low serum calcium levels. These convulsions sometimes result in spontaneous fractures of the limbs. If the condition has not advanced too far then it can be corrected by the administration of calcium either in the food or by injection.

Iodine Deficiency Iodine deficiency may occur where the cat is fed a mainly meat diet. Affected kittens cease to grow and show a sparse coat with a rather thickened skin. There may be swelling of the head due to oedema (fluid in the skin). The animal is slow moving, gentle and affectionate. Sexual activity may not occur at puberty but less severely affected queens may conceive and carry the litter to term, when they may have difficulties in kittening and show a tendency to produce kittens with open eyes and cleft palates (see BREEDING).

Vitamin A Deficiency Vitamin A deficiency is probably more common in the cat than is generally realized, as many of the usual foodstuffs of the cat's diet, with the exception of liver, are rather low in their content of vitamin A. Symptoms of deficiency are loss of weight due to muscle wastage, poor coat with rough, scaly patches on the skin, conjunctivitis with reddish staining of the fur in the corners of the eyes, dryness and inflammation of the cornea of the eye (keratitis), fear of light (photophobia), failing vision, infertility, abortions around the fiftieth day, and kittens with nervous defects such as deafness, ataxia (staggering gait), intention tremors and spasticity of the limbs due to over-growth of the bones of the skull and the spinal column. An excess of vitamin A is just as damaging as a deficiency resulting in a crippling overgrowth of the bones of the neck with resultant pressure on the spinal nerves.

Vitamin D Deficiency Vitamin D deficiency is rare in the cat as the requirement for this vitamin is remarkably small in this species. Deficiency may cause rickets in the growing kitten with bowed legs and swollen joints.

Vitamin E Deficiency Deficiency of vitamin E may result from the feeding of certain types of fish or excessive amounts of cod liver oil. The deficiency causes the condition known as 'Steatitis' or 'Yellow Fat Disease', in which a yellow-brown or orange pigment is deposited in the fat around the shoulders and in the abdomen, causing the fat to become very firm to touch. Affected kittens lose their appetite, become very quiet and apparently have difficulty in moving around.

Vitamin B^1 Deficiency Vitamin B^1 or Thiamin deficiency occurs in the cat as a result of feeding a diet in which the vitamin has been inactivated by processing or by the action of thiaminase, an enzyme present in the tissues of certain fish. Symptoms are loss of appetite and weight, inflammation of the peripheral nerves (neuritis) with pain in the limbs and an exaggerated response to touch (hyperaesthesia), heart disorders, and convulsion due to haemorrhages in the brain.

Vitamin B^6 Deficiency Vitamin B^6 or Pyridoxine may be destroyed by heat during canning, so deficiency may occur in cats fed on a tinned diet. Symptoms are loss of appetite and weight, convulsions, anaemia, kidney disease and stone formation in the urinary tract.

Nicotinic Acid Deficiency Deficiency of this vitamin leads to diarrhoea, loss of weight with severe emaciation, ulceration of the tongue followed by death within a period of about three weeks.

Meat Meat is the skeletal muscle of food animals, usually herbivores. In addition cats obtain 'meat' from rats, mice and birds. Butcher's fresh lean meat consists of about 20% protein of high biological value, 5% fats mainly saturated, 1% mineral ash and 74% water. Cheap cuts may have 20% or more fat. Fresh meat is highly acceptable to the cat, useful in tempting a fickle appetite, but cats will not eat stale or tainted meat. In the past whale meat, similar in composition to butcher's meat, has been extensively used by the canning industry for cat foods. Meat supplies all the essential amino acids needed by the cat, and the fat is a good source of energy. Fresh meat is a good source of the B vitamins – thiamine, nicotinic acid and riboflavine. Iron in meat is available to the cat. Carcass meat when fed as the sole item of diet results in deficiency of calcium, iodine and vitamin A, deficiencies which can be made good by appropriate additions during processing or by feeding a mixed diet containing bone salts, bone meals or bones, liver etc., as well as meat.

Fish Fish contain about 10% protein of high biological value, and the fat percentage ranges from 1% in whitefish to 8–15% in oily fish. Fishroes are high in protein – 20–25% in the case of cod and herring roe. The fat-soluble vitamins A and D are found in all fish species in fairly large amounts. Fish are not, however, a particularly good source of minerals unless the bones are consumed. Fish on the whole contains more iodine than mammal or bird flesh. A number of fish species contain an enzyme called thiaminase, which destroys any thiamin (see VITAMIN B[1] DEFICIENCY) which may be present in the food. Thiaminase, however, is destroyed by cooking. Tuna fish should not be fed in large quantities, as it contains oils that oxidize very readily, thus destroying vitamin E present in the flesh. Consequently, unless supplementary sources of vitamin E are fed, a diet of pure tuna may result in diseases associated with vitamin E deficiency.

Pregnancy Diet Pregnancy in the cat lasts approximately nine weeks. It will not be necessary to modify the diet during the first four or five weeks of pregnancy, and pregnancy diagnosis is not usually made until three weeks after the animal has been mated. It is, however, advisable to give a varied but balanced diet during this period. Towards the end of the fifth week, the quantity of food given should begin to increase. It is preferable to feed two small meals daily rather than one large one. The amounts given should be steadily increased until the cat is having up to twice its normal daily intake at the end of the seventh week.

It has been found that the feeding of generous quantities of high quality protein (e.g. red meat) during pregnancy prevents the breeding queen from losing condition after kittening. In the last ten days or so of pregnancy, the feeding of carbohydrates to the mother will help build up food reserves in the kittens.

A good vitamin/mineral supplement will help to ensure that the queen receives all the substances essential for the health and that of the kittens.

Nursing Queen Diet It has been found from research that the greatest nutritional requirements of a breeding queen occur during the latter part of lactation, particularly if the litter is large. The nursing queen should have up to twice as much food as she would normally receive during the first two weeks of lactation, and this quantity should be gradually increased until the end of the fifth week. The owner should aim to wean the kittens by the time they are six weeks old. It is important that the queen has access to water at all times. Useful foods during lactation include milk, fish, eggs and good quality meat. A vitamin/mineral supplement may be beneficial, but should only be given on veterinary advice.

Invalid Diet Generally speaking, the same rules apply to feeding invalid cats as to feeding human patients. The food should be bland, plain and lightly cooked, preferably by boiling or poaching. Fried foods should not be offered. Dishes should be scrupulously clean, and small amounts should be given at frequent intervals. Plenty of fluids, e.g. water, glucose solution or barley-water should be available at all times, unless the veterinary surgeon advises otherwise.

Nystagmus Nystagmus is a side-to-side flicking of the eyes. It usually occurs as a result of brain damage and is a common sequence of concussion.

Congenital nystagmus is incurable.

Obesity Obesity refers to excessive body weight of a degree sufficient to cause interference with the normal bodily functions and be a danger to health. An obese cat cannot easily lose excess heat from its body because the fat layers act as insulation. The extra weight puts a strain on the limbs, causing a decrease in the amount of exercise taken voluntarily by the cat. This in turn reduces bowel tone and tends to cause sluggish circulation. Fatty infiltration of organs such as the liver and kidneys may occur, impairing their function. They are more likely to suffer diseases such as atherosclerosis and arteriosclerosis. Obesity increases the risk for surgical work, and difficulties are encountered when incising and suturing as a result of the fat.

A number of different factors may be responsible for obesity. Neutering has been implicated without factual evidence. Straightforward overfeeding is without doubt the most important cause of obesity. Since many pets express obvious pleasure at receiving food, the inevitable reward to owners precipitates more feeding. Diseases such as thyroid disorders are very rarely a cause of obesity.

Special commercial diets containing very small quantities of carbohydrate are now available for obese cats. Unfortunately cats do not always take readily to a new diet. Reduction in the quantities of the diet to which a cat is accustomed is the only means of reducing weight. A modest, but constant weight loss should be achieved, ½% of the cat's total bodyweight per day representing a reasonable reduction. It is advisable to keep a record of the animal's weight at least once a week. As the total weight gradually falls, the daily intake of food will require to be altered, so that veterinary examination of the animal will be needed at intervals to re-evaluate the case. Dieting should be undertaken on veterinary advice and under the supervision of a veterinarian.

Ocelot *Felis pardalis* is one of the most beautifully marked cats and so unfortunately its fur has great commercial value: because of this it is in very grave danger of becoming extinct.

The distinctively spotted coat has a background colour varying from greyish-beige to cinnamon; the

The Ocelot, *Felis pardalis*

spots are elongated and border a deep buff centre. The ground colour of the sides of the body is paler than the back and the underparts are cream. The head has two straight dark lines which run from the sides of the nose to the top of the forehead, which is spotted and there are two stripes on each cheek, the whisker pads and chin are cream and there are four or five parallel stripes on the neck. The upper side of the tail is marked with dark blotches. Colouring varies from one area to another.

The Ocelot measures about 4 ft including the tail which may be about 12–15 in. A large male may weigh up to 35 lb., the females being about a fifth less.

Distribution ranges from the extreme south of the U.S.A., where it is now almost extinct, through the tropics to Ecuador and Northern Argentina. An excellent climber it spends much of its time resting in branches of trees but hunts mostly on the ground, its prey varying from small to medium sized rodents, opossum, deer fawns, tree lizards and snakes; it has also been known to kill lambs and young calves, and being a good swimmer, fish may also form part of the diet.

Reputed to be reasonably docile in captivity, it often sleeps with its owner, but the degree of docility depends greatly on the understanding of animal psychology and the fact that it is nocturnal, and play has been known to suddenly turn into attack.

Ocicat Developed in the first place in the U.S.A., from a kitten which appeared as a result of a cross-mating between a Chocolate-pointed Siamese male and a cross-bred Abyssinian-Siamese female, this variety has now been produced in two colours, Dark and Light Chestnut. Both have short silky fur of pale cream, with the former having dark chestnut spotting and the latter spots milk chocolate in colour. Both too have tabby markings on the throat, legs and tail, and golden eyes. Championship status has not yet been granted.

This variety is as yet unknown in Britain and on the Continent few breeders have taken them up.

Odd-eyed White see WHITE LONG-HAIR and WHITE SHORT-HAIR

Oedema This refers to the accumulation of fluid in the tissues. See ANAEMIA and Oedema of the Larynx under LARYNX DISORDERS.

Oesophagus Disorders The oesophagus is subject to bacterial and viral infection, to obstruction and neoplasia.

Bacterial and viral infection is usually seen in cats that have previously suffered from similar infections in the respiratory passages. The organisms migrate from the nose via the pharynx and so enter the oesophagus. If the inflammatory condition of the oesophagus is severe, bleeding, difficulty in swallowing, pain and regurgitation of foodstuffs may be apparent.

Oesophageal obstruction is sometimes seen in kittens suffering from a congenital defect known as persistent right aortic arch. Food is regurgitated after each meal. The condition is corrected by surgery.

Neoplasms may compress the oesophagus from the outside, or develop within the oesophagus wall causing partial or complete blockage.

Oestrus Strictly speaking the term oestrus means the period of the reproductive cycle when the female will accept the male, but it is more generally used to denote the whole of the oestrous or heat period. The latter can actually be divided into:

1. Pro-oestrus – the stage in which the ovarian follicles are ripening and which covers the courtship period (see BEHAVIOUR).
2. Oestrus – the stage of acceptance of the male.
3. Metoestrus – the stage which gradually merges into pregnancy if conception occurs.
4. Anoestrus – the period when the female is sexually quiescent.

The different stages outlined above can be distinguished by an examination of the cells obtained by a vaginal smear technique, but for practical purposes, sufficient information can usually be derived from careful study of the cat's behaviour.

Oil see Dangerous Liquids under ACCIDENTS

Olive Oil This is a vegetable oil, and is produced by crushing white olives. It has a number of uses in the cat.

1. *Dietary Supplement* Because it is a good source of vitamins and fats, olive oil is often added to the diet, and helps to promote a shiny coat.
2. *Aperient* A number of cat-owners use olive oil to promote regularity. Since it is utilized as a food, however, its effectiveness is doubtful. Liquid paraffin is more useful.
3. *Cleansing Agent* Warm olive oil is a useful agent for cleaning mildly soiled ears. It may also be used for floating foreign bodies out of the eye in an emergency.

Orange-eyed White see WHITE LONG-HAIR and WHITE SHORT-HAIR

Orphaned Kittens see FOSTER MOTHER

Os Penis This is a small tunnel-shaped bone which resides in the penis of the cat, and through which passes the urethra, the tube carrying urine from the bladder to the outside. It is one of the important factors in precipitating urethral obstruction in the cat, since being bone it is rigid and will not expand to allow the passage of large pieces of sand – see

Bladder Sand under BLADDER DISORDERS.

Osteomyelitis Osteomyelitis is comparatively common. It tends to occur in the 'long' bones – the femur, humerus, tibia and fibula and radius and ulna, and usually affects the shafts rather than the joints. One of the most frequent causes of osteomyelitis is the introduction of infective organisms by a deep bite. Generally only the most superficial parts of the bone are affected, but sometimes organisms may be carried by the blood that supplies the bone into the central cavity of the bone. Infection of the bone marrow may have serious consequences. The condition is painful. The temperature is usually slightly elevated. X-ray techniques may help to diagnose the condition. Treatment consists of resting the limb together with antibiotic therapy. See also BONE DISORDERS.

Otitis see EAR DISORDERS

Otodectes cynotis see MITES

Ounce see SNOW LEOPARD

Outcrossing see BREEDING

Ovary Disorders Ovarian disorders are uncommon in the cat however ovarian cysts may arise. These affect the cat's behaviour. It behaves as if it were constantly in oestrus which is extremely trying for the owners. A cat with cystic ovaries rarely conceives following mating. Surgical removal of the ovaries is the only effective treatment.

Occasionally sexual behaviour persists in spayed cats. This may be due to small fragments of ovary having been accidentally left in the abdomen at the time of the operation, or because the adrenal glands have started to produce female sex hormones.

Ovariohysterectomy see SPAYING

Overalls see COATS

Overweight see OBESITY

Pads The pads are areas of thickened, horny skin on the feet which enable the cat to walk on comparatively rough surfaces without injury. There is one pad on the undersurface of each digit, and a fifth pad behind the digits, corresponding to the 'heel' of the human hand. All these pads contact the ground during movement. There is a sixth pad, the 'stopper' pad on the rearward-facing surface of the foreleg, a short distance above the paws.

Injury to the pads is comparatively rare, but glass splinters, thorns, caustic chemicals and hot surfaces may cause damage. The pads can also be made sore as the result of long journeys undertaken on foot after a move of house by the owners. Epsom salts (magnesium sulphate crystals) may be used in solution for bathing the pads in order to harden them, should this be desirable when minor cuts and soreness occur. See also PAWS.

Pain Perhaps one of the most difficult problems for the veterinarian is to decide when an animal is in pain. Pain, being subjective, is difficult to identify and quantify objectively. Realistically one decides on the degree of pain by comparison with humans suffering the same degree of injury or disease and by careful observation of an animal's behaviour. The ability to feel pain depends on the development of the nervous system and it seems unlikely that an earthworm can feel pain as intensely as higher animals. The cat, however, being a mammal fairly high in the evolutionary scale, undoubtedly feels pain in a similar way to man and should be given the benefit of any doubt. Care should be used when administering pain killers to cats. See MORPHINE.

Pallas's Cat *Felis manul* is described as having two distinct coat colours; one predominantly silvery-grey and due to the fur on the back being black at the base and tip, with white in the middle, and the other a basically orange-brown. Both types have grey foreheads with black spots and white and black rings round the eyes. The most remarkable feature of this cat is the very low forehead and the wide spaced ears which are similar to the Sand Cat's and suggests hunting by sight rather than by sound; crouching behind small rocks it would go unseen.

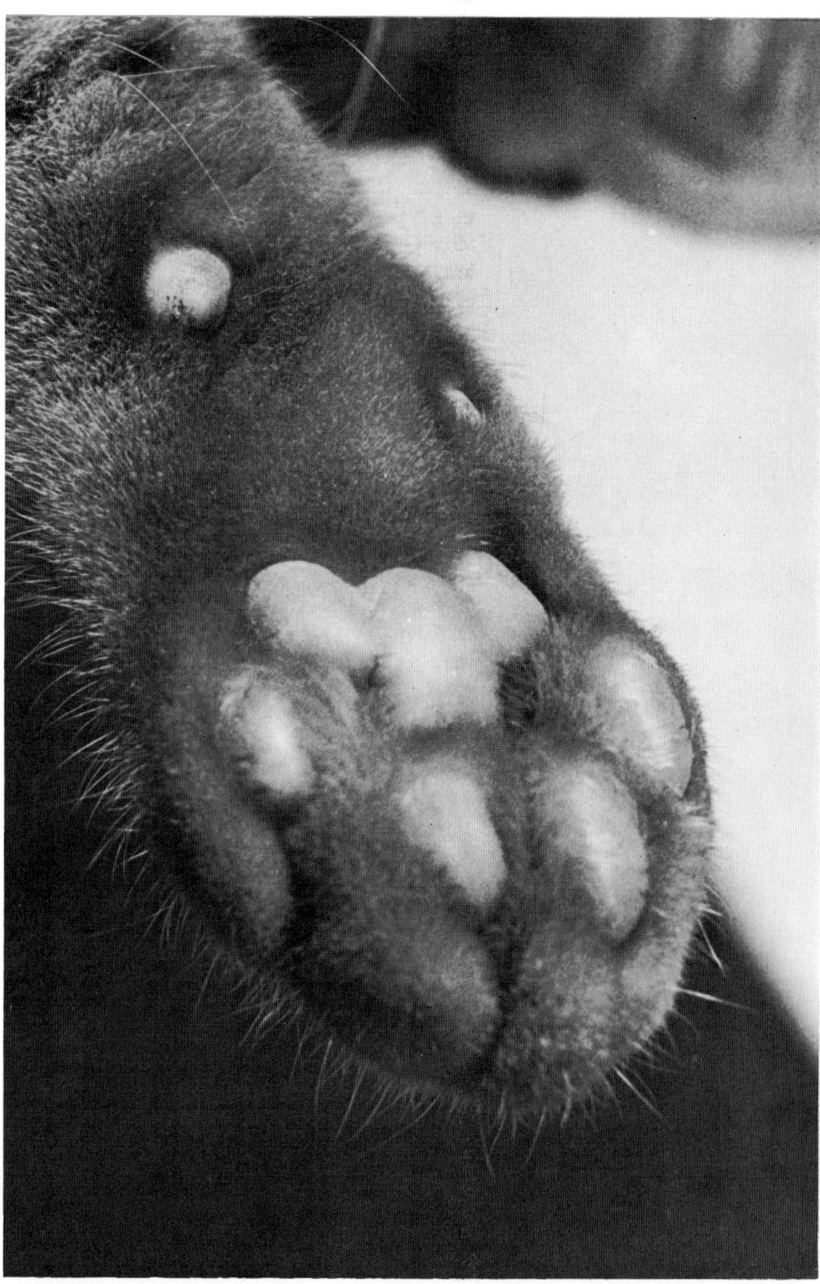

With stripes on the side of the face slanting downwards, very expressive eyes and long cheek fur it is a most handsome and unusual cat. The tail is bushy with a ring towards the end and a black tip.

The combined length of the head and body is from 1½–2 ft, the tail is from 9–12 in. and weight is about 6–7½ lb. The male may be rather heavier and larger than the female.

Distribution is from the east of the Caspian Sea to Persia, Tibet, Mongolia and Western China. It lives very much as the European Wild Cat in the wooded areas and mountainous country; but also lives in the steppes and deserts of China. It subsists on pikas or mouse-hares as well as rodents.

Palsy, Bell's see FACIAL PARALYSIS

Pampas Cat *Felis colocolo* is a species about which very little is known and it is feared that it is in very great danger of becoming extinct as, due to the devastating encroachment of civilization, its habitat is disappearing. At one time it was widely dispersed throughout the Argentine and Uruguay where it inhabited both grasslands and reeds in swampier conditions, and prey consisted of the small mammals and birds. It is mainly nocturnal.

The Pampas Cat is about the size of the domestic cat and has a comparatively long tail; the fur is silvery-grey, becoming lighter on the underparts, and there are reddish-brown markings running obliquely along the back and sides with a dark line along the centre of the back. Faint lines run above the eyes and reach to the ears; a pink nose-pad and spotted whisker pad makes the head most attractive.

Panleucopaenia Feline panleucopaenia or Feline infectious enteritis, is a highly infectious, acute disease mainly of young cats with a high death rate. The name panleucopaenia refers to the marked diminution in the numbers of the white cells of the blood which is a feature of the disease. The infection is caused by a virus which affects only members of the cat family, both domesticated and wild. It is thought that about 30% of the cat population is immune to the disease and it is probable that subclinical infection occurs with the creation of carrier animals.

The incubation period varies from 4 to 10 days. The symptoms are a high initial fever with sudden loss of appetite, listlessness, vomiting, rapid dehydration, depression, coma and death. The most constant symptom is the vomiting of a small quantity of bile-stained fluid or froth. This may occur on two or three occasions only, or may be repeated frequently throughout the early stages of the disease. The vomiting is distressing to the cat and is apparently attended by pain. Affected animals seek cold surfaces to lie on often sitting, hunched up in the sink or a drain. The cat will often seek water but will seldom attempt to drink, sitting crouched with head hanging over the water bowl. Despite the popular name of enteritis, diarrhoea is not a feature of the disease unless the cat survives for more than a few days. In hyperacute cases death may occur within twenty-four hours of the onset of the disease. Unless there is a concurrent infection with one of the respiratory viruses, there is no discharge from the eyes or nose and no sneezing or coughing. The abdomen appears to be painful and any pressure to that area tends to evoke a moan of pain.

The female may infect her unborn offspring. This can produce abortion in the early stages of pregnancy but in the later stages it gives rise to the condition known as Cerebellar Hypoplasia (Ataxia). Affected kittens are apparently quite normal until the age of between 8–16 weeks, as the symptoms are at first regarded as being the usual unsteadiness of the young kitten which has persisted for a longer period than usual. Symptoms include a lack of coordination, limb spasticity and a high-stepping gait particularly of the hindlegs, and the kitten frequently topples sideways and may actually fall over. Postmortem examination shows that part of the brain is markedly underdeveloped.

Treatment of panleucopaenia is generally supportive in character. The broad-spectrum antibiotics will limit the secondary bacterial infection which exacerbates the condition. It is essential to counter dehydration by the infusion of fluids. The cat must be kept warm, often an airing cupboard making a good sick bay. Small quantities of fluids such as glucose or brandy and water should be given frequently by mouth.

Immunization with vaccines produced in tissue culture provides a strong degree of protection against the disease. Vaccination is best performed at about 10 weeks of age. The cat's immunity should be boosted by an annual injection of vaccine.

Panther see LEOPARD

Panther, Black see LEOPARD

Panthera leo see LION; ***P. onca*** see JAGUAR; ***P. pardus*** see LEOPARD; ***P. tigris*** see TIGER; ***P. uncia*** see SNOW LEOPARD

Papilloma Papillomata are benign neoplasms rather similar in appearance to warts. They rarely cause trouble unless they become knocked and begin to bleed. Occasionally they are responsible for ear disease. See EAR DISORDERS and WARTS.

Paracentesis see under ASCITES

Paraffin (Kerosene) see Dangerous Liquids under ACCIDENTS

Paralysis Paralysis is a descriptive term which relates to an animal's inability to use a group of muscles. The usual cause is damage to the nerve which supplies the muscle group. Hemiplegia refers to paralysis of one side of the body while paraplegia is used to describe paralysis of the hind end of the body. The latter condition is seen in the cat usually as a result of a broken back following a road accident. See also FACIAL PARALYSIS.

Paraplegia see PARALYSIS

Parasites A parasite is an animal or plant which has adapted its life style until it is totally dependent for its existence on another animal or plant. It lives at the expense of the host and so causing it variable degrees of harm. A very wide range of animal and plant orders and species have adapted this way of life and have developed some fascinating if rather repugnant methods of propagation in order to complete their life cycles.

Parasites, Prevention of Prevention of infestation of an animal by parasites depends in most instances upon breaking the lifecycle of the parasite. It is therefore essential that the lifecycle of each parasite should be known so that the weakest links in the chain can be chosen for attack. Unfortunately it has not yet been possible to unravel the lifecycles of all the parasites of the cat, although research is progressing in this sphere. Prevention of the important feline parasites is described elsewhere, but one or two examples can be given to illustrate the principle.

The common tapeworm of the cat, *Dipylidium caninum,* has a lifecycle which includes a stage where the worm egg is swallowed by the larvae of a flea. The egg develops within the larvae and the subsequent adult flea, and if the latter is, in turn, swallowed by a cat during grooming activities, the tapeworm develops in the cat's intestine. Prevention of infestation in this case rests upon the elimination of the flea. The flea itself lays its eggs in the coat of the cat, from whence they fall to the ground there to hatch into maggot-like larvae in the dirt and dust in corners of the cat's bed or general environment. The larvae feed on micro-organisms and other protein material in the dirt and develop into adult fleas. Prevention here lies in frequent cleansing of the cat's environment in order to deny the flea larvae shelter and food supplies coupled with treatment to kill the adult fleas before more eggs are laid. See also WORMS, TICKS, ANAEMIA, TOXOPLASMOSIS, FLEAS, LICE and MITES.

Parti-colored see BI-COLOURED

Parturition see BIRTH and BEHAVIOUR

Paws The paws consist of the digits and the claws. Claws may be retracted or extended voluntarily by the cat. As well as the important part they play in locomotion the paws are used for washing, digging holes, burying, attack, chastizing kittens, for play and for experimenting with new substances. Cats also scoop fish out of water with their paws.

Injury to the bones of the paws is comparatively rare as impact is usually transmitted to the bones higher in the leg. Indeed, most cases of fracture of the bones of the paw are caused by crushing. The claws are sometimes broken or torn, and, although this is a particularly painful condition and bleeding is copious the claws usually grow again unless the nailbed is destroyed. Infections of the paws, which may be the result of bite wounds, and fungal infections of the nailbed, can cause trouble for fairly long periods, but usually respond to treatment. See also CLAWS and PADS.

Peat Moss This is a product which forms naturally as a result of the decomposition of moss in moorland bogs over a period of hundreds of years. Peat moss, although expensive, is clean and pleasant-smelling, and makes excellent litter for dirt-trays. It does not cling to the cat's feet and get spread about the house, and its absorbent properties make it particularly suitable for use by a large number of cats – perhaps a mother and kittens. Peat moss is available from good pet and garden shops, but only the best quality, which is free from metal and stones, should be used.

In the U.S.A. clay is the most commonly used material instead of peat moss. See LITTER BOXES.

Pedigree A pedigree refers to the ancestors of an animal. This becomes important in breeds which have specific characteristics and where it is important to identify the ancestors and thereby ensure the breeding quality. It is common to talk about the length of the pedigree which is absurd since all pedigrees are the same length. It is the quality that is so important.

Peke-faced Red see RED SELF

Penicillin see ANTIBIOTICS

P.D.S.A. The People's Dispensary for Sick Animals is a welfare organization which was founded in 1917 to provide free treatment for animals of the poor. Qualified veterinarians are employed in a few of its clinics.

People's Dispensary for Sick Animals see P.D.S.A.

Peridontal Disease see TEETH CARE

Peritonitis The peritoneum is the membrane which lines the abdominal cavity and invests the abdominal organs. Peritonitis, inflammation of the peritoneum, is usually bacterial in origin but may be due to a specific virus infection (see below). Bacterial peritonitis may arise following abdominal surgery, navel infection in newborn kittens, rupture of an abscess in the abdominal organs, or perforation of the alimentary canal or uterus. Symptoms of the condition are depression, loss of appetite, thirst, vomiting, and a fairly rapid loss of condition and abdominal pain. Initially the temperature may be quite high but later falls to slightly over normal. There is usually an increasing abdominal distension due to the accumulation of inflammatory fluid within the abdominal cavity. Treatment is difficult and the disease often has a fatal outcome. The cat should be anaesthetized, the abdomen opened, any perforation or rupture repaired, all exudate removed and the abdominal cavity irrigated with sterile saline and large doses of antibiotics instilled. These measures should be combined with large systemic doses of the broad spectrum antibiotics and infusions of suitable fluids to combat dehydration.

Tubercular Peritonitis Infection of the peritoneum with the tubercle bacillus, *Mycobacterium tuberculosis*, is now comparatively rare in the cat and usually results from extension of the disease from an infected focus in the intestine or the mesenteric lymph nodes. Symptoms are similar to those seen in the other forms of bacterial peritonitis but the disease runs a more chronic, protracted course and is associated with emaciation and a fluctuating or persistently high body temperature. Diagnosis can be made by bacteriological examination of samples of the fluid withdrawn from the abdominal cavity. Treatment is not justifiable in view of the dangers of infection of human contacts, particularly children.

Feline Infectious Peritonitis Feline infectious peritonitis is a fatal chronic viral disease of cats which appears to be increasing in incidence. The causal virus is very similar to that causing Feline leukaemia (see LEUKAEMIA). The mode of transmission and the incubation period are not known but it seems likely that the latter is prolonged and may be measured in weeks rather than days. The disease affects mainly young cats under 3 years of age, but animals of all ages and breeds and of both sexes appear to be susceptible to infection. Recent evidence suggests that the large feral cats, such as lions and leopards, are also susceptible to the disease. Symptoms are an initial fever, general listlessness and depression, loss of appetite, a progressive and marked loss of bodily condition, slight anaemia and the development of ascites (see ASCITES). In a proportion of cases there may be respiratory distress following extension of the disease to the thorax. Usually there is no vomiting or diarrhoea but there may be jaundice in the terminal stages of the disease. The illness pursues a chronic course lasting for weeks or even months, but almost invariably proves fatal. Postmortem examination reveals the presence of variable amounts of fluid within the abdominal cavity with an associated peritonitis, in which there is deposition of a fibrinous exudate on the abdominal organs. Treatment is generally ineffective but recovery has been reported. No method of immunization is currently available.

PERSIAN Long-haired Brown Tabby

Persian The first long-haired cats known in Europe were the Angoras from Ankara in Turkey, but soon afterwards they were followed by cats from Persia (now Iran). The heads were a little larger and broader, the noses shorter and the colours more various, but it was not until the first official cat show in 1871 that these differences were really appreciated and the early fanciers showed a preference for the Persians.

Mr Harrison Weir in his 'Points of Excellence', a book published in Britain in 1889, set out the first standards for the judging of cats, and said that the fur of the Persian was fine, silky and very soft, while that of the Angora was slightly woolly in texture. Miss Frances Simpson, a well known British cat judge, writing at the beginning of the twentieth century, considered the differences between the two were of so fine a nature that she preferred to refer to the long-hairs as Persians, ignoring 'the class of cat commonly called Angora, which seems gradually to have disappeared from our midst'.

The early colours recognized were the Whites, Blacks, Blues, Chinchillas, Smokes, Tortoiseshell, Tortoiseshell and White, Red, Brown, Grey and Silver Tabby and soon prize-winning Persians of the various varieties were being exported to many countries to form the nucleus of the majority of the cat fancies throughout the world today.

For many years in Britain, all cats with long fur were referred to as Persian, but eventually the name was dropped, and they are now known simply as 'Long-haired cats'. 'Persian' is still used by many people, particularly when speaking of the Blues, and in the U.S.A. and Canada, the term is still in general use.

Perspiration Perspiration or sweat is a watery secretion produced by specialized glands in the skin. Although the skin of the cat contains glands similar to the sweat glands of man, these only appear to be functional in the pads of the feet. The act of perspiration or sweating is controlled by sweat centres located in the central nervous system. These centres are stimulated by heat, by changes in the composition of the blood and by various psychic states such as fear or anxiety. In the cat perspiration appears to have very little effect on heat control, cooling being achieved more in this species by panting and by flattening of the hair coat. Perspiration from the foot pads can often be seen when the cat is frightened or anxious.

Petshops Some petshops are unfortunately most unreliable, and this has served to bring the whole trade into disrepute. Many petshop owners and employees have some knowledge of the care of pets, and can offer advice to their customers. The Pet Trade Association has recently set up a scheme whereby those in the trade take examinations leading to a formal qualification. The syllabus was developed with the collaboration of the British Veterinary Association.

When buying cats or kittens from a petshop, the customer should ensure that they have no purulent eye discharge, diarrhoea, 'snuffles', external parasites or injuries. In the event of buying an animal which the customer considers to be in poor health, he should seek veterinary advice at once. Reputable petshop owners will agree to pay veterinary fees or give a discount, should the customer detect a minor, remediable fault in an animal. If a customer buys an obviously diseased cat from a petshop out of pity, he should be prepared for the veterinary fees and to carry out a good deal of nursing. The most satisfactory way of purchasing cats from petshops is to arrange with the manager to be notified as soon as the animals become available. In this way, unless they are 'incubating' disease or are ill on arrival at the petshop, it should be possible to purchase sound, healthy stock.

Pharyngitis Inflammation of the pharynx may result from secondary bacterial invasion often in association with dental conditions. Pharyngitis also occurs in feline influenza, in which case it is acute, and may be accompanied by ulceration. Pharyngitis may also follow trauma to the pharynx by foreign body.

Signs of pharyngitis are refusal to eat, salivation and, in painful cases, pawing at the mouth. The condition usually responds to antibiotics.

PERSIAN Chinchilla

Pharynx see RESPIRATORY ORGANS and PHARYNGITIS

Picornavirus Infection see FLU

Placenta see AFTERBIRTH

Plants Eaten The cat is wholly carnivorous in the wild or feral state; his diet consists of small rodents and birds, together with the larger types of insect. The stomach and intestines of nearly all of the small animals contain a considerable amount of semi-digested vegetable matter which therefore forms a part of the cat's diet. The domestic cat, fed mainly on meat and fish, requires, for perfect health, a supplement of vegetable food as a source of vitamins and as an aid to stool formation. If these are not provided the cat will augment his diet by eating grasses and other wild plants such as cat nip, which are reputed to be attractive to him.

A cat living in a flat or where there is no ready access to grass must have his diet augmented by vegetable matter, not so much for its food value as for its content of fibrous material. Many cat foods contain vegetable additives for this purpose. Alternatively, a box of rich soil sown regularly with grass seed will serve the same end.

Play see BEHAVIOUR and TOYS

Pleasure Cats register pleasure in a number of ways. Purring, which is one of the most familiar, varies from barely audible vibrations to the loud and intermittently shrill sound of the ecstatic cat. Zoologists still do not fully understand the mechanism of purring, but some authorities consider it is partly due to alterations in the turbulence of the blood. Purring can be felt in the area of the larynx. Cats also purr when frightened, for example when being handled, and this could be an attempt at placation by showing friendliness to the handler.

Lowering of the forequarters and raising of the hindquarters, with tail erect is yet another sign of pleasure, and is probably sexual in origin. Rolling is a related form of behaviour.

Siamese and Burmese have a complex vocabulary of approving words, best understood by devotees of these breeds.

Pleasure may also be expressed by sudden bouts of kittenish behaviour, by a rhythmic kneading action of the forepaws, with the claws extended, or sucking the fabric of clothes while being nursed.

Pleasure at the company of another cat may be shown by washing and grooming, and some cats show a tendency to lick the hands of people.

Pleura Disorders *Hydrothorax* Hydrothorax is a condition in which there is accumulation of a watery fluid within the thoracic or chest cavity. In the cat hydrothorax occurs during the course of two different disease conditions: (1) Lymphosarcoma of the anterior mediastinal lymph nodes (see LEUKAEMIA), and (2) Congestive heart failure. In the former condition the pressure exerted by the growing tumour on the great veins of the area causes obstruction of the circulation and fluid is forced out of the blood into the chest cavity. In the case of heart failure, which is extremely rare in the cat, a similar condition arises in that the return of venous blood to the heart is dammed back by the overloaded heart and again fluid percolates from the blood vessels into the thorax. Symptoms of the condition are those of pressure collapse of the lungs due to the mounting pressure of the fluid within the chest. There is increasing respiratory distress and the cat tends to crouch on its sternum with its head and neck extended and its elbows held away from the sides of the chest. Respirations become gasping in character, the cat breathes with open mouth, and the visible mucous membranes of the mouth and eye become dull purplish in colour (cyanosis). If relief is not forthcoming the animal will die of asphyxia. Treatment depends upon the cause of the condition.

Pleurisy Pleurisy is inflammation of the pleura, the membrane lining the interior of the chest and investing the lungs. The pleura of the cat appears to be particularly prone to suffer inflammatory change to which it responds by the outpouring of considerable quantities of inflammatory exudate. The cause of the pleurisy is usually bacterial in origin. Symptoms of pleurisy are similar to those seen in hydrothorax, viz. those of pressure collapse of the lungs, but there may be more signs of pain in the chest and the disease may be so acute that cats may be found dead without any premonitory symptoms being shown. Postmortem examination shows considerable quantities of a foul smelling brownish-red or yellow exudate in the chest floating in which are flakes of fibrin. The pleura is thickened and inflamed and often covered by a greyish fibrinous coating. Treatment is difficult as any handling of the cat may produce a fatal respiratory crisis. It is essential to drain off as much of the exudate as possible and partially replace it with antibiotic solutions. This must be performed under a local anaesthetic as general anaesthesia is out of the question in most cases. The systemic administration of large doses of the broad spectrum antibiotics is a necessary corollary to chest drainage. Unfortunately most cases end fatally.

Pneumothorax Pneumothorax is a condition in which air collects within the thoracic cavity. The condition is uncommon in the cat but may result from a penetrating wound of the chest wall following a road accident. The presence of air within the thoracic cavity acts in a similar way to the accumulation of fluid, causing a pressure collapse of the lungs. Symptoms of the condition are therefore similar to those seen in hydrothorax or exudative pleurisy but are usually much more acute and there is a rapidly increasing respiratory distress as more air gains access to the cavity. Treatment is by withdrawal of the imprisoned air either through a hypodermic syringe or a water drain, puncture of the chest being performed at the highest point as the air tends to rise within the chest. Any obvious wound of the thoracic wall must be repaired to prevent further ingress of air.

Pleurisy see PLEURA DISORDERS

Pneumonia Pneumonia refers to an acute infectious inflammation of the lung. It is characterized by high temperature, difficult breathing, reluctance to eat and a cough. The cat is often very miserable, and shows a reluctance to move. It may result from infections with bacteria, viruses, fungi and parasites either alone or more commonly in combination. Treatment consists of antibiotic therapy and specific chemicals for parasites if present. Careful diligent nursing is still of considerable importance for successful treatment of pneumonia. Animals should be kept warm in a constant temperature, hygiene of environment and animal maintained and, where prescribed by the veterinarian, inhalations instituted.

Pneumothorax see PLEURA DISORDERS

Poisons With the increasing complexity and diversity of chemicals in our environment the study of poisons and their effects have become a very important branch of medicine, known as toxicology. Fortunately, as a consequence of the fastidious feeding habits of cats, poisoning is very rare.

The cat may, however, ingest poisons together with a rat, mouse or bird which has itself been poisoned, it may inhale poisonous fumes or absorb toxic substances through the skin. Notable among the latter are compounds derived from coaltar.

The list of poisons and the variety of symptoms they produce is so extensive that to list them here would be meaningless. An animal which shows severely abnormal behaviour should be taken to the veterinarian. If a poison is suspected it should be reported and preferably the container produced.

Poisons can produce vomiting, diarrhoea, fits, sleepiness, convulsions, blindness and death. Cats, unlike dogs, are rarely seen in the act of consuming poisons so the problem is not recognized until symptoms appear. In the unlikely event of an animal being caught in the act, emetics should be administered immediately to make the cat vomit. Washing soda crystals, mustard, salt water and soap are possible emetics. When poisoning is suspected the animal should be kept warm and quiet and veterinary advice sought immediately. If the poison is known an antidote may be possible. In the absence of specific information on the constitution of the poison, symptomatic treatment will be instituted.

Polydactylia see BREEDING ABNORMALITIES

Pot Belly This term is used to describe a pendulous, dilated abdomen. It is often a sign of malnutrition or of heavy roundworm infestation in the kitten.

It also occurs in the older animal suffering from Ascites (dropsy). In this disease fluid collects in the abdomen.

Diseases of the uterus may also give the cat a bloated, pot-bellied appearance.

Powders Powders given by mouth are comparatively rare nowadays, as most drug manufacturers produce tablets or pills. If the powder will dissolve in water it is easier to make the powder into a solution and give it by means of a teaspoon. Should the powder have to be given by itself, it should be placed on the back of the tongue in the same way as is a tablet, and the cat should be allowed access to water afterwards. Dry powders tend to cause the cat to splutter and cough.

External powders are fairly straightforward to apply. Care should be taken to ensure the patient does not lick them from the coat. It may be necessary to apply dressing over a wound or burn on which powder has been placed. Ear and eye powders are extremely uncommon, drops and ointments being generally more favoured.

Prefixes see AFFIXES AND PREFIXES

Pregnancy see GESTATION

Pregnancy Diet see NUTRITION

Premature Birth Premature birth may be defined as the birth of an animal before the end of the normal period of gestation or pregnancy. In the cat the duration of gestation averages about 65 days with a range of between 60 and 71 days, so a premature kitten is one born before the 60th day of pregnancy. It is unlikely that kittens born before the 56th day of gestation will survive. Premature kittens show varying degrees of hairlessness, they are rather somnolent and reluctant to move, and tend to suffer from respiratory difficulties. Such kittens should be placed in a warm environment, if possible in an oxygen rich atmosphere, and may require hand-feeding as they are often too weak to suckle effectively and the queen may not come into full milk for a few days after the birth. See also BIRTH.

Premier A neuter, the Premier is the equivalent of a male or female Champion.

A neutered pedigree cat can compete in the shows in the specific classes put on for neuters. The same regulations apply as to being registered and if there has been a change of ownership the cat must have been transferred to the new owner at least three weeks before the show.

Premier certificates are given to the winners of the open neuter classes should the judges consider they are up to the required standards.

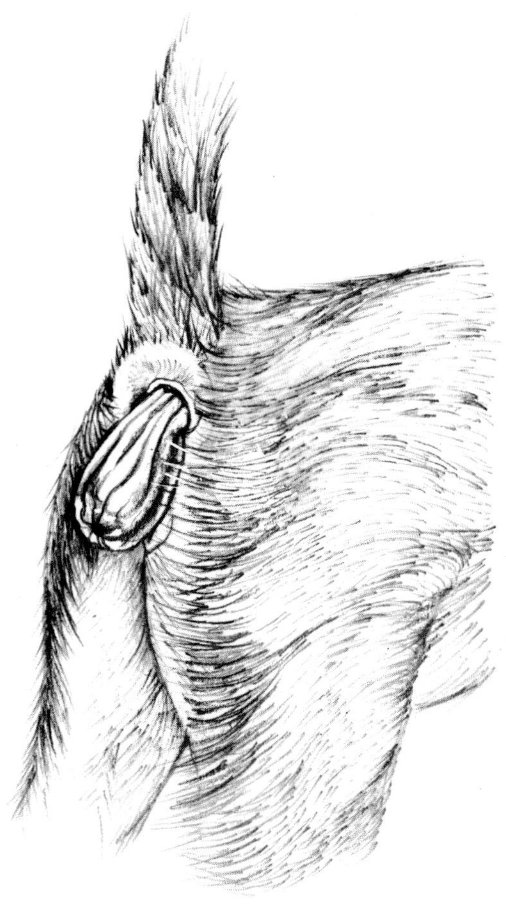

Prolapse of the rectum

The winning of three such certificates at three shows under three different judges, subject to approval by the Governing Council of the Cat Fancy, entitles the cat to bear the title 'Premier'.

The majority of the Premiers are magnificent animals, and being neutered make most decorative house pets.

Pro-oestrus see OESTRUS

Prognosis The prognosis is the prediction made as to the outcome of a disease or an injury at the time the diagnosis is established, or in the period following diagnosis when the patient's response to treatment may be observed. It is made in the light of published information on the disease condition and of the diagnostician's personal experience. Other factors influencing the prognosis are the age, resilience, immunological status, temperament and general condition of the patient; and the amount of care that the owner is able to devote to the patient during the rest of its life. To take a hypothetical case, the prognosis for a well-fed, strong three-year-old cat sustaining a fracture of the femur could be favourable. It would have a reasonable amount of resilience enabling it to overcome the shock of the accident. Such a cat would constitute a good 'anaesthetic risk', because his healthy liver and kidneys would facilitate detoxification of anaesthetic agents given into the bloodstream. Following an operation to reduce the fracture, the healing of the bone and soft tissues would be rapid and the patient should soon be using the erstwhile fractured leg. On the other hand, if the animal sustaining such a fracture were ill-nourished and suffering from nephritis and respiratory infection, and 14 years old, the prognosis would be considerably less favourable. Indeed the veterinarian might suggest that the chances of an operation enabling the animal to return to active life were so few as to make euthanasia a kinder proposition.

Prolapse Prolapse of an organ means its turning inside out and, in the case of hollow organs, everting through the orifice to which it is attached. For example, prolapse of the rectum involves the passage through the sphincter of part or all of the rectum, whose lining is thus penetrated. The organs whose prolapse is most commonly reported are the rectum, and the uterus.

Rectal Prolapse This happens most often in kittens, and the immediate cause is diarrhoea. The animal strains in an attempt to pass the diarrhoea, and the rapid succession of rectal contractions is sufficient to make the hollow organ fold up upon itself, as the finger of a glove may be pushed inside out. It then passes through the anus. This condition is accompanied by shock and dehydration. Treatment consists of replacing the rectum and treating the diarrhoea.

Uterine Prolapse This occurs after parturition. Either one horn or both horns of the uterus may prolapse. This condition precipitates a state of shock in an animal already suffering from exhaustion. Treatment consists of replacing the uterus under general anaesthetic and, if the patient is to be used again for breeding, suturing the uterine horns to the lining of the abdomen to prevent them everting again. If no further breeding is anticipated, the uterus may be replaced and the animal spayed.

Proteins see NUTRITION

Protozoan Parasites see COCCIDIOSIS and TOXOPLASMOSIS

Pruritus This word simply means itchiness, a state of irritation. Pruritus may occur in response to parasites, insect bites, exposure to allergens, irritant chemicals or heat. It is an almost constant feature of dermatitis. A persistent or widespread pruritus may make a cat extremely restless and even prevent sleep. Modern therapy for conditions involving pruritus often includes the use of cortisone derivatives which tend to reduce inflammation. Since self-mutilation inhibits treatment of skin conditions which produce pruritus its reduction with anti-inflammatory drugs hastens cure. See SKIN DISEASES and PSEUDORABIES.

Pseudorabies Aujeszky's Disease or Pseudorabies is an infrequent acute viral infection of cats. It is believed that transmission of infection occurs through ingestion of the virus and since the disease also occurs in rats, the latter are probably a source of infection. The incubation period of the disease ranges from 2–9 days, usually averaging 3–4 days, and the infection is invariably fatal within 48 hours of the onset of symptoms. The disease commences with the cat showing a complete loss of appetite, a tendency to hide, adoption of the crouched position, and occasionally mewing as if in pain. Paralysis of the throat muscles usually occurs with consequent difficulty in swallowing and the drooling of saliva. The characteristic symptom is the appearance of intense itching (pruritus) of a localized area, from which the disease gets its popular name of 'Mad Itch'. The cat licks, rubs and gnaws at the affected area producing severe mutilation of the skin and the subcutaneous tissues. Twitching of the muscles of the head and neck and of the lips may occur and there may be convulsions. In some cases the cat becomes quite frenzied and will attack inanimate objects or other animals. No effective treatment is known.

Puberty Puberty is the age of sexual maturity. Cats that are brought up in large groups of the same age, e.g. litters that are raised in catteries seem to reach puberty earlier than those kept as individual pets. The time of birth may also affect puberty. Many cats mature in the spring months. Thus a female born in December may have her first oestrus cycle in April, whereas one born in June may not have hers until the following March or April. Males are influenced by factors such as the presence of females in oestrus. See also BEHAVIOUR.

Pulex iritans see FLEAS

Pulse Rate The easiest place to feel the pulse in the cat is on the inner aspect of the hind leg, just above the stifle (knee joint). With much experience, it is possible to qualify the character of the pulse. Timing of the pulse rate, can, however, be achieved without long practice, and the value obtained may be useful in first-aid and home nursing. The normal value for an adult cat is 110–130 per minute. Kittens have a rather higher rate. Fever, excitement and exercise will all raise the pulse rate.

Puma *Felis concolor* is a very big cat, but nevertheless it is a true member of the genus *Felis* as it does not 'roar'. The body of a large male can measure about 5 ft, with another 3 ft for the tail. The weight of such an animal has been recorded up to 260 lb. On the other hand, a small male might weigh only 80 lb. This difference in size can give rise to the conjecture that there are different species, as indeed it is referred to as the 'Cougar', 'Mountain-Lion' as well as many Indian names. This is also probably due to the fact that originally it covered a very wide range from the deserts of Patagonia to the mountains of British Columbia, but with the destruction of much of its habitat, together with its relentless persecution and slaughter, its range has been considerably reduced.

The summer coat of the Puma is generally a reddish brown with white underparts and upper lips; there is usually a darker ridge along the back and tail which ends in a black tip; there are dark lines above the eyes and the whisker pads are dark, giving good 'expression'. The Puma can vary in colour and some have been noted which are light fawn to an almost black, but the latter is considered to be a melanistic form and does not constitute a separate species. In type it somewhat resembles a lioness, but the head is rounder.

The Puma is an avid hunter and of very great strength. It is known to eat anything from slugs or mice to a horse and has been seen attacking a buffalo; its prey is killed swiftly.

Very much more could be written about this beautiful and intriguing cat.

Punishment Cats do not seem to respond very well to punishment. One is likelier to achieve better results by rewarding good behaviour than by punishing bad.

When cats develop bad habits, these can often be cured by breaking the habit, rather than by punishment. For example a cat that takes to soiling the carpets suddenly may be corrected by removal of the particular carpet or rug he is using, or by moving the furniture around, or possibly even by putting him outdoors or on his dirt-box at a different time.

The concept of punishment clearly has a place in the psychological processes of the cat, however, for mother cats frequently chastise their kittens.

Purring see PLEASURE

Pyaemia Pyaemia is a condition in which pus-producing organisms gain access to the bloodstream and are distributed around the body causing abscesses wherever they are arrested. Such abscesses occur usually where there are small calibre capillaries and may be confined to the subcutaneous tissues of the skin, but, more seriously, they may develop in any of the internal organs. Pyaemia usually arises during the course of sepsis, often resulting from the bite of another cat. Affected cats show loss of appetite and bodily condition, a slight fever, and a variable number of abscesses in different parts of the body. Where these abscesses are in the internal organs then symptoms referable to those organs mainly involved are seen. For example an abscess in the brain will give rise to serious nervous symptoms. Treatment is usually rather disappointing and consists of the administration of large doses of broad spectrum antibiotics coupled with drainage of any accessible abscesses.

Pyloric Stenosis Pyloric stenosis is a condition in which the opening from the stomach into the duodenum, the pylorus, is narrowed and may be fibrosed. This results in obstruction to the passage of food from the stomach into the intestines. The stenosis may be congenital and permanent in character or acquired and spastic in type. The symptoms are similar in both cases in that the cat is obviously hungry and eager to eat but soon after feeding shows signs of discomfort and regurgitates the food with some force – projectile vomiting. The regurgitated food may be eaten again and retained or again vomited back. Diagnosis can be confirmed by X-ray examination of the stomach after the administration of a barium meal. There is a progressive loss of condition as the cat is unable to retain sufficient food for proper nourishment. Treatment may be medical or surgical. Particularly in the spastic type of case, which is often associated with extreme nervousness, medical treatment in the form of antispasmodic drugs may be quite successful. Surgical treatment consists of making incisions in the muscular ring around the pylorus, which results in a relaxation of the sphincter.

Pyometritis Pyometritis refers to a serious condition of the uterus in which large quantities of pus accumulate. It causes considerable systemic upset in the animal which usually shows symptoms of listlessness, excessive thirst, vomiting and dehydration. It is often accompanied by large quantities of pus from the vagina.

Treatment consists of surgical removal of the infected uterus and the ovaries. The animal is usually in a state of toxaemia from the breakdown products of the pus. Prognosis is poor. Since many female cats are spayed when young this condition is rare.

Q, R

Quarantine The purpose of quarantine in the U.K. is to prevent the virus disease rabies from entering the national mammalian population. The incubation period of rabies, the time between an animal being infected by the virus and the appearance of clinical symptoms of disease, may be up to six months. In fact, recent research shows it could be more, but the authorities still consider six months to be a reasonable quarantine period. Therefore, any cat entering the U.K. which has been in contact with another animal suffering from rabies, should develop the disease whilst in quarantine. Quarantine kennels are carefully designed and rigorously inspected.

Owners are normally allowed to visit their pets at the quarantine kennels, but it is important that they obey all the rules of the establishment, in the interests of public and animal health.

The law requires cats to be isolated in quarantine kennels for a six month period, and to be vaccinated against rabies during that time. Cats are normally penned individually, unless an owner quarantines two or three, and requests that they share accommodation. See EXPORTING and RABIES.

Queen Queen is the term used to describe an entire (unspayed) female cat. Usually it is used for female cats which have produced at least one litter.

Queen, Nursing Diet see NUTRITION

Rabies Because of their hunting instincts, cats are constantly exposed to the 'reservoir of rabies' in wildlife: rodents, skunks, bats, and other vectors. The disease is caused by a virus which is only excreted from the body in the saliva of infected animals. In nature, it is transmitted from animal to animal by means of a bite and contamination of the wound with the virus-bearing saliva. Rarely, rabies may be transmitted by virus contamination of fresh, already existing wounds. Virus may be present in the saliva of animals several days prior to the onset of recognizable symptoms and the animal may transmit the disease through biting at a very early stage of the disease.

In cats the disease is generally characterized by viciousness and excitation. Swift movements and erratic behaviour are more marked in rabid cats than in dogs, and their bites are considered dangerous because they are generally of the deep puncture type. Rabid cats attack suddenly, biting and scratching viciously. They have a tendency to grab with their teeth and to hold on until rendered unconscious. Death occurs within 10 days of the first clinical symptom.

The course of the disease can be divided into three phases: prodromal (commonly called 'dumb' rabies), excitative, and paralytic. During the early stages of infection, slight temperature elevation, dilation of the pupils, a sluggish corneal reflex, and resentment of handling may be confused with symptoms of other diseases. It is quite possible to be bitten or exposed to saliva bearing the rabies virus while examining the animal during this period.

Signs of the disease are most easily recognized during the excitative stage which lasts from 3 to 7 days. The cat becomes increasingly restless, irritable and nervous and is intolerant to light or sudden stimuli of light or sound. Early in this stage, it may shun people, hide in dark places, mew continually, scratch the ground, and snap at imaginary objects or eat unusual things. This stage is most dangerous because of the tendency to bite anything that is encountered. After several days of the excitative stage, the animal becomes paralyzed, eventually goes into a coma, and dies.

This unpleasant and deadly disease exists in Europe, Asia, Africa and America. Only one human being has to date survived following clinical symptoms. It is fortunately absent from the U.K. Stringent quarantine regulations continue to arrest its spread to these islands.

Radial Paralysis Radial paralysis refers to paralysis of the extensor muscles of the fore-limb as a result of nerve damage. Radial paralysis may be transient or permanent depending on cause and severity. Slight trauma to the nerve may not result in permanent damage, as a certain amount of healing is possible. Similarly, the application of pressure may not permanently affect the nerve. In cases of irreversible radial paralysis, amputation of the limb may be suggested as there is some risk of infection ascending from the useless limb into adjacent structures. Patients subjected to amputation normally adjust extremely well, although the sight of a three-legged cat is unpleasant to some people.

Radiography This aid to diagnosis is of particular importance to veterinary surgeons where patients can themselves provide little information as to the location of any internal discomfort or injury. X-rays are generated by passing a very high voltage across an electronic vacuum tube. The energy of the electrical current is converted into a beam of X-rays – a radiation similar to visible light but of sufficient energy to penetrate through many of the tissues of the body. The harder and denser structures such as bone, absorb the beam to a greater degree than fat or muscle, and this selective absorption by portions of the body makes radiography possible because the beam throws a 'shadow' of the internal organs which can be recorded on photographic film.

It is important that a radiograph should not be blurred by movement of the patient during its exposure to X-rays. Therefore, while the cat is normally a good patient from the radiographers point of view it may occasionally require to be sedated or anaesthetized before a film is taken.

The animal's bones show up particularly well in a radiograph and this enables the veterinary surgeon to assess the full extent of any fractures and dislocations and also to check that such injuries have been corrected and are healing satisfactorily.

The fact that radiography also visualizes the fine detail of bone structures makes its use important in the diagnosis of other conditions of the skeleton such as tumours, infection and nutritional disorders.

The air-filled lungs also show up well in a radiograph enabling the veterinary surgeon to assess some of the chest conditions affecting the cat. For example, lung lobes affected with pneumonia are more opaque to the beam than the normal lung parenchyma and this change can be visualized in a radiograph.

Many abdominal organs are of equal density, a fact which makes them difficult to differentiate on a plain X-ray film. To examine their shape and function it is necessary to administer a *contrast agent* – a substance which is opaque to X-rays. Barium sulphate is one of these and is used to outline the gastro-intestinal tract – one example of this examination is called a barium meal.

Iodine compounds are similarly used to show the internal structure of the heart and blood vessels after an appropriate injection has been made. When the compound is eliminated from the bloodstream by the kidneys it allows the urinary tract to be visualized.

Another medical use of X-rays is, of course, in the treatment of various forms of cancer. While this is sometimes undertaken in cats and other veterinary patients, the ordinary diagnostic X-ray machine is not suitable for this purpose and such treatment can only be carried out at institutions possessing the much more intricate equipment required for this purpose.

Ranula A ranula is a swollen sublingual salivary gland. Affected salivary glands respond to treatment consisting of the administration of an anaesthetic, incision of the swelling and application of a chemical cauterising agent. If the condition persists, the whole salivary gland is sometimes removed.

Rectum Disorders Conditions of the rectum include foreign bodies, neoplasms, rectal prolapse, rectal impaction and constipation. For rectal prolapse and constipation, see PROLAPSE and CONSTIPATION.

Foreign Bodies Some foreign bodies that are ingested by the cat pass through the alimentary canal without damage and then lodge in the rectum. They may usually be removed relatively easily by the use of forceps or fingers, although a general anaesthetic is often required for this procedure.

Neoplasms of the Rectum Neoplasms of the rectum have been reported.

Rectal Impaction This occurs in longstanding cases of constipation and is due to solidification of faeces with the rectum. The condition is relieved by the administration of enemas or suppositories or by physical emptying of the rectum using forceps or gloved hands.

Red Abyssinian see ABYSSINIAN

Red Burmese see BURMESE, NEW COLOURS

Red Point see HIMALAYAN and SIAMESE

Red Point Short-hair see SIAMESE, RED POINT

Red Self Developed in the first place from the Red Tabby, this is a very rare variety, due to the difficulty in producing a cat with the deep rich red fur completely free from tabby markings. The standard is as for other long-haired varieties, and the large round eyes should be a deep copper colour. The Red Selfs that do appear at the show invariably have some tabby markings on the face and tail.

A good Red Self would be most useful for mating to a Black and White Bi-colour in an endeavour to produce Tortoiseshell and Whites or mating to a Black or Tortoiseshell for Tortoiseshells. The type is usually very good.

As well as the Red Self in the U.S.A. there is also a variety recognized known as the Peke-faced Red. This was developed from the Red Tabby and the

Red Self kittens

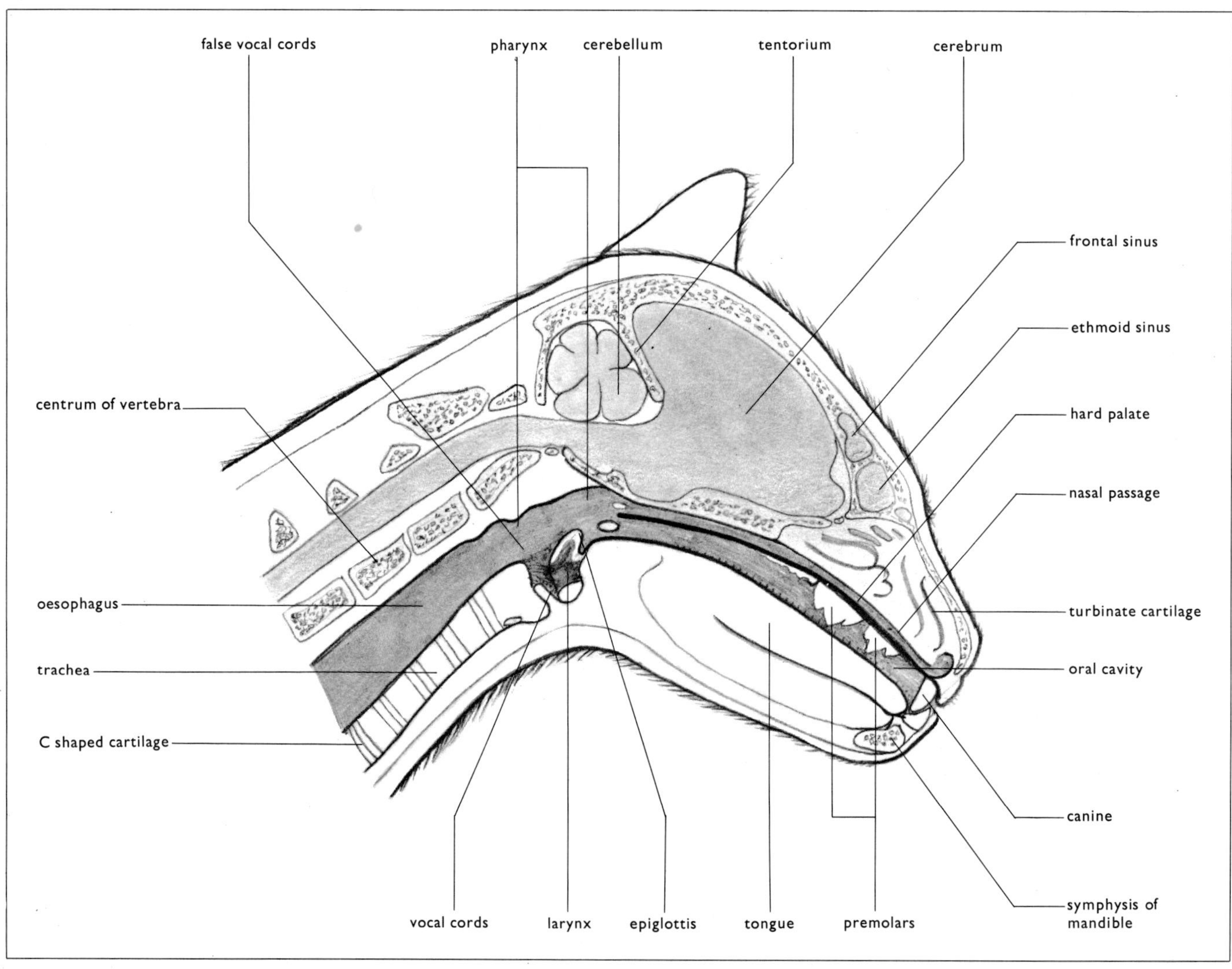

RESPIRATION Respiratory organs of the head

Red Self, and may be either a Red Self or Tabby, but the head should resemble that of the Pekinese, with the nose being very short and depressed, even indented, between the eyes. Faults are irregularities of the teeth and underjaw.
See colour plate 37, *page 147.*

Red Tabby see TABBY LONG-HAIR and TABBY SHORT-HAIR

Red Tabby Point see SIAMESE, ANY OTHER COLOUR

Registration of Breeds In Britain pedigree cats and kittens may be registered with the Governing Council of the Cat Fancy on payment of a small fee, a form for which purpose may be had from the Registrars. This form asks for full information of the name proposed, the colour, the names and breed numbers of the parents and the grandparents, and the name and address of the breeder.

If intending to go in for breeding seriously, it is advisable to register a Cattery name, known in Britain as a prefix, as well. This is a distinguishing name used before the cat's own special name, and may only be used by the breeder registering it. In the U.S.A. affixes are also allowed. This not only enables kittens from certain catteries to be identified at once, but also makes the choosing of the names much easier.

Repeats are not permitted for at least twenty years, and single names that have not been used before are exceedingly difficult to find.

A register is kept of all cats and kittens so recorded, and once registered and given a number, it is not possible to make any changes or additions, even if sold to a new owner. When there is a change of ownership, this should also be registered with the Governing Council on one of their special transfer forms.

At the moment, there are nine registering bodies in the U.S.A. In Europe too the various countries

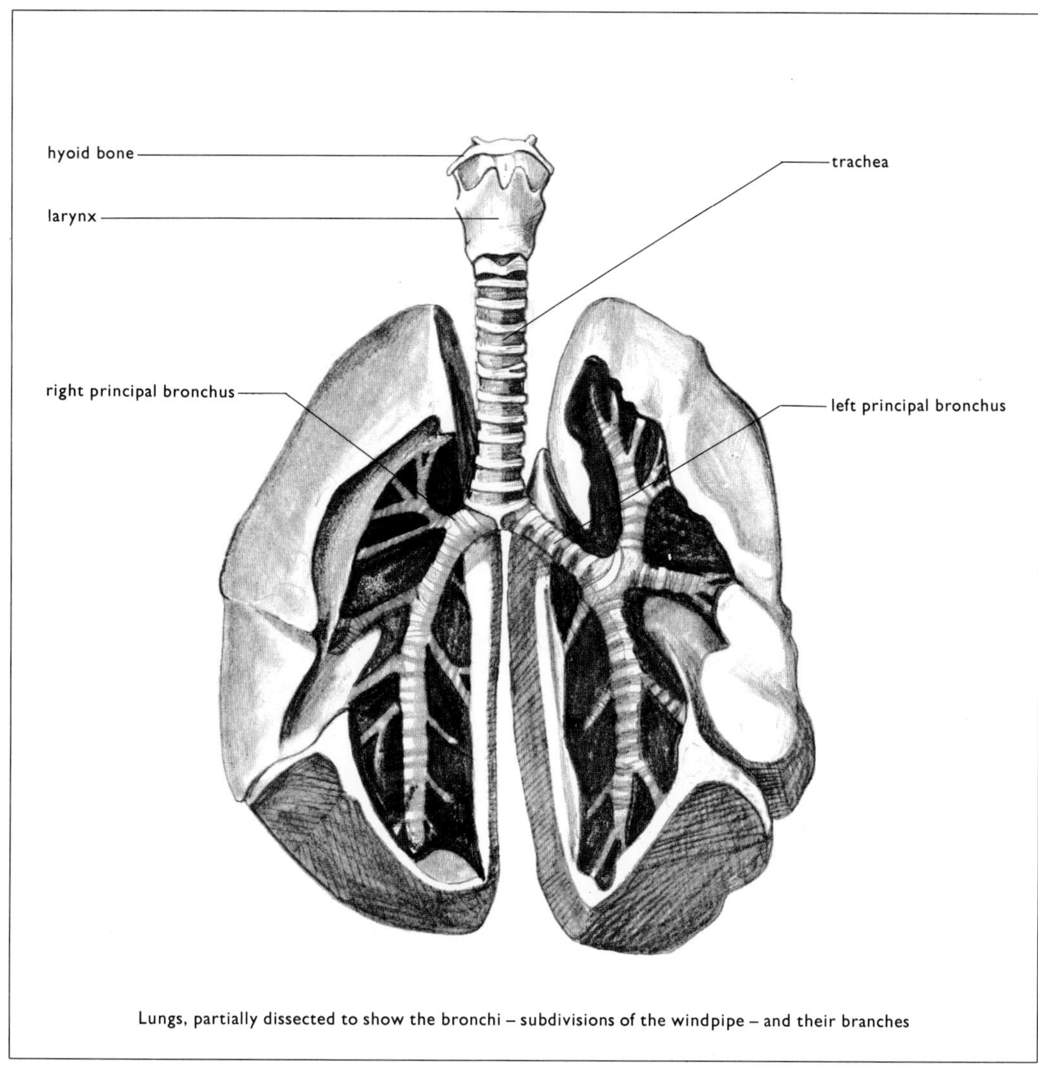

Lungs, partially dissected to show the bronchi – subdivisions of the windpipe – and their branches

RESPIRATION The lungs

have one or more such bodies. All carry out the same functions as given for the Governing Council of the Cat Fancy in Britain and the procedure is much the same.
See also AFFIXES AND PREFIXES.

Respiration see BREATHING

Respiration Rate The normal respiration rate for a cat is 25–30 respirations per minute. Generally speaking, the respiration rate will increase with an increase in temperature, so that a raised rate is often a sign of ill-health, usually a fever associated with infection. Healthy cats may, however, show an increased respiration rate after exercise, or when excited. Panting may occur if the cat is extremely hot. Owners who wish to measure the respiration rate of their cats should do so when the animals are relaxed, undisturbed and sitting quietly in familiar surroundings. Respiration rate falls considerably during sleep.

Respiratory Organs The organs concerned in respiration are the nasal cavities, the pharynx, the larynx, the trachea, the paired bronchi and their branches (the bronchioles), and the lungs. The pharynx is separated into an upper and lower chamber by the soft palate, which serves to keep the air-passage and the food-passage separate.

The larynx is a box-shaped structure made of cartilage; its entrance is guarded by a 'lid' known as the epiglottis, which is closed when food is being swallowed, preventing it from entering the respiratory tract.

The trachea is a tube of smooth muscle supported by a number of C-shaped cartilages, which prevents it from collapsing. The trachea divides into two branches, the bronchi. They also contain cartilage in their walls which helps to maintain their rigidity. They in turn divide into many smaller branches, the bronchioles. They are covered by cilia, fine hair-like projections, which beat to keep a layer of mucous material moving across their surface. The branches of the bronchioles become finer and finer, until they eventually terminate in the alveolar sacs of the lung tissue. These sacs resemble bunches of hollow grapes. They consist of moist membranes through which gases easily pass, and are richly supplied with blood capillaries. It is here that oxygen from the inhaled air diffuses into the bloodstream. At the same time carbon dioxide passes out of solution in the blood, into the air within the sacs.

The lungs themselves, while being made up entirely of masses of sacs, which gives them a spongy texture, are also divided into well-marked zones or lobes. The right lung has four lobes and the left lung three.

Respiratory movements of the lungs are assisted by movement of the muscular chest walls and the diaphragm.

Rex see CORNISH REX and DEVON REX

Rheumatism Rheumatism is a disease of the connective tissues of the body involving the muscles, tendons and joints, and giving rise to stiffness and pain. The term includes arthritis, myositis and fibrositis. It is doubtful if rheumatism as recognized in man actually occurs in the cat, but a rare condition known as 'rheumatoid arthritis' has been described in this species. The disease occurs mainly in the older cat, over eight years of age, and the main feature is that it involves several joints in the body, particularly the smaller joints which are the counterparts of the fingers and toes in man. The affected joints become swollen, hot and painful to move and X-ray examination shows that new bone is deposited around the joints. The affected cat is reluctant to move and progressively becomes more and more immobilized. There may be lameness in one or more limbs. There is often loss of appetite and the body temperature is usually slightly raised, probably due to pain. There is a progressive loss of condition and the cat may become quite emaciated. Treatment is difficult but alleviation of symptoms can usually be achieved. See also ARTHRITIS.

Rhinitis see CATARRH

Rhinotracheitis, Viral see FLU

Rickets see NUTRITION

Ringworm Dermatomycosis or Ringworm is due to invasion of the skin, the hair and the claws by certain species of fungus which have become adapted to grow on the keratin contained in these structures. The most frequent fungus involved in ringworm in the cat is *Microsporon canis*, but infection with *Trichophyton mentagrophytes*, which is commonly found in mice, may also occur. The symptoms produced by either species of fungus are essentially the same in character. The clinical form of the disease is usually seen in young animals, or those which are debilitated by intercurrent disease or malnutrition. Some cases in adult animals are symptomless and the cat is then a carrier capable of spreading the infection to susceptible animals including human contacts. The lesions vary a good deal from cat to cat and even from site to site on the same animal. In some cases the infection is acute and causes a severe inflammatory response with raw, moist patches developing coupled with breaking off and loss of hair. The characteristic lesion of ringworm is a circular area which spreads peripherally, in which there is breaking off and loss of the hair associated with scaling of the skin. Often the centres of such lesions become pigmented and healing takes place from within outwards. The usual sites of infection are the head, particularly the forehead and ears, and the feet and claws. The latter become roughened and pitted on their surface and show scaliness of the skin round the base of the nail. In some cases there is a generalized scaling of the skin with an associated thinning of the hair.

Diagnosis of ringworm infection is made by examination of the cat under Wood's Light (see WOOD'S LIGHT) in the case of *Microsporon*, examination of selected hairs under the microscope, and by cultivation of the organism on suitable media.

Treatment is difficult, prolonged and expensive, and one must always be conscious of the fact that infection can easily spread to human contacts, especially children. The treatment of choice is the administration of a specific antibiotic. The application of fungicidal shampoos in addition is beneficial. The antibiotic must be continued for some weeks. Any bed or bedding must be destroyed and any utensils soaked in warm 5–10% formaldehyde for at least 12 hours. Cages, etc., may be disinfected by soaking in the same solution or by flaming with a blow lamp. See also WOOD'S LIGHT.

Roaming The cat is by nature a hunting animal, and most cats that are allowed outdoors will not confine themselves to their own gardens, but cover wide areas in search of prey. They also tend to establish territories (see BEHAVIOUR). Unfortunately, a few individuals will spend long periods away from home, and often stay several days in another household in the locality. Entire tomcats are notorious for this behaviour, although neuters may show it. It is often impossible to cure, although neutering may moderate the roaming tendency. The best plan is to confine cats to the home a certain amount each day during kittenhood, and to have them neutered fairly early (4–6 months in the case of a male). In the U.S.A., where the problem is greater than in the U.K., total confinement is advocated.

Rodent Ulcer Rodent Ulcer is a condition of the skin of the lip region which affects cats of all ages, although it is infrequent in the kitten. The name Rodent Ulcer was applied to the condition under

colour 44 Siamese Seal Point
45 Siamese Seal Point kitten
46 Siamese Tortie Poin
47 Siamese Tabby Poin

colour 48 Smoke Long-hair

right Rodent ulcer, the cause of this condition is not yet clear

the erroneous belief that it was similar to the disease of that name in man. Technically it is an eosinophilic granuloma. The cause of the condition is not yet clear, but it is probably a low-grade, chronic staphylococcal or streptococcal infection of the skin, which is aggravated by the licking action of the rasp-like tongue of the cat.

Symptoms are that a shiny, pink flattening or depression appears on the upper lip towards its central division. This gradually extends into an erosion and thickening of the upper lip. Eventually, the entire lip may become eroded, with exposure of the gums, drooling of saliva, and possibly difficulties in feeding.

Treatment is difficult but in the early stages complete removal may be successful. Medical treatments have sometimes proved effective in individual cases. The most successful treatment is irradiation of the lesion.

Röntgen Rays see RADIOGRAPHY and X-RAYS

Roundworms see WORMS and POT BELLY

Royal Cats of Siam see SACRED CATS and SIAMESE

R.C.V.S. The Royal College of Veterinary Surgeons was given its first Royal Charter in 1844 to administer to and protect the interests of the veterinary profession. It remains the governing body of the profession in the U.K. responsible to Government for the administration and discipline of the profession. All qualified veterinarians are members of the Royal College in the U.K. and can only practise so long as they retain their membership.

Royal College of Veterinary Surgeons see R.C.V.S. above.

R.S.P.C.A. The Royal Society for the Protection of Animals is a charity whose responsibility for the welfare of animals is known worldwide. In the U.K. it maintains inspectors in all parts of the country who are constantly endeavouring, both by invoking the law and education, to improve the well being of animal life. In addition the Society runs a number of clinics and hospitals where the poor are able to obtain free qualified veterinary attention.

Royal Society for the Prevention of Cruelty to Animals see R.S.P.C.A. above.

Ruff see FRILL

Rumpy see MANX

Runt Used in the phrase 'the runt of the litter' signifies a noticeably smaller kitten than the rest. Perfectly capable of developing into a normal adult, it is often found that the runt is the most active, is

first to reach the milk supply, and develops more character than the heavier and more lethargic kittens. On the other hand if the small size is due to some genetic or congenital failure or to a pathological cause the runt will probably fade out after a few days or weeks. It will also die if it is so much smaller than the others that it gets pushed aside at feed times. Its survival will depend on the cause and degree of its condition, and if it lives it may fail to grow normally and be in poor condition compared to the other kittens.

Rupture see HERNIA

Russian Blue There has always been speculation as to the origin of the Russian Blue. It is assumed by many that they are the descendants of the blue cats brought from Archangel many years ago by sailors and travellers. However, cats with short blue fur have also been known as Maltese, Spanish, American or just Blue, so where they actually came from is still a matter of conjecture. It must be confessed that the Russian Blues of today have been produced by carefully planned breeding, producing graceful animals with foreign type and unique double coats, having a distinct silvery sheen. Their skulls are flat and narrow, resulting in heads with receding foreheads and short wedged in shape. The whisker pads are prominent and the almond shaped eyes vivid green. The large pointed ears differ from those of other cats in that the skin is thin, almost transparent, with very little fur covering. The slim bodies

are on long legs with dainty oval feet. The coat may be a medium to dark blue in colour, but should be the same all over and be short, thick and fine, standing up almost like seal skin. Faults are white hairs in the fur, tabby markings and rings on the tail.

Quiet by nature, they live happily in flats if necessary, becoming very attached to their owners. Although agile, they are not given to climbing indoors or scratching the furniture.

See colour plate 38, *page 148*.

Rusty-spotted Cat *Felis rubiginosa* is a small species weighing approximately 3 lb. and is very elegant. Its length is 1½ ft with a tail length of about 9 in. It varies from a fawn to rust in colour with white underparts. The spots are distributed rather differently from the Leopard Cat which it somewhat resembles; they are more pronounced on the back and are elongated, they often become less pronounced on the sides but more dense on the flanks; the tail is comparatively free of markings but darkens towards the tip. The head striping resembles the Leopard Cat.

The habitat is Southern India and Ceylon where it is very rare although it is not killed for its skin on account of its small size. It frequents long grassland and brushwood where it hunts small birds and small mammals.

It is reputed to be quite easily tamed if the kittens are taken young.

Russian Blue

S

Sacred Cats Delving back into the past in an endeavour to trace the origin of many of the breeds, not infrequently it is said that the first cats of a particular variety were the guardians of the temples, being looked after by the priests, or they belonged to members of the royal family of the country in question and were, therefore, looked on as 'sacred'.

On the face of it, as many countries have this story, this may all seem rather farfetched, but on consideration there is probably some element of truth behind the tales. In the East, in Turkey and other countries, cats of unusual colouring or coat length, were considered of high value, and it is quite feasible that as such they would be given as presents to royalty or taken into the temples for greater safety to be looked after and fed by the priests.

The first Siamese cats seen in England were known as the 'Royal Cats of Siam', as they were said to have come from the King's Palace. France, from which the first Birmans, the Sacred cats of Burma, came, has the legend of how these cats were guardians of the temple and were much revered by the priests as oracles. See also GUARD CATS and SIAMESE.

Saline Saline is a solution of salt. A solution of saline which contains similar amounts of salt to the blood is known as physiological saline.

Saline is a useful solution with which to bathe wounds. It is also used, as a sterilized solution, to inject into cats who have become dehydrated – lost body fluid.

Salivation Salivation describes the production of saliva and its discharge into the mouth. Saliva is secreted by a number of paired glands lying in the tissues under the tongue and the floor of the mouth, and it enters the mouth by means of small tubes called salivary ducts. Salivation is stimulated by the presence of food. The function of saliva is to moisten the material ingested, thus facilitating both mastication and swallowing. Although the saliva produced by humans and some other species contains digestive juices, feline saliva contains a negligible amount of such substances, food is retained in the mouth for such short periods that there would not be sufficient time for salivary enzymes to function before it reached the stomach.

Salmonellosis *Salmonella* infection is usually contracted by contact with infected faeces of other animals or by eating infected milk, meat, eggs or rodents. Acute infection is usually seen in kittens and gives rise to an acute gastro-enteritis with vomiting, diarrhoea, dysentery, dehydration, collapse and death. Mild cases may show only an intermittent diarrhoea. Abortion due to infection with *S. cholerae-suis* has been reported. Treatment with the broad-spectrum antibiotics is usually effective but carriers may persist and form something of a public health hazard. See also FOOD POISONING.

Sand Cat *Felis margarita* is about the size of the domestic cat and has a most interestingly shaped head with very short muzzle and expressive eyes; the ears are very widely spaced – almost at the side of the head – and are wide at the base with a black patch on the back. The body colouring varies from yellow-brown to grey-brown and is plain except for a few stripes on the legs and three bands on the tail which is black tipped. The paws are rather unusual as they have a thick covering of fur, no doubt to assist its life in the sandy areas. In good coat this animal is most beautiful.

The Sand Cat's habitat is North Africa, where it lives in semi-desert areas and rocky wastes, Arabia, and parts of the Middle East extending as far north as southern Russia.

Very little is known of its habits, but it is considered to be nocturnal and hunts such animals as ground squirrels and hares. As it is said to dig shallow burrows in the sand and rocks where it bears its young and hides during the daytime, this mode of living would undoubtedly account for its unusual features.

Sanitary Trays see LITTER BOXES

Scalds see ACCIDENTS

Scottish Fold First seen in Scotland in 1961, this variety has ears which are folded forward and downward. Similar mutations have also appeared in Germany and Belgium. Short coated, any colour and coat pattern is possible. The variety has not yet been granted recognition by the Governing Council of the Cat Fancy. Several have been imported into the U.S.A., but no standard has yet been recognized. *See colour plate* 39, *page 173*.

Scottish Wild Cat see EUROPEAN WILD CAT

Scratching see PRURITIS, PSEUDORABIES and SKIN DISEASES

Scratching Posts Many cats take great delight in sharpening their claws on the best furniture and curtains. Since punishment is rarely effective, the only remedy is to exclude cats from any rooms in which you wish to preserve the fittings and furniture. Prevention, as in many behaviour problems, is better than cure – cats brought up with a scratching-post generally content themselves with using that.

Scratching posts may be made out of lengths of trees with a rough bark (e.g. elm) or planks of a non-splintering type. Posts with a special rough surface are obtainable from petshops. Non-wooden scratching boards may be improvized at home by sewing a length of coconut matting or strong sisal cord carpet on a suitable frame.

The secret is to make the scratching post or board available to the cat as early in its life as possible, so that it acquires a habit of using the post in preference to other things.

Scurf see DANDRUFF

Scrotum The sac containing the testicles is made of comparatively thin and sensitive skin, and shows a tendency to be affected by dermatitis, particularly if irritant chemicals contact it. It is also quite easily penetrated by sharp objects, so that bacterial infection may affect the testicles as a result of bite wounds. Castration is usually the best solution, although antibiotic therapy might be attempted with a valuable stud cat.

Seal Point see HIMALAYAN and SIAMESE

Seborrhea see DANDRUFF

Sedatives This is a composite description of a large number of drugs which effectively sedate an animal. Cats are notoriously diverse in their response to drugs and have until recently been difficult to sedate safely and effectively. The barbiturates and more recently the promazine tranquillizers have considerably improved the situation.

Serval *Felis serval* is an extremely distinctive cat and its head shape quickly distinguishes it from other species, it is comparatively small while the

A scratching pad is an alternative to a scratching post

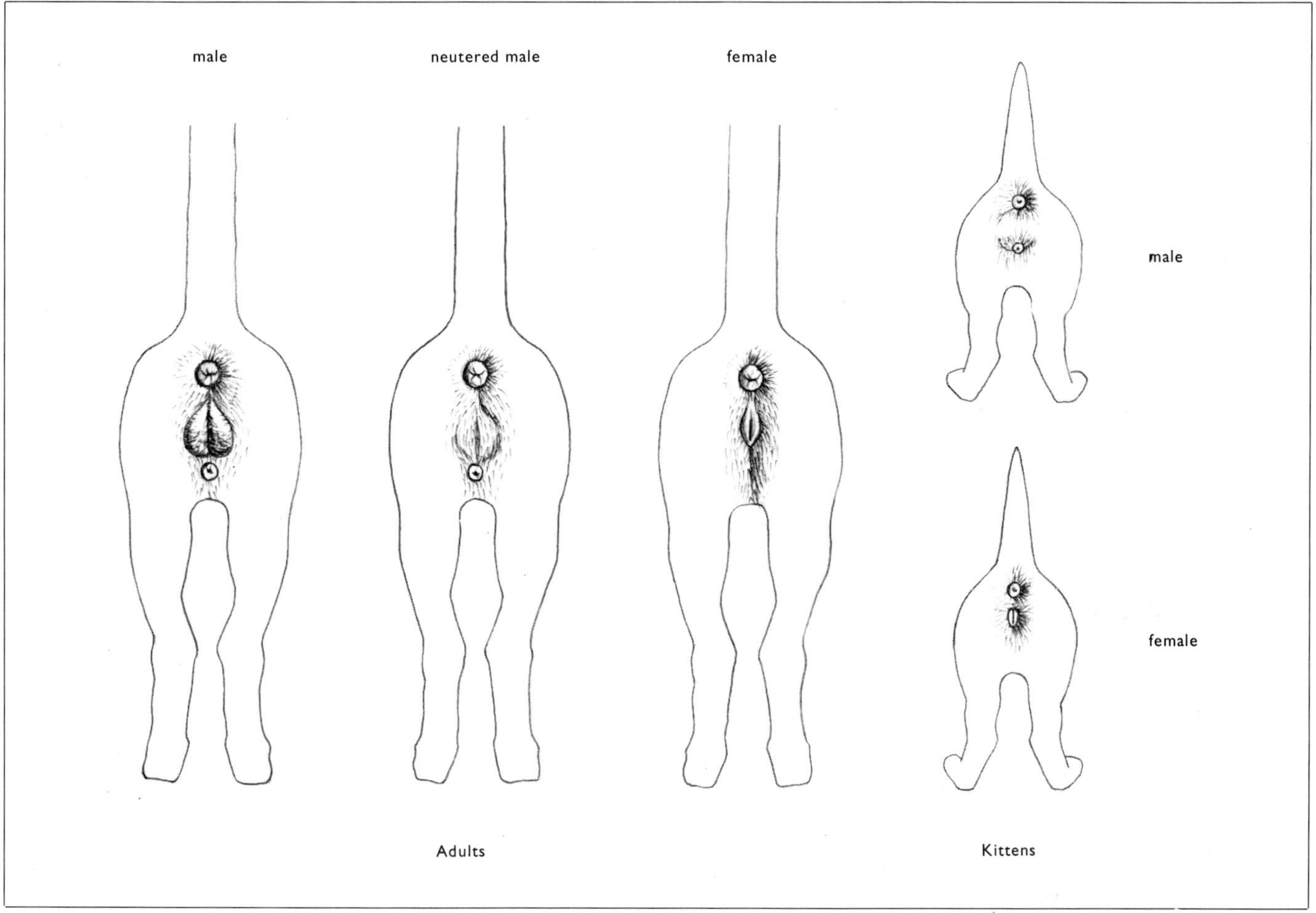

left A scratching post saves damage to furnishings

above Sexing cats and kittens

ears are very large and set high on the head with almost no space between; the tips are slightly rounded. It has none of the usual stripes on the face, but a row of spots run from the nose upwards to the ears and appear again on the cheeks; the nose is black with a pink central patch. The coat colouring varies from tawny-grey to reddish-yellow. There are stripes on the neck giving a 'bib' effect. The body is spotted with large dense black spots which, on the spine run horizontally but do not form a stripe; they become larger on the flanks, but decrease in size towards the legs and are very small on the paws. The tail is ringed with a black tip. The fur on the underparts is almost white. A black coated form (Denis 1964) is also recorded. The head and body measure about 3 ft and the tail measures about 9–12 in. The general build is light and it is long legged.

The habitat is Africa where it is found over a wide area but it frequents broken country as opposed to dry desert, lying up in bush and reeds and not far distant from a water supply. It is mainly nocturnal and its prey consists of small mammals up to the size of steinbok, and birds up to the size of guinea fowl and francolins; an expert climber, it is also able to take roosting birds.

Sexing Cats are perhaps a little difficult to sex for the untrained eye. It is, however, a relatively simple practice. Lift the tail and observe the anus. Now observe the distance between the anus and the genital opening below it. In females the distance is very small while in males it is greater. Also in males the swelling of the scrotum containing testicles is apparent in entire, unneutered animals.

Sexual Behaviour see BEHAVIOUR

Shaded Silver Long-hair At the beginning of the century, the Shaded Silvers were recognized in Britain, but at that time there was a great deal of confusion in the judging between those with lighter coats and darker-coated Chinchillas, and so their classes were dropped. They are still recognized in North America and other parts of the world.

The coat should be pure unmarked silver in colour, with definite shadings down the sides, face and tail; the general effect being much darker than that of the Chinchilla. The eyes should be blue-green, and the nose brick red. Faults are bars, and cream or brown tinges in the fur. The general characteristics are as for other Long-hairs.

Shadow Point see SIAMESE, TABBY POINT

Shampoo see BATHING

Shock The medical term 'shock' is generally considered to mean a state of circulatory disturbance such that the cardiac output is decreased and the total circulating blood volume reduced. As a result the tissues receive less oxygen and the body temperature falls.

Signs of shock include reduced response to stimuli that would normally alert attention, weakness of the limbs, or collapse. The mucous membranes of the gums, lips and eyes become pale pink in colour, and, in severe cases where oxygen depletion is marked, they may appear bluish. The feet become cold to the touch, the pulse is weak and rapid, respirations may be shallow, rapid and possibly laboured, and if the animal is conscious, it may show signs of thirst.

Shock follows a road accident or the infliction of any wound causing severe internal or external haemorrhage; exposure to extremes of temperature, electrocution, thermal or chemical burns, near-asphyxiation, major surgery, severe loss of body fluids, following vomiting or diarrhoea, and prolonged and difficult parturition. In some situations the onset of shock can be anticipated and measures taken to minimize its extent. Early treatment of shock may easily save an animal's life. Once shock progresses beyond a certain point it becomes irreversible, and the prognosis is grave. No time should be lost in taking a shocked animal to the veterinarian.

First aid: Keep the patient warm by wrapping it in blankets, but do not apply local heat, e.g. hot-water bottles, since these can cause vasodilation which actually aggravates the condition. Avoid disturbing the patient, and, if transporting the patient, make sure he is well cushioned against jolting of the vehicle. Do not give fluids by mouth. Stimulants such as brandy should not be given.

Show Standards Each exhibit at a show is judged according to the set standard, that is they should conform very closely to a number of characteristics, as given in the standard of points approved by the Governing Council of the Cat Fancy in Britain, and by the various governing bodies in the U.S.A. and on the Continent; the latter following the British standards.

The scale of points is set out under various headings, with points totalling one hundred in all being allocated between the colouring, the markings or lack of them, the coat, the body, tail, head, ears and eyes. The number of points under each heading vary considerably as to the importance placed on a particular feature for the variety in question. For example, in Britain in the Cream Long-hairs 30 points are given for the coat colour alone, but in the Blue Long-hairs 25 is allowed for the head and only 20 for the coat. In the U.S.A. the standards are very similar, with slight variations in the points allocated.

The nearer to the show standard a cat is, the more chance it has of winning its class, but the perfect cat has yet to be born, and most exhibits have some slight fault.

Condition too is very important and points are awarded for this. It is of little use for a cat to come close to the required standard, but to be in poor condition.

Shortened Tails see BREEDING ABNORMALITIES

Showing or Exhibiting *Britain* Throughout the British Isles, cat shows are held under the auspices of the Governing Council of the Cat Fancy. There are three categories, all one day only: the Championship show where Challenge Certificates are given (see CHALLENGE CERTIFICATES); Sanction shows, which are really rehearsals for Championship shows, but where Challenge Certificates are not given; and lastly the smaller Exemption shows, which are ideal for beginners, where Challenge Certificates are not given and the rules are not so stringent as that of the other two shows, but well-known judges officiate so that it enables new exhibitors to learn and compare the merits of their cats, and to understand how shows are run.

To enter a show, a schedule and entry form should be obtained from the show manager. These are ready about eight weeks before the show day. The schedule contains details of the classes (see CLASSES AT SHOWS); the names of the judges; the entry fees payable; the prize money, and details of the cups and specials offered by the various clubs. Clubs may put on special classes for their own members only. It is not necessary to belong to a club to enter a show, but there are advantages in reduced entry fees, if it is the one organizing the show; and the Club's cups and special prizes for which to compete. A cat must be registered to be entered, unless it is competing in the household pet classes only. If not bred by the exhibitor, it must have been owned and transferred to him three weeks or more before the show day.

The entry form requires details of the cat's name and various particulars as given on the registration or transfer form. The numbers of the classes chosen (not more than twelve) should be filled in carefully, making sure they are the correct ones for the cat. The entry form must be correct in all details, as otherwise disqualification may follow, when the catalogue is checked by the Registrar. The correct amount of entry fees must be enclosed and it must be received by the show manager before the closing date.

It is inadvisable to enter any kitten or cat at a show that has not been inoculated against Feline Infectious Enteritis.

About ten days before the show a tally, giving the number of the pen the cat will occupy in the hall, together with vetting-in and passing-out cards, are sent to the exhibitor. Each exhibit is thoroughly examined by a veterinary surgeon before it is allowed to enter the hall, so that it is useless to take a cat along that is not in first class condition. Fleas in the coat, dirty ears, inflamed gums or any other sign that all is not well may mean non-passing by the veterinary surgeon and the forfeiting of the entry fees. The cat must be taken to the show in a basket or other proper container, never on a lead or carried.

A warm white blanket and a suitable litter tray must be provided, and once in the show, this should be placed in the numbered pen corresponding to the tally put on white tape or ribbon and tied around the cat's neck. Peat moss is usually provided in the hall. Feeding dishes and toys are not allowed in the pen, but cats may be fed about lunch time, when the open classes have been judged. Judging may go on all day, with the results lists going up on the award board as they are received from the judge. Prize cards are put on the pens but prize money is not paid out for several weeks until all winning entries in the catalogue have been checked by the Registrar.

The judge goes to each pen accompanied by the steward who carries the table, the towel and the bowl with disinfectant. The steward takes the cat out of the pen for the judge and places it on the table for her inspection. Should the cat prove exceedingly difficult to get out of the pen or object violently to being handled at its first show, it is inadvisable to continue to show it.

Some shows now have 'Best of Breed' instead of 'Best in Show'. 'Best of Breed' means that the best of each variety with championship status is chosen by the judges, probably winning a rosette. 'Best in Show', that is best adult, best kitten and best neuter, is chosen by a panel of judges in each section – Long-hairs, Short-hairs, Siamese or other type.

On returning from the show, the cat should be given a little brandy or whisky in milk, wiped all over with a little mild diluted non-toxic disinfectant, given a good feed, and should be isolated from other cats and kittens for a few days at least, as even if inoculated against Feline Infectious Enteritis, it may still bring home some other ailment.

North America The biggest difference between the British shows and those held in North America and on the Continent is that the latter are usually two-day shows, being held on Saturday and Sunday. Shows in Britain are one-day only; the majority taking place on a Saturday, but a few are held mid-week, due to the difficulty of finding suitable halls.

The method of entering and exhibiting at any show is much the same throughout the Cat Fancy world, starting with the sending off for the schedule or premium sheet about two months before the show. The entry forms or entry blanks, as they are called in North America, have to be filled in with details as on the cat's registration certificate and returned by the closing date, or before, with correct fees to the show manager.

The shows are run by clubs under the sponsorship of the various registering Associations. In North America frequently there are four shows being held in the hall at once, with the same cats taking part in three of them or more. There will probably be two All-Breed, one Long-hair Speciality and one Short-hair Speciality, with the Club actually running the show being responsible for one of the All-Breeds.

The cats are vetted in, and both in North America and on the Continent, as the judges do not go to the cats, the owners are allowed to hang curtains inside the pens and to display any ribbons or rosettes won at previous shows at the back, any won on the day being hung on the outside.

In America, as each class is called, the cats are taken to the judging rings by a steward or the owner. There are no miscellaneous or club classes as in Britain, and the appropriate breed class entered will depend on the cat's achievements in the past (see CLASSES AT SHOWS). A cat can go forward at the show, if it wins its class, to be judged against the winner of the next, for example, the winner of the Novice class will be compared with the winner of the Open class until eventually by elimination a Best Cat is chosen and also a Best Opposite Sex, referred to as BOX for short. Ribbons are given to all the winners with special rosettes or ribbons for the Best cats. The Best of each variety is also chosen and also the best neuters. Kittens are judged separately and their Bests do not compete with the cats. There may also be classes for Household pets.

There are various All-American awards and winning cats at the different shows are awarded points according to the number of wins and also the number of cats beaten, until the cat with the highest score becomes Cat of the Year.

Continent On the Continent the Best in Show is chosen by a panel of judges, as at the majority of the shows in Britain. Ribbons and rosettes are given to the Best cats. Prize money is not awarded, but special prizes, frequently presented by exhibitors, are given to the winners. Many British judges officiate at these shows and are then entitled to be called International judges.

Shows On an average there are about forty cat shows organized by the various cat clubs each year in the British Isles under the auspices of the Governing Council of the Cat Fancy (see SHOWING OR EXHIBITING). In size they range from the small exemption show with less than one hundred cats to the largest cat show in the world: this show is organized by the National Cat Club and held at Olympia in London, attracting an entry of more than 2,000 cats.

At all these shows approved judges officiate in a purely honorary capacity, receiving only travelling and hotel expenses, giving their services entirely free.

As far as possible, the shows are held with a two-week interval between them, as cats may not be exhibited more than once within fourteen days. Due to the scarcity of halls, it is not always practical to have such an interval, and some shows may even be held on the same day.

At the British shows, the prize monies are small. Cups or wins on cups are offered at the shows and also special prizes. As well as the Club organizing the shows, many of the other clubs also guarantee classes for their members only. The prize money is not paid out on the day, as all entries in the catalogues have to be checked to make sure the details given about each cat are correct, and this may take several weeks.

The Continental shows are run on slightly different lines, and tend to be smaller than the British ones. Whereas in Britain the judge goes to the pen with the steward, who gets the cat out and places it on the judge's table for inspection, in many countries in Europe, the cats are brought by the stewards to the judge at the end of the hall. It is also usual for the cats belonging to the same owner to be penned together or next to one another regardless of the breed instead of the colours and varieties as in Britain. There are not nearly so many classes and gifts, frequently donated by other exhibitors, are given to the winners. As the judges do not go to the pens as in Britain, exhibitors are permitted to hang curtains around and to display in the pens the ribbons and rosettes won by the cats.

A similar system of judging is carried out in North America, with pens being curtained and ribbons displayed. The owners take the cats to the judges in a judging ring. The classes are few, one big entry fee is paid, with cats being judged under various classifications and dropping out as they are beaten, until the Best finally emerges. Cash prizes and special awards are frequently offered by cat food and similar companies for the Best Cats, but there is no prize money as such. Ribbons are awarded to the Best in Show, the Best of Colour, Best Opposite Sex, Best Grand Champion and so on. As in Britain rosettes may only be offered by clubs and not by individuals.

Siamese Introduced into Britain in the 1870s, those with seal points were known as the 'Royal Cats of Siam', as it was said they had come from the Royal Palace in Siam. Chocolate points were also among the first arrivals. The early cat fanciers fell in love with the unique coat pattern and fascinating blue eyes of these cats. However, the kittens proved to be delicate and susceptible to the most minor ailments. Eventually, by using common sense in upbringing and selective breeding, Siamese were produced which were as healthy and even more prolific than many of the other pedigree breeds. The numbers increased rapidly, until today they are the most numerous of all the registered cats.

The early Siamese had roundish heads and far from slender bodies, differing greatly from the modern variety, medium in size, with long slender bodies on slim legs, long tapering tails and long, well-proportioned wedge-shaped heads, with large pricked ears. There are now seven recognized point colourings, not counting the 'Any Other Colour Siamese' which caters for any further possible colour variations in the points, such as Blue Creams etc.

The general standard is the same for all Siamese: *Head:* Long and well proportioned, with width between the eyes, narrowing to a fine muzzle. Ears rather large and pricked, wide at the base. *Shape:* Medium in size, body long and svelte, legs slim, the hind legs being slightly higher than the front ones: small oval feet: tail long and tapering, straight or very slightly kinked at the end. *Eyes:* Clear brilliant deep blue, oriental in shape, and slanting towards the nose. No squint. *Coat:* Very short and fine in texture, glossy and close-lying. Faults are white toes, bad kinks, and squints, brindling in the points.

When first born the kittens are white all over, with no signs of the coloured points which develop as the fur grows. It may be as long as three months before the definite colour is seen, although long before that it should be possible to distinguish one point colour from another. They develop much earlier than many other breeds, and by the age of four weeks may be running all over the place.

They mature young, and this should be borne in mind, as a female may call when only five to six months old, and a male may be capable of siring when not much older. Neither should be allowed to breed at such an early age, and if not required for breeding should be neutered. The veterinary surgeon will advise as to when this should be done as it depends on development.

Grooming Condition is all important if a cat is to look well-groomed; this means correct feeding and general good care. Siamese love grooming, but should never be brushed too hard or combed too much. Over-brushing will take the undercoat out and over-combing may leave track marks in the short fine fur. More than anything they love hard hand grooming, with the hand being drawn firmly from head to tail. Finishing off with a rub with a chamois leather will produce a wonderful sheen. The ears should be inspected to make sure there is no sign of ear mites, which may need veterinary attention. Any dirt or dust may be removed gently with a little cotton wool, taking care not to poke too hard. The occasional use of a fine steel tooth comb is recommended to make sure that the fur is completely flea-free, particularly if the cat is to be shown, as fleas may mean disqualification.

Showing Competition is high in the Siamese section at the shows, so any cat or kitten entered must look at its best. Every entry is inspected by a veterinary surgeon before being allowed into the show hall, and if the cat has dirty ears, fleas in the coat, is running a slight temperature, or is obviously off colour, he will be disqualified, with the entry fees being forfeit.

Seal Point The points, that is the mask, ears, legs, feet and tail should be a clearly defined seal brown,

Siamese Seal Point and Tabby Point kittens

Siamese Tabby Point

with the mask being connected by tracing with the ears, and the body colour should be cream, shading into pale warm fawn on the back.

The Seal Point is the most popular of all the Siamese varieties, and many come close to the set standard.

See colour plates 44 *and* 45, *page 201.*

Blue Point A Blue Point is first said to have been registered in 1894, but little is known as to how it was bred. There appears to be no definite evidence as to how the first Blue Points were produced; whether they were 'sports' or from cross-breeding.

The points should be blue, all being the same colours, and the ears should not be darker. The body should be a glacial white, shading gradually into blue on the back. The eyes should be a clear, bright vivid blue.

See colour plate 40, *page 174.*

Chocolate Point Although the Siamese with chocolate points were said to have been among the earliest known in Britain, it was not until 1950 that they were recognized, and given a separate breed number.

The points should be the colour of milk chocolate, including the ears, with the body colour being ivory all over – shading, if at all, to the same colour as the points. The eyes should be a clear bright vivid blue.

See colour plate 41, *page 175.*

Lilac Point Lilac Points were called Frost Points at first in the U.S.A., being known there for many years before they were recognized in Britain. Lilac mated to Lilac proved to breed true and before long these cats with their delicate colouring had become very popular, and today their classes at the shows are well filled.

The points should be pinkish grey, with the nose-leather and pads being of faded lilac; the body

colour should be off-white (magnolia), shading, if any, to tone with points. Eyes: Clear, light, vivid blue (but not pale).
See colour plate 42, *page 175.*

Tabby Point It is believed the earliest Tabby Points known in Britain were produced from a Siamese mating with a farm tabby in 1952. One of the kittens with Siamese type was mated to a Seal Point male, producing Siamese with tabby points, which, at first, were known as Lynx Points. Further matings followed, some with Silver tabbies, others with brown tabbies. They were shown in the 'Any Other Variety' classes in the early 1960s and as well as 'Lynx' were also known as 'Shadow Points', but the name eventually agreed on, although not liked by all, was 'Tabby Point'. After several years of selective breeding, recognition was granted in 1966.

The type is as for the other Siamese. The body colour should be pale conforming to the recognized standard for the particular points colouring.

The ears should be solid coloured bearing the impression of a thumbmark, with no stripes. There should be clearly defined stripes on the mask, especially around the eyes and nose, and distinct markings on the cheeks, with darkly spotted whisker pads. The legs should be marked with various sized broken stripes, with solid markings on the backs of the hind legs, and the tail should be ringed with varying sized clearly defined rings, but ending in a solid tip. The eyes should be a brilliant clear blue.
See colour plate 47, *page 201.*

Red Point After the 1939–45 War several fanciers became interested in the possibilities of producing Siamese, with even more varied coloured points, such as Red. Both in the U.S.A. and in Britain experimental breedings were carried on on very much the same lines, involving cross-matings with Seal Point females and Short-haired red tabby males. It took many years to perfect the bright reddish-gold points colouring, and it was not until 1966 that recognition was granted. At first the majority produced were males, any females having tortoiseshell points, but eventually both sexes were produced.

The early Reds were known as Red Point Short-hairs. Many carried shadow tabby markings which it was feared would be introduced into other Siamese points colouring, and it was not until after the appearance of Tabby Points that the Red Points were allowed to be called Red Point Siamese.

The characteristics are as for the other Siamese, but the body should be white, shading to apricot on the back; points, ears, mask, legs, feet, tail a bright reddish-gold, and the eyes a bright vivid blue.
See colour plate 43, *page 176.*

Tortie Point These are invariably an all-female variety, and are most attractive with their tortoiseshell markings. Produced in the first place from Red and Tortoiseshell short-hairs, mated to Siamese, they are a recently recognized variety. The body colouring may be cream or fawn, and the tortie markings should be restricted entirely to the points. The ears should be seal coloured, sprinkled with red, or red sprinkled with seal. The mask too should be seal defined with tracings up to the ears, the distribution of cream and seal to be in equal proportions, but the patches need not be even. The legs and feet should be in accordance with the mask, and the tail should have the same basic colour as the mask, and may be brindled with cream. The eyes should be a brilliant deep blue.
See colour plate 46, *page 201.*

Any Other Dilution Siamese It was realized some time ago that there were a number of possible colour variations in the points of the Siamese in addition to those already recognized, and selective breeding has now produced a number of different colours. Formerly shown under Any Other Colour Siamese these are now known collectively as Any Other Dilution Siamese. They are as follows:

Cream Point
Blue Cream Point
Chocolate Cream Point
Lilac Cream Point

Blue Tortie Point
Chocolate Tortie Point
Lilac Tortie Point

Red Tabby Point
Cream Tabby Point

Tabby Tortie Point

It is possible that there will be other colour variations, but the type and general characteristics are as given for the other Siamese, and all should have the striking blue eyes, so much admired.

In the U.S.A. there is also the Albino Siamese, having white fur and a pinkish skin. It is not yet known in Britain or on the Continent.

Siberian Tiger see TIGER

Silver Mau see EGYPTIAN MAU

Silver Tabby see TABBY LONG-HAIR and TABBY SHORT-HAIR

Sinusitis see CATARRH

Si-Rex see DEVON REX

Skeleton The skeleton consists of the bony structures that go to make up the rigid framework of the body. All vertebrate species have a skeleton, and it fulfills a number of functions. The bones of the limbs, vertebral column, pelvis and chest make up a system of rigid levers: the effect of the muscles pulling on these levers is movement of various kinds, e.g. walking, respiratory action, twitching of the tail, etc. Many bones, for example, those of the

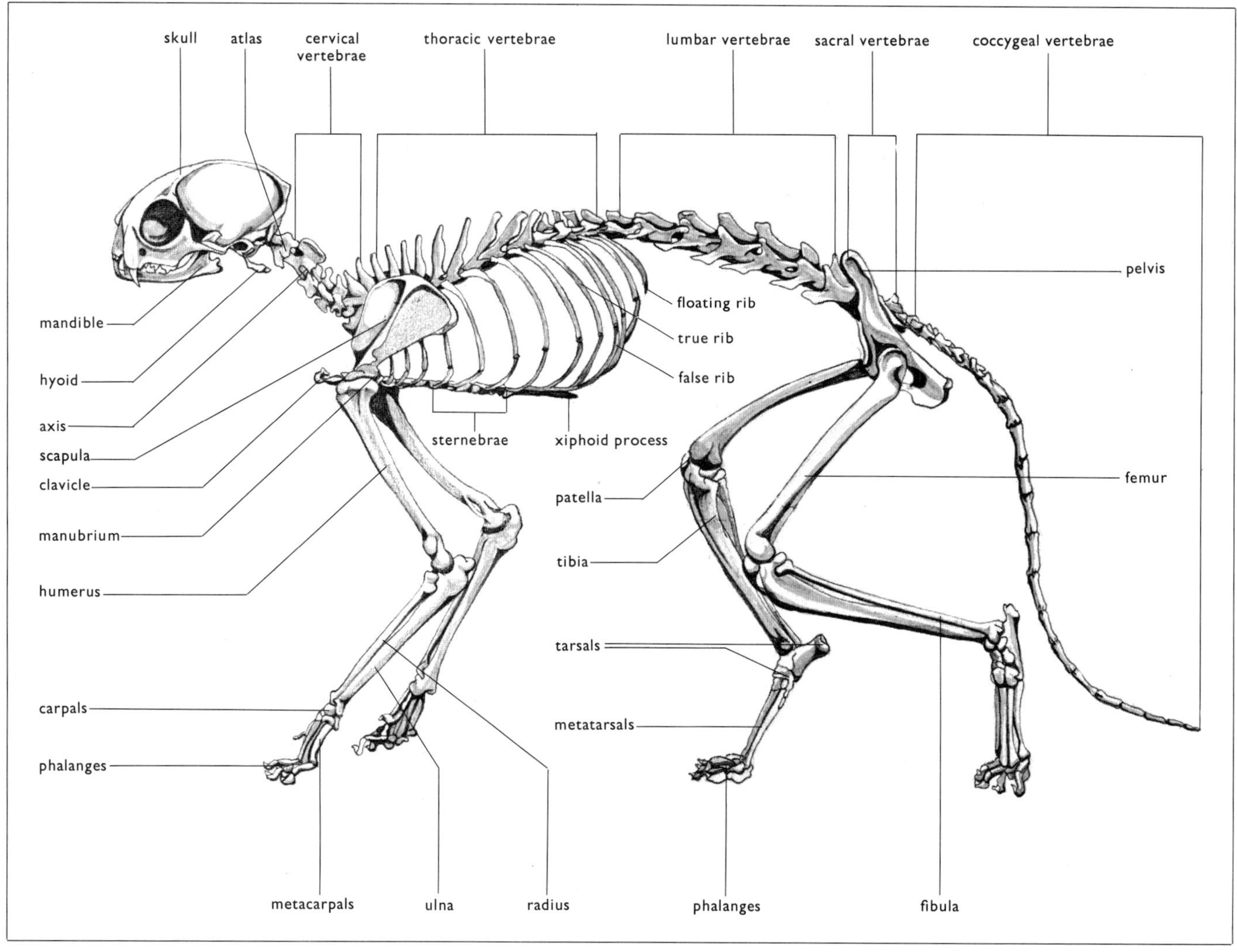

The skeleton of a cat

skull, pelvis and chest, serve to protect vital and delicate organs from mechanical injury. The ribs and the long bones and the vertebrae all contain cavities in which blood cells are manufactured. The bones are supplied with nutrient substances that enable them to grow and maintain themselves by means of blood vessels. They are surrounded on their outer surfaces by a tough, protective membrane, the periosteum. Where two adjacent bones come into contact with one another and articulate together to form a joint, a layer of smooth hard cartilage is found overlying the bone surface. This ensures smooth joint action.

Bones consist of various categories. There are long bones, such as the femur or humerus, which are roughly cylindrical in shape, with a hollow medulla in which bone marrow is found; short bones, which are made up of a core of spongy bone surrounded by compact bone; flat bones such as those of the skull and pelvis, which are made up of two layers of compact bone with a fine layer of spongy bone sandwiched between them; and irregular bones, such as the vertebrae which resemble short bones but are irregular in shape.

Skull This structure encloses the brain. The lower jaw is attached to the cranium and articulates with it. The whole skull is made up of a number of flat bones that fit together rather like jig-saw pieces. During the early life of the kitten the union between these bones is not complete and soft areas may be felt in the skull. It is important to prevent injury occurring to these vulnerable parts. The skull is pierced by a number of holes through which nerves – those nerves that link the brain with organs like the ears and eyes – emerge. Injury to the skull is comparatively rare, although a hard blow can result in depressed fracture, with a danger of brain damage occurring.

Vertebral Column The vertebrae are basically cylindrical in shape, the hollow part being termed the neural canal. The spinal cord runs through the neural canals of successive vertebrae, rather as a

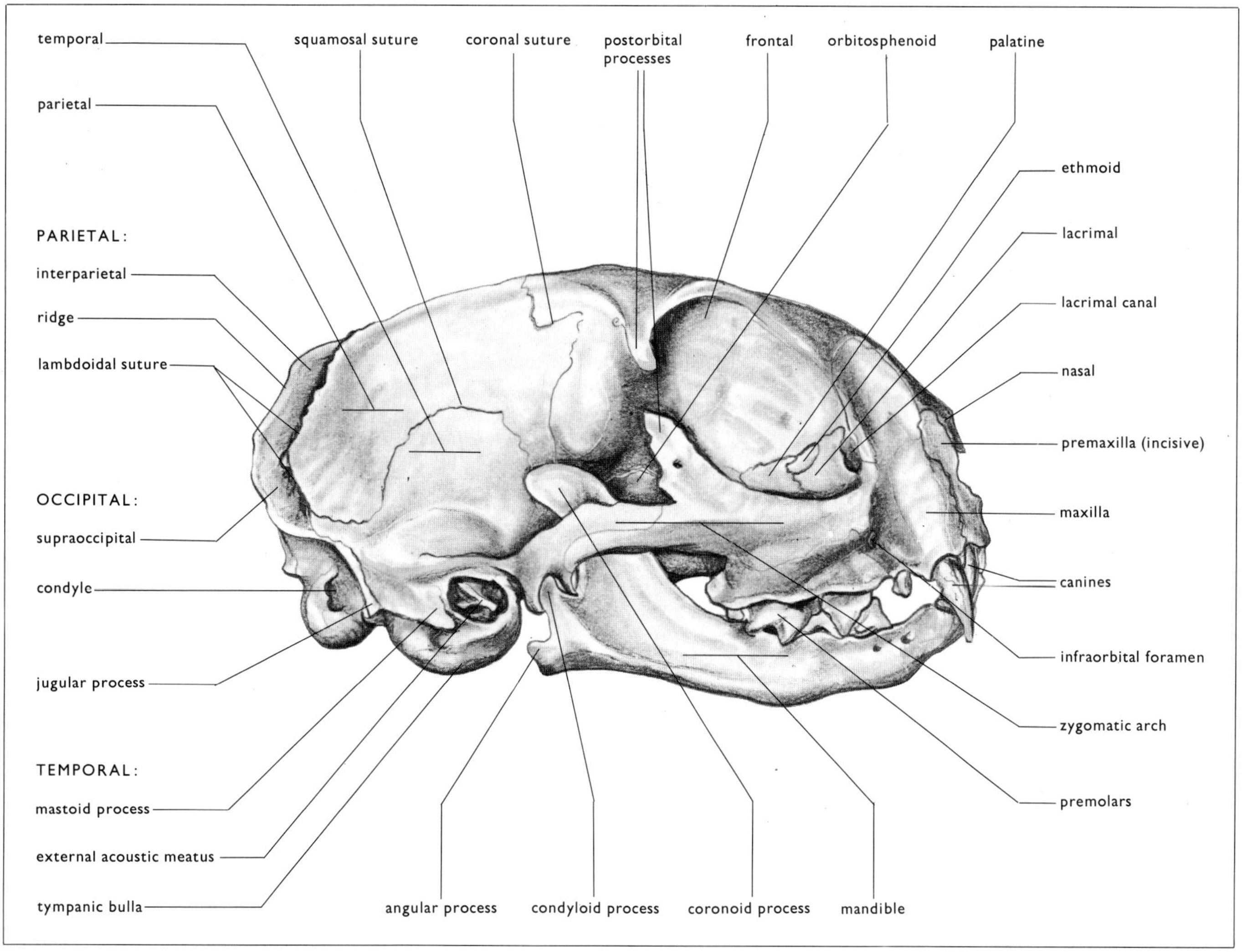

temporal
squamosal suture
coronal suture
postorbital processes
frontal
orbitosphenoid
palatine
parietal
ethmoid
PARIETAL:
interparietal
ridge
lambdoidal suture
lacrimal
lacrimal canal
nasal
premaxilla (incisive)
OCCIPITAL:
supraoccipital
maxilla
condyle
canines
jugular process
infraorbital foramen
zygomatic arch
TEMPORAL:
mastoid process
external acoustic meatus
tympanic bulla
premolars
angular process
condyloid process
coronoid process
mandible

above A cat skull; *right* a cross-section of the vertebral column

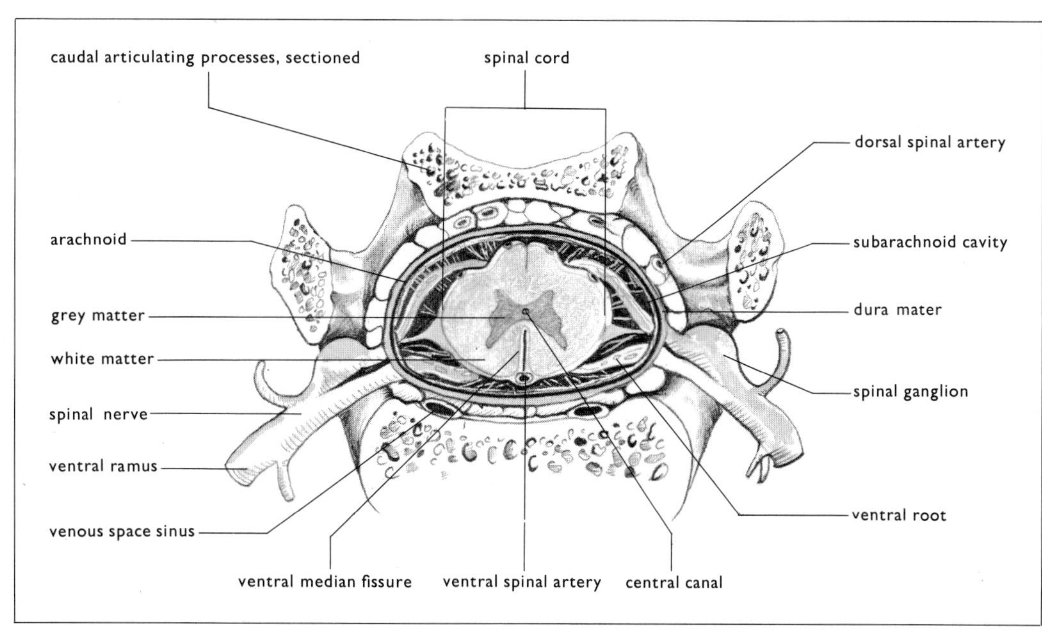

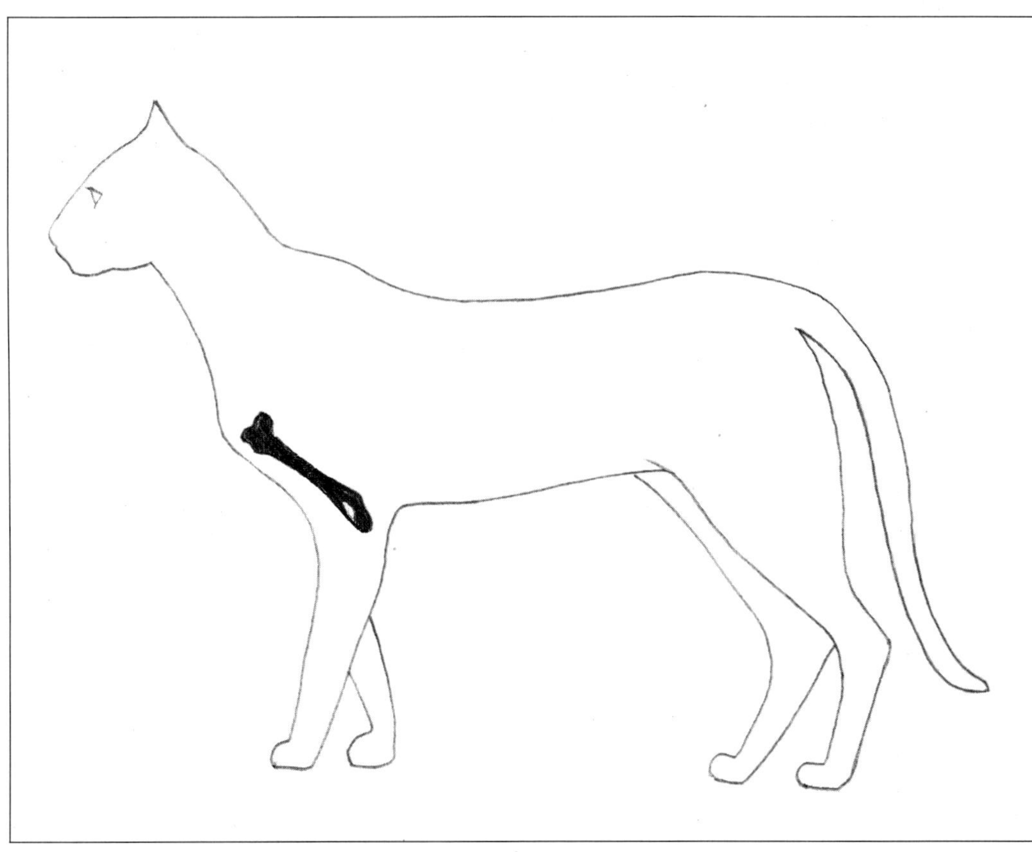

left A diagram showing the situation of the humerus; *below left* the humerus

colour 49 Spotted, Silver kitten

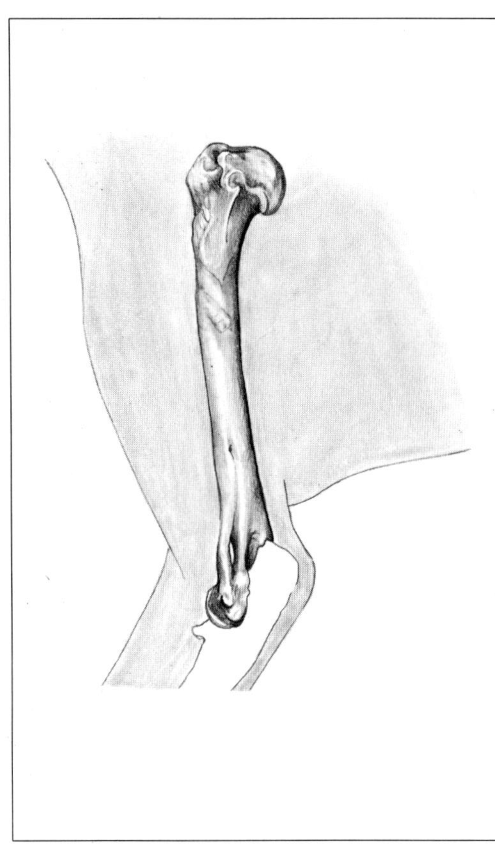

string is passed through beads. The vertebrae also possess a number of projections which serve as attachment points for the muscles of the back. They are divided up into regions since their structure is found to be modified according to the part of the spine in which they are situated.

The cervical vertebrae are found in the neck and are seven in number. The first two are highly specialized to permit nodding and rotatory movements of the head.

The thirteen thoracic vertebrae are those of the chest.

The lumbar vertebrae, which are found in the upper abdomen are seven in number and have very large transverse processes, to which are attached the muscles of the abdominal wall.

There are three sacral vertebrae, but they are fused together to form a bony mass known as the sacrum. This structure articulates with the bones of the pelvis. The coccygeal vertebrae are found in the tail, and their number varies according to its length. They have a very simple structure, with almost negligible processes. Those at the very end of the tail lack a neural canal, and are little more than solid cylinders of bone.

Ribs These are flattened, elongated bones that form a cage-like structure to which are attached the muscles that make up the chest wall. They are attached dorsally to the thoracic vertebrae, and

colour 50 Tabby Long-hair Brown
51 Tabby Long-hair Red and kittens

right A diagram showing the situation of the femur; *below right* the femur

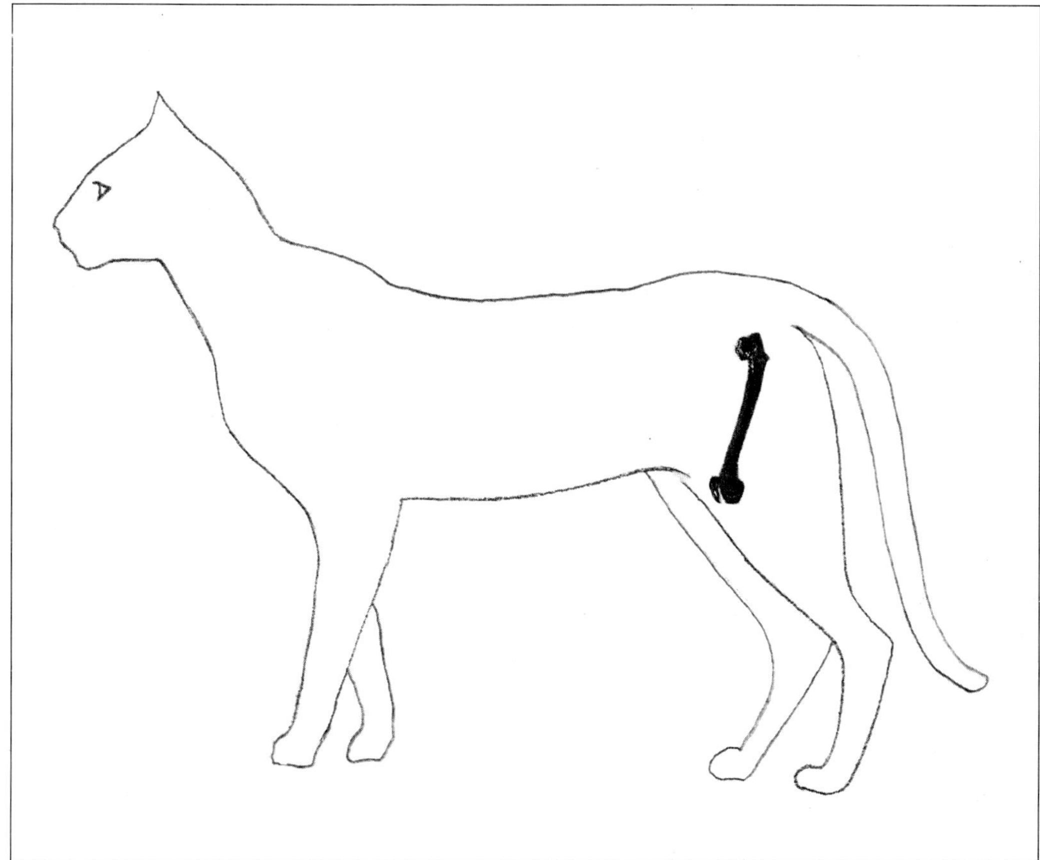

ventrally to the breast bone (sternum). There are usually thirteen pairs of ribs, and, although they are not hollow, they contain a substantial amount of red marrow, and hence play an important part in blood cell production. The movements of the chest wall which are made possible by the ribs enable the volume of the chest-cavity to be varied, allowing the lungs to fill and empty.

Forelimb Bones The scapula or shoulder bone forms the uppermost part of the forelimb. The clavicle ('collar bone') is present only in rudimentary form, and does not articulate with any other bones.

The humerus articulates with the scapula at its upper end and with the radius and ulna at its lower end.

The radius and ulna are parallel bones that go to make up the forearm. The radius, situated slightly inside the ulna also articulates with the humerus.

The forepaw is made up of three groups of parallel bones: the carpals which are situated immediately below the radius and ulna; the metacarpals, situated below the carpals; and the phalanges, corresponding to the human fingers, each set of which constitutes a digit.

Hindlimb Bones The femur or thigh bone is a very long and comparatively fragile bone. The upper-

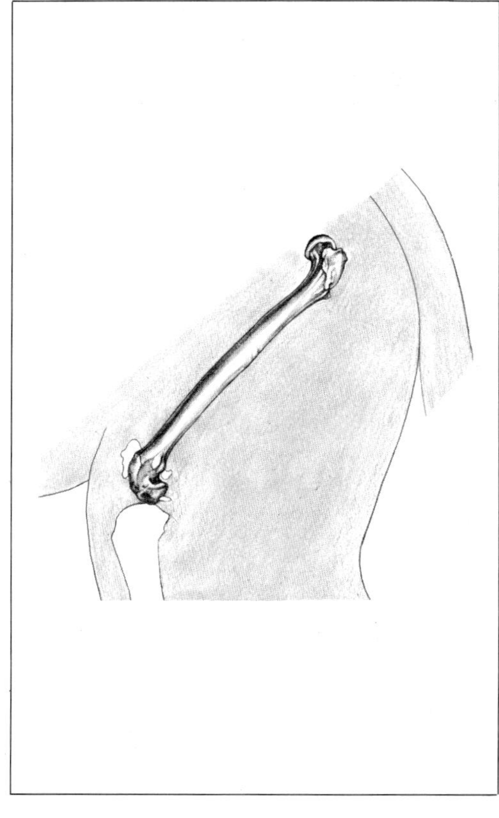

most end, usually called simply the femoral head, makes the ball of a ball-and-socket joint with the acetabulum of the pelvis. The lower end articulates with the tibia and fibula.

The tibia and fibula are basically rather similar to the radius and ulna, but the fibula is very fine in comparison with the tibia. The articulation of the upper ends of the tibia and fibula with the lower end of the femur constitutes the stifle or knee joint, together with small bones, the patella and the fabella.

The bones of the hind paw correspond approximately to those of the forepaw, and are called the tarsals, metatarsals and phalanges.

Pelvis This structure is a system of flat bones fused together, and is attached both to the sacrum and the femurs by ligamentous connections. All the bones of the pelvis are paired, and it may be thought of as consisting of two hip-bones (coxae) which have joined together. Each coxa comprises an ilium, an ischium and a pubis, which join at the acetabulum. The ilium is a large, roughly paddle-shaped projection, whose free end articulates with the sacrum. The pubis forms the forward part of the floor of the pelvis and the ischium forms the hindermost part of it.

Skin Diseases The skin is a very complex organ with numerous parts and several functions. It reflects not only specific conditions which relate only to its own malfunction but it can be diseased as a result of general bodily disease. The diagnosis of skin conditions presents the veterinary and medical clinician with a considerable problem since several different causes can produce similar lesions making a differential diagnosis extremely difficult.

Parasites remain a major cause of skin disease. Great care must be exercised to ensure that they are absent. See PARASITES.

Eczema is a term used in connection with skin disease. It is now so loosely used particularly by the lay public as to have lost any real meaning, and it is best avoided.

After parasitic infection one of the commonest types of skin conditions seen in the cat is known by a variety of names including Milliary dermatitis, Milliary eczema, Eczema and Fish eczema, the latter so-called from an erroneous belief that the disease is due to an entirely fish diet. The cause of the disease is not yet clear although it is probably complex and involves nutritional, hormonal and possibly parasitic factors. The condition appears first as numerous small, scabby areas in the skin, distributed mainly along the back on each side of the spine and around the base of the tail. The spots are apparently rather itchy as the cat licks, bites, scratches and rubs at the affected areas causing raw, moist places to develop. If the small scabs are removed then circular ulcers are left, appearing as raw, red, moist spots. There is a loss of hair over the affected areas of skin and the remaining coat is often stained brown from the cat's saliva during licking. The condition tends to spread slowly until the entire body surface may be affected. Even if the spots are not visible, if a hand is passed over the skin one can feel the small scabs in the depths of the coat.

Treatment is difficult as the essential cause of the condition remains unknown. Thorough grooming of the coat is an essential adjunct to successful treatment, any loose or dead hair being removed by combing and brushing. Scabs may be removed by bathing with warm, soapy water or olive oil, the raw areas dried and a soothing dressing applied. The cat should be carefully examined for the presence of fleas, as some authorities believe the condition is a manifestation of flea-bite allergy. Certainly many cases improve if parasiticidal measures are taken. The administration of the B complex vitamin, Biotin, by injection, has proved effective in a number of cases, suggesting that a possible deficiency or faulty metabolism of this vitamin may be a cause of the condition. Hormonal treatment, usually the administration of the male sex hormone, testosterone, in the form of an implant, has also been attended by a fair degree of success. The addition of thyroid extract to this therapy is to be recommended. Recently the use of the female sex hormone has been reported as highly effective in this condition and this would now seem to be the treatment of choice. The itching and acute eczematous type reactions can be controlled by the systemic use of cortisone derivatives but their long-term use is not without its dangers.

In view of the considerable problems associated with diagnosis veterinary advice is essential where a skin condition is present. Laboratory aids have greatly improved the chance of diagnosis and successful treatment, thus skin scraping, skin biopsy, sensitivity tests, culture of secondary bacteria autogenous vaccines and Wood's lamp are examples of the armoury now at the veterinary clinician's disposal.

Slipped Disc see SPINAL DISC PROTRUSION

Smell The sense of smell is highly developed in the cat as it is in most carnivorous animals. The stimulus for the sensation of smell is the presence of minute odorous particles in the air which is inspired during breathing or sniffed into the nose. There are sensitive nerve endings in the mucous membrane of the olfactory area of the nasal cavity in the form of delicate filaments – the olfactory hairs. From these nerve fibres run to nerve cells in the membrane which are connected to the olfactory centre in the front portion of the brain by the olfactory nerve – the first cranial nerve. It would seem that the odorous particles must become dissolved in the watery mucous bathing the olfactory hairs before chemical stimulation of the nerve endings can occur.

Smell is used mainly in the cat as an aid in the

search for food but it is also related to the sexual life and the protective reactions of the animal. The cat will often lose its appetite when the sense of smell is impaired due to inflammation of the nasal mucous membrane.

Smoke Long-hair Known as 'the cat of contrasts', the Smoke, when fully adult, has a most striking coat of black and silver, differing from all other long-hairs, although the general characteristics are the same. The undercolour of the fur should be white, tipped with black, so that the cat appears to have a jet black coat showing gleams of silver as he walks. The face should be black enframed with a silver frill, the ear tufts also being silver; the feet should be black, and the eyes deep orange or copper in colour.

A Smoke may be mated to another Smoke, or an occasional outcross to a Black may be used to improve type.

The kittens are nearly always black when born and it may be time before a true smoke colouring is seen.

Grooming is all important if a Smoke is always to look its best, and the coat must be well brushed away from the body to give the undercoat a chance to show through the dense black.

It is also possible to have Blue Smokes by crossing a Smoke with a Blue. This is also a recognized variety, with the same standard, but blue replacing the black.

In the U.S.A. short-coated Smokes are recognized, with black tippings to the short white fur.
See colour plate 48, *page 202.*

Smoke Short-hair see SMOKE LONG-HAIR

Snake-bite There are not many cases of cats suffering from snake bite in U.K. due to the paucity of venomous snakes and the fact that their habitat (wet, marshy ground) is not particularly attractive to cats. Treatment requires the administration of anti-venom to victims of snake-bite. This is only available from major hospitals, and its transport in time of emergency could well raise problems. In cases of animals being bitten on the leg by a snake, the application of a tourniquet as a first aid measure is advised. This prevents the venom being circulated around the body by the bloodstream.

Snow Leopard *Panthera uncia* is also referred to as the Ounce, but Ounce and Leopard are misleading names, for although it is classified as of the same genus as the ordinary Leopard and one of the five big roaring cats (the others being the Lion, Jaguar, Tiger and Leopard) there are some peculiarities of its skull and it has a shorter muzzle. There is debate as to whether it has ever been heard to properly 'roar' so that some zoologists consider it worthy of a genus of its own.

The soft luxuriant coat, longer and thicker in winter, is pale grey shading to tinges of yellowish-buff with white underparts which are longer than the body fur; the black rosette markings diminish to solid spots on the head and lower limbs. The ears are very small – no doubt due to the cold it has to withstand – and black edged with a white spot behind. The long tail is very bushy and is marked with rosettes. Measurements of head and body are approximately $4\frac{1}{4}$ ft and the tail may be a further 3 ft. Shoulder height is 2 ft or thereabouts and the weight is similar to the Leopard.

Found in the mountain ranges of central southern Russia, such as the Pamirs, the Hindu Kush in Afghanistan, and from there eastwards to Tibet and the Himalayas, and further north to the Tian Shan and Altai Mountains into Mongolia and Western China, it tends to live in the regions between the tree-line – around 12,000 ft and the permanent snow – around 18,000 ft; it descends into the upper valley bottoms in the winter.

Prey varies with its habitat, and includes makhor, ibex, musk deer, blue sheep, urial, pikas, snow cocks and other birds.

Rare in every region that it inhabits, the estimated number is now no more than 400 or 500, as it is ruthlessly persecuted for its fur and to satisfy the hunting skill of the average hill man. Various countries are endeavouring to protect it but although many prohibit the export or import of skins, 'made up articles' often are not covered, and poaching is difficult if not impossible to control. The U.K. Government (March 1972) imposed a ban on the import of skins, and the U.S. Secretary of the Interior signed a similar order, but this may be too late to save it.

South African Cat Clubs There are five Cat Clubs in South Africa which are grouped together under the Governing Council of the Associated Cat Clubs of South Africa and each Club holds one or two Shows a year in the city in which it has its headquarters, i.e. Cape Town, Durban, Johannesburg and Port Elizabeth. Many breeders are members of all the Clubs and send their cats by air to compete at all Championship Shows. Siamese, in all their colour varieties, outnumber other breeds but about thirty recognized breeds appear regularly on the show bench. New stock is imported from time to time from well known overseas breeders but in the opinion of several judges who have visited shows in England and the Continent, South African bred cats could hold their own anywhere in the world. All breeds are judged to standards laid down by the Governing Council of the Cat Fancy in England with the exception of the Korat which is at present only recognized in America and South Africa.

The number of cats exhibited at shows varies between 200–300, a feature of the larger shows being the large proportion of unregistered or 'alley' cats that are entered. Education in cat care and instruction in breeding and showing are included in the service given to members of the various Clubs. Film

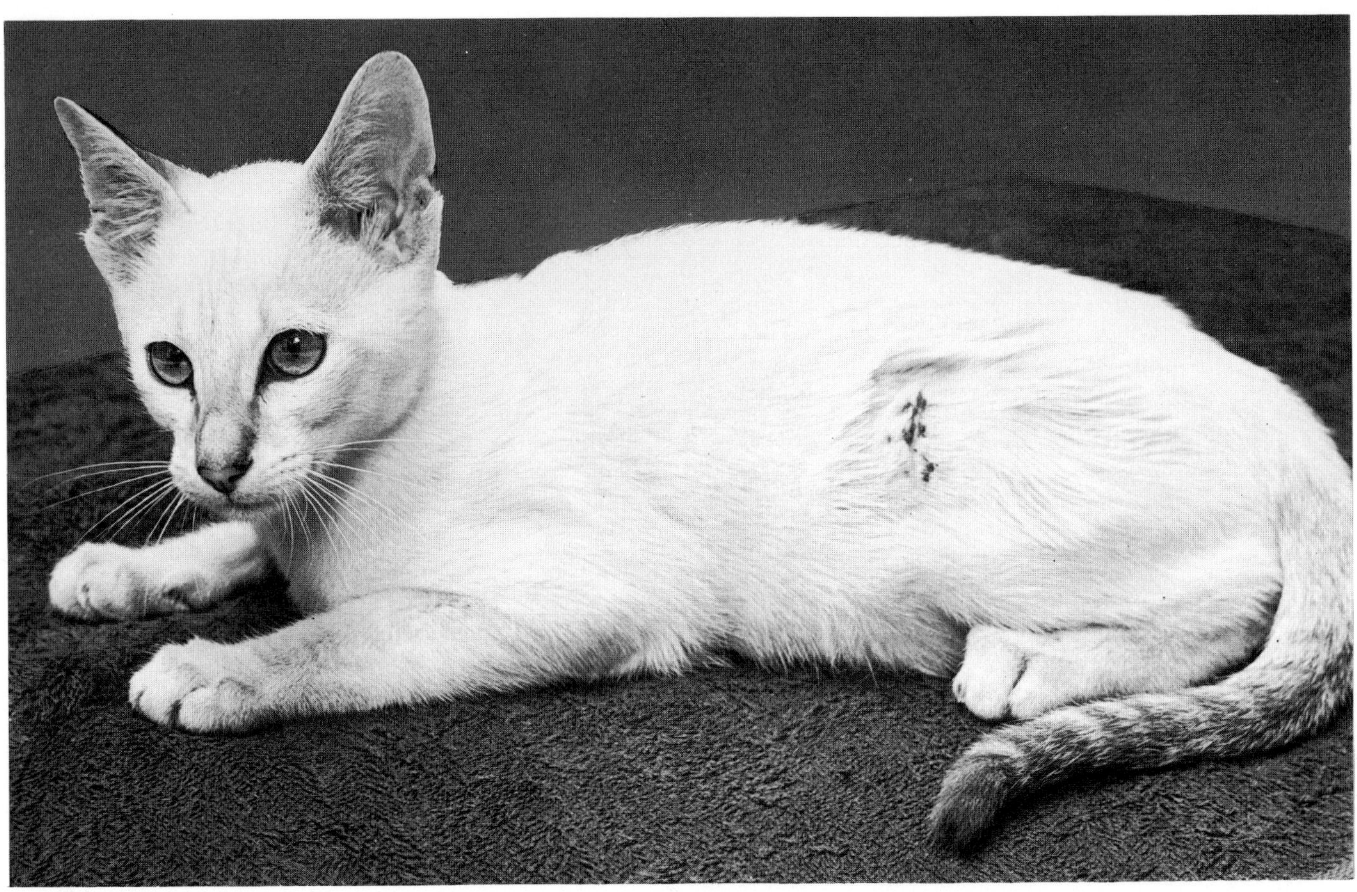

shows and other social activities also are arranged.

Interest in the different breeds, particularly the newer ones, is on the increase in South Africa although the comparatively low white population means that there are fewer breeders of cats than in some countries.

There is a strict training for would-be judges comprising lectures and a good deal of study, culminating in oral, written and practical tests.

Spaying Spaying is the term used to describe the operation for the removal of the ovaries and uterus in the female cat. This procedure prevents the animal from coming into oestrus and therefore from having kittens.

The operation can be performed at any age but is usually undertaken when the animal is four to five months of age.

It should be remembered that spaying is a major operation and carries all the risks of abdominal surgery. Modern surgical and anaesthetic techniques however have ensured that the death rate for this operation is extremely low indeed. The cat seems particularly resilient to this operation and recovery is usually rapid and uneventful.

Spinal Disc Protrusion (Slipped Disc) Clinical symptoms of a slipped disc in the cat are extremely rare. In spite of obvious degenerative changes which occur and can be seen post mortem they very rarely produce clinical signs.

Spleen This is an abdominal organ, shaped rather like a flattened cylinder and lying adjacent to the stomach. It is dark red in colour and has a plentiful blood supply. The boundaries of the organ are formed by a fibrous capsule, and the central part consists of dense, soft tissue, rather like the liver.

The spleen acts to purify lymph from bacteria or foreign matter that may have gained access to it. It is also a site of the breakdown of exhausted blood cells, and appears to act as a reservoir for blood. When heavy haemorrhage occurs, the size of the spleen is often found to be very much reduced, indicating that its blood reserves have been discharged into the circulation.

Despite the variety of functions performed by the spleen, the animal is able to continue a reasonably healthy life if this organ is removed for health reasons.

Split-foot see BREEDING ABNORMALITIES

Spotted Many wild cats have distinctive spotted markings, and it is said that the oldest domestic cats known were spotted. They were exhibited at the

SPAYING *above* A young female whose stitches have just been removed

right Brown Spotted

early cat shows, but then for many years were practically unknown, appearing by accident from chance matings. One or two were shown but it was not until 1960 that a definite breeding programme was planned. By cross-mating silver tabbies with black short-hairs, breeders were successful in producing some outstanding Spotties. Other cross-breeding was tried and eventually Spotties were produced in a variety of colours, including Silver, Red and Brown, with the numbers gradually increasing.

The type is usually typically British, the heads being broad, the ears small and the bodies powerfully built. Any background colour is now recognized, but the spotting must be distinct, with the spots standing out clearly from the background colouring. Ideally the cats should be spotted all over, as stripes and barrings are considered faults, but tabby markings are allowed on the face and head. The eye colours should conform with the coat colour.
See colour plate 49, *page 219.*

Spotted Cat, Little see TIGER CAT

Spotties see SPOTTED and TABBY SHORT-HAIR, SILVER

Sphynx see MEXICAN HAIRLESS

Spraying see BEHAVIOUR

Squint Squint, or Strabismus, describes eyeballs that do not move in a co-ordinated fashion. The best-known form of squint is when both pupils move to the inner border of each eye, giving the subject the appearance of focusing on his own nose. Squint may, however, be manifested by any independent movement of both eyeballs. The condition is typically seen as an inherited trait in the Siamese, but in this species it does not seem to reduce visual powers. Strabismus may also result from other diseases of the eye, particularly damage to the muscles controlling the eyeball, or the nerves, and the formation of tumours in the orbit (eye-socket). Some experts have attempted correction of congenital strabismus by covering the 'good' eye, which means that the other eye has to work proportionately harder, and to focus on objects in the field of vision. After a time, the covered eye is brought back into use, after which the eyes should operate more as a pair. See also BREEDING ABNORMALITIES.

Staphylococcal Infection The organisms, *Staphylococcus albus* and *S. aureus,* are normal inhabitants of the skin, nose and throat of the cat. They are liable to cause disease when implanted into the skin by wounds, or when some factor, such as viral infection, lowers the resistance of the tissues they inhabit. Staphylococci are pus-producing organisms. They are found quite frequently in abscesses and in purulent occular and nasal discharges. These

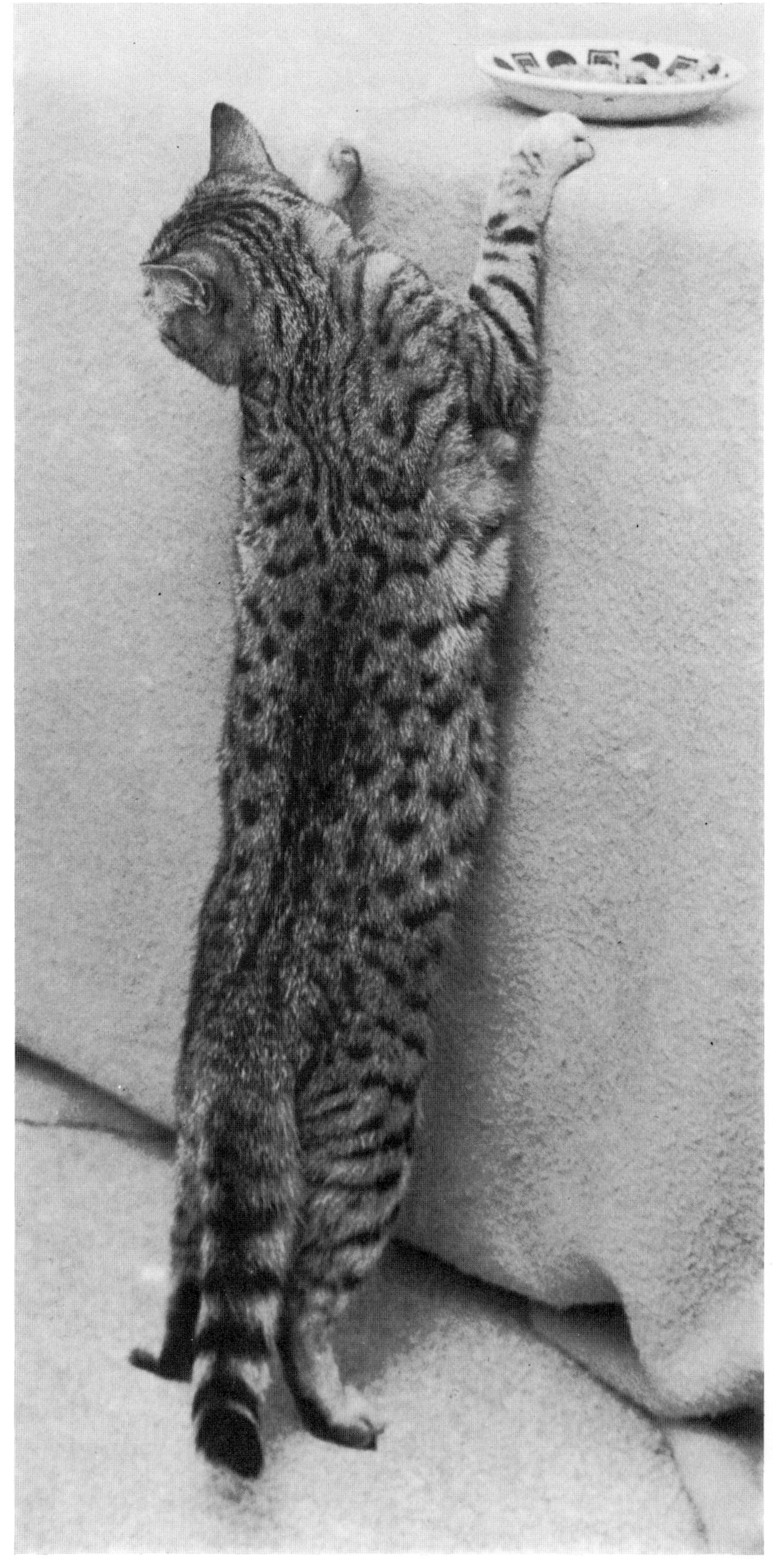

bacteria are now resistant to many antibiotics but fortunately are sensitive to the more recent synthetic penicillins. Persistent staphylococcal infections can be treated by injections of staphylococcal toxoid or of an autogenous vaccine.

Stale Food Unlike dogs, cats are extremely fastidious, and tend to reject food which is dried-up, rancid or decaying. Although attracted by strong-smelling foods such as herrings and game birds, cats seem capable of detecting food which is unfit for consumption.

Cats do not need to be protected from the ill-effects of eating stale food, since they will usually reject it voluntarily.

Steatitis Steatitis, or yellow-fat disease, is a condition in which the fat, particularly that around the abdomen, is very dark yellow or orange in colour. Cardiac lesions are also often present. The disease is caused by the feeding of certain fatty acids, such as are present in red tuna fish and rancid fish liver oils that have been spoilt by storage. The addition of tocopherol (vitamin E) to such oils whilst they are fresh prevents them from turning rancid. Red tuna should only be given occasionally, and then in small quantities.

Sterility see APHRODISIACS and IMPOTENCE

Sternum The sternum or breast bone anchors the ribs at the lower part of the chest. It runs from the anterior part of the chest between the forelegs to end at the posterior aspect of the chest cavity.

Stewards At British shows each officiating judge has a steward, who is usually chosen well in advance by the judge personally. Carrying a small table, the bowl for washing the hands or suitable disinfectant, and a towel, the steward accompanies the judge to the pen. There the exhibit is taken out to be judged and placed on the table for the judge to examine and assess its qualities. The steward should check that the number on the pen and on the tally are the same and whether the cat is male or female. Occasionally a male may be entered in a female class or vice versa in error.

The way a steward handles a cat is all important. It should never be held by the scruff of the neck, and the best way to get an exhibit out of the pen is to bring it out backwards, taking care that the back is not dragged against the somewhat low doorway. While the judge is examining the cat, the steward should be ready and alert to grab the animal should it endeavour to escape. The majority of the cats entered for a show behave very well and make no fuss at all about being handled, but there is the occasional miscreant who will not hesitate to use tooth and claw if it feels so inclined.

When the judge has examined all the exhibits in a particular class and made a decision, he or she will enter the results in the judging book in triplicate. The steward should make sure that these are entered correctly and when several classes have been judged, should also check that the judge has not cross-judged, i.e. placed one cat first in one class with another cat as second, and in another class has reversed them. Two slips from the judging book have to be taken up to the show manager's table by the steward, so that one may be put up on the award board and the other copied into the book. In due course, from these results the prize cards will start to go up.

Silver Spotted

Stewards must also be on hand to carry up exhibits for the Best in Show judging, where cats nominated for this honour are individually handled by a selected panel of judges.

To become a steward to a judge, one first starts by assisting generally in some way or other at a show. People are needed to put up prize cards or slips on the award boards, to enter the results in the book, and even just to take coffee around to the judges. In this way eventually the general show routine will be understood. Some judges are prepared to have a second steward to assist the first, and this is an excellent way for a beginner to really learn to cope with a steward's duties.

After breeding cats for a number of years and stewarding at many shows, in time it is possible that one of the specialist clubs may be prepared to nominate a steward of really proven worth as a probationer judge.

A steward's duties in North America are rather different to those in Britain, as the judging is carried out in rings, with each judge having a show ring, a ring steward and a clerk. Stewards are used to carry the cats from the hall to the ring, but owners are also allowed to do this.

In the ring a row of pens is provided behind the judges' table with each class of cats to be judged being placed in them in turn. The steward's job is to make sure that the pens are disinfected and the paper changed quickly, so that as soon as one class is finished, the pens are ready for the next. Another duty is always to be ready with a bowl, towel and disinfectant for the judge to wash after handling each exhibit on the table to assess its points. A steward must also be prepared to handle the cat if asked to do so by the judge, but has nothing to do with the judge's book as in Britain, to make sure that there is no cross-judging. It is the clerk who is responsible for seeing that the judge's book is entered up correctly, and who prepares a summary sheet showing the awards made and ensures that the winning cat goes up into the next class until it is beaten (see CLASSES AT SHOWS). As the judge awards ribbons to the first, second and third prizewinners, the clerk is expected to have them set out ready for the judge to put on the cage.

The clerk is also responsible for keeping the public out of the ring, although they are permitted to watch from the sides, and must see that the award slips marked by the judge are displayed for all to see as soon as to hand. A catalogue must also be marked ready for the judge on completion of judging.

Some continental shows are now run on similar lines to that in Britain, with stewards officiating in the same way, but others have the judging carried on in a separate room, away from the public, with a number of stewards bringing the cats to the judges. They too have a number of pens for comparison of the cats by the judges should they so wish.

Stifle The stifle is the term given to the joint in the hind leg which corresponds to the knee joint in the human. It is a complex joint between the femur and the tibia and incorporates the patella or kneecap. See also SKELETON.

Stings The first-aid measure for bee and wasp stings is to apply an antihistamine (available from chemists) to the area. If the sting is visible, it should be removed with a pair of eyebrow tweezers. If the cat is stung in the mouth or eye, take it to the veterinary surgeon immediately, and watch for signs of respiratory distress en route. It may be necessary to give artificial respiration if swelling of the site prevents the cat from breathing.

Strabismus see SQUINT

Straying Straying from one home to another seems to be one of the characteristics of cats. At first they merely visit a house or garden while they are out hunting, then they meet the occupants of the house, and become bolder about going into all the rooms, and eventually they may visit on a regular basis, demanding food when they arrive.

Occasionally they may actually move into another household in the vicinity. Cats that indulge in this sort of behaviour may inexplicably decide to return to their original home after a period spent away.

Entire tom cats and male cats that were neutered late in life seem especially prone to straying, and this may be associated with their territorial behaviour. It is impossible to cure straying.

Streptococcal Infection Streptococci resemble the staphylococci in many respects particularly in that they are found as normal inhabitants of the body. Like the staphylococci, many of the organisms are pus-producing. They are often found in abscesses, and nasal or ocular discharges. They have been incriminated as a cause of various infective conditions including fading and still-births in kittens, abortion and metritis (inflammation of the womb) in queens, umbilical infection (navel-ill) in kittens, cerebral (brain) abscesses and otitis (canker) in adult cats. Occasionally one sees an acute streptococcal septicaemia in the cat where the symptoms, dehydration, prostration, coma and death within a short space of time, resemble those seen in Panleucopaenia. Fortunately most streptococci remain sensitive to Penicillin.

Strike, Blow-fly see MYIASIS

Stud Management see BREEDING

Stud Tail Stud Tail is a condition seen in the entire male cat or stud in which there is a seborrhoeic dermatitis in a localized area on the upper surface of the base of the tail. At this point there is a collection of sebaceous and apocrine glands known as the Supracaudal Organ. The sebaceous glands are stimulated by the male sex hormone, testosterone, resulting in an excessive secretion of sebum. This tends to dry on the skin surface collecting dust and dirt leading to clogging of the outlets of the glands and forming comedoes (blackheads). The blocked glands become distended with retained sebum, the skin of the affected area swells causing the hairs to stick up. Secondary bacterial infection of the distended glands may occur which combined with licking and rubbing of the region may result in the development of a raw, moist area. Treatment consists of antibiotic therapy in combination with anti-inflammatory and hormonal drugs. The condition may be prevented by careful cleansing of the base of the tail in the stud cat to prevent the excess sebum drying and collecting dirt.

Stumpy see MANX

Sub-mental Organ Infection Infection of the Sub-mental Organ, so-called 'Feline Acne', is occasionally seen in the cat. The Sub-mental Organ consists of a complex of sebaceous and sweat-type glands situated in the skin in the area of the chin. In disease of the Sub-mental Organ, there is excessive secretion of oily sebum which collects dust and dirt forming blackheads which block the dusts of the glands. The glands continue to secrete sebum and become distended with retained secretions, which form a suitable medium for bacterial multiplication leading to inflammation and sometimes pus production. The chin becomes rather swollen and tender, and the skin is hot and reddened. The cat will often show difficulty in feeding as any contact of the inflamed chin with a feeding dish causes pain and the animal will back away, often spitting and snarling its displeasure. Close inspection will reveal the blackheads at the entrance to some of the gland ducts, others will have a little inflammatory fluid or pus oozing out when gently pressed.

Treatment is to open up the ducts by frequent bathing with warm water coupled with the administration of the broad-spectrum antibiotics. Once the ducts are unblocked then local applications of antibiotic ointment will prove useful.

Sulpha Drugs The sulpha drugs, also known as the sulphonamides, are a group of complex organic chemicals. They do not occur in nature, all of them having been synthesized in the laboratory. They are, however, chemically similar to certain naturally-occurring substances. The simplest member of the sulphonamides group, sulphanilamide, was discovered in 1908, but its implications in medicine were not realized until 1935. Since then a vast number of sulphonamide drugs have been synthesized. The mechanism by which these drugs achieve their anti-bacterial effect is interesting. Bacteria are heavily dependent on several B vitamins for their healthy existence. The sulpha drugs, upon entering the body of the patient, render such vitamins unavailable to the bacteria. This prevents the organisms from growing and reproducing, although it may not kill them. This effect of bringing bacterial multiplication to a standstill is known as bacteriostasis. Once bacteriostasis is achieved, the natural body defence mechanisms are frequently able to overcome the remaining bacteria, so that the disease usually subsides. Sulpha drugs are used in the cat both in the treatment of infections of the gut, and in the form of powders for application to wounds.

Sumatran Tiger see TIGER

Sunshine Cats seem to derive considerable pleasure from all sources of warmth, and they love to bask in the sun. A cat may usually be relied upon to seek out the sunniest and most sheltered spot in the garden, and there indulge in sunbathing. Vitamin D is produced in the skin by the action of the sun's rays. The ultra-violet rays present in sunlight which are primarily responsible for this vitamin production also kill germs on the surface of the cat's body, so that plenty of sunshine may help to correct or prevent skin infections, and helps the animal to recover from minor diseases. Glass blocks ultra-violet rays, so that sunshine coming through a closed window is of little health benefit, despite the fact that it warms the cat and makes him contented.

Superfoetation Superfoetation is the development of one or more further foetuses after other foetuses are already present in the uterus. To put it another way, the term denotes the presence of two or more foetuses of different ages in the womb at the same time. The condition is rare but occurs where there is fertilization of ova (eggs) released from the ovary at successive heat or oestrous periods. This means that it is possible for kittens in the same litter to have different sires and that some of the litter may be born several days after the other members of the litter. See also DUAL MATING.

Supracaudal Organ see STUD TAIL

Swimming In common with most mammals, cats are able to swim. Few pet cats will however be seen swimming unless they accidentally fall, or are thrown, into deep water.

The basic 'stroke' used when swimming is dog paddle, being identical to a slow trotting gait. The head is held high to prevent water entering the mouth and nostrils, and the tail is often held out straight behind, to act as a stabilizer.

Feral cats, especially lions and tigers, appear to enjoy swimming. They have been observed swimming while towing fairly large prey. Cubs frequently play in water.

Turkish cats, alone among the domesticated varieties, are renowned for their love of swimming.

Swiss Mountain Cat The small wild cats of the world are now quite well documented and it is undoubtedly *Felis silvestris silvestris* – the European Wild Cat, which frequents the Swiss Alps. Some gradation in coat thickness, intensity of ground colour due to geographical position could naturally occur, and some variation in size is also possible where food distribution varies, but there is nothing to support claims that a new species of cat exists in the Swiss Alps.

There is the possibility of hybridization occurring in this region and it cannot entirely be discounted since it is reported that breeders in Germany and elsewhere in Europe are now making crosses with the Abyssinian, the Ocelot, the Margay Cat, the Jungle Cat and the Leopard Cat. The Leopard Cat in its natural state prefers the hilly and mountainous regions.

With the movement of so many wild species for the purpose of pets, or for the purpose of breeding experiments which have on occasion escaped and become feral, it could easily lead to speculation that a new species existed in the Alps.

T

Tabby Any cat with stripes and bars seems to be referred to as 'Tabby', and the original domestic cats were thought to have tabby markings. Indeed it is said that if all the domestic cats throughout the world today were to inter-mate, the result would be that eventually all the cats would be tabby.

'Tabby' is given in the dictionary as 'A brindled or mottled or streaked cat; a kind of waved or watered silk'. The word is derived from the 'Attibiya' quarter in Bagdad where centuries ago a type of patterned or watered taffeta or silk was first made. The material was known as 'tabby', and a cat with similar markings was also so-called.

The tabby markings on a cat's coat can vary considerably, but the more usual are referred to as 'blotched' or classic, while flecks all over the coat resembling the fish is known as 'Mackerel'. Another form of markings may be seen in the 'Spotties'.

Tabby Long-hair The pattern of markings required for the Tabby Long-hairs is the same as that for the Short-hairs. On the head there should be clear pencil markings, with swirls on the cheeks, spectacles around the eyes, and an 'M' mark on the forehead. There should be two rings around the chest, known as the 'mayoral' chains, with three dark bars along the back, with other bars and swirls along the flanks. On looking down on the shoulders a distinct impression of a large 'butterfly' may be seen. The stripes should be quite distinct with no brindling, but this effect is more difficult to achieve in the Long-haired Tabbies. It is much easier to detect in the Short-hairs.

In Britain, there are three recognized colours in the Long-haired Tabbies; the Brown, the Red and the Silver, the pattern of markings being the same in each case. In North America, Blue, Cream and Cameo tabbies are also recognized.

Brown Tabby A very old, and once very popular variety, but one that is seen but rarely these days. The background colouring should be a rich tawny sable, and the markings dense black. The large round eyes may be hazel or copper in colour. As it is difficult to find a suitable out-cross to improve the type, this is often not so good as that of the other long-hairs.

Silver Tabby Long-hair kitten and mother

Faults are a white chin and a white tip to the tail.
See colour plate 50, *page 220*.

Red Tabby The coat colouring of this variety should be a deep rich red, with the pattern of markings an even richer darker red, so that it stands out well from the body colouring. The type is frequently very good, with short noses, broad heads, and excellent round copper-coloured eyes. The numbers are few, but there is a steady demand for the kittens as very striking pets.

Contrary to popular belief a Red Tabby is not always a male. There are more males than females for the simple reason that Red Tabbies do appear in the litters of Tortoiseshells and Tortoiseshells and Whites, when the red kittens will be male and those like the mothers female. Red Tabby mated to Red Tabby will produce kittens of both sexes.
See colour plate 51, *page 220*.

Silver Tabby Once a very popular variety, said to have been used in the early days of cat-breeding to produce the Chinchilla, there are comparatively few about now. A good specimen is most attractive with the background fur a pure pale silver in colour and a distinctive dense black pattern of markings. The eyes may be green or hazel. It is exceedingly difficult to produce a cat with clear markings, too often they are smudged or brindled, not clearly marked at all. Often too there are brownish tinges in the fur, which is a definite fault.

There have been, and still are, one or two outstanding champions, but the difficulty is to find suitable crosses that will improve the type without loss of markings.

The kittens are born dark, with the silver appearing as the fur grows. They are much liked as pets.
See colour plate 52, *page 245*.

Tabby Point see SIAMESE

Tabby Short-hair In Britain there are three colours recognized for the Tabbies, the Brown, the

Red and the Silver, while in the U.S.A. it is also possible to have Blue, Cream and Cameo Tabbies. The contrasting pattern of markings required is the same for each, that is running down the face should be delicate pencil markings, with swirls around the cheeks, markings as of spectacles around the eyes and a mark resembling an 'M' on the forehead. There should be two necklaces around the chest usually referred to as the 'mayoral chains'. Three dark bars should run along the spine, with the flanks and saddle having deep bands of contrasting colour. Looking down on the shoulders, there should be distinct markings forming the shape of butterfly wings. Both the legs and tails should be ringed. All these markings should be clear and distinct, not smudged, blurred or brindled. It is difficult to get perfection in the pattern, and frequently the tail rings are too solid, and the markings on the back not distinct enough.

Another pattern of markings is also recognized. This is known as the Mackerel Striped. The markings are dense, the rings being narrow and numerous running from the spine to the ground, like flecks, resembling those seen on the mackerel fish, hence the name. The colours are various, but the Silver with the black markings are the most distinctive.

Brown Tabby One of the oldest breeds known, but comparatively rare as a pedigree variety, due to the difficulty of finding the right stud to use to improve the type and the markings. Mating Brown Tabby to Brown Tabby indefinitely invariably seems to result in loss of type.

The ground colour should be a deep rich sable brown, with the contrasting pattern of dense black markings, 50 points are allowed for these. The eye colour may.be orange, hazel, deep yellow or green. There must be no white hairs in the coat, on the chin or around the mouth. The white chin is a fault which appears quite frequently. The type should be typically British, but as yet does not appear to be as good as that of the British Blue.
See colour plate 53, *page 245.*

Red Tabby A prize-winning pedigree Red Tabby has a wonderful dark red coat with the pattern of markings of even a richer dark red – 50 points are allowed for these in the standard; the colour being nothing like that of the sandy pets seen around. The eyes may be hazel or orange in colour. White spots or white hairs anywhere in the coat are bad faults, as is a white tip to the tail. The type is usually very good.

It is quite untrue to say that all Red Tabbies are males or that they are sterile. Given pure red breeding on both sides, the results will be pure red kittens, with both male and female in the litter. If however, one parent is not pure bred, the result may be Red males and Tortoiseshell females.

Red Tabbies are sometimes used as mates for the all-female Tortoiseshells and the Tortoiseshells and Whites in an endeavour to produce kittens like the mothers. It is not such a good idea as it may seem, as often tabby markings are introduced, which prove exceedingly difficult to breed out.

The Reds make most attractive, very decorative pets, and there are rarely sufficient kittens around to meet the demand.
See colour plate 54, *page 245.*

Silver Tabby Considered by many to be the most attractive of the short-haired tabbies, the Silver should have a ground colouring of pure clear silver, with a distinctive dense black pattern of markings, 50 points being allocated for this in the set standard. There should be no white hairs in the fur, and white chins and any brown markings on the coat are considered bad faults. The type of the Silver Tabbies is usually typically British and the pattern of markings can be exceedingly good.

When newly born, the markings on the kittens may be seen quite clearly, but as the fur grows, it tends to look greyish until it clears when they are about three months old.

The Silver Tabbies are now appearing in ever-increasing numbers at the shows. They are being used to breed the recently re-recognized 'Spotties' which are also becoming very popular.

Affectionate, self-sufficient cats, they make sturdy, hardy pets, and with very little grooming, always seem to look immaculate.
See colour plate 55, *page 245.*

Tabby Tortie Point see SIAMESE, ANY OTHER COLOUR

Taenia taeniaformis see Tapeworms under WORMS

Tails It is not uncommon for cats to have their tails caught in doors. This can cause considerable damage requiring surgical amputation. See AMPUTATION.

Talking While Siamese and Burmese are particularly renowned for their oral communication, nearly all pet cats have a vocabulary of some kind whereby they converse with, and frequently give orders to, their owners.

A very loud, long call may mean 'let me in quickly, it's cold outside', or 'help, I'm stuck in a tree' or simply 'I'm back, come and welcome me indoors'. Demands for food tend to be a variation of this first sound, volume being reduced because less projection is required. Some very reserved or polite cats have an extremely quiet mew for indicating that it is dinner time, almost as though they are reluctant to be considered greedy.

Then there is a rather short, noncommittal sort of mew, frequently made by cats as they cross a room, heading for nowhere in particular. This may mean 'I don't like the weather today, what do you think

Silver Tabby Short-hair

of it?' or 'I wish you'd stop doing the football pools and remember you are meant to be entertaining me, but I don't really care if you don't make a fuss of me'. Or it may mean 'kindly note that I am crossing the room, and may therefore require the door to be opened shortly', and so on. It is the duty of the owner to use his imagination and make a study of the cat's likes and dislikes in order to be able to interpret this kind of sound.

Thirdly there is a staccato, muted, almost bleating type of sound made by cats that are watching exciting events from windowsills. A classic example of the cat who can see about twenty birds feeding at a birdtable outdoors. It is probably too cold for him to go out, and in any case he is so entranced with the sight that he cannot drag himself away from the window and go out of the door, but he is very stirred at the events going on, and feels a need to share his experience with the humans in the room, so he communicates vocally.

Yet another sort of mew is made by cats that have been stroked to the point where they are purring double-time and are so ecstatic that they express their pleasure by mewing and purring at the same time. This slightly resembles trills played on the high notes of a piano.

Cats also talk to one another, of course, and a mother will call to her kittens if they are playing and she wishes to recall them to the nest. Females often call to toms when they are in season – this form of speech is not much appreciated by the human ear and has been called 'caterwauling'. See also BEHAVIOUR, SEXUAL.

Tallies A week or two before the show, each exhibitor is sent a vetting-in card, together with a small disc with a hole in it. Both the vetting-in card and the disc, referred to as a tally, should bear the same number, which will correspond with the pen provided in the hall for the cat. Should there by a discrepancy between the card and the tally, the owner should inform the show manager before the show. In the case of two or more exhibits being entered, the names as well as the numbers should be on the vetting-in card, to enable the owner to know which tally belongs to which. On the morning of the show great care must be taken to make sure the correct tally is around the right neck, as otherwise a cat may be put in the wrong pen and incorrectly judged and disqualified afterwards. The number on the tally is entered in the judge's book in the appropriate classes to be judged.

The tally must be worn around on the neck on a piece of narrow plain white tape or ribbon or thin rounded elastic. Care must be taken to see that it is not too tight so that it causes distress, or too loose so that the cat gets its paws into it and pulls it off, or even gets it between the teeth.
See also SHOWING OR EXHIBITING.

Tapeworms see WORMS and PARASITES

Tar see Dangerous Liquids under ACCIDENTS

Tartar see TEETH, TEETH CARE and GINGIVITIS

Teats Teats, or nipples, are the fleshy projections on the mammary gland that enable the young to extract milk from the mother. In the cat, each teat has a number of tiny orifices, although the milk may appear to be coming from a single hole. Occasionally, a teat may become blocked, and there is then some danger of mastitis occurring.

Blind teats are a congenital abnormality in which there are no openings at the end of the teat communicating with the teat canal. The condition is not uncommon in the cat and usually passes unnoticed. When the associated mammary gland commences lactating for the first time, there is increasing pressure from the imprisoned milk and this tends to curtail and eventually suppress further milk formation. The gland then atrophies and becomes nonfunctional. Occasionally a secondary bacterial infection of the blocked gland results in a mastitis with heat, swelling, tenderness, reddening of the overlying skin and possibly abscess formation. See also MAMMARY GLAND and MASTITIS.

Teeth The adult cat has 30 teeth – 12 incisors, 4 canines, 10 pre-molars and 4 molars.

The temporary teeth are smaller, sharper and less dense in structure than the permanents; indeed the temporary incisors are only just visible in kittens. These deciduous teeth are acquired at 4–6 weeks of age.

Change from temporary to permanent dentition, the period normally described as 'teething', commences between 15 and 17 weeks of age and all the permanent teeth are through by 6 months and fully developed at about 7 months old. The first teeth to be changed are the central pairs of incisors, followed about 1 week later by the laterals and then the corner incisors. The canine teeth or fangs change at $4\frac{1}{2}$ months, the tip of the permanent canine appearing at this time; these fangs, the largest teeth, are fully erupted at 7 months of age.

Pressure exerted by the permanent teeth in the gums on the roots of their temporary counterparts causes pressure atrophy (withering) of these roots and the crown of the tooth drops off. Baby teeth are seldom shed complete with roots so owners do not need to worry if they see rootless crowns lying on the carpet. Persistence of temporary teeth after the permanents erupts is very rare in the cat although common in the dog.

Kittens seldom show any signs of discomfort or decreased health during teething unless gingivitis, inflammation of the gums, develops. This is sometimes seen, usually at about 5–6 months of age, and can be recognized as a fiery red line where the gum meets the tooth. There may be a foul smelling breath. Kittens sometimes show reluctance to eat, obviously due to discomfort, and may dribble saliva.

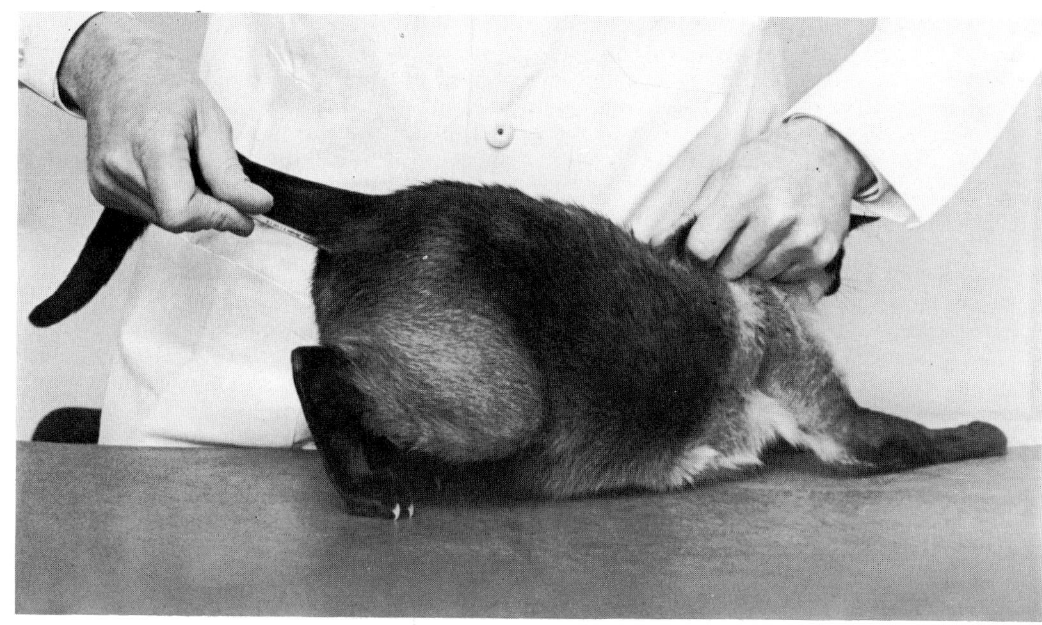

THERMOMETERS When taking its temperature hold a cat firmly

Veterinary advice should be sought in severe cases. Although careful attention to diet, especially vitamins and minerals, is recommended, antibiotics may be necessary to deal with secondary infection.

Teeth Care Care of the teeth starts during kittenhood, and should continue throughout the cat's life. Regular examination of the mouth by the owner is essential.

The deciduous (milk) teeth are shed between the fourth and sixth months of life. It is wise to examine the mouth occasionally to ensure that the milk teeth do not persist as the permanent teeth would develop at the wrong angle.

Dental tartar may begin to form about the third or fourth year of life, but many cats teeth remain white and clean until late in life. Predisposing factors for tartar formation are not well understood. Although bones and hard foods may help dislodge loose pieces of tartar there is no evidence that they help to prevent its formation. It is thought, rather, that the degree of acidity or alkalinity of the saliva of the individual plays an important part in tartar growth. Whatever the cause, it is advisable to have teeth scaled when required. If it builds up the gums are pushed back from the teeth and gingivitis develops. Delaying tartar removal may also result in decay of whole teeth, infection of the mouth and gums which may cause systemic disease.

Caries refers to the common problem associated with human teeth-holes in the enamel. This is very rare in the cat. Symptoms which reveal its presence include reluctance to eat, salivation and rubbing of the mouth with the paw.

Peridontal disease refers to a severe form of infection of the gums and teeth which results from neglect. Tartar builds up causing the gums to recede from the tooth root. Between the tartar and gums is a red inflamed area suitable for secondary bacterial growth which causes pus formation. This produces offensive smell and toxins which can affect the cats breath. Treatment consists of removing any loosened teeth, scaling and antibiotic treatment of the affected gums.

Temminck's Golden Cat *Felis temmincki* is a deep red-gold on the back graduating to a paler colour on the underparts, only showing very faint stripes – except on the face and head, which are pronounced blackish streaks with white intermingled; there are prominent ones from the eyes to the neck. This colouring however is variable according to locality and may veer to grey. The coat is soft and thick. The head and body combined may measure from 29–34 in. and the tail a further 18 in.

Distribution is wide and ranges from Tibet, south-western China, north India, Burma, Indo-China, Thailand, Malaya and Sumatra. There are said to be some three varieties, which would be natural in such a wide distribution and climatic variation. Little is known of its habits and it has only been observed in zoos, but it is thought to be a forest animal living both on the ground as well as in trees, so its prey may include mammals as large as small deer. Some have been shot while raiding domestic stock.

There are interesting reports of it being easily tamed if taken young, obeying commands and performing tricks like a dog.

Temper see BAD TEMPER

Temperature The normal body temperature of cats is 101·5°F. This will in fact fluctuate between 100·5°F and 102·0°F without significance. If however the temperature falls outside these limits and is accompanied with signs of disease, veterinary advice should be sought. See also THERMOMETER.

Territorial Behaviour see BEHAVIOUR

Testicles The testicles, or testes, are paired ovoid masses of relatively hard tissue lying in the scrotum (see SCROTUM). Each is covered by a layer of peritoneum called the tunica vaginalis, and its interior consists of masses of fine coiled tubes known as the seminiferous tubules. The walls of these tubules are made up of cells that produce spermatozoa (male reproductive cells) together with cells that secrete a nutrient substance. The seminiferous tubules of each testis discharge their contents into the epididymal duct, a long, coiled duct lying on the border of the testis itself. The fluid is stored in this duct until maturation of the spermatozoa has taken place, after which it passes on into the deferent duct, a comparatively large tube that joints the tube to the urethra the exterior lying in the penis. Ejaculation of spermatozoa thus takes place along this tube. The testicles are also responsible for the secretion of a number of male hormones that affect the secondary sexual characteristics of the cat. See also SEXING.

Tetanus Tetanus in the cat is quite rare, less than a dozen cases being recorded. The symptoms shown in the reported cases were stiffness of the muscles and joints of the limbs, the muscles of the back being almost board-like. The cats sometimes had great difficulty in getting on to their feet. The third eyelid was drawn across the eye and there was a greatly increased response to various stimuli, e.g. light, sound or touch, and these tended to provoke violent tetanic spasms in which the head and tail were drawn towards each other and the back arched. Some cases showed trismus (lockjaw). Treatment is difficult and most of the recorded cases died. The cat should be nursed away from all stimuli, i.e. in a quiet, darkened room. Penicillin and tetanus antitoxin should be given in large doses together with tranquilizers and muscle relaxants to prevent the tetanic spasms.

Thermometer Body temperature of animals can only be accurately recorded by inserting a suitable clinical thermometer into the rectum.

The most suitable thermometer for use in the cat is the small so-called stubby-ended thermometer, in which the mercury-containing bulb at the business end is shorter and thicker than that of an ordinary clinical thermometer. Overall length is 3 in. (7·75 cm.) and the bulb is $\frac{3}{8}$ in. (0·75 cm.) in length.

Cats do not like having a strange object inserted into the rectum so care should be taken to do it as efficiently and gently as possible. Make sure the mercury column is shaken down. The bulb of the thermometer is lubricated with petroleum jelly (vaseline) to facilitate insertion. One person restrains the cat's front and while another grasps the root of the tail and raises it to expose the anus, the thermometer is gently inserted into the anal orifice, a rotary movement often helps. The thermometer must enter the rectum for 1–1$\frac{1}{2}$ in. otherwise rectal temperature will not be recorded; the sphincter muscle in the anus often creates resistance when the thermometer is only $\frac{1}{2}$ in. in and gentle, firm pressure must be maintained until the thermometer slides further in; at this point the cat often cries out quite piteously – this is not pain but a despairing wail at its lost dignity! Once inserted keep hold of the protruding part of the thermometer, do not let it go, gently deflect it sideways to ensure that the bulb comes into contact with the lining of the bowel wall. Most thermometers are designed to register temperature within half a minute but there is some individual variation in speed of registering and it is therefore customary to keep the instrument in position for one minute whenever possible.

Thermometers should be carefully washed in *cold* water after use and then steeped in a suitable antiseptic solution which must be wiped off with cotton wool before being used again.

A full size clinical thermometer is a perfectly suitable alternative if the small type described above is not available; it should also be stubby-ended.

Thirst Thirst is the sensation associated with the need of the body for water. The sensation is believed to arise in the nerve endings in the pharyngeal region when this area has less than its normal water content, but the exact mechanism governing thirst is not yet known. It has been shown that the signal for water drinking is a deficit of water in the body relative to the other constituents. When this deficit amounts to 0·5% of the bodyweight, then water is drunk in amounts proportional to the deficit, but ingestion stops before absorption of the water has had time to take place. Most of the water drunk by an animal during a 24-hour period is taken within 2–5 hours of feeding irrespective of the time of eating. If the animal is starved this greatly reduces the 24-hour water intake. Thirst is an important symptom of disease.

Thrombosis, Aortic see HEART DISEASE

Throwback A throwback is an individual who has reverted to ancestral characteristics which have not appeared in recent generations. This phenomenon is due to the reappearance of old characters due to the recombination of the genes required for their production and which had become separated during the history of the animal's pedigree.

An *Ixodes* tick larva

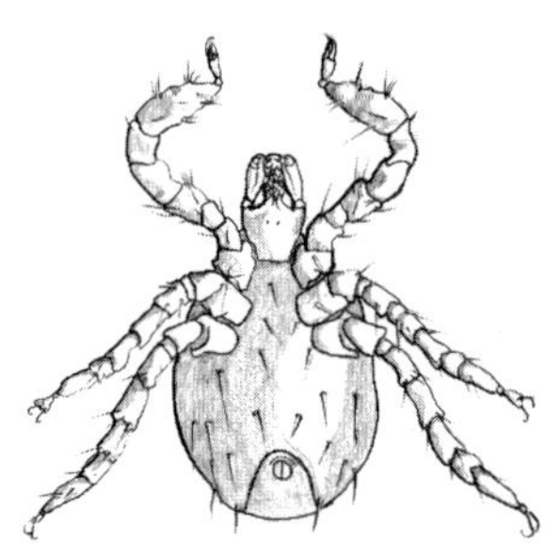

Tick Infestation Infestation with ticks of the species, *Ixodes*, is quite common in rural areas. The ticks congregate in vegetation and attach themselves to any warm-blooded animal that passes. Usually the sites of attachment are the head and the limbs of the cat. The ticks appear to cause little irri-

tation to the affected animal and once they become engorged after about 10 days, they fall off. In severe cases, the cat's environment, viz, the cattery, may become infected with ticks which are then extremely difficult to eradicate. The ticks appear as brown or slatey blue oval bodies varying in size from a pin-head to that of a small haricot bean, attached to the skin by their mouth parts and remaining immobile on the skin surface. Owners often mistake these parasites for a tumour or a cyst due to this immobility. Treatment depends upon the number of ticks present on the cat. Single parasites can be removed by applying a little chloroform or ether to relax the mouthparts and then pulling the tick away from the skin. If removal is attempted without such anaesthetization of the tick, the head parts are often left behind in the skin and this results in the development of a chronic sore area which is very slow to heal. Treatment of the whole body area with pyrethrum, derris or sulphur at fortnightly intervals will usually prevent the ticks becoming attached.

The Tiger, *Panthera tigris*

Tiger The Tiger *Panthera tigris* is very variable. Its original distribution was wide and extended from Eastern Turkey and the Caspian Sea to the coast of Manchuria and southwards through China, India, and South East Asia as far as Java and Bali, but today its distribution is vastly reduced and it is in great danger of becoming extinct throughout its entire range. This is due to the destruction of its habitat by man; to the many wars over the last thirty years in such places as Burma, Malaysia, India, China, Korea, Pakistan, and in particular Vietnam through the use of the poisonous defoliating chemicals which have turned vast areas into semi-deserts, destroying the tigers, their habitat and also their food supply. Not only has this taken grim toll, but such pressure as land reclamation schemes, hydro-electric schemes and the vast commercial exploitation of their skins have reduced their numbers of some 30,000 in 1939 to about only 1,960 over the entire area (Waller in 1971). This figure will undoubtedly be much lower now. Although the Indian

Central Government banned the commercial export of skins in 1969, and the U.K. Government, as well as the U.S. Secretary of the Interior signed a similar order prohibiting their import (1972) and some other countries are imposing restrictions, poaching has become such an acute problem that it threatens plans for conservation. Skins are showing 'underground' taxidermy, and the method of killing is usually by agricultural poisons which cause agonising death.

Although usually only three races of tiger are listed, there are in fact eight and Mountfort, 1970, lists them as follows:

Bali tiger, *P. tigris balica,* extinct; Javan tiger, *P. t. sondiaca*, maximum 12 animals; Siberian tiger, *P. t. altaica,* 120–130 animals; Caspian tiger, *P. t. virgata,* maximum 50 animals; Chinese tiger, *P. t. amoyensis,* very scarce, perhaps extinct; Sumatran tiger, *P. t. sumatrae*, maximum a few hundred; Indo-Chinese tiger, *P. t. corbetti,* rapidly declining; Bengal tiger, *P. t. tigris,* 2,000.

The colouring as well as the striped pattern varies from one individual animal to another, but it is sometimes possible to distinguish between the inhabitants of different areas, although it may be difficult. The tigers of Siberia and China are somewhat paler, with longer fur; and usually they tend to be lighter in the northern areas and darker in the southern. Size varies also, and animals in the north are larger than those in the south. Colouring varies from buffish-fawn to shades of rich brown, with dark brown stripes, the width and number can vary considerably. Starting in the centre of the back they run vertically except on the legs. The head is evenly striped, but the nose is without markings; the ears are dark with a pale patch. The stripes form a 'bib' effect on the chest. The tail is ringed; the underparts of the body are pale.

The 'White Tigers' are a dilute form, they have an almost white body-colour with charcoal tinged with brown stripes; they have blue eyes and pink nose-pad.

The combined length of head and body of males varies from 5–7½ ft; tigresses are smaller, from about 5–5½ ft. The tail may be from 2½–3 ft. The weight range is considerable and can vary from about 300–500 lb.; a tigress may weigh only 200 lb.

Tigers swim well and will visit islands in order to hunt, their prey consisting of a variety of animals according to the area to which they belong. They will attack animals as big as elephants.

Tiger Cat *Felis tigrina,* also known as the Little Spotted Cat is very easily confused with the Ocelot and the Margay Cat. It generally tends to be an intermediate variety measuring about 2½–3¼ ft of which 10–17 in. may be tail. The size, however, is not a reliable guide to identification as the Margay Cat varies quite considerably. The most distinguishing feature is possibly the difference in striping on the forehead; in the Tiger Cat, the striping is not very pronounced and does not follow such a definite pattern as in the other two species. For example, the Ocelot has two straight dark lines which run from the sides of the nose to the top of the forehead, with spots in-between while the Margay Cat has similar lines which tend to be 'pear-shaped' and the 'filling in' spots are elongated and narrow, while the spots on the Tiger Cat tend to be somewhat indistinct. The Tiger Cat has white streaks above and below the eyes, the latter merging with the cheeks and a dark line runs from the eyes across the cheeks; the whisker-pads are pale with dark spots and the ears are not quite so rounded as the Margay's and the insides are lighter. Coat colour is normally yellowish-fawn shading to creamy-white underparts, which are interspersed with spotting. A dark line of spots runs down the centre of the back and the markings along the flanks towards the tail tend to break up into rosettes with a tawny centre. The spots become much smaller on the legs fading out on the paws; the upper side of the tail is ringed with large dark blotches.

Distribution is from Costa Rica in Central America to northern South America where the forests and woodlands are preferred. They are excellent climbers and hunt birds and small mammals. By nature rather vicious little cats, especially as they age, they do not make good pets and so great suffering and many deaths have resulted through attempts to tame them. Hunted for their skins they are in grave danger of becoming extinct.

Tinned Food see NUTRITION

Tom Tom is the name given to the male cat. The term usually implies an entire male or Stud cat, being qualified by the adjective neuter(ed), when referring to the castrated male animal.

Tongue Disorders *Inflammation* Known as glossitis this is characterized by redness and swelling of the organ; vesicles (small blister-like sacs filled with fluid) may form and rupture to cause ulceration. A painful condition, the cat tends to salivate and refuses to take food. Glossitis may be due to infection of the mouth with a virus, in response to burns or the presence of irritant substances or sharp foreign bodies in the mouth.

Tumours Not uncommon, the one most frequently reported being squamous cell carcinoma, a most unpleasant tumour of the cancerous variety, also seen in other structures of the mouth, such as the gums and in the tonsils. This is a grave condition since the formation of secondary growths is almost inevitable.

Tortie A commonly used abbreviation for Tortoiseshell.

Tortie Burmese see BURMESE, NEW COLOURS

Tortie Point see HIMALAYAN and SIAMESE

Tonkinese A very rare variety produced in the first place by cross-matings between Siamese and Burmese, they have been bred in Britain and in the U.S.A. The type is Foreign and the bodies of medium length. It has not yet been recognized.

Tortoiseshell Long-hair Cream, black and red in well-defined patches evenly distributed over the coat, the typical long-hair type, neat ears, short nose and deep copper or orange big round eyes, are the requirements for a show Tortoiseshell. As it is one of the oldest varieties known, being featured in many paintings, and appearing often from mongrel breeding, it is looked on by some as quite commonplace. Few people realize how difficult it is to breed a true Tortoiseshell with no tabby markings or white hairs.

Invariably female, any males born usually proving sterile, they are exceedingly difficult to produce to order, and breeders may try a number of crosses, using a self-coloured male without one Tortoiseshell appearing in the litter, but there will certainly be a wonderful selection of kittens in the litter.

The fur should be long and flowing, with the patches of colouring being quite distinct and not mixed with any other colouring. This is quite difficult to achieve in the long-hair. There should be patches on the legs, tail and head, and even the ears should have small patches. A blaze of cream or red running down the centre of the face is liked, although not specially stated as a requirement in the standard.

See colour plate 56, *page 246*.

Tortoiseshell Short-hair One of the oldest of the British Short-hairs is the Tortoiseshell with a short close coat of black and red (light and dark) patching. The colours should be as bright as possible, with the patches being entirely separate from one another, with no overlapping. They should be all over the body, with the tail, the legs and feet, even the ears, having small patches. Tabby markings and white hairs are bad faults. A red mark, known as a blaze, running down from the forehead to the nose is liked, and certainly adds to the attractiveness of the breed.

An all-female variety, the choice of stud is limited, but a self-coloured Black or Cream may be used. Any cat with tabby markings should be avoided, as this could introduce markings that would prove exceeding difficult to breed out. It is not easy to produce Tortoiseshells, and most litters from them are very mixed, sometimes not even containing a kitten like the mother. Tortoiseshell kittens are very dark when first born, the coloured patching appearing as the fur grows.

In the British and Continental standards 25 points are given for the colour and 25 for the eyes, which may be orange, copper or hazel; for American, see American standards.

Probably because of the cross-breeding, the variety is known for its intelligence, sturdiness and extreme playfulness.

See colour plate 57, *page 246*.

Tortoiseshell and White Long-hair Like the Tortoiseshell, this too is a patched cat, having the same coloured patches of red, cream and black but interspersed with white. More striking in appearance but just as difficult to produce to order, another all-female variety, a male could be chosen from one of the self-colours of the coat in the hope of a tortoiseshell and white kitten appearing in the resultant litter. One breeder in Britain has been most successful in carrying out a planned breeding programme for this variety which involves the use at stud of the recently recognized variety, the Bi-coloured Long-hair.

Known in American as the Calico cat because of the patched coat pattern, the patches should be entirely separate, and there should not be too much white. The type is usually quite good, and before now a Tortie and White has been Best in Show.

From time to time a Tortoiseshell and White male appears and there are rumours of his being worth a terrific price. This rarely comes to anything, as invariably when adult he turns out to be sterile, incapable of siring kittens and even if he were not sterile he would hardly be of any more value than any other cat.

From Blue and White Bi-coloured matings with Tortoiseshell and Whites, a strikingly-coloured new variation, the Blue Tortoiseshell and White, has been produced. It can be bred in both Long and Short-hairs, but has not yet been recognized.

See colour plate 59, *page 246*.

Tortoiseshell and White Short-hair Also referred to in the U.S.A. as the Calico cat, the Tortoiseshell and White is one of the most colourful of the Short-hairs, with its brilliant colouring of black, light and dark red and cream, evenly balanced with white. Usually white predominates, but this is a fault. The patches should be clear and well defined, with no brindling, or tabby markings, and there should be no white hairs in the patches. A white streak (the blaze) running from the centre of the forehead to the nose is liked. The eye colours may be orange, copper or hazel.

This is an all-female variety, and exceedingly difficult to produce to order. A male of one of the colours in the coat, such as black or white, could be tried as a stud, or one of the Bi-colours. A tabby mating should be avoided, as this could mean the introduction of bars and the very persistent stripes.

See colour plate 58, *page 246*.

Torula utilis see YEASTS

Touch Sense The cat's skin, like that of other mammals, contains tiny sense organs that respond

TOYS *left* A cat showing affection for a toy stuffed with catnip; *right* an easily made toy which may amuse a cat for hours

to tactile stimuli. These small organs when stimulated transmit impulses along the sensory nerves, informing the brain of their activation.

The whiskers, or vibrissae, also play an important part in keeping the cat informed about the immediate environment. They are rigid enough not to collapse on contact with relatively hard surfaces, and so carry pressure to the sensitive whisker pads.

Toxascaris leonina see Ascarids under WORMS

Toxins see POISONS

Toxocara cati (mystax) see Ascarids under WORMS

Toxoplasma gondii see under TOXOPLASMOSIS

Toxoplasmosis Toxoplasmosis is the disease resulting from infection of the cat with the protozoan parasite, *Toxoplasma gondii.* This parasite, which was first found in a small desert rodent, the Gondi, hence the name, is now thought to be a protozoan organism whose natural host is the cat. In the intestine of the cat the toxoplasms go through the typical coccidian life cycle culminating in the oocyst which passes out in the faeces and constitutes the infective agent. Occasionally the parasites stray from the intestine and are carried to various parts of the body by the blood or lymph streams. Here they become encysted in the tissues and become quiescent but may cause damage to the host by virtue of their presence. Two types of toxoplasmosis are recognized in the cat – an acute form in which the symptoms depend upon which organ is mainly involved and which is mainly seen in young animals where it often assumes a pneumonic form, and a chronic type seen in older animals giving rise to symptoms of brain disorders or ataxia (swaying gait), or to intestinal granulomata (see GRANULOMA) with associated weight loss, diarrhoea and anaemia. Diagnosis is difficult and depends upon rather complex laboratory tests. Treatment is not very satisfactory. Human contacts usually suffer a subclinical infection, but infection during pregnancy may lead to abortion, stillbirths, and congenital abnormalities.

Toys Toys for kittens should be chosen very carefully, as they may be harmful if destroyed, but adults are fairly sensible on the whole and do not often chew and swallow things.

Balls of wool, although very tempting to kittens, particularly if one is knitting, and the ball jumps and rolls in a tantalizing fashion at the end of each row, should not be used as toys. If the kitten is allowed to play with them while the owner is supervising him, he is likely to 'help himself' to one while left alone, and if he gets the end of the wool stuck in the back of his throat he will take in more and more wool in trying to free himself. Cats have choked in this way and others have died a slow death from damage done to the intestines by the wool. There is also a danger that a kitten encouraged to chase balls of wool will accidentally swallow a needle that has been left in one. It is far better to give your kitten a solid rubber ball to play with, or one of the hard plastic type with holes in – provided the holes are not large enough for him to trap his feet in them, and are sufficiently

TOYS *above* A well made adventure playground
right simple toys provide great fun out of doors

widely spaced to prevent his teeth getting caught if he picks it up.

It is amazing how inquisitive little paws can satisfy the cat's proverbial curiosity, but they tend to pay for the experience!

Objects such as ping-pong balls and stuffed fabric mice may be suspended from a rail or chair, and kittens amuse themselves by their pendulum motion. Elastic is the best material to use for this kind of toy – string does not stretch if the cat's claws get caught. Stuffed toys in general should have securely fitted eyes or no eyes at all, and dyes used in the fabric should be non-toxic. 'Catnip' mice, which contain dried herbs relished by cats are available.

Some cats get a lot of pleasure out of a garden swing – a small rubber tyre from a child's bicycle, tied by a rope by a tree may be used for this.

Other good, cheap toys are a cardboard grocery box and an old blanket or sheet – kittens will leap in and out of the box, ambush one another and 'play tents' beneath the sheet. Discarded children's gloves stuffed with kapok or rags are also often popular.

Trachea see RESPIRATORY ORGANS

Training see MANNERS IN THE HOUSE

Tranquillizers see SEDATIVES

Transfusion This term means the removal of fluids from one animal and their administration into the body of another. It is most frequently applied to blood and plasma. (The giving of mineral salts in solution, artificial blood-volume expanders and pre-digested foodstuffs into the bloodstream is generally known, by contrast, as an infusion.)

Blood transfusion may be necessary because the patient has lost blood; because it is anaemic; or because it is short of blood clotting factors. Plasma transfusion is used to replace the watery part of the blood that tends to be lost in large quantities when an animal is burned or suffering from an exudative type of lesion. Plasma may also be used in lieu of blood during surgical operations.

Administration of blood is through a vein or, less frequently, into the marrow cavity of a long bone or straight into one of the body cavities (usually the abdominal cavity).

Transportation Most cats travel fairly well. The cat should be accommodated in a strong, comfortable box for security and safety.

Car Transport Cats may lie contentedly in cars, but should preferably be placed in boxes as above. Being rather unpredictable creatures, there is a danger that the cats will distract the driver and cause an accident if they are loose. There are also unpleasant cases recorded of cats that escaped from the windows of moving cars. The driver should, of course, avoid abrupt clutchwork, fast cornering, sudden harsh braking and taking hump-bridges at speed, in order to arrive with placid passengers and minimize in-transit sickness. See CAR SICKNESS.

Anti-emetic sedative type drugs are very useful for administration before car transportation. Large meals less than six hours before travelling should be avoided.

Rail Transport U.K. railway regulations stipulate that cats should be in an enclosed container. It is wise to check that ventilation is adequate, and provide absorbent bedding and a water pan (fixed to the cage if possible) if the journey is lengthy. Sometimes special arrangements may be made with the guard to check on the cat at intervals. Adequate labelling is vital – the cage should bear the sender's name and address and phone number as well as those of the recipient, in case the cat is not collected from the destination station.

Sea Transport Arrangements for the housing of cats on board ship are made in accordance with the export and import laws, which vary from one country to the next. The crew is normally responsible for the day-to-day care, so it is wise to ship one's cat with a line of good reputation or, better still, to send the cat on a boat that has passengers and arrange for one of them to check on its welfare from time to time. People sending large batches of cats by ships often hire an animal attendant to escort them.

Air Transport Again, the airlines have their own regulations about the conditions in which animals are flown, and will not normally allow cats to accompany their owners on the passenger-deck. Fibreglass boxes are much better than wooden ones for air travel, because of their lightness. Cardboard boxes are sometimes allowed, but are definitely not recommended. Engine noise seems to worry cats less than might be expected, but sedation is indicated in cats which are sensitive to loud noise.

Travelling While cats adapt quite well to travel, they are happier in their own environment. It is inadvisable to take one's cat on holiday. The chances of the animal getting lost in its strange surroundings are extremely high, and even if confined to the house, it will take quite a long time to familiarize itself with all the new sights, sounds and smells in order to settle down. It is a scientifically proven fact that all species suffer to a greater or lesser degree as a result of being moved from one point to another. This stress can be reduced by the administration of sedatives that render the animal less sensitive to the commotion.

See also EXPORTING.

Travel Sickness see TRANSPORTATION and CAR SICKNESS

52 53
54 55

colour 52 Tabby Long-hair Silver
53 Tabby Short-hair Brown
54 Tabby Short-hair Red
55 Tabby Short-hair Silver

overleaf 56 Tortoiseshell Long-hair
57 Tortoiseshell Short-hair
58 Tortoiseshell and White Short-hair
59 Tortoiseshell and White Long-hair
60 Turkish

57
59

61

62

Trench Mouth see GINGIVITIS

Trichodectes canis see LICE

Trichophyton mentagrophytes see RINGWORM

Trismus see TETANUS

Trombicula autumnalis see Harvester Infestation under MITES

Tubercular Peritonitis see PERITONITIS

Tuberculosis Feline tuberculosis appears to be diminishing in frequency in the U.K. This is undoubtedly due to the eradication of bovine tuberculosis from the national dairy herd since the majority of cases in the past were due to infection with the cattle strain of *Mycobacterium tuberculosis*, only about 4% being due to the human strain. The incidence of the disease until comparatively recent years was estimated at about 2–3% of the cat population.

Most cases of infection resulted from drinking infected cows milk and the primary sites of the disease were found in the alimentary tract either in the throat region or in the intestine. Tuberculosis of the chest cavity is infrequent in the cat. The symptoms shown vary with the site of the disease. With a throat infection, the tonsils and the associated lymph nodes become inflamed and enlarged and the latter may burst and discharge a watery, blood-stained fluid. There may be difficulty in swallowing, excessive salivation, and the cat may cry out when it opens the mouth. With an intestinal lesion, there is a progressive loss of condition even though the cat eats quite well. As the disease progresses the animal becomes listless, emaciated and anaemic. There may be attacks of vomiting and blood tinged diarrhoea. Tuberculous peritonitis may result from the rupture of a tuberculous abscess and fluid accumulates in the abdominal cavity producing swelling of the abdomen (see ASCITES). In the case of thoracic infection there is usually an exudative pleurisy with a progressive collection of fluid in the chest cavity. This leads to increasing respiratory distress and eventually to asphyxiation and death. Involvement of the skin may result from the bite of an infected cat and lead to the formation of flattened circular areas which are firmly adherent to the underlying tissues. Treatment of feline tuberculosis is not recommended in view of the danger to human health.

Tumours see NEOPLASIA

Tumours of the bone see BONE DISORDERS

colour 61 White Long-hair, Orange-eyed
62 White Short-hair, Odd-eyed

Turkish This is one variety that differs in the standard required from the majority of the other long-hairs, and is akin to the Angoras, the first cats with long fur seen in Europe. Imported in the first place direct from Turkey, they have Angora type; the head being a short wedge in shape, the round eyes light amber in colour, the nose longish, and large upright ears. The sturdy body should be long on legs of medium height, and the full tail of medium length. Although the first Angoras were said to be all white, this variety from the area around the Van lake in Turkey has auburn markings on the face and a tail of similar colour with deeper auburn rings. The long and very silky fur should be chalk white, with no trace of yellow. The coat is very full in winter, with most being shed in the summer.

The Turkish cats have the reputation of being fond of water, and apparently in that country, they enjoy swimming in warm pools and shallow rivers. They are frequently referred to as the Swimming cats.

The litters are small, with more males being born than females. The kittens make most distinctive and decorative pets, being very intelligent and readily showing affection to their owners.
See colour plate 60, *page 247.*

Types The word 'type' is used throughout the Cat Fancy to denote the particular structure of a cat. The term is used generally when speaking about distinct breeds of cats, that is one refers to Long-hair or Persian type, Foreign type, British type, Siamese type, Angora type and so on.

The Long-hair or Persian type is always taken to mean that such a cat should have a round broad head, big round eyes, small rounded ears, cobby body on short sturdy legs, and a short full tail, while a cat with Foreign type has a wedge-shaped head, almond shaped eyes, large pointed ears, a long svelte body on high slender legs and long tapering tail. Cats with Foreign type include the Siamese, Abyssinians, Russian Blues, Burmese, Havanas and the Rex, but there are slight variations in the type required.

The British type, known as European on the Continent, is seen in the short-haired cats with broad round heads, large round eyes, full cheeks, shortish noses, and small rounded ears. Their bodies are powerful, on legs of good substance, and the length of the thickish tails should be in proportion to the bodies.

The Exotic Short-hairs in America have short fur but the type is akin to that required for the Persian, while the American Short-hairs have broad heads too but should have noses of medium length, with gentle curves, and round and wide eyes, with a very slight slant. The bodies should be medium to large, on medium length heavily muscled legs, and the tails should be of medium length.

The Angora type may be seen in the Angoras and Turkish with the fur not being quite so long as in the Long-hairs, and the heads being more wedge-shaped than round, with noses of medium length, with large upright ears. The bodies are longish and the tails full, but slightly tapering.

Ulceration Ulceration is the formation of a round or irregularly-shaped, circumscribed mass of tissue on a surface with a chronically inflamed base. In the cat ulceration is seen in certain skin conditions such as eosinophilic granuloma, tuberculosis and leprosy, in the eye in keratitis, in the tongue and the mouth in the respiratory viral infections, chronic kidney disease and leukaemia, and more rarely in the intestine. Treatment depends upon the cause and the site of the ulceration but mainly consists of either surgical excision of the ulcer or cauterisation to stimulate the healing processes.

Umbilical Cord The umbilical cord consists of the blood vessels and other attachments that link the abdominal area of the foetus with the afterbirth. In these blood vessels are carried the substances required by the foetus for growth during the period it is within the uterus. The umbilical cord normally breaks or is bitten through by the mother when the kitten is born. It is helpful to allow blood to flow from the placenta into the kitten before doing so. The stump of the umbilical cord is somewhat susceptible to bacterial infection during the first few hours of life, so steps should be taken to ensure that the housing for a new litter of kittens is clean. See also BIRTH and BEHAVIOUR, MOTHERING.

Umbilical Hernia see BREEDING ABNORMALITIES

Uncinaria stenocephala see Hookworms under WORMS

Urethral Obstruction see BLADDER DISORDERS

Urinary Disease see NEPHRITIS and BLADDER DISORDERS

Urination Urination or Micturition is the act of passing urine. To some extent this is a reflex action under the control of nerve centres in the spinal cord which are stimulated when the pressure of the urine in the bladder reaches a certain level, but this can be over-ruled by other centres of the brain, making house-training of kittens possible. The desire to urinate arises from stimulation of nerve endings in the wall of the bladder by stretching and contraction of the musculature. The cat follows a certain ritual of urination in which a hole is excavated either in the soil or in the litter of a sanitary tray, urine is passed into the hole which is then covered up again. Urination also has a sexual connotation in the male cat as he will spray urine around the borders of his territory to demarcate its extent to other males. If this is prevented or the male is moved to other surroundings for mating purposes then there may be an inhibitory effect on his sexual behaviour. See also Spraying under BEHAVIOUR.

Uterus The uterus or womb is part of the female reproductive system. It is in this Y-shaped organ that the kittens are nurtured during development before birth. The afterbirth of the young are attached to its wall for nutrients throughout gestation. See also PYOMETRITIS, GESTATION and AFTERBIRTH.

Vaccinations Vaccinations may be given to protect the cat against certain infectious diseases. The only vaccination routinely recommended in the U.K. is against feline infectious enteritis (feline panleucopenia). It should be administered between 6 and 12 weeks of age. A second injection is usually required 7–14 days after the first one, this has the effect of boosting antibody production so as to prolong a state of immunity. Boosting doses are also needed at regular intervals during the remainder of the cat's life.

Vaccine against a number of respiratory syndromes to which the cat is prone have also been prepared. Unfortunately the immunity they confer is short-lived, and, in any case a cat that is immunized with such agents may easily be exposed to infectious organisms of a different type, so that their efficiency is limited.

Rabies vaccine is available in countries where rabies is prevalent. Cats entering British quarantine kennels also receive rabies vaccine during their quarantine period by law.
See also IMMUNITY.

Vagina The vagina is the passage leading from the vulva to the cervix in the female.

Vaginitis is indicated by unproductive attempts to urinate, licking of the vulva and possibly a discharge of mucus or pus. Vaginitis usually responds well to the application of antibiotic. See also VULVA.

Vesical Calculi see Cystic Calculi under BLADDER DISORDERS

Viral Rhinotracheitis see FLU

Viruses Viruses are very small micro organisms which require living cells in order to live and reproduce. By parasiting the cells of higher animals they often destroy them causing disease. Common virus diseases of cats include Flu, Panleucopaenia, and Rabies (see under relevant headings).

Vitamins see NUTRITION

Vivisection The very sound of this word is enough to strike fear and disgust in the hearts of many catlovers, but the truth is that a large number of misconceptions are held by the general public in U.K. on this topic. Medical research is necessary to increase knowledge of the normal functions of the body, the functioning of the body during disease, and the action of drugs upon the body. Both animals and human volunteers are used in these investigations. All research involving experimental work on animals is rigidly controlled by the Home Office. Animal welfare societies maintain a constant and useful vigilance which helps to maintain a sense of balance. As an indication of the interest shown in animal welfare by medical research workers, a society has been formed by them with the express purpose of devising methods whereby research can be effected without using animals.

The term 'experiment' may be used to describe a very wide range of procedures, many of which cause the animal little or no discomfort. An example of this is palatability testing on foodstuffs, when the animals are offered several alternative dishes, and their reactions recorded. Behaviour tests likewise rarely have a detrimental effect on the animal.

The percentage of 'terminal' experiments – i.e., those in which the animal is painlessly destroyed at the end of the tests – is relatively low.

It is arguable that human beings do not have the right to use animals for experimental purposes, but in view of the number of human and animal lives that have been saved as a result of research such a concept remains extreme.

Vulva The vulva is the external opening of the female reproductive tract. From it leads the vagina or vestibule which receives the male penis during copulation. See also VAGINA.

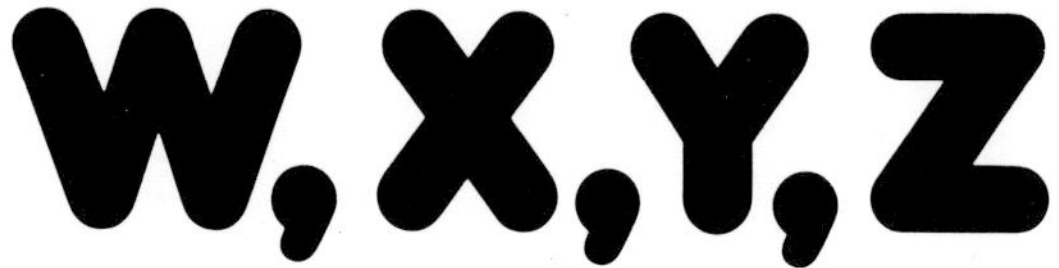

Warts Warts or Papillomas are benign tumours of the skin which are found quite frequently in the cat. It is possible that these growth may be the result of a virus infection. Warts affect cats of all ages but are more often seen in elderly animals. The growths may be single or multiple and are usually found in the skin of the head and neck, the shoulders, the chest and abdomen, the feet, the eyelids and the external genitalia. They are often attached to the skin by a stalk but may be nodular or cauliflower-like in shape. Although warts are benign they may cause trouble by virtue of their presence in certain sites, e.g. a wart on the eyelid will often give rise to a conjunctivitis or even a keratitis. As they project from the skin they are very susceptible to damage and may bleed or undergo secondary bacterial infection. Treatment is not usually necessary but removal can be accomplished by ligation of the stalk where present, cauterization or surgical excision. See also PAPILLOMAS.

Water Fresh water must be provided for cats at all times; a cat which is deprived of fresh water suffers greatly. For this reason, the water bowl should be shaped like a shallow, truncated cone, being wider at the base than at the top, so as not to be easily knocked over and the water spilled. Water bowls may be made of china, of tinned or enamelled iron or of plastic. The size of the bowl will depend upon how many cats or other animals are kept as well as upon the habits of the owner. Should the owner keep very irregular times or on occasion, stay away from home overnight, the bowl should be large enough to satisfy the cat's needs until his return. A half litre bowl is sufficient for one or two cats.

It is important to keep the water bowl in a place from which the cat cannot be accidentally excluded should a door be shut inadvertently, and where it is not exposed to direct sunshine. The bowl should be washed and refilled daily, whether the water has been used or not.

Weaning For the first 3–4 weeks of life kittens will be solely dependent on the queen's milk but by 6–7 weeks of age should be able to feed themselves adequately. The art of satisfactory weaning is to maintain the kittens' growth rate without any check and weaning must therefore be a gradual process.

Between 3 and 4 weeks of age kittens should be encouraged to lap milk; cat's milk is more concentrated than cow's milk, therefore the latter needs to be supplemented rather than diluted as so many owners do. It is probably better to use a proprietary powdered milk food, either one specially designed for kittens or one for human infants.

Lapping can often be encouraged by allowing the kittens to imitate their mother and join her in taking milk from a saucer; failing this just gently dipping the kitten's nose and mouth in the milk will make it lick it off its own muzzle. By 4–4½ weeks most kittens should be able to lap efficiently. At about 4½ weeks kittens may be introduced to solid food. Remembering that they are essentially carnivorous, animal protein is next to be introduced. Good quality lean raw meat finely scraped, or minced, may be offered once a day initially. Simultaneously the milk may be augmented by mixing in a suitable cereal. When the kittens can take solids efficiently, finely chopped cooked fish, rabbit, meat or chicken may be given.

Over the period 4–6 weeks of age the number of supplementary feeds is increased and at the same time access of kittens to the queen is reduced so that by 5–6 weeks of age the kittens are suckling the dam only during the night.

From 6–8 weeks of age kittens should be receiving five meals daily, three with a milk basis and two with an animal protein basis; at this stage they should be ready to leave the dam and continue an independent existence.

Whiskers The whiskers, called vibrissae by anatomists, play an important sensory role in the life of the cat. It is said that the distance from the tips of the whiskers on the right cheek to those of the left cheek represents the broadest portion of the cat's body. Thus when the head of the cat is placed in a hole or gap, the animal may ascertain if it will be able to squeeze its body through. Should the whiskers be compressed by the walls of the hole, then it is too small to admit the cat. Care should be taken to avoid hurting the sensitive whiskers during play and grooming. See also TOUCH SENSE.

White Long-hair There are three recognized varieties of Whites with long fur, the variations being solely in the eye colour. Each variety should have typical long-haired type, and long flowing pure white coats. Spectacular cats, they have become increasingly popular in recent years, and there is a steady demand for the kittens.

The three eye-colours are orange, blue, and odd-eyed with one eye orange and the other blue. The early Whites were the Angoras with blue eyes, the first long-hairs known in Europe, and then, as now, there was an association with these coloured eyes and deafness. It is possible to breed from certain strains that have good hearing, so breeders are now concentrating on this. Due to the difficulty in cross-breeding to improve the type without losing the blue eyes, the type of this variety has not until now been very good. Several Odd-eyed Whites who excel in this, however, have appeared recently, and this has been a great help to the breeders of the Blue-eyes. The eyes should be as deep blue in colour as possible.

The Odd-eyed is useful for breeding both the Orange-eyed and the Blue, and may also appear in litters of both varieties. Each eye should be a good deep colour. It is now recognized, but has not yet been granted Championship status in Britain, as is the case in the U.S.A.

The number of Whites with orange eyes are rapidly increasing in numbers. Having excellent type and good eye colouring, they are frequently Best in Show. It is not such an old variety as the Blue-eyed, happening by accident in the first place, when breeders tried using other self colours, such as a Blue or a Black to improve the type of those with blue eyes. At shows, those with orange eyes invariably won, and in time, both colours were recognized; recognition of the Odd-eyed following very much later.

Whites may be produced by matings to Whites, Blacks, Blues and Creams, with white kittens and other colourings appearing in the litters. They may also be used as studs for the Tortoiseshells and Whites and the Bi-coloured.

Whites need constant and careful grooming if they are always to look their best, and a number of breeders believe in bathing them a few days before a show, so they present an immaculate appearance. Any yellowing staining in the coat is considered a fault, the tail particularly being affected in this way, especially that of the male.

See colour plate 61, *page 248.*

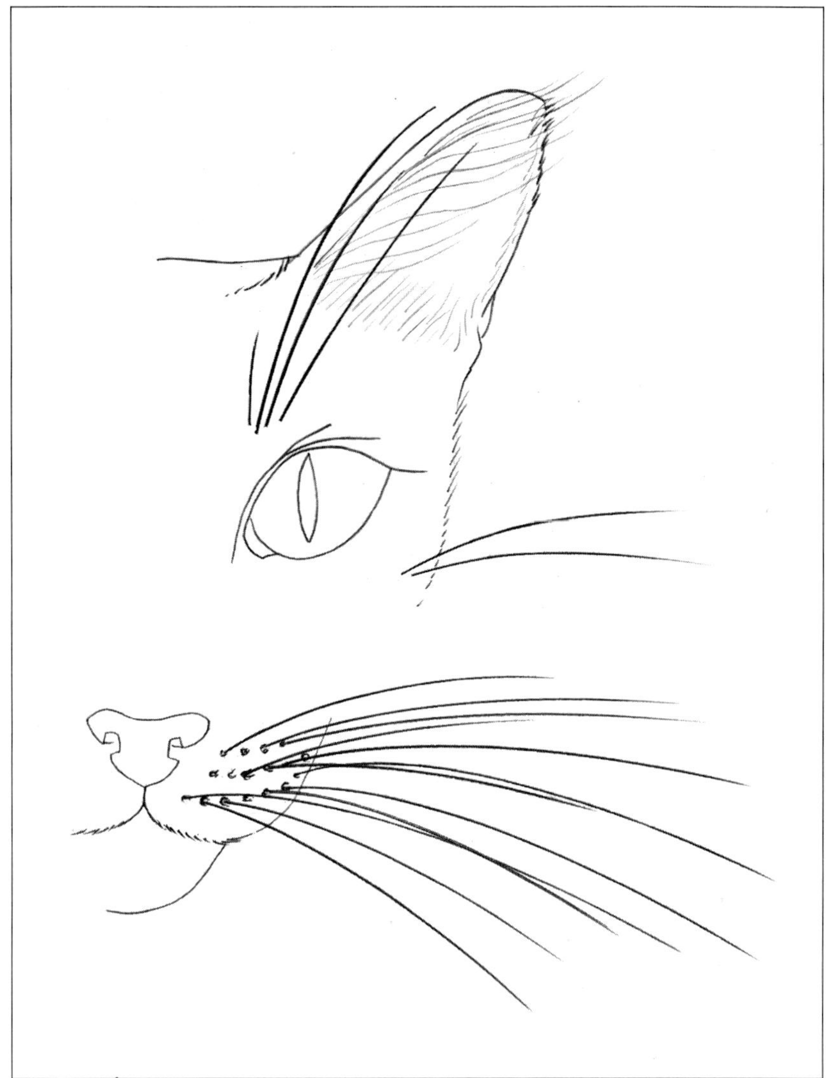

Whiskers are important sensory organs

White Short-hair Although the British White Short-hairs have been with us for a very long time, they are still comparatively rare. In some countries they were considered unlucky.

In Britain, three breed numbers have been granted to differentiate between the eye colouring – White with Blue-eyes, White with Orange-eyes and White with Odd-eyes having one eye of each colour.

The oldest variety is probably that with the blue eyes, but possibly because of the deafness which is known to affect them, and some other white-coated animals, the numbers have been very few. They are not all deaf, those being born with a black smudge, known as a thumbmark, on the head, which may fade with age, usually proving to have good hearing. Deep blue eyes are an essential characteristic of this variety, but it is difficult to know when young what colour the eyes will be, as the eyes of all kittens are blue when first opened and may not change for some weeks. The deeper the shade of blue, however, the more likely it is to remain so.

The Orange-eyed variety is easier to breed as it may be cross-bred with other short-haired varieties, such as the Black, Tortoiseshell and White, and the Bi-colours, without losing the eye colour. Odd-eyed kittens may appear in the litters of either varieties, and are very much liked for breeding both.

The standard for all three varieties is the same, that is, the bodies should be powerful, with full and broad chests; the legs should be of good substance

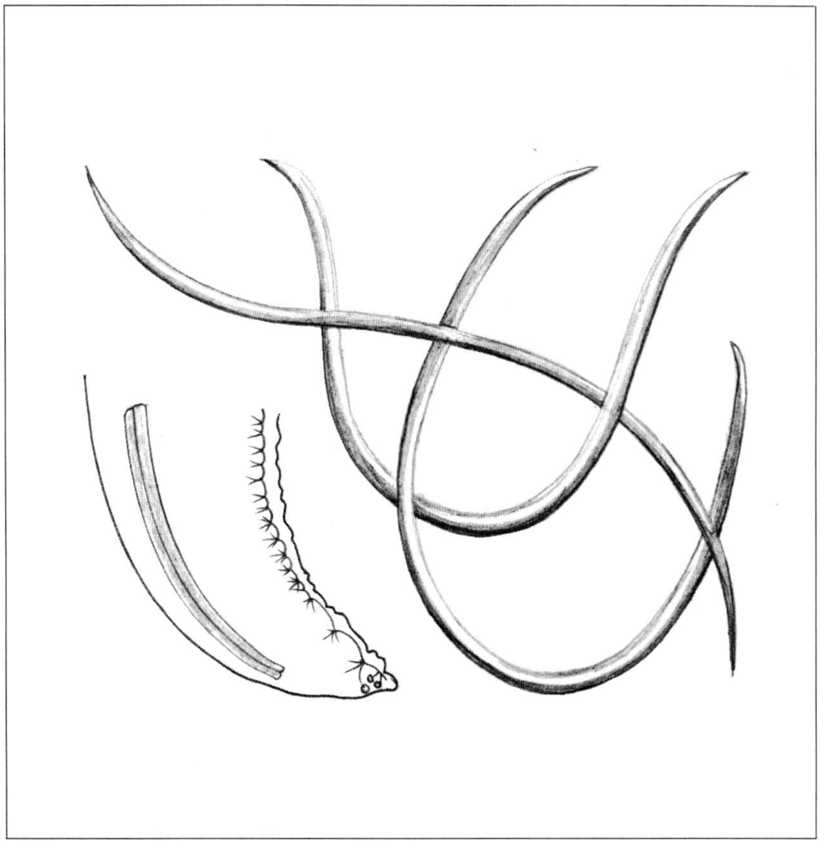

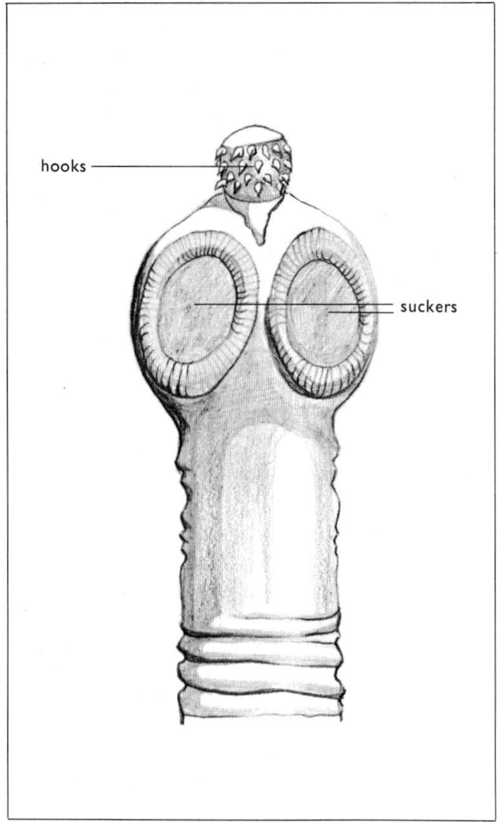

above Intestinal roundworms, *Toxascaris leonina*, and an enlargement of the posterior end of a male; *left* head of the tapeworm, *Dipylidium caninum*, showing the hooks and suckers by which it anchors itself to the intestinal wall

on neat feet, and the tail thick at the base and of medium length. The heads should be broad, with well developed cheeks, the noses short and the ears small. The pure white fur should be untinged with yellow and short, fine and close.

The kittens may have a pinkish appearance when first born, but this vanishes with the growth of the plush-like fur. White kittens are now very much sought after possibly due to their appearance in television advertisements.
See colour plate 62, page 248.

White tigers see TIGER

Wild Cat, African see AFRICAN WILD CAT; **European** and **Scottish** see EUROPEAN WILD CAT

Wood's Light Wood's light is light produced by an apparatus invented by the American physicist, Robert Williams Wood, consisting of an ultraviolet lamp, the bulb of which is made of glass containing nickel oxide and screens off most of the visible light rays. When Wood's light falls upon hair infected with ringworm fungi of the *Microsporon* species, the hair fluoresces a bright pastel green colour. The light is used for the detection of ringworm infection in the cat particularly in the subclinical or symptomless cases.

Worms The parasitic worms of the cat can be divided into two main groups, 1. Roundworms and 2. Tapeworms.

1. *Roundworms* This group can be further subdivided into (a) Ascarids, (b) Hookworms, and (c) Lungworms.

(a) *Ascarids* These are the intestinal roundworms of the cat and are of two species, *Toxocara cati (mystax)*, and *Toxascaris leonina*, the former being by far the more common. Toxocara worms live in the small intestine where they lay eggs which pass out in the faeces. After further development the egg becomes infective and if swallowed by a cat it hatches into a larva, which migrates through the liver and the lungs returning to the bowel to complete its development into the adult worm. Toxascaris has a more simple lifecycle, the larvae not undergoing a migration but developing in the wall of the intestine.

Unless present in large numbers, roundworm infestation is usually symptomless. Unthriftiness, diarrhoea, a pot-bellied appearance and possibly anaemia may occur with a heavy worm burden. Children may very rarely become infected by eating infective eggs and this gives rise to the condition known as 'visceral larva migrans'. In this disease the larvae hatch out of the eggs and migrate to various parts of the body, including the liver, the lungs, the eye and the central nervous system, where they may produce severe damage to vital organs.

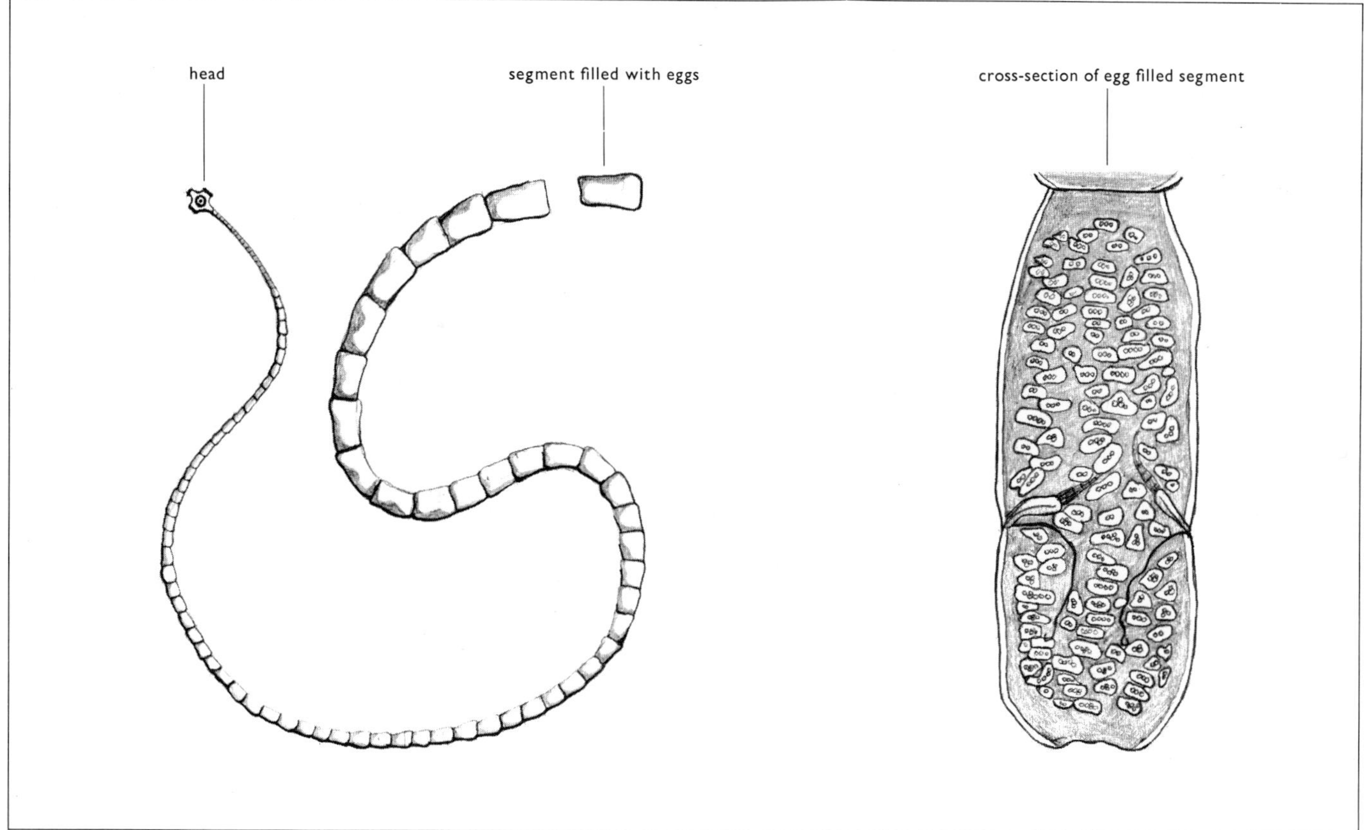

The tapeworm, *Dipylidium caninum*

Treatment consists of the administration of Piperazine compounds. Prevention of infection depends upon good sanitation measures in the cattery. Cats should not be kept on earth runs which are impossible to disinfest of worm eggs. Concrete runs, which can be washed and scrubbed down thoroughly, or even flamed with a garden flame gun, are much more advisable. Any faeces should be removed and burnt as soon as possible after being voided to prevent development of worm eggs to the infective stage.

(b) *Hookworms* Two species of hookworms occur in the cat, *Uncinaria stenocephala*, and *Ancylostoma tubaeforme,* the latter being the more dangerous infection. These worms live in the small intestine and lay eggs which pass out in the faeces. In suitable moist surroundings, the eggs hatch into larvae which develop to the infective stage within about a week. The infective larvae can enter the cat either through the intact skin or by being swallowed, and usually undergo a migration through the lungs before returning to the intestine to develop into adult worms. The parasites attach themselves to the mucus lining of the intestine and suck blood. The chief symptom of hookworm infestation therefore is anaemia, associated with unthriftiness, sometimes emaciation, and general weakness. Sometimes areas of itchy dermatitis develop where the larvae have entered the skin. There may be diarrhoea which may be blood-stained or tarry in appearance. Treatment is by the administration of thenium compounds which are often combined with piperazine for simultaneous control of roundworms. Prevention of infection again depends upon good cattery hygiene and keeping runs as dry as possible, as the infective larvae are susceptible to dessication. Sunlight is a good disinfecting agent.

(c) *Lungworms* *Aelurostrongylus abstrusus* is the common lungworm of the cat. The presence of the worm in the lung may produce coughing, wheezing, sneezing, symptoms of pleurisy and pneumonia.

The lifecycle of the worm is indirect as an intermediate host is required for its completion. The eggs are laid in the lung arteries and are scattered by the bloodstream throughout the lung tissue. Here they hatch into first stage larvae and pass through the passages to the back of the throat where they are swallowed. After excretion in the faeces, they enter slugs or snails to become infective larvae. The larvae when the slug or snail is swallowed by a cat burrow out through the intestinal wall and enter the mesenteric lymph nodes where they become adult. They then gain access to the lymph stream, pass into the blood and arrive in the lungs via the heart.

Diagnosis of infection depends upon finding the first stage larvae in the faeces. Treatment is difficult, but recently the drug Tetramisole given orally has been found to be effective.

2. *Tapeworms* The commonest tapeworm of the cat is *Dipylidium caninum*, but infection with *Taenia*

taeniaeformis may also be seen. These worms seldom cause any ill-health in the cat but may produce digestive disturbances and loss of bodily condition. Owners become concerned because of the presence of motile worm segments in the faeces or in the fur around the anus. *Dipylidium* eggs are passed out in the segments in the faeces and they are then eaten by flea larvae (see FLEAS), developing into the infective cysticercoid stage in the adult flea. If the flea is swallowed by a cat then the cysticeroid is liberated by the digestive processes and reaches the intestine where it develops into the adult tapeworm. In the case of *Taenia*, the cysticercoid develops in the livers of mice, rats, rabbits and squirrels. Treatment of these infestations is difficult. Prevention of infection rests upon elimination of fleas in the case of *Dipylidium* and preventing the cat catching rodents in *Taenia* infestations.

X-rays X-rays or Röntgen Rays differentiate between the densities of tissues through which they pass. The image of the varying densities is recorded on a photographic plate which then acts as a permanent record of the internal situation of the animal at the time of exposure. These rays have greatly improved the clinicians ability to diagnose with accuracy. See RADIOGRAPHY.

Yeasts Yeasts are microscopic plants belonging to the fungi; not possessing chlorophyll they live on carbohydrate and other food materials manufactured by green plants and are thus classed as saprophytes. Various species of yeast are cultivated and used by man to bake bread and ferment sugars to produce alcohol. Dried yeast, especially *Torula utilis,* is a good source both of proteins and vitamins of the water soluble B group – thiamine, riboflavin and nicotinic acid. It can be added to food directly in small quantities, strictly limited by its bitter flavour. Yeasts are grown and processed to provide both protein and protein-free extracts. The latter are found in some flavouring agents often well liked by cats when suitably diluted in their food. Research is striving to improve the yield of food protein from yeasts grown on substrates (materials) which would otherwise be waste products.

Yellow-fat Disease see STEATITIS

Zibelines see Brown Burmese under BURMESE